子連れ狼

LONE
WOLF
AND
CUB

story
KAZUO KOIKE

art
GOSEKI KOJIMA

DARK HORSE COMICS

translation
DANA LEWIS

lettering & retouch
DIGITAL CHAMELEON

cover artwork
FRANK MILLER with **LYNN VARLEY**

publisher
MIKE RICHARDSON

editor
MIKE HANSEN

assistant editor
TIM ERVIN-GORE

consulting editor
TOREN SMITH for **STUDIO PROTEUS**

book design
DARIN FABRICK

art director
MARK COX

Published by Dark Horse Comics, Inc. in association
with MegaHouse and Koike Shoin Publishing Company.

Dark Horse Comics, Inc.
10956 SE Main Street, Milwaukie, OR 97222
www.darkhorse.com

First edition: January 2001
ISBN: 1-56971-506-8

1 3 5 7 9 10 8 6 4 2

Printed in Canada

To find a comics shop in your area, call the
Comic Shop Locator Service toll-free at 1-888-266-4226

BLACK WIND

子連れ狼

By KAZUO KOIKE

& GOSEKI KOJIMA

VOLUME

5

A NOTE TO READERS

Lone Wolf and Cub is famous for its carefully researched re-creation of Edo-Period Japan. To preserve the flavor of the work, we have chosen to retain many Edo-Period terms that have no direct equivalents in English. Japanese is written in a mix of Chinese ideograms and a syllabic writing system, resulting in numerous synonyms. In the glossary, you may encounter words with multiple meanings. These are words written with Chinese ideograms that are pronounced the same but carry different meanings. A Japanese reader seeing the different ideograms would know instantly which meaning it is, but these synonyms can cause confusion when Japanese is spelled out in our alphabet. *O-yurushi o* (please forgive us)!

LONE WOLF AND CUB

子連水狼

TABLE OF CONTENTS

the twenty-fourth

Trail Markers

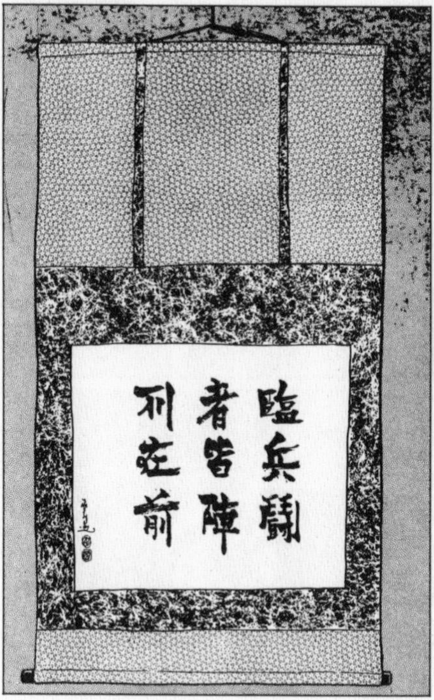
臨兵闘
者皆陣
列在前

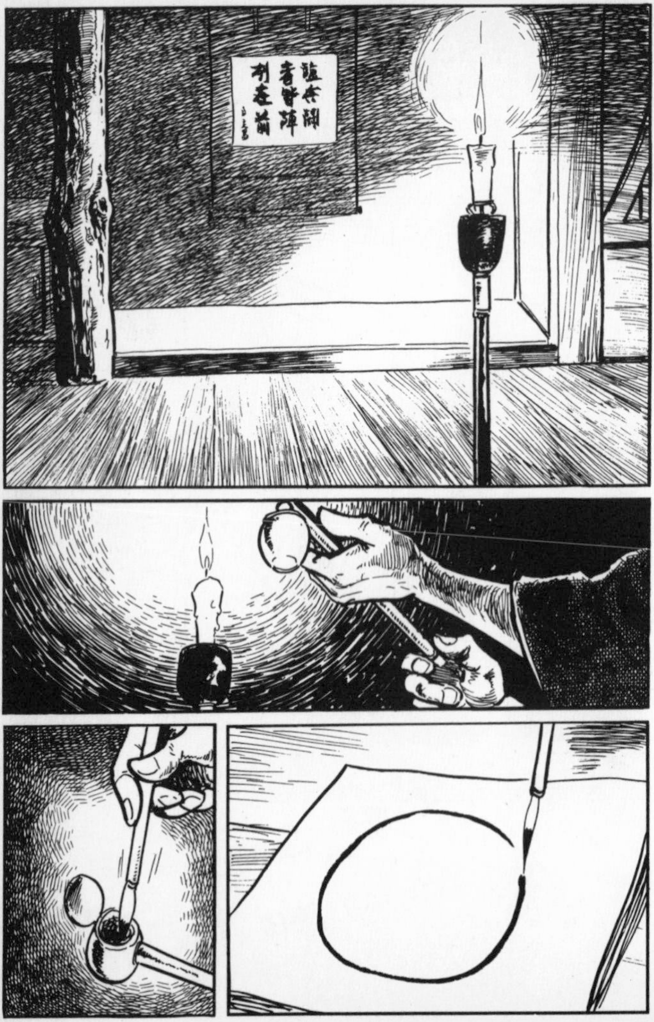

臨兵闘者皆陣列在前

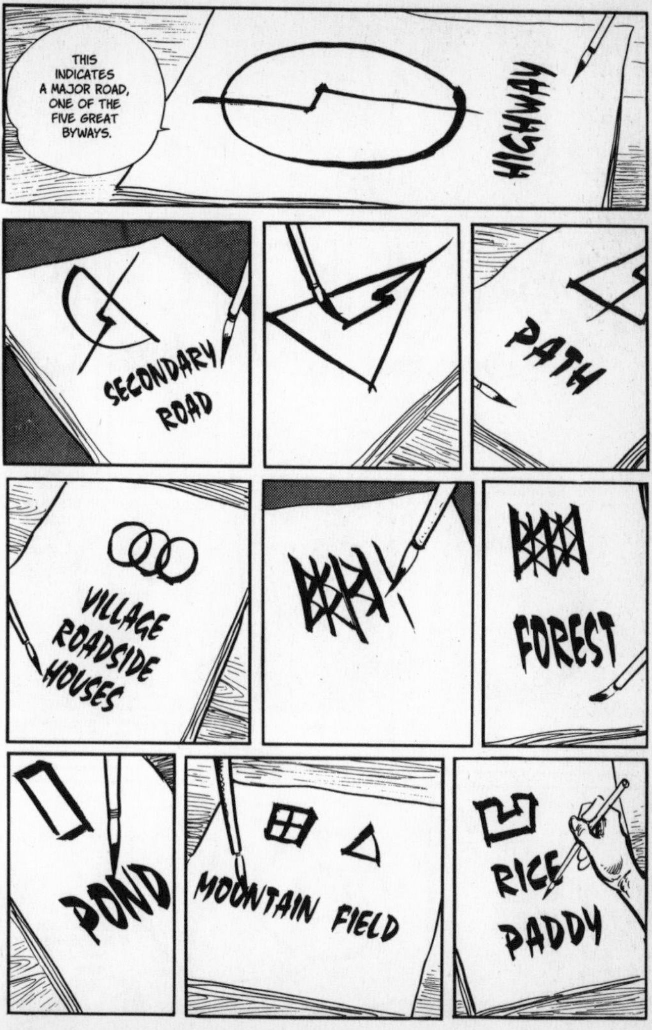
THIS INDICATES A MAJOR ROAD, ONE OF THE FIVE GREAT BYWAYS.
HIGHWAY
SECONDARY ROAD
PATH
VILLAGE ROADSIDE HOUSES
FOREST
POND
MOUNTAIN FIELD
RICE PADDY

RIVERS ARE DIVIDED INTO THREE CATEGORIES.

OCEAN

BROOK CREEK

RIVER

GORGE

CASTLE

FORT

BUT THIS.

THIS IS HIS ENCAMPMENT!

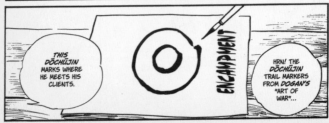

THIS DŌCHŪJIN MARKS WHERE HE MEETS HIS CLIENTS.

ENCAMPMENT

HRN! THE DŌCHŪJIN TRAIL MARKERS FROM DOGAN'S "ART OF WAR"...

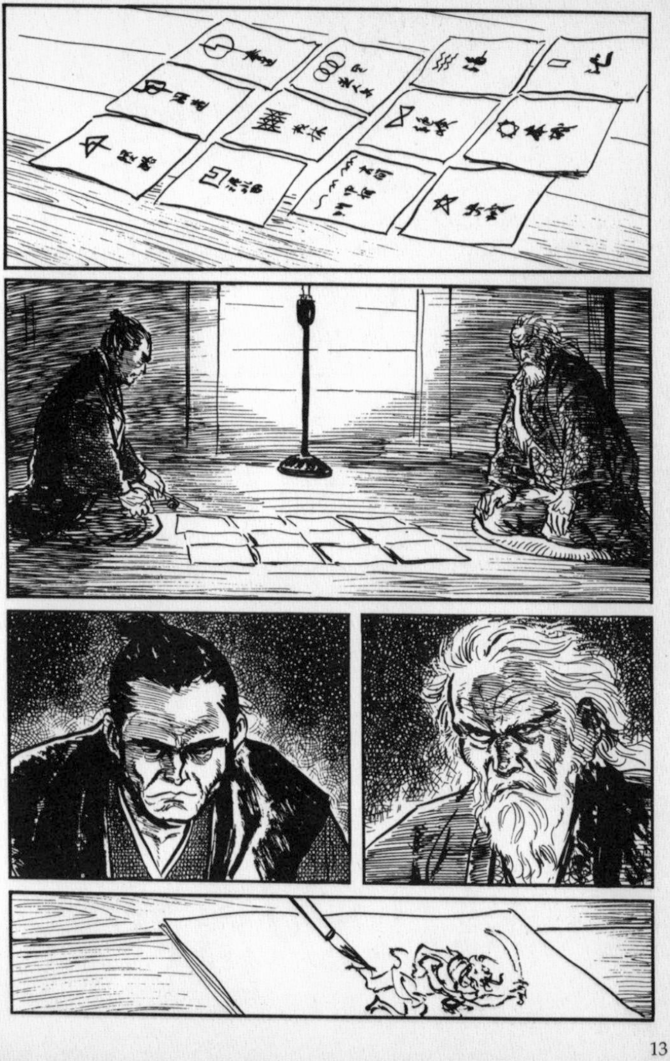

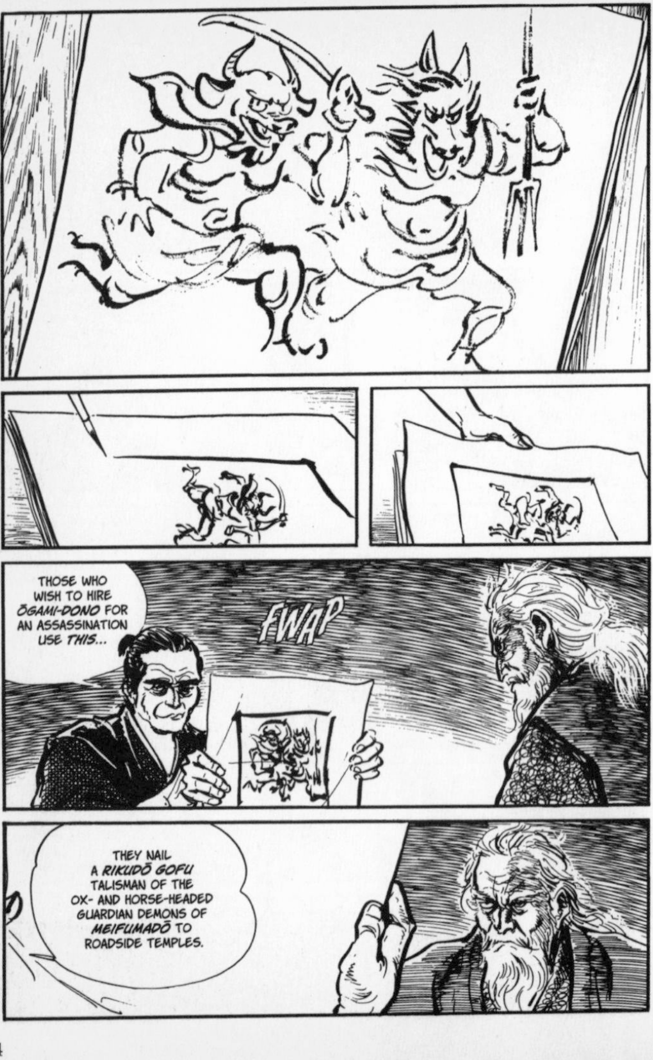
THOSE WHO WISH TO HIRE ŌGAMI-DONO FOR AN ASSASSINATION USE THIS...
FWAP
THEY NAIL A RIKUDŌ GOFU TALISMAN OF THE OX- AND HORSE-HEADED GUARDIAN DEMONS OF MEIFUMADŌ TO ROADSIDE TEMPLES.

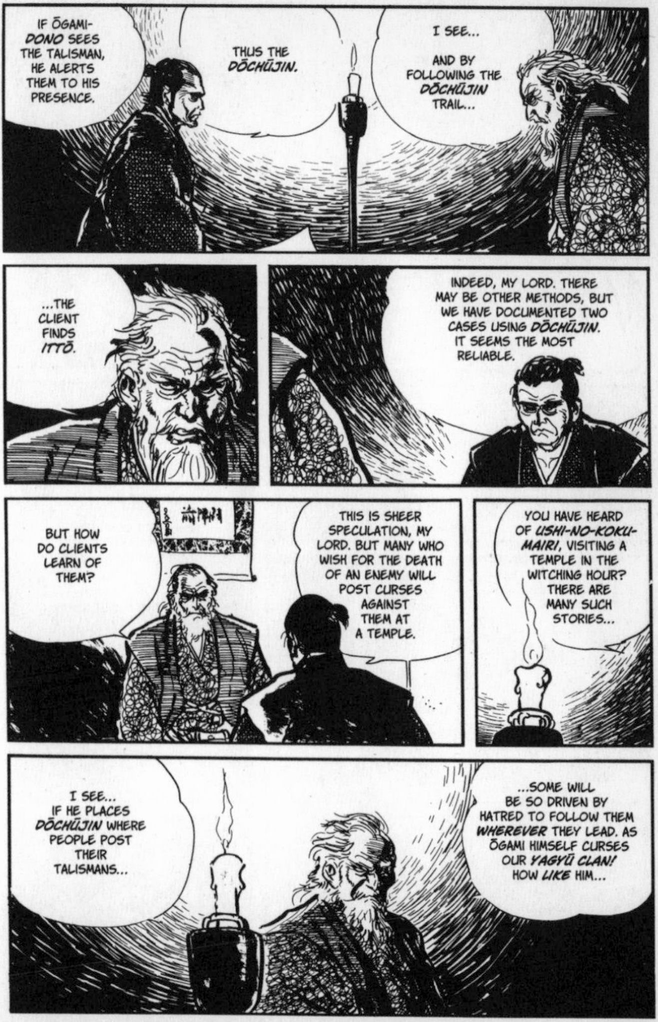
IF ŌGAMI-DONO SEES THE TALISMAN, HE ALERTS THEM TO HIS PRESENCE.
THUS THE DŌCHŪJIN.
I SEE... AND BY FOLLOWING THE DŌCHŪJIN TRAIL...
...THE CLIENT FINDS ITTŌ.
INDEED, MY LORD. THERE MAY BE OTHER METHODS, BUT WE HAVE DOCUMENTED TWO CASES USING DŌCHŪJIN. IT SEEMS THE MOST RELIABLE.
BUT HOW DO CLIENTS LEARN OF THEM?
THIS IS SHEER SPECULATION, MY LORD. BUT MANY WHO WISH FOR THE DEATH OF AN ENEMY WILL POST CURSES AGAINST THEM AT A TEMPLE.
YOU HAVE HEARD OF USHI-NO-KOKU-MAIRI, VISITING A TEMPLE IN THE WITCHING HOUR? THERE ARE MANY SUCH STORIES...
I SEE... IF HE PLACES DŌCHŪJIN WHERE PEOPLE POST THEIR TALISMANS...
...SOME WILL BE SO DRIVEN BY HATRED TO FOLLOW THEM WHEREVER THEY LEAD. AS ŌGAMI HIMSELF CURSES OUR YAGYŪ CLAN! HOW LIKE HIM...

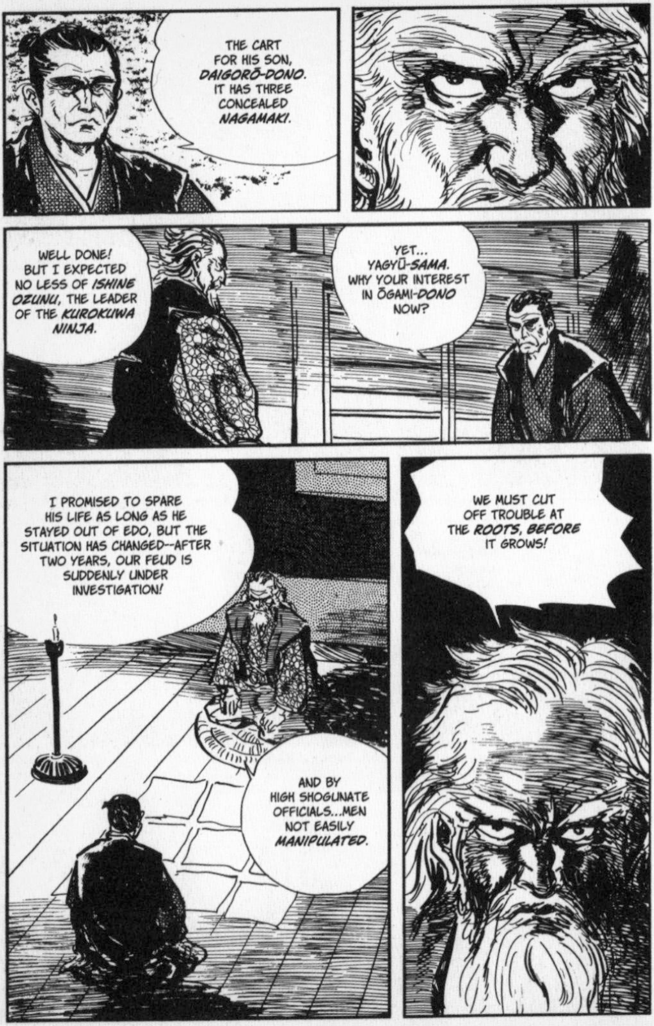
THE CART FOR HIS SON, *DAIGORŌ-DONO*. IT HAS THREE CONCEALED *NAGAMAKI*.
WELL DONE! BUT I EXPECTED NO LESS OF *ISHINE OZUNU*, THE LEADER OF THE *KUROKUWA NINJA*.
YET... YAGYŪ-*SAMA*. WHY YOUR INTEREST IN ŌGAMI-*DONO* NOW?
I PROMISED TO SPARE HIS LIFE AS LONG AS HE STAYED OUT OF EDO, BUT THE SITUATION HAS CHANGED--AFTER TWO YEARS, OUR FEUD IS SUDDENLY UNDER INVESTIGATION!
AND BY HIGH SHOGUNATE OFFICIALS...MEN NOT EASILY *MANIPULATED*.
WE MUST CUT OFF TROUBLE AT THE *ROOTS, BEFORE* IT GROWS!

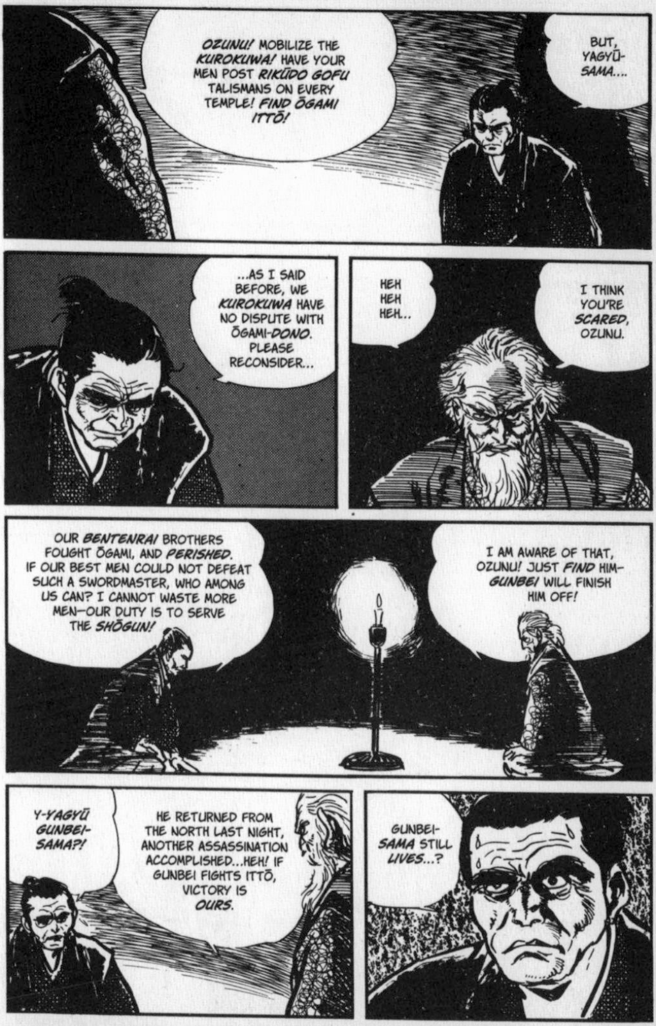
OZUNU! MOBILIZE THE KUROKUWA! HAVE YOUR MEN POST RIKŪDO GOFU TALISMANS ON EVERY TEMPLE! FIND ŌGAMI ITTŌ!
BUT, YAGYŪ-SAMA....
...AS I SAID BEFORE, WE KUROKUWA HAVE NO DISPUTE WITH ŌGAMI-DONO. PLEASE RECONSIDER...
HEH HEH HEH...
I THINK YOU'RE SCARED, OZUNU.
OUR BENTENRAI BROTHERS FOUGHT ŌGAMI, AND PERISHED. IF OUR BEST MEN COULD NOT DEFEAT SUCH A SWORDMASTER, WHO AMONG US CAN? I CANNOT WASTE MORE MEN—OUR DUTY IS TO SERVE THE SHŌGUN!
I AM AWARE OF THAT, OZUNU! JUST FIND HIM-GUNBEI WILL FINISH HIM OFF!
Y-YAGYŪ GUNBEI-SAMA?!
HE RETURNED FROM THE NORTH LAST NIGHT, ANOTHER ASSASSINATION ACCOMPLISHED...HEH! IF GUNBEI FIGHTS ITTŌ, VICTORY IS OURS.
GUNBEI-SAMA STILL LIVES...?

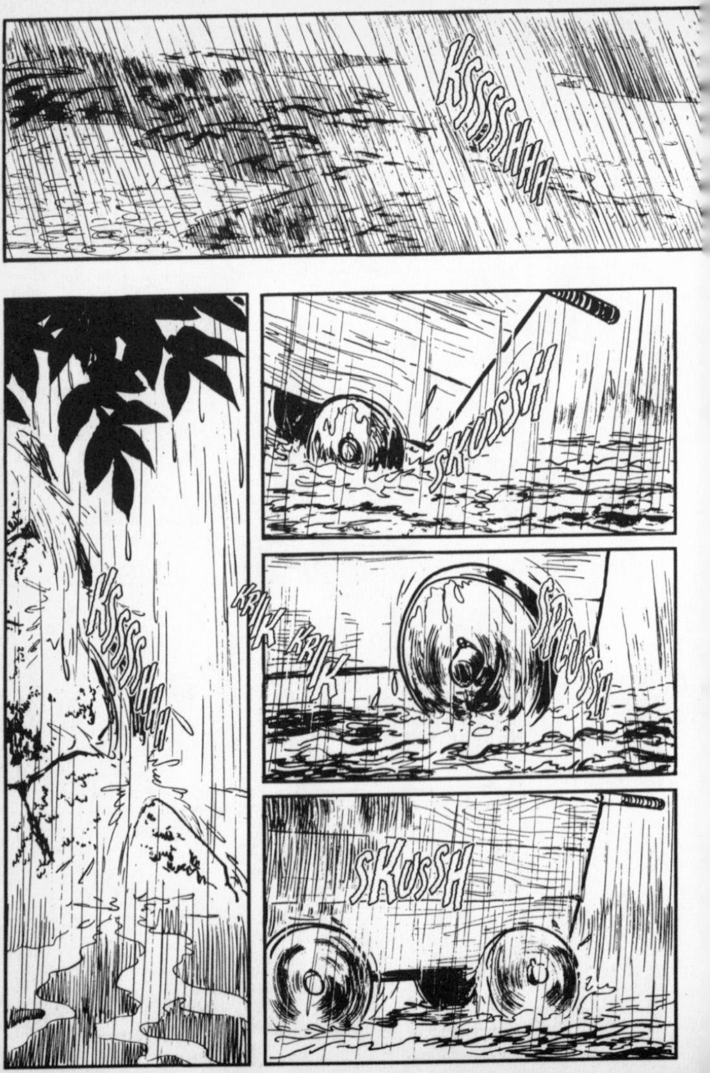
KSSSSHHH
SKUSSH
KSSSSHHH
KRIK KRIK
SPLUSSH
SKUSSH

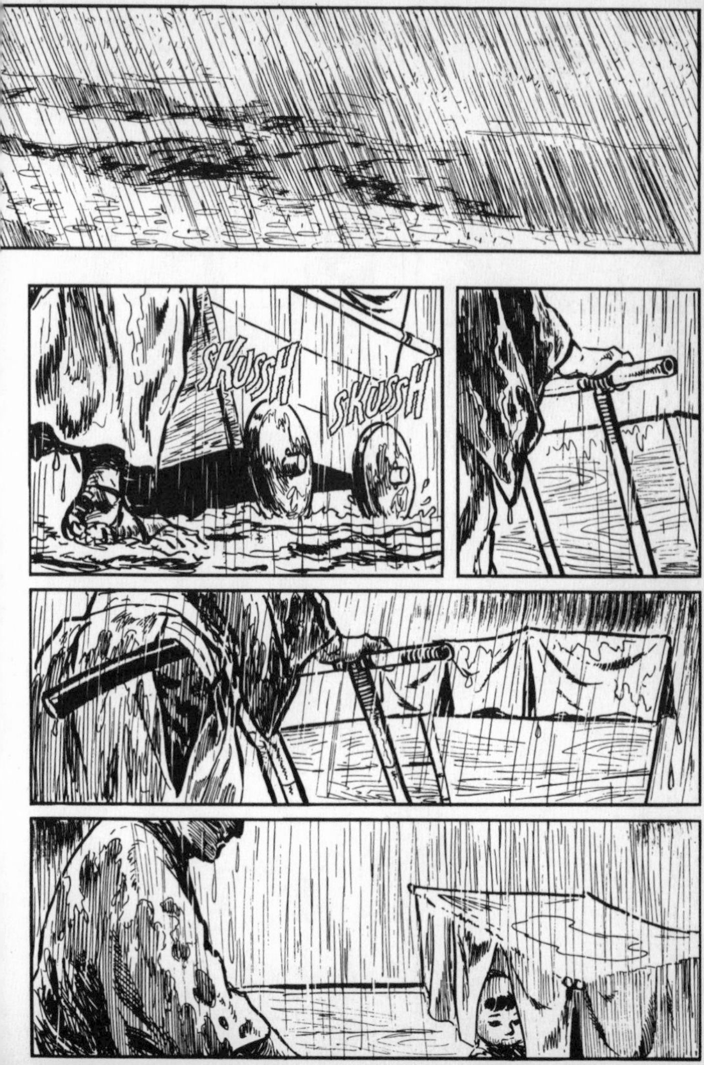
SKUSSH
SKUSSH

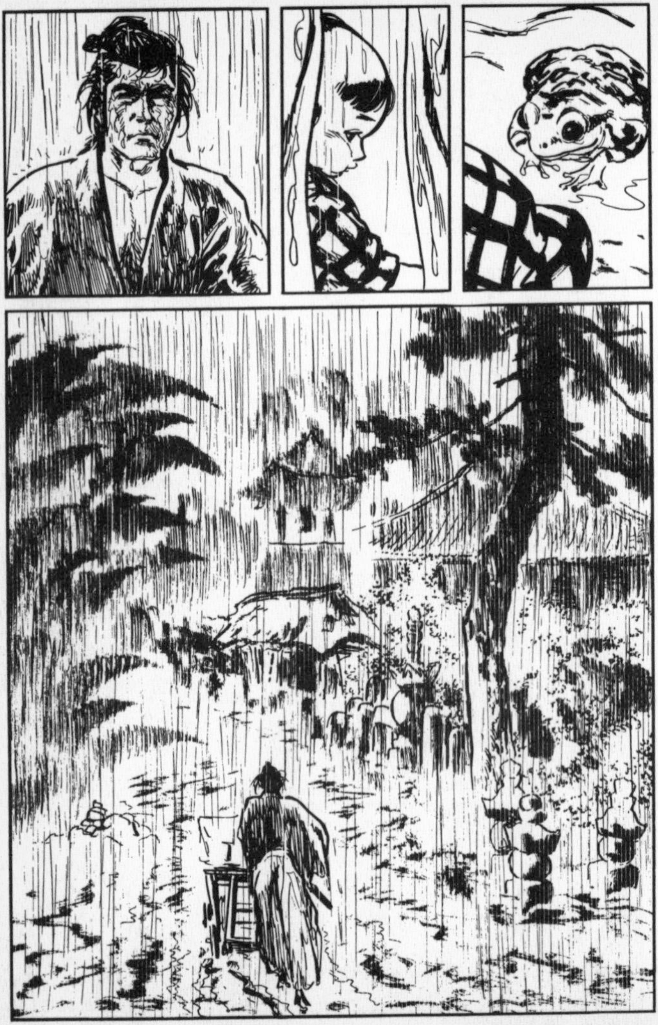

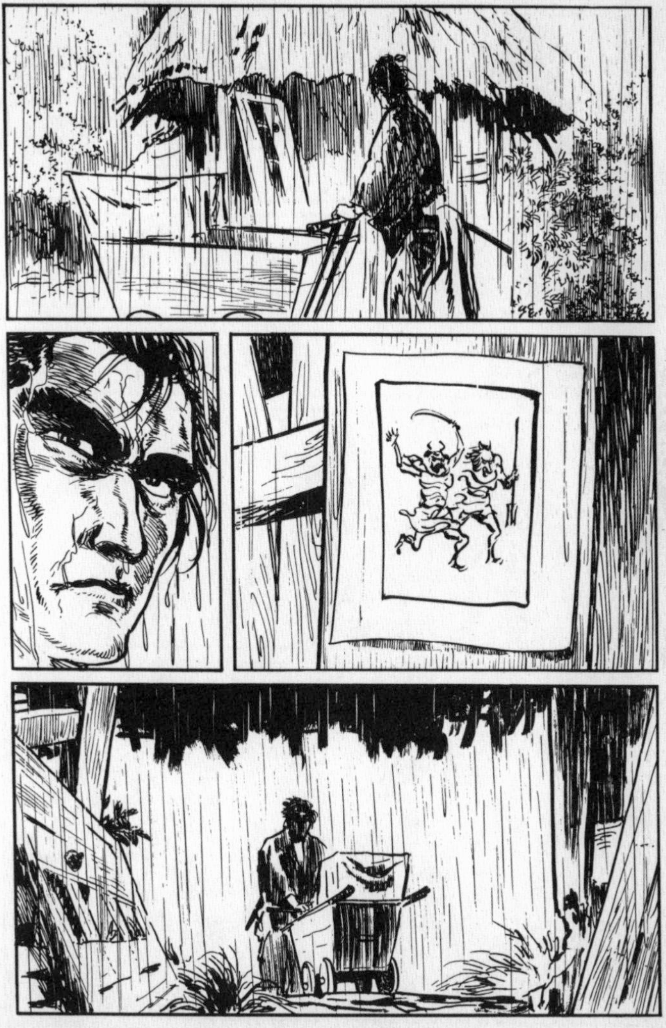

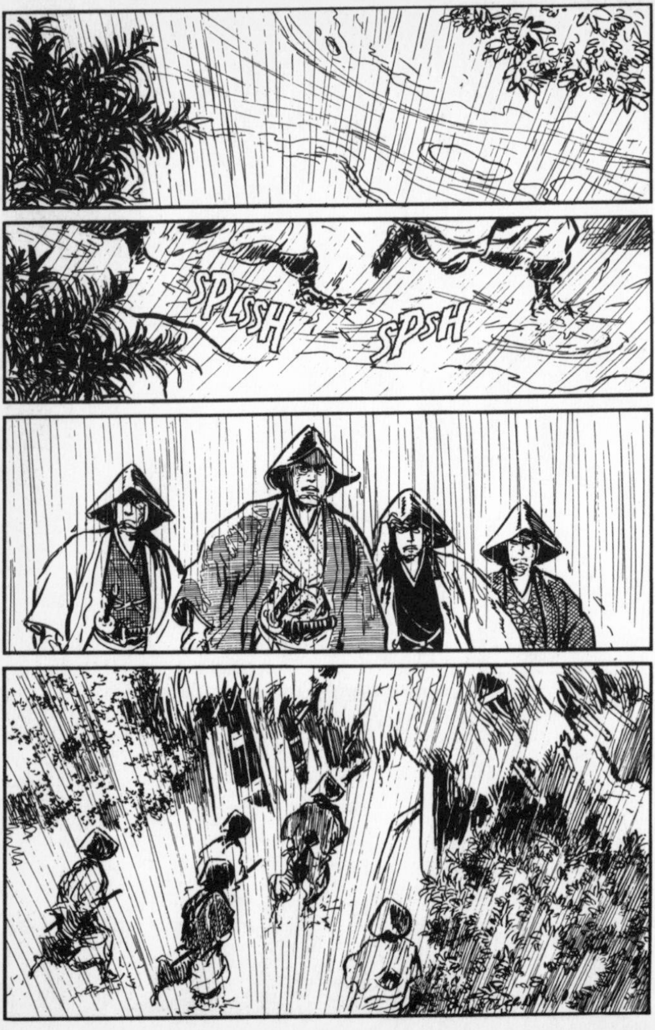
SPLSSH
SPSH

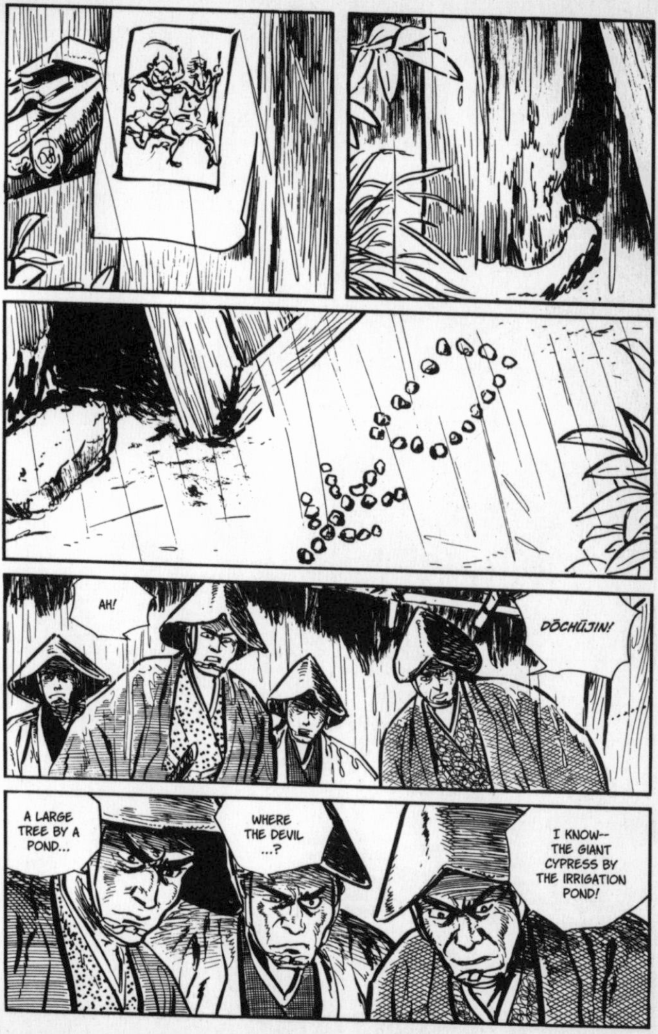
AH!
DŌCHŪJIN!
A LARGE TREE BY A POND...
WHERE THE DEVIL ...?
I KNOW-- THE GIANT CYPRESS BY THE IRRIGATION POND!

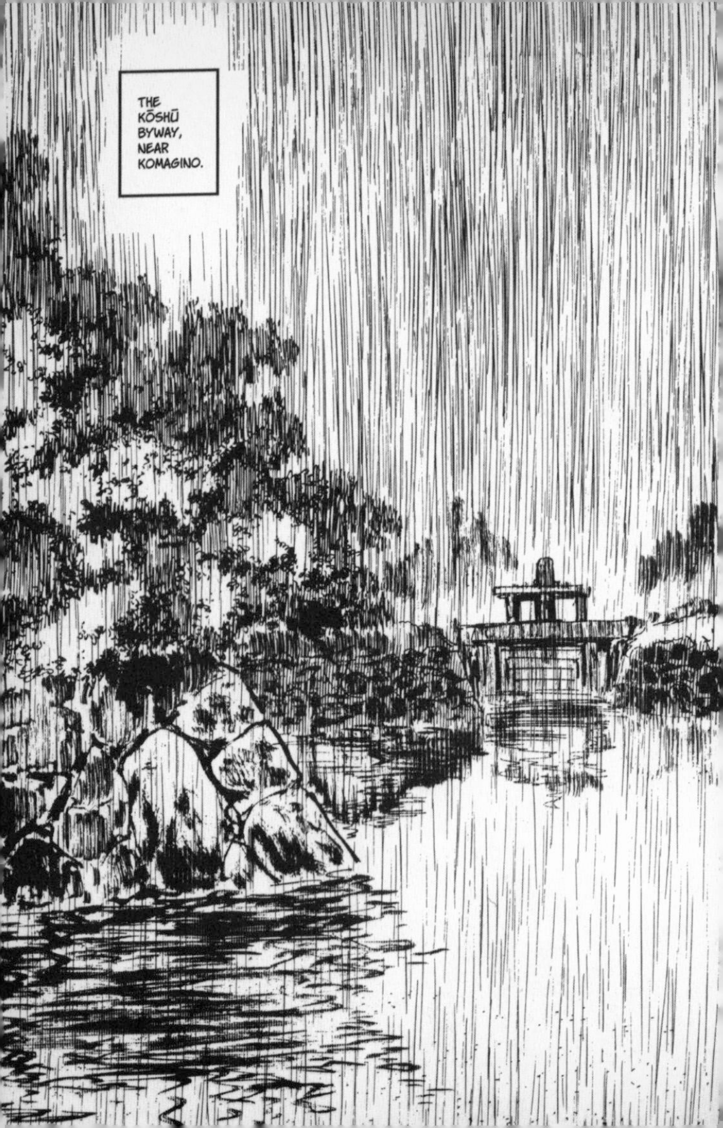
THE KŌSHŪ BYWAY, NEAR KOMAGINO.

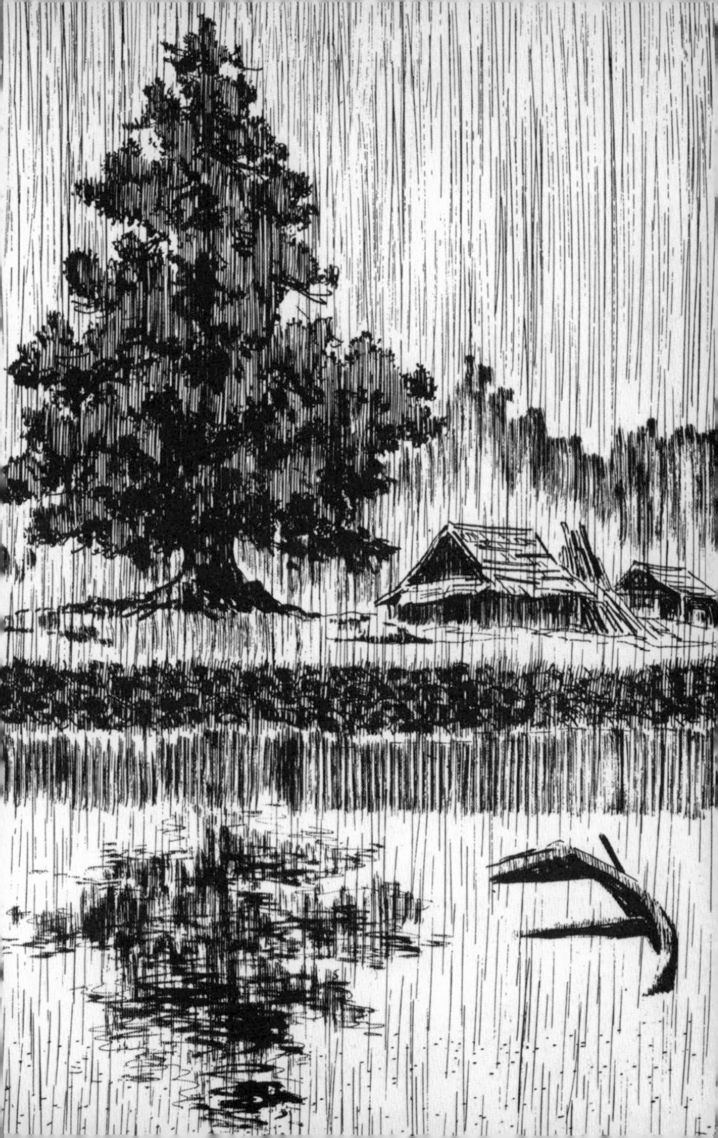

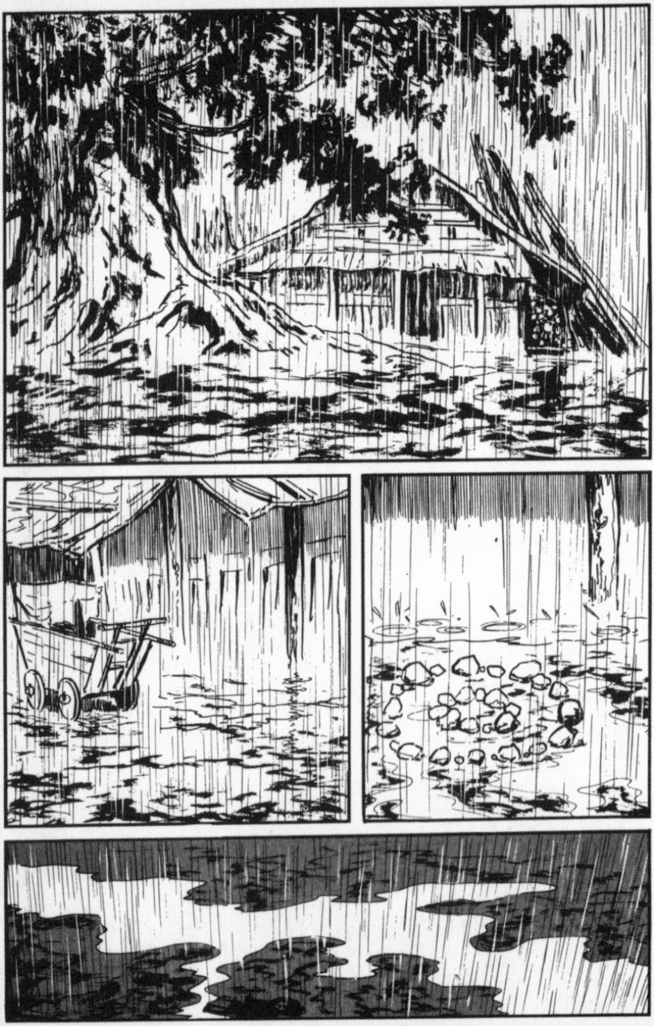

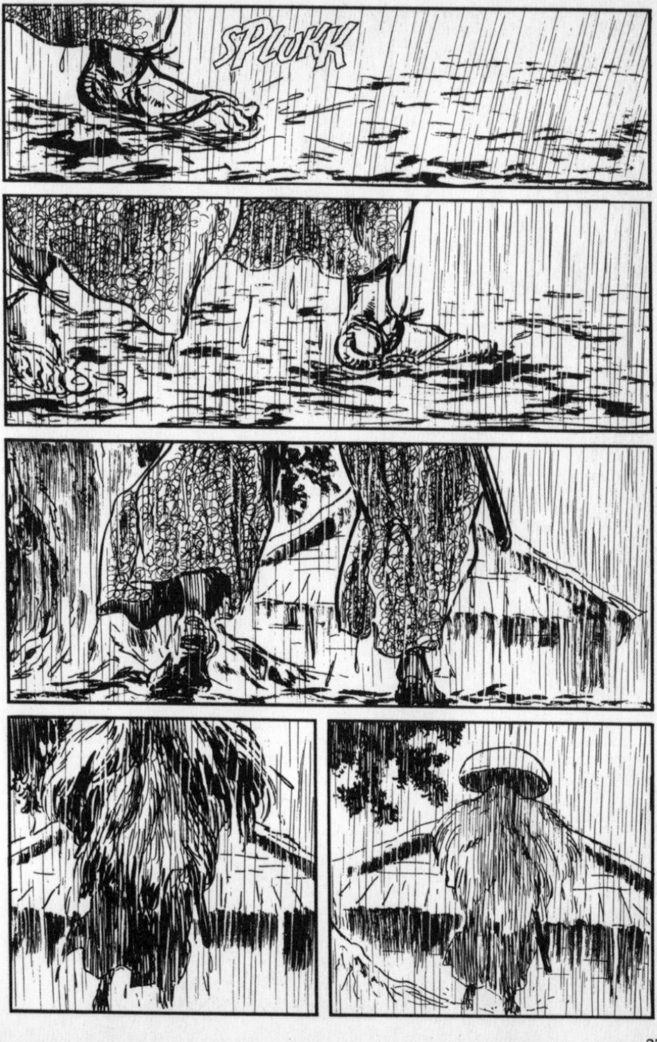
SPLUKK

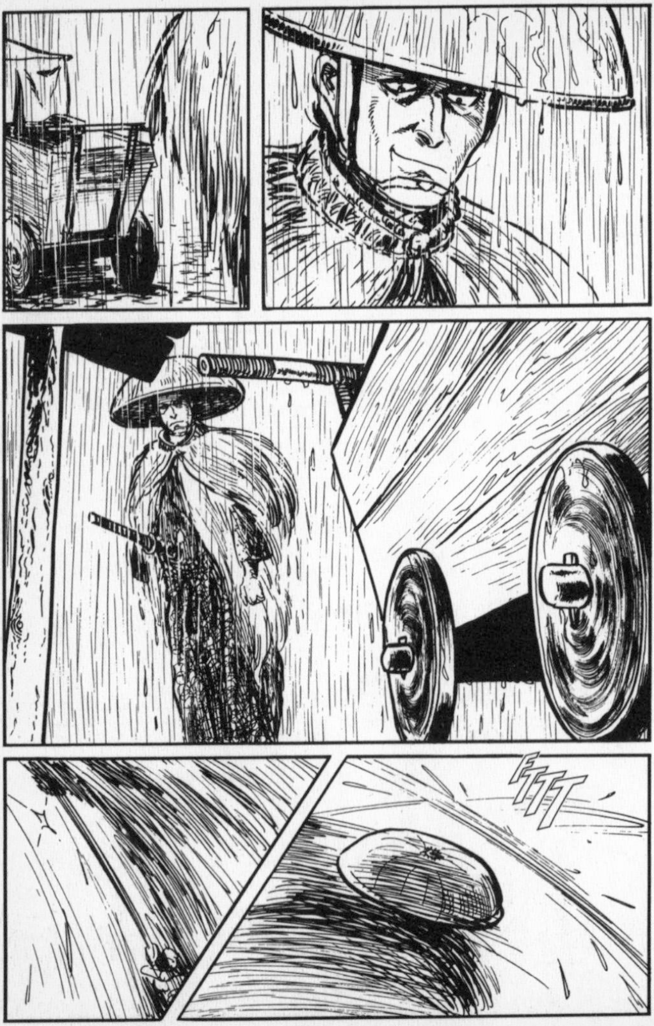
FTTT

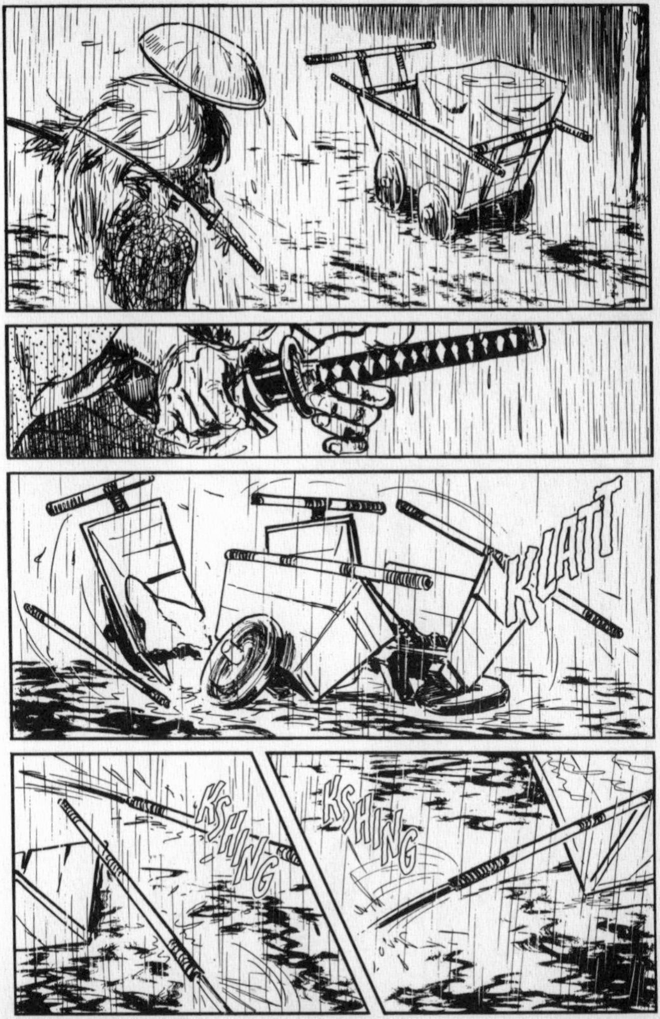
KLATT
KSHING
KSHING

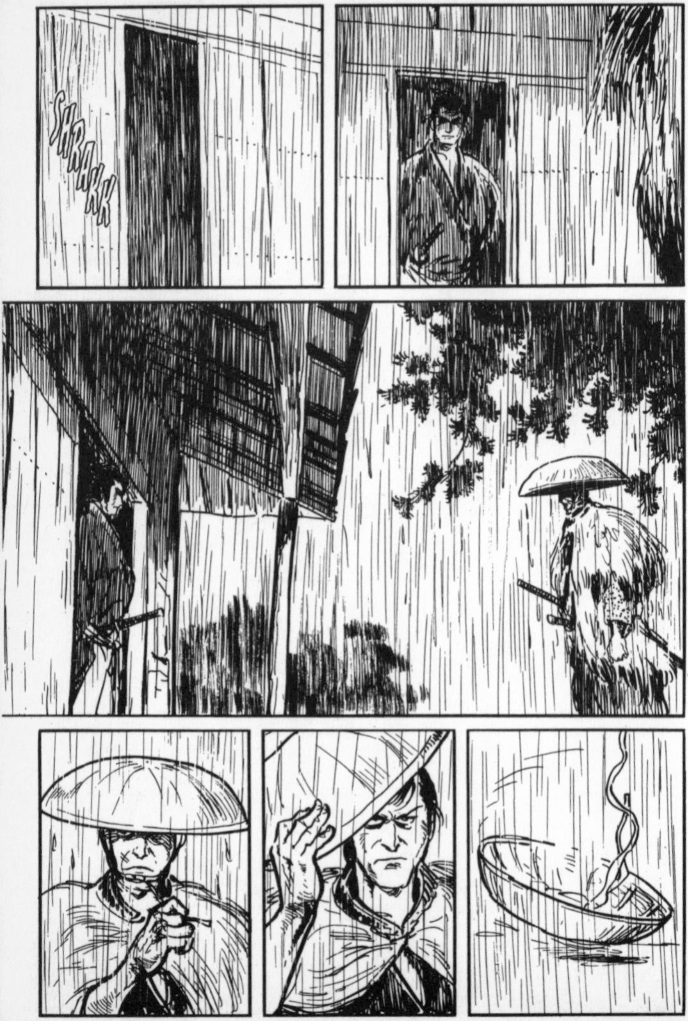
SHRAKK

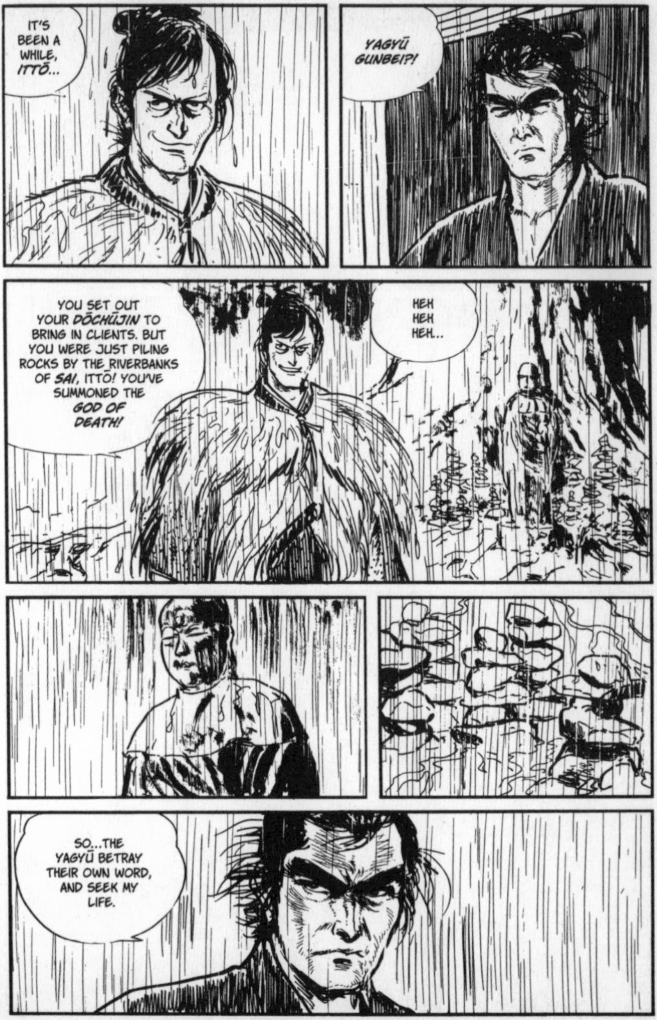
IT'S BEEN A WHILE, ITTŌ...
YAGYŪ GUNBEI!?!
YOU SET OUT YOUR DŌCHŪJIN TO BRING IN CLIENTS. BUT YOU WERE JUST PILING ROCKS BY THE RIVERBANKS OF SAI, ITTŌ! YOU'VE SUMMONED THE GOD OF DEATH!
HEH HEH HEH...
SO...THE YAGYŪ BETRAY THEIR OWN WORD, AND SEEK MY LIFE.

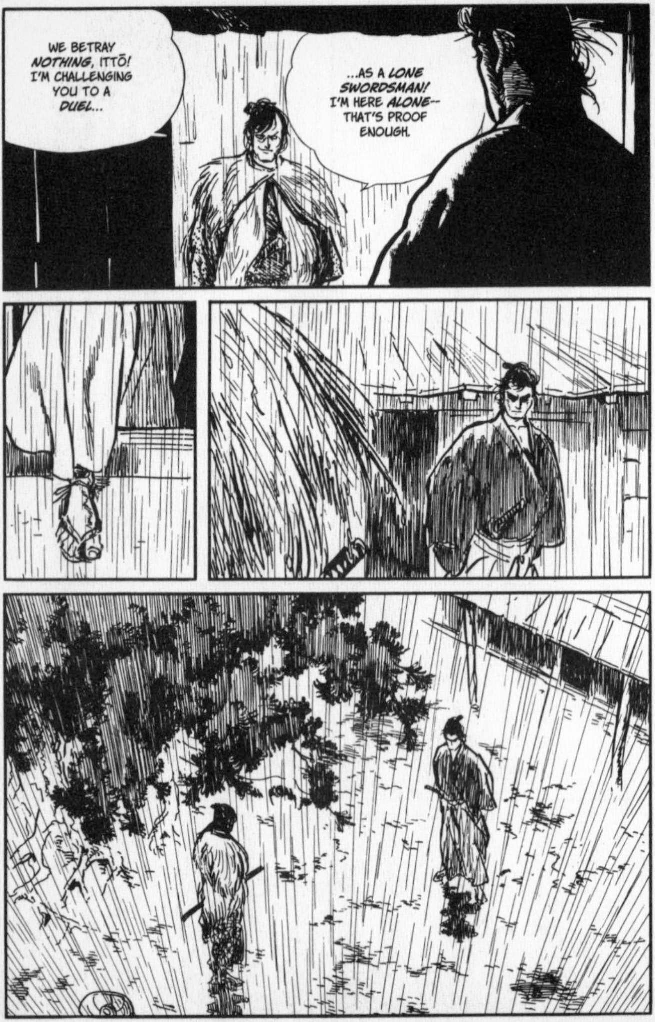

WE BETRAY NOTHING, ITTŌ! I'M CHALLENGING YOU TO A DUEL...
...AS A LONE SWORDSMAN! I'M HERE ALONE-- THAT'S PROOF ENOUGH.

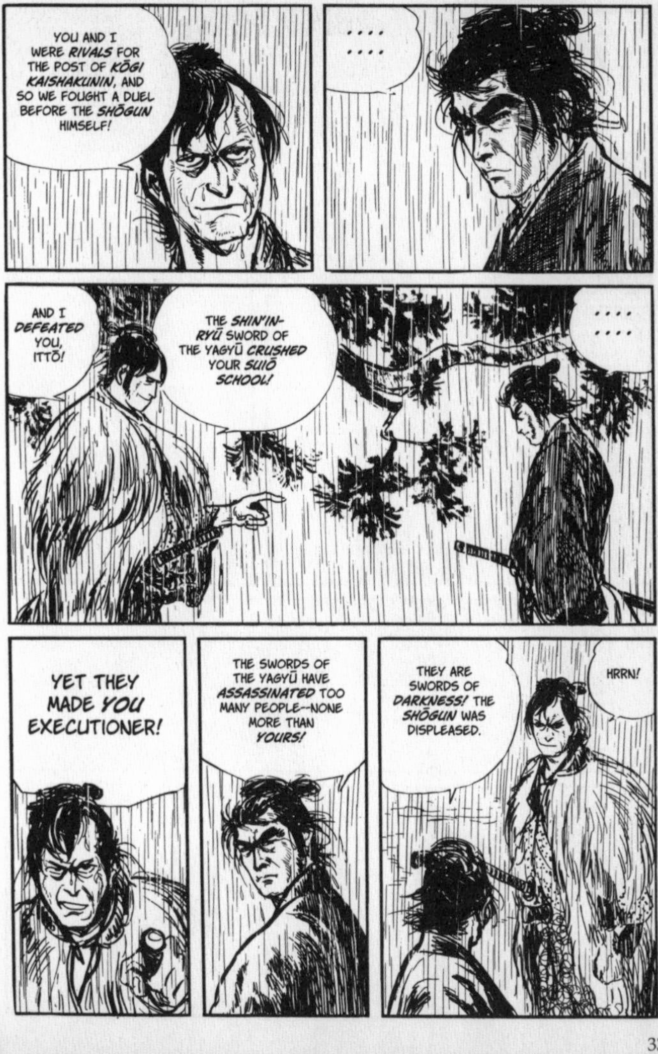
YOU AND I WERE RIVALS FOR THE POST OF KŌGI KAISHAKUNIN, AND SO WE FOUGHT A DUEL BEFORE THE SHŌGUN HIMSELF!
....
....
AND I DEFEATED YOU, ITTŌ!
THE SHIN'IN-RYŪ SWORD OF THE YAGYŪ CRUSHED YOUR SUIŌ SCHOOL!
....
....
YET THEY MADE YOU EXECUTIONER!
THE SWORDS OF THE YAGYŪ HAVE ASSASSINATED TOO MANY PEOPLE--NONE MORE THAN YOURS!
THEY ARE SWORDS OF DARKNESS! THE SHŌGUN WAS DISPLEASED.
HRRN!

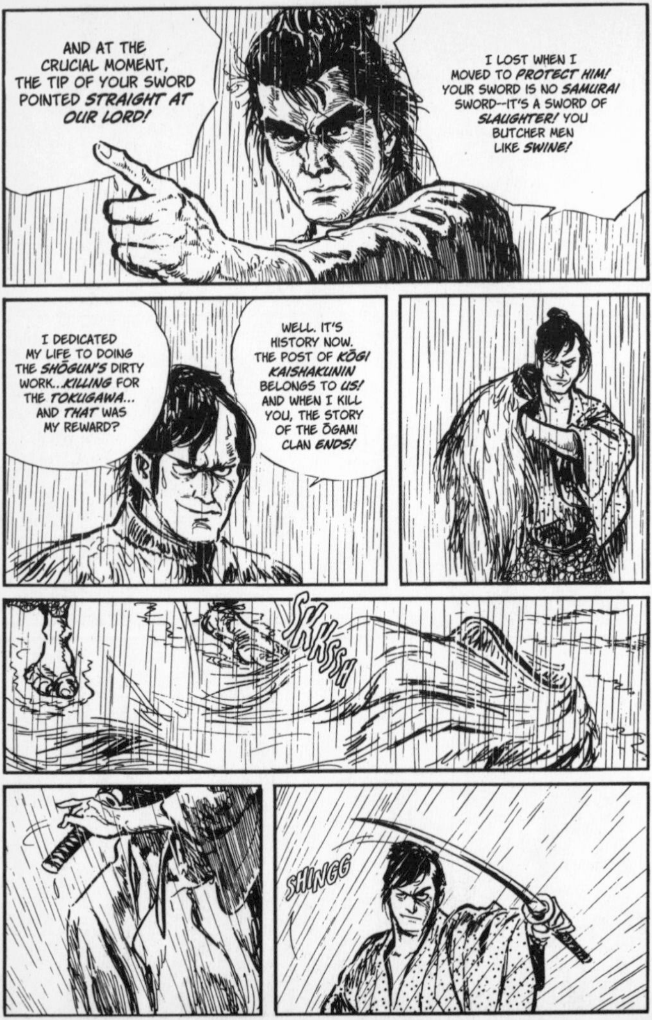
AND AT THE CRUCIAL MOMENT, THE TIP OF YOUR SWORD POINTED *STRAIGHT AT OUR LORD!*
I LOST WHEN I MOVED TO *PROTECT HIM!* YOUR SWORD IS NO *SAMURAI* SWORD--IT'S A SWORD OF *SLAUGHTER!* YOU BUTCHER MEN LIKE *SWINE!*
I DEDICATED MY LIFE TO DOING THE *SHŌGUN'S* DIRTY WORK...*KILLING* FOR THE *TOKUGAWA*... AND *THAT* WAS MY REWARD?
WELL. IT'S HISTORY NOW. THE POST OF *KŌGI KAISHAKUNIN* BELONGS TO *US!* AND WHEN I KILL YOU, THE STORY OF THE ŌGAMI CLAN *ENDS!*
SKKSSSH
SHINGG

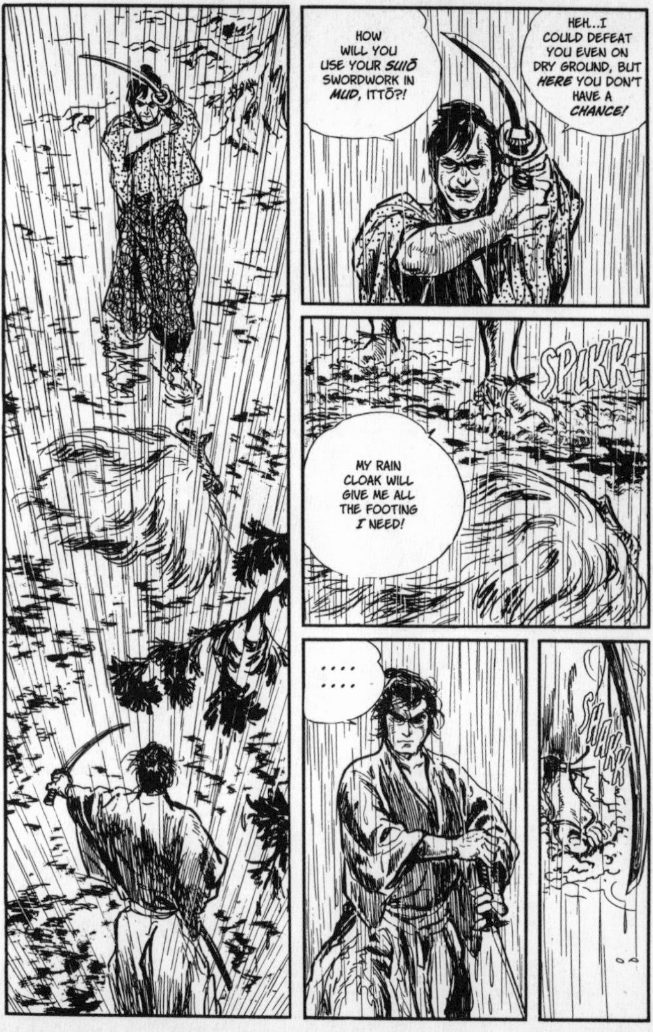
HOW WILL YOU USE YOUR *SUIŌ* SWORDWORK IN *MUD*, ITTŌ?!
HEH...I COULD DEFEAT YOU EVEN ON DRY GROUND, BUT *HERE* YOU DON'T HAVE A *CHANCE!*
SPLKK
MY RAIN CLOAK WILL GIVE ME ALL THE FOOTING *I* NEED!
....
....
SHAKK

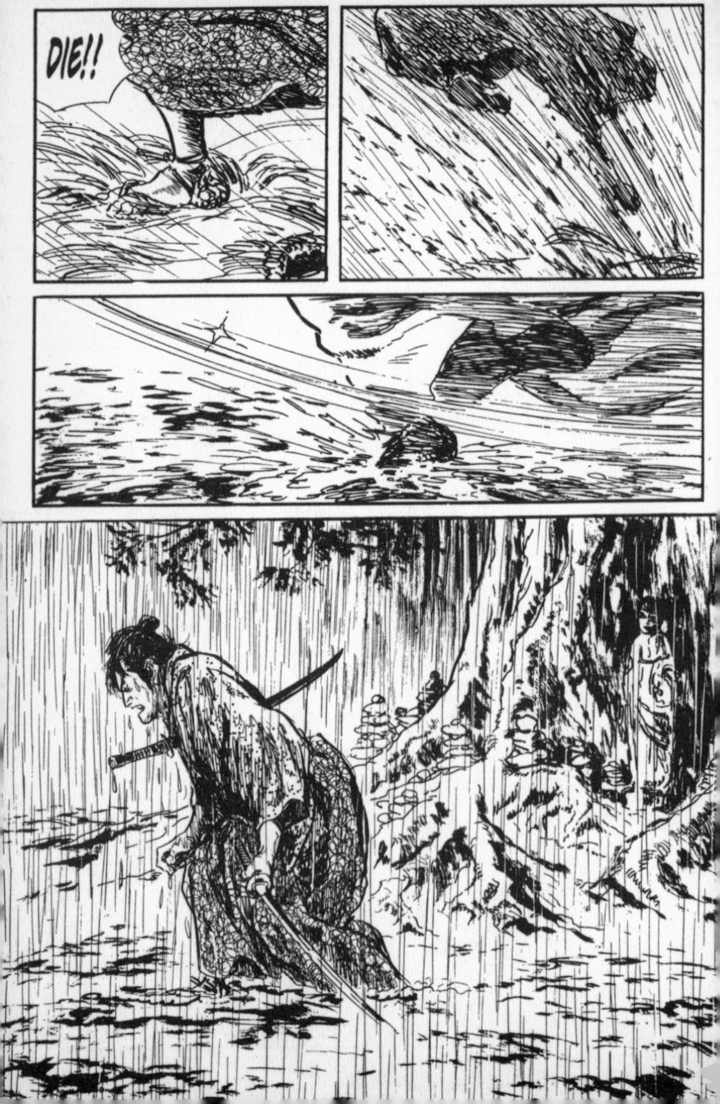
DIE!!

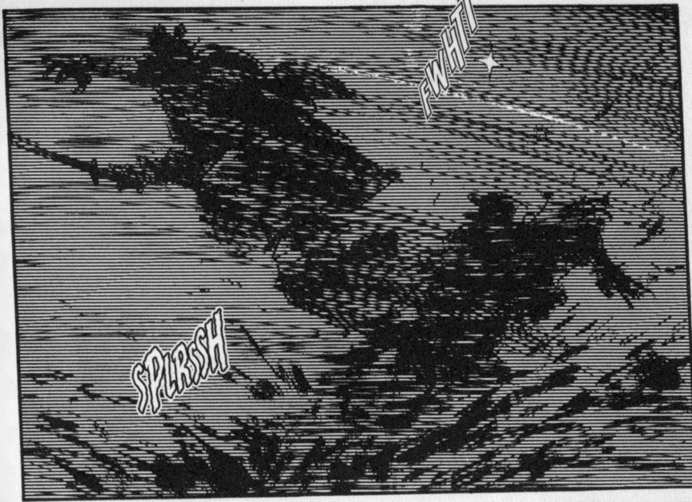
FWHT
SPLASSH

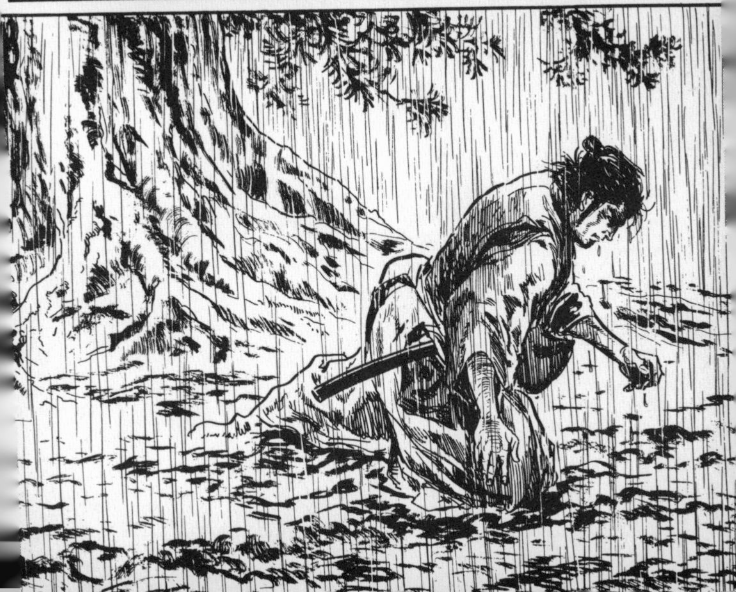

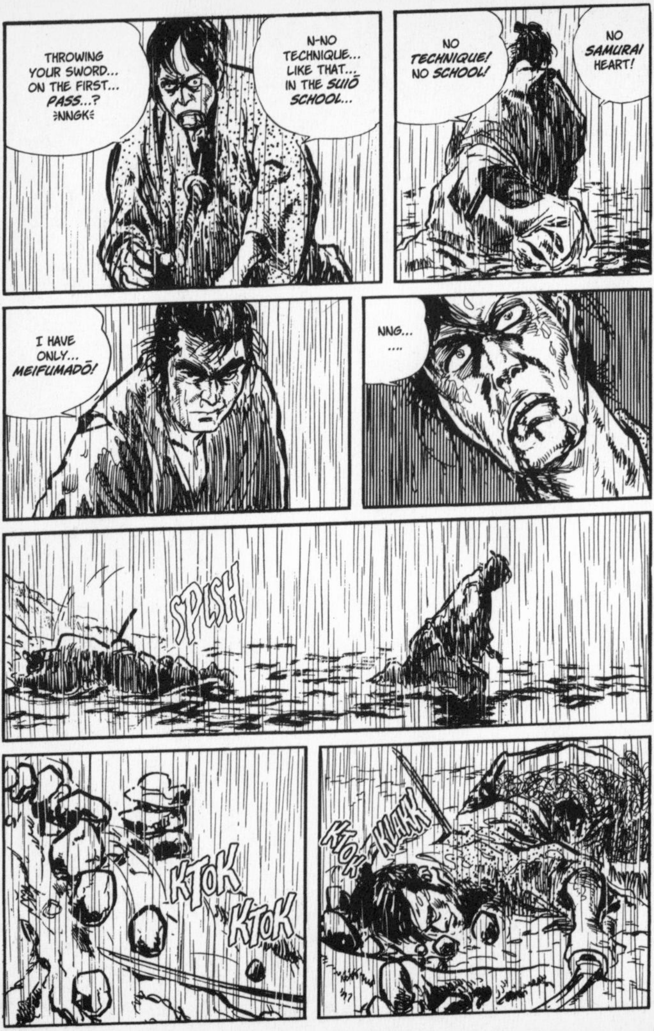
THROWING YOUR SWORD... ON THE FIRST... PASS...? ≷NNGK≶
N-NO TECHNIQUE... LIKE THAT... IN THE SUIŌ SCHOOL...
NO TECHNIQUE! NO SCHOOL!
NO SAMURAI HEART!
I HAVE ONLY... MEIFUMADŌ!
NNG... ....
SPLSH
KTOK KTOK
KTOK KLAKK

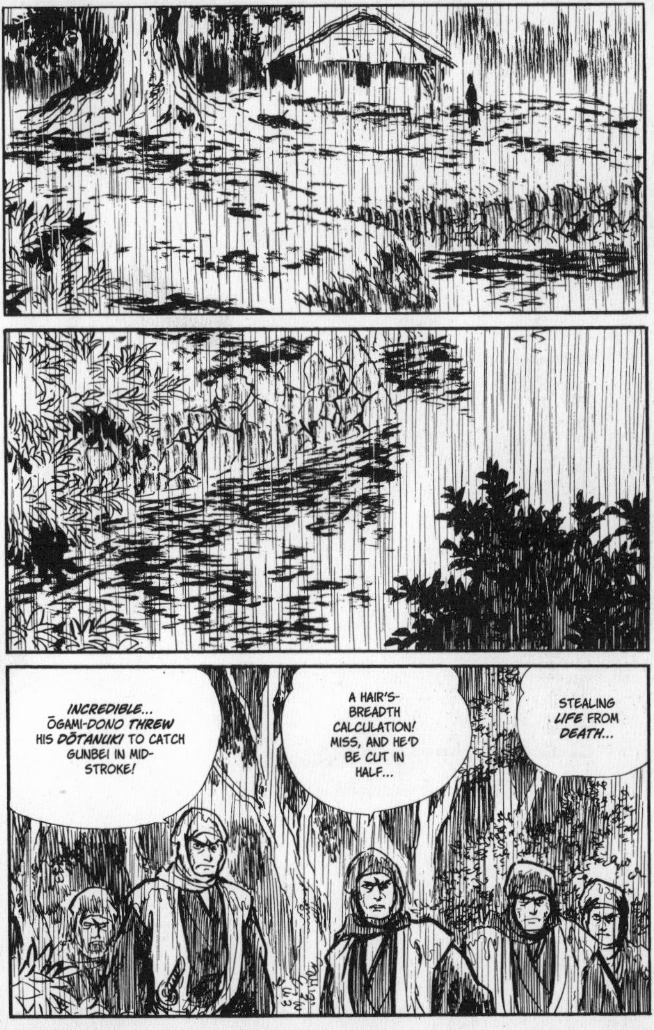
INCREDIBLE... ŌGAMI-DONO THREW HIS DŌTANUKI TO CATCH GUNBEI IN MID-STROKE!
A HAIR'S-BREADTH CALCULATION! MISS, AND HE'D BE CUT IN HALF...
STEALING LIFE FROM DEATH...

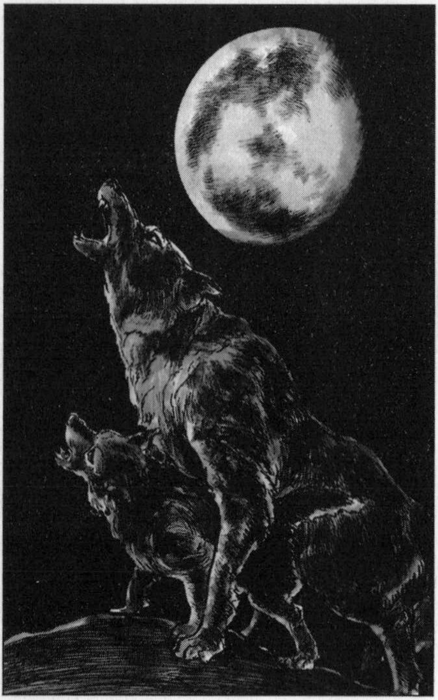

the twenty-fifth

Executioner's Hill

礼記

君子曰く
皐はその自ら生ずる所を楽しむ
礼はその本を忘れず
古の人に言あり
曰く狼死て正しく丘に首するは
たなり

楚辞
鳥は飛んで故郷に反り
狼は死するに必ず丘に首す

TRUE JOY IS TO TAKE PLEASURE
IN ONE'S OWN ACCOMPLISHMENTS;
COURTESY IS TO LEARN FROM THE MODELS OF THE PAST.
DID NOT THE ANCIENTS SAY, IN DEATH THE WOLF
TURNS HIS HEAD TOWARD THE HILLS?
THIS IS VIRTUE.

THE BIRDS FLY, RETURNING TO THEIR HOMELAND;
AND WITHOUT FAIL, THE DYING WOLF
TURNS HIS HEAD TOWARD THE HILLS.

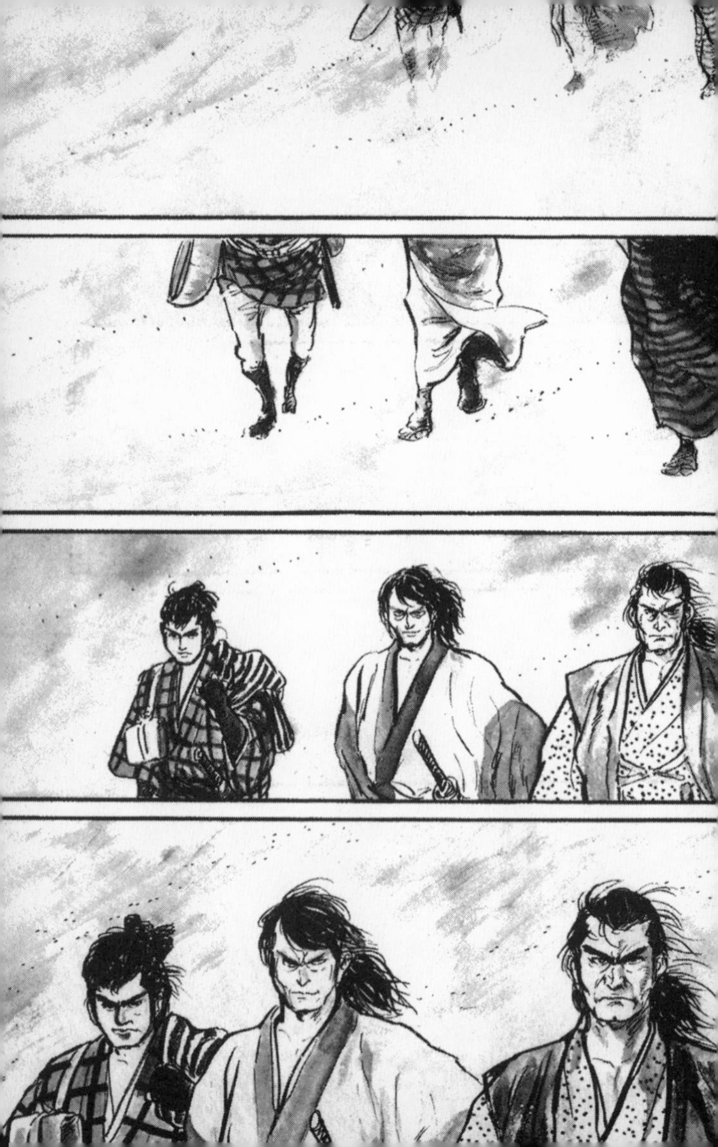

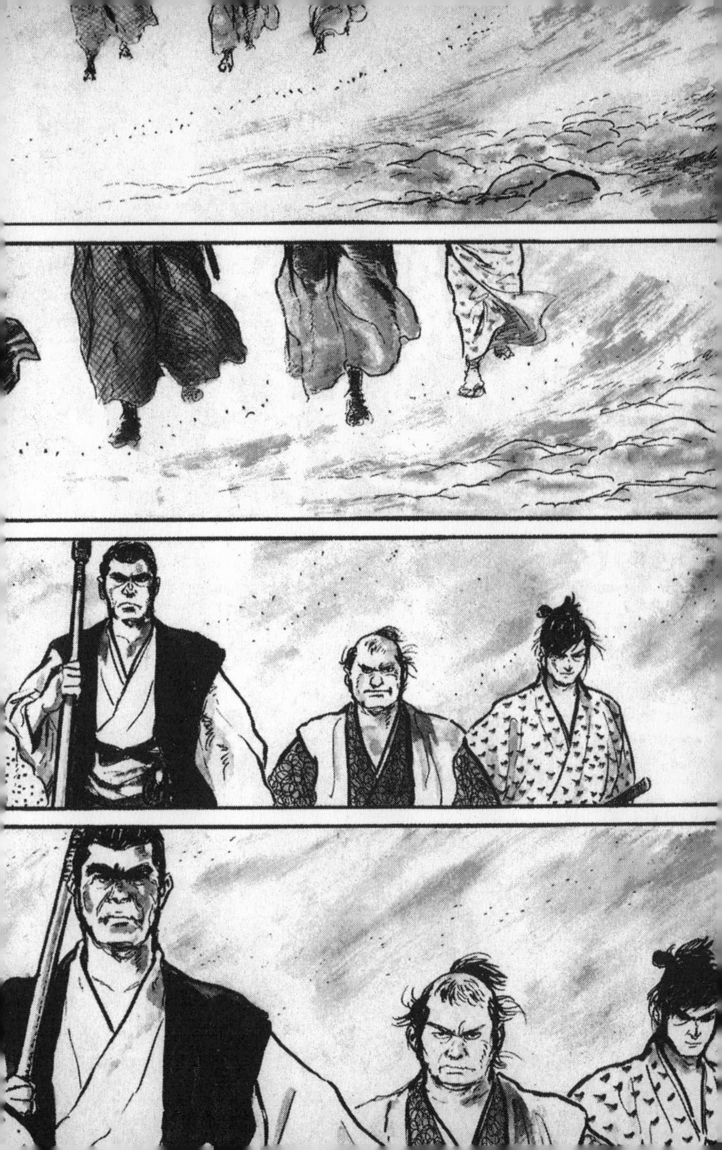

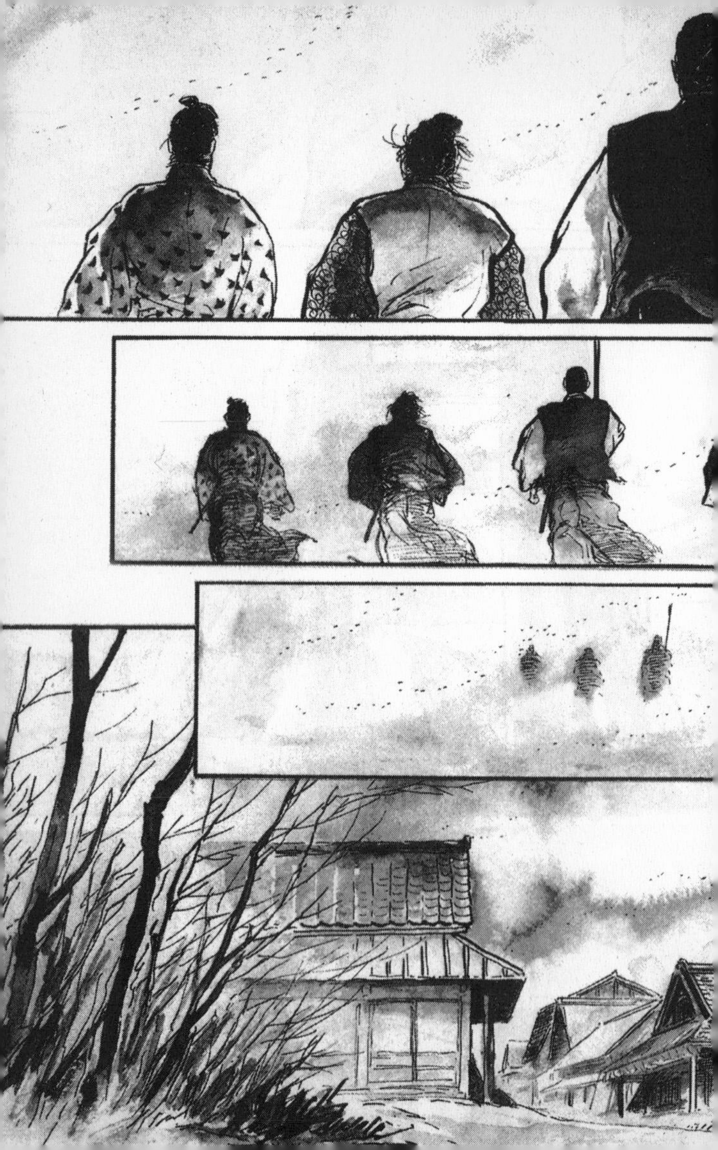

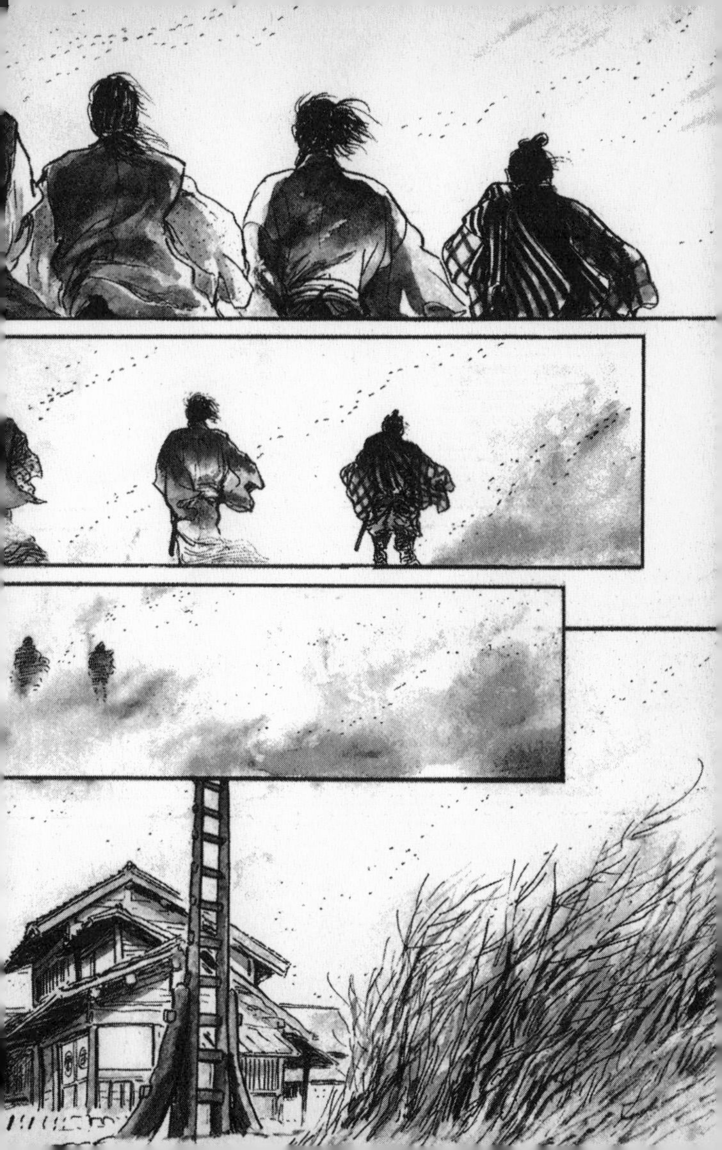

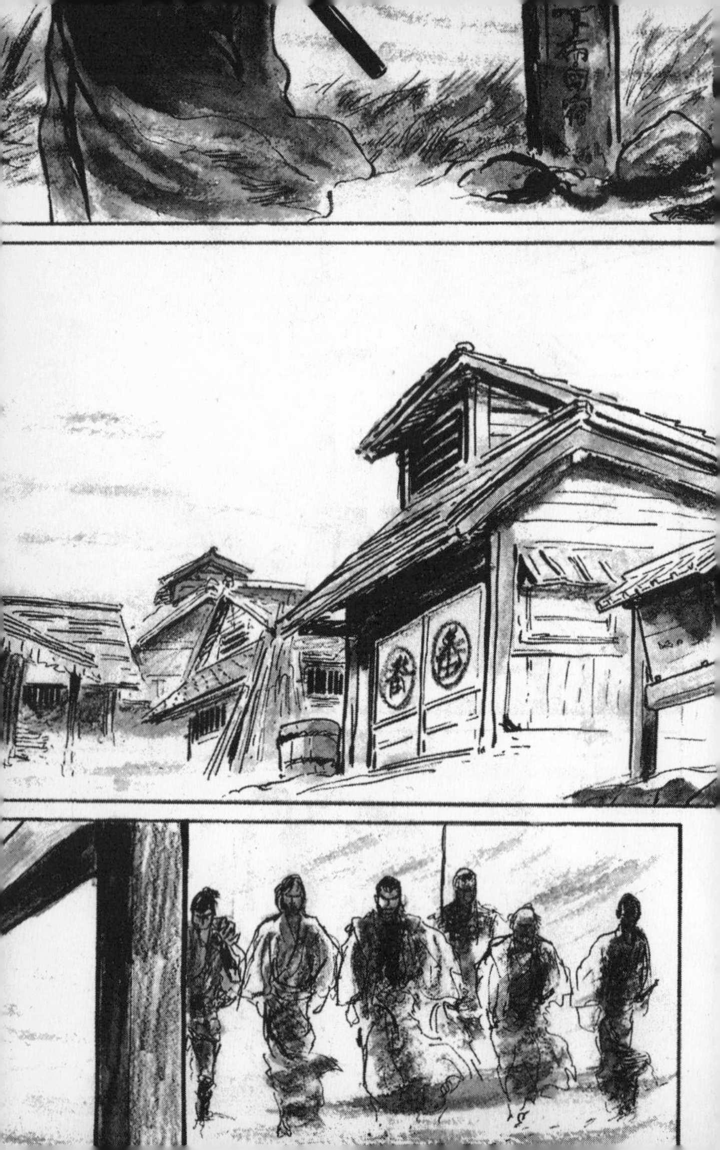
番
番

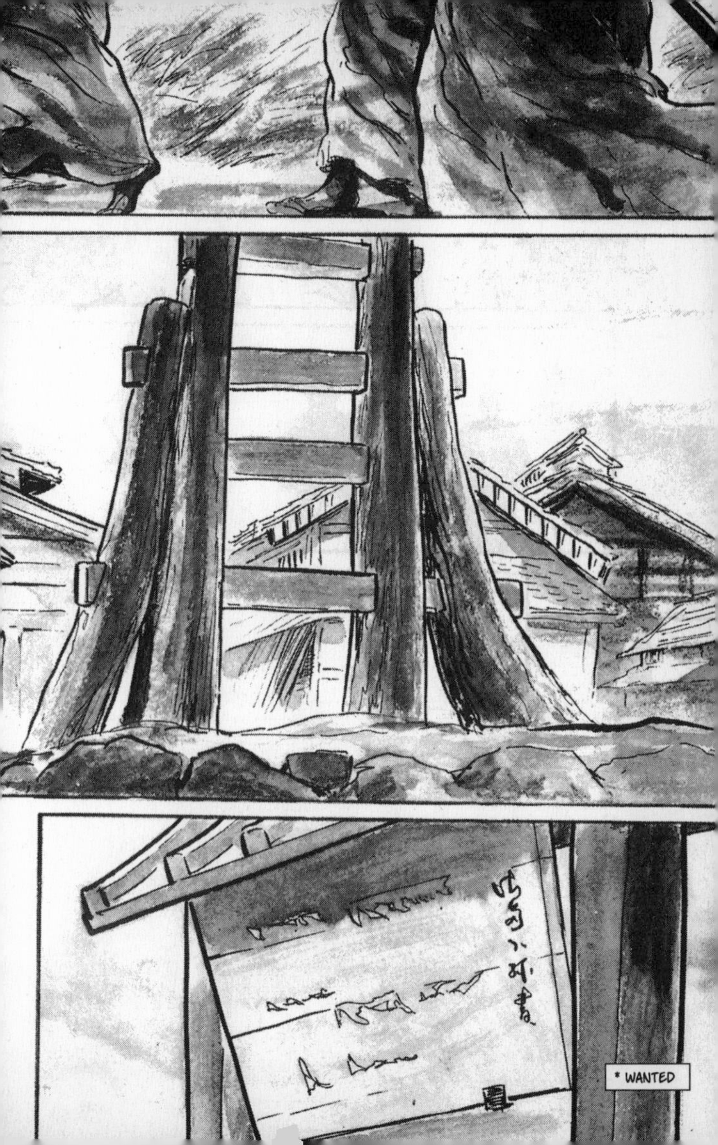
* WANTED

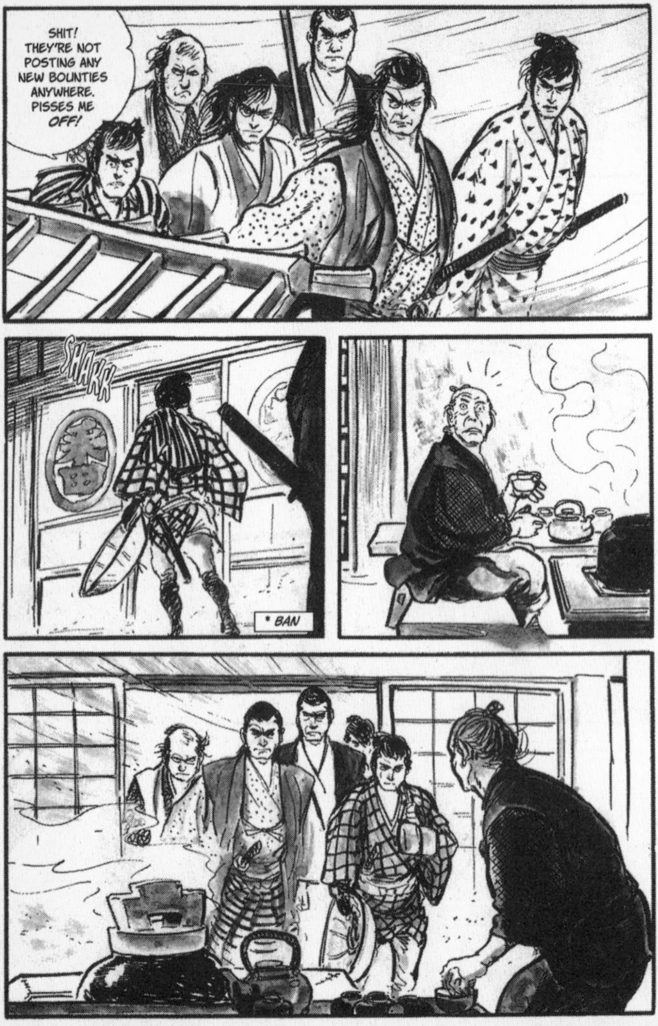
SHIT! THEY'RE NOT POSTING ANY NEW BOUNTIES ANYWHERE. PISSES ME OFF!
SHAKK
* BAN

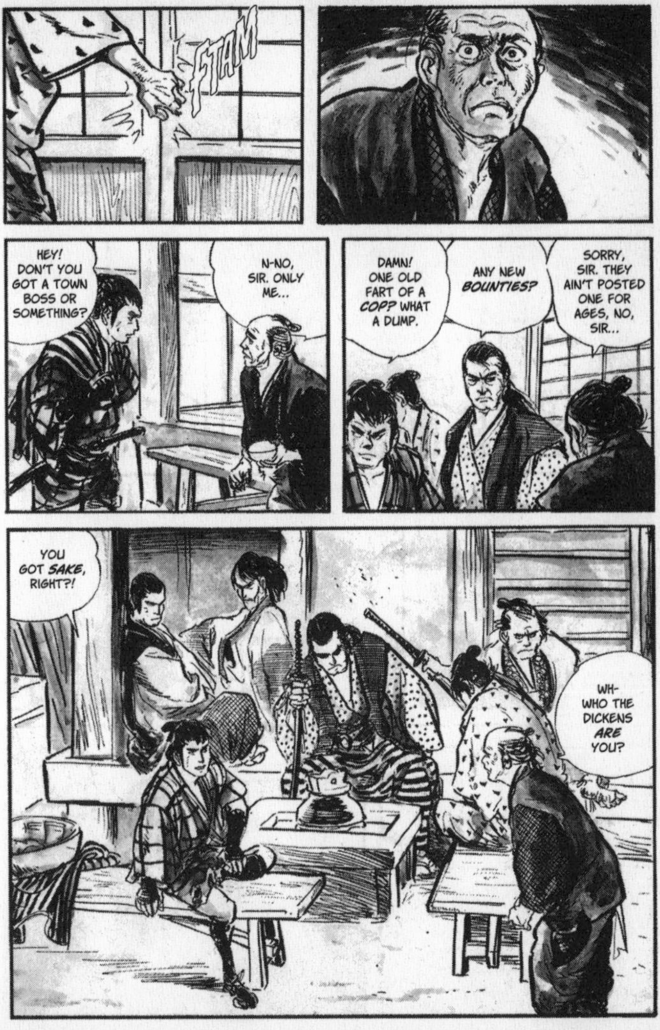
FTAM
HEY! DON'T YOU GOT A TOWN BOSS OR SOMETHING?
N-NO, SIR. ONLY ME...
DAMN! ONE OLD FART OF A COP? WHAT A DUMP.
ANY NEW BOUNTIES?
SORRY, SIR. THEY AIN'T POSTED ONE FOR AGES, NO, SIR...
YOU GOT SAKE, RIGHT?!
WH- WHO THE DICKENS ARE YOU?

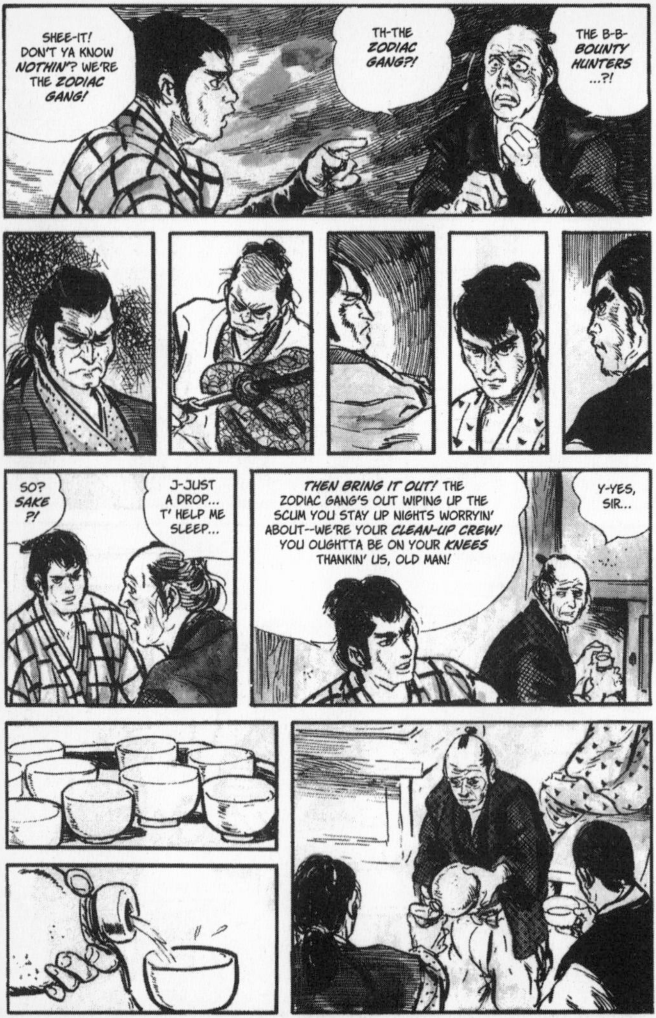
SHEE-IT! DON'T YA KNOW NOTHIN'? WE'RE THE ZODIAC GANG!
TH-THE ZODIAC GANG?!
THE B-B-BOUNTY HUNTERS ...?!
SO? SAKE ?!
J-JUST A DROP... T' HELP ME SLEEP...
THEN BRING IT OUT! THE ZODIAC GANG'S OUT WIPING UP THE SCUM YOU STAY UP NIGHTS WORRYIN' ABOUT--WE'RE YOUR CLEAN-UP CREW! YOU OUGHTTA BE ON YOUR KNEES THANKIN' US, OLD MAN!
Y-YES, SIR...

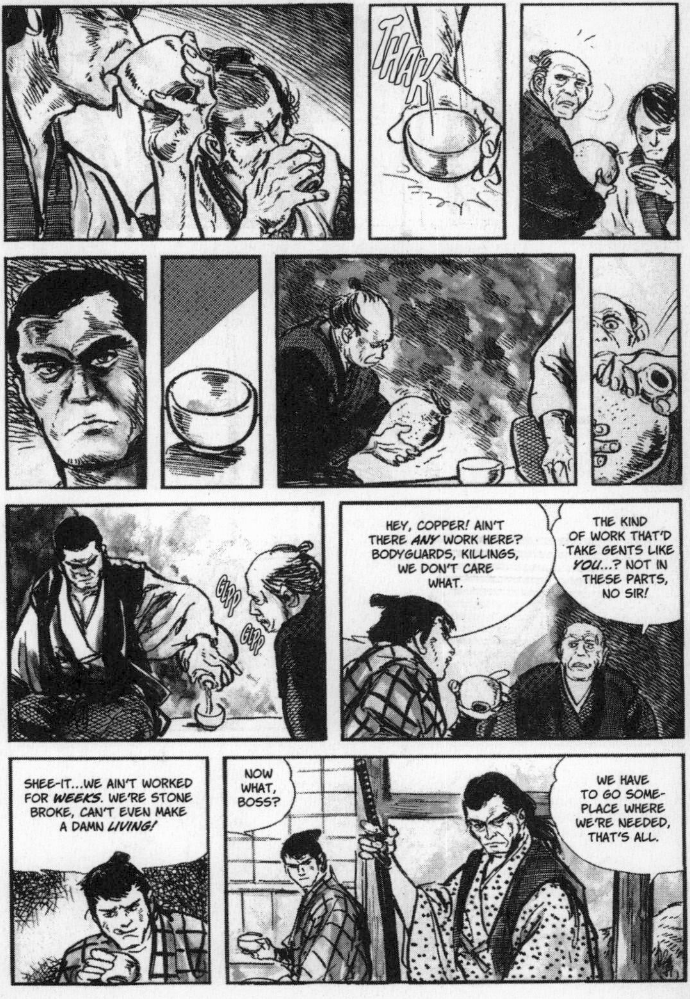
THAK
GLPP
GLPP
HEY, COPPER! AIN'T THERE ANY WORK HERE? BODYGUARDS, KILLINGS, WE DON'T CARE WHAT.
THE KIND OF WORK THAT'D TAKE GENTS LIKE YOU...? NOT IN THESE PARTS, NO SIR!
SHEE-IT...WE AIN'T WORKED FOR WEEKS. WE'RE STONE BROKE, CAN'T EVEN MAKE A DAMN LIVING!
NOW WHAT, BOSS?
WE HAVE TO GO SOME-PLACE WHERE WE'RE NEEDED, THAT'S ALL.

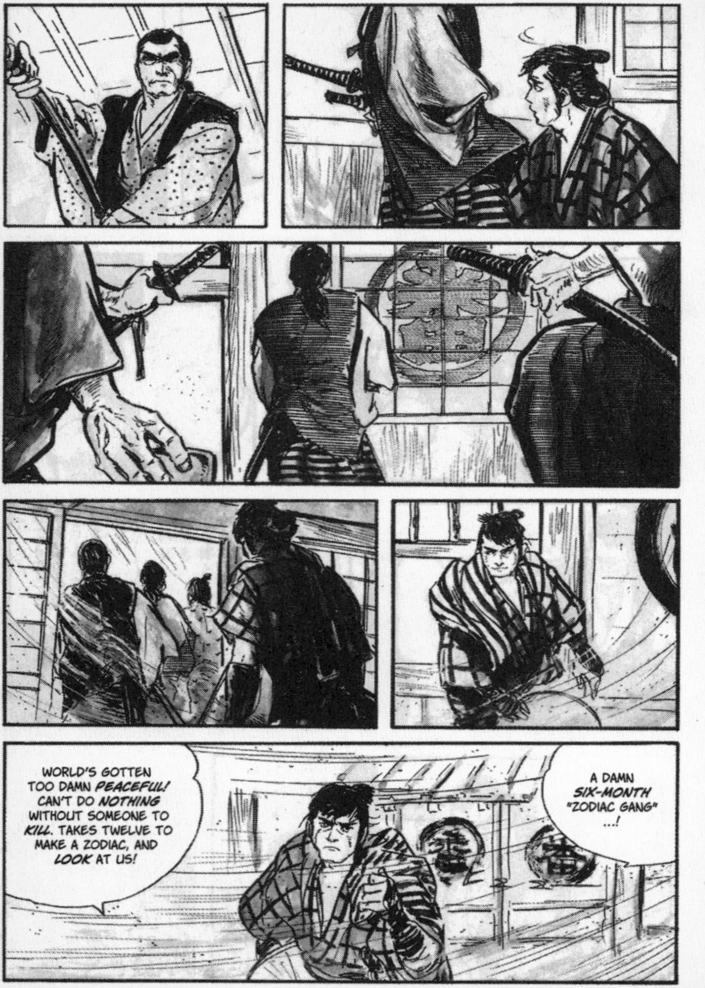
WORLD'S GOTTEN TOO DAMN *PEACEFUL!* CAN'T DO *NOTHING* WITHOUT SOMEONE TO *KILL*. TAKES TWELVE TO MAKE A ZODIAC, AND *LOOK* AT US!
A DAMN *SIX-MONTH* "ZODIAC GANG" ...!

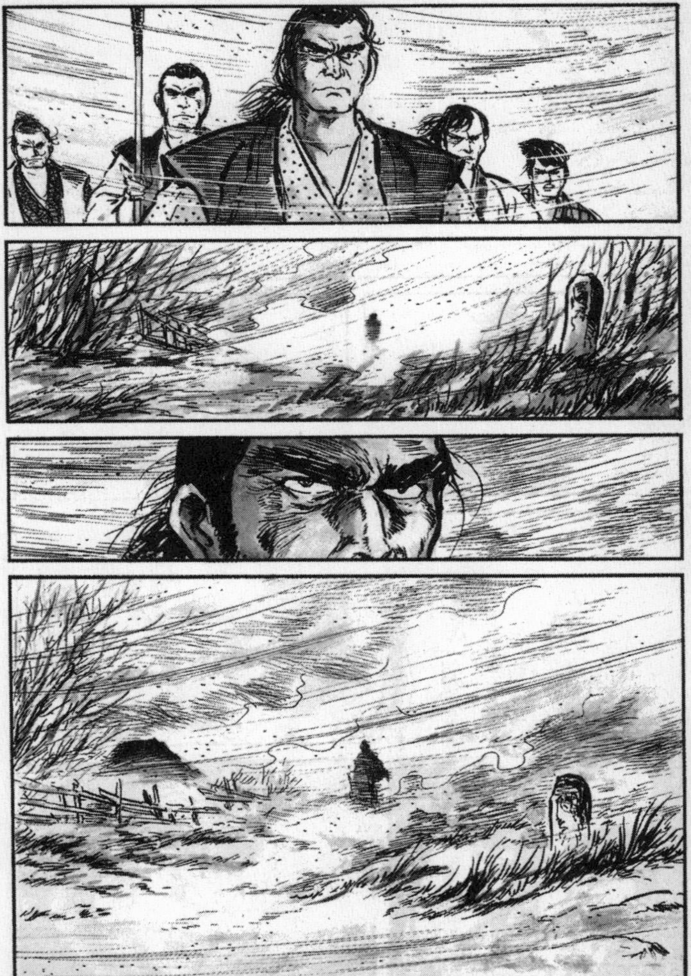

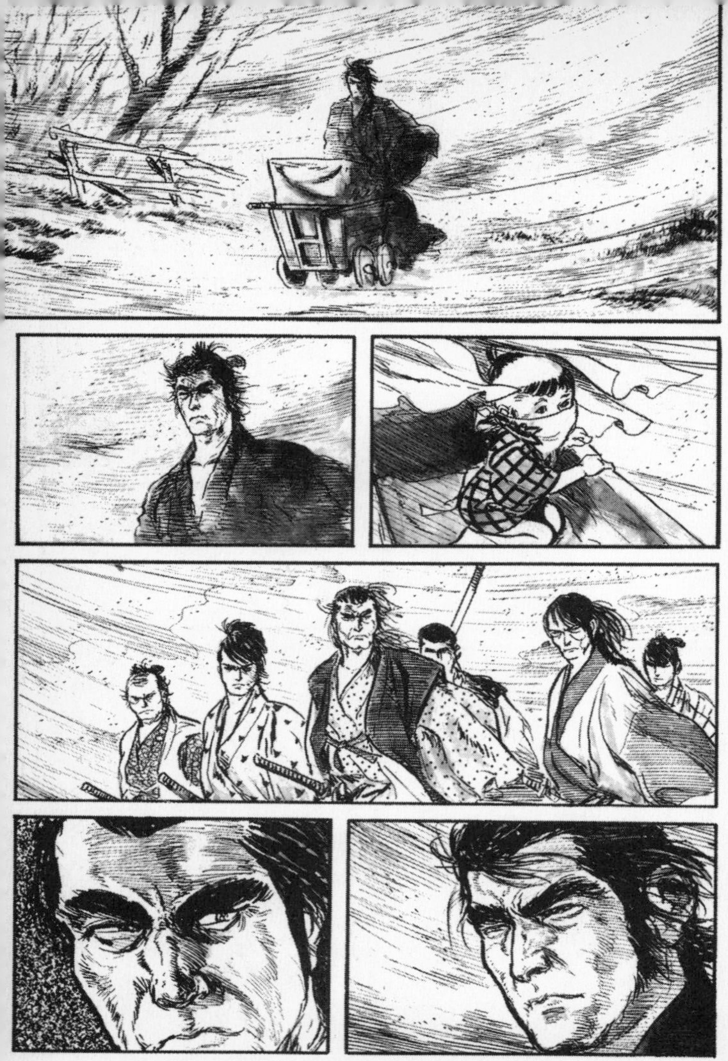

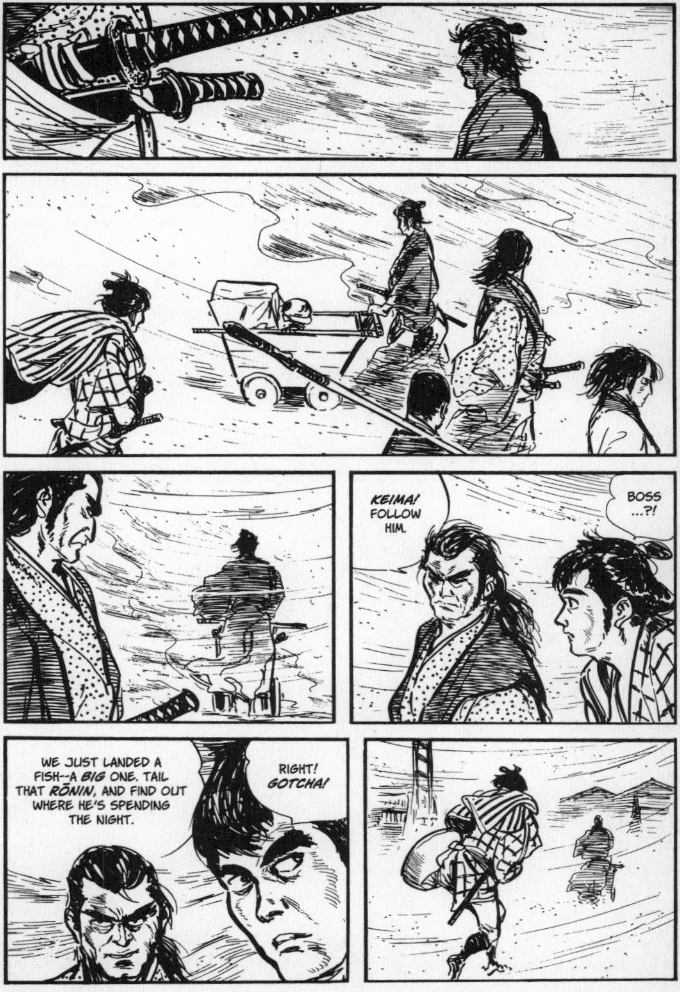
KEIMA! FOLLOW HIM.
BOSS ...?!
WE JUST LANDED A FISH--A *BIG* ONE. TAIL THAT *RŌNIN*, AND FIND OUT WHERE HE'S SPENDING THE NIGHT.
RIGHT! *GOTCHA!*

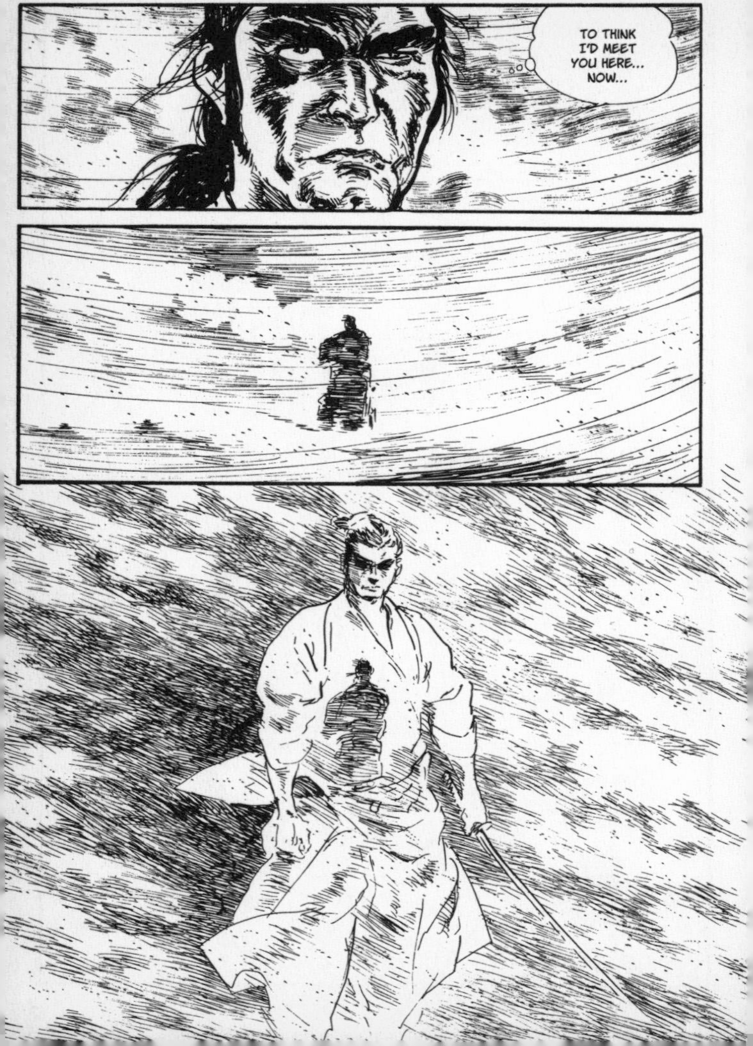
TO THINK I'D MEET YOU HERE... NOW...

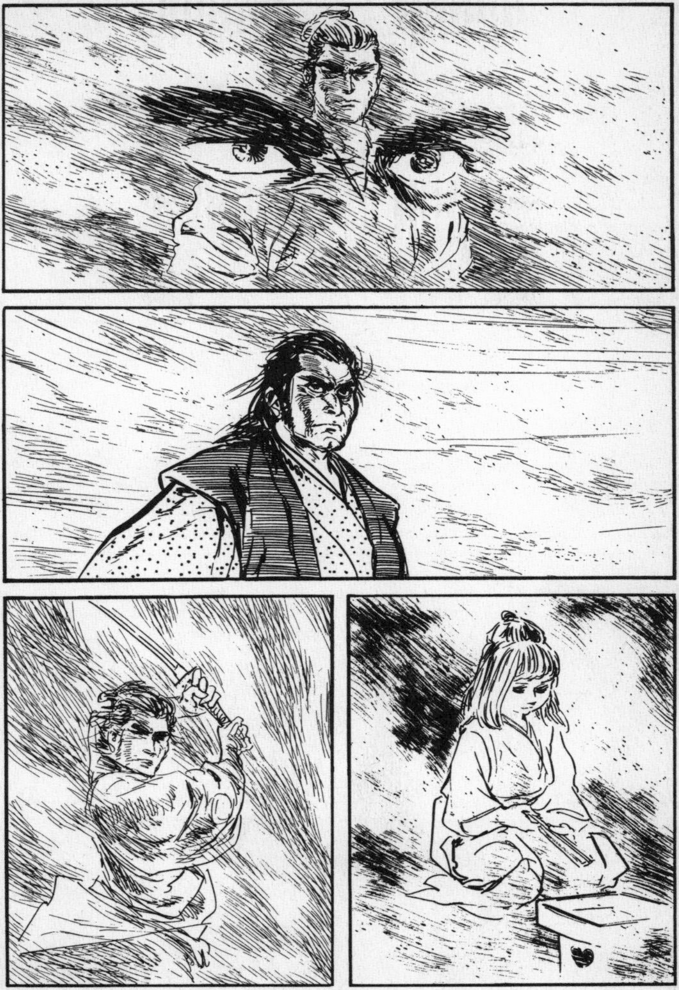

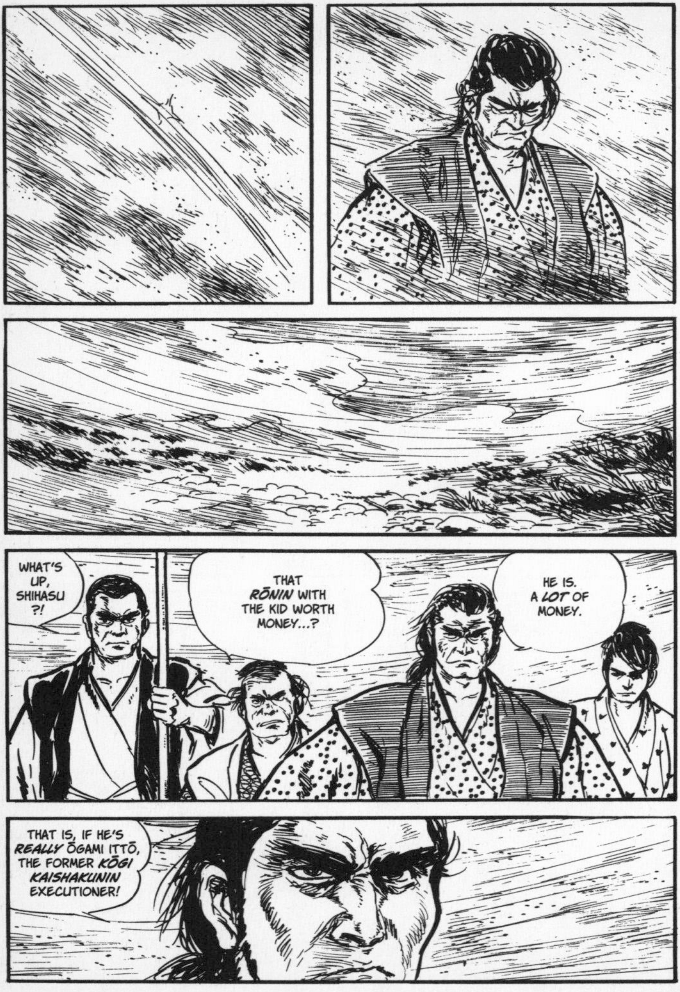
WHAT'S UP, SHIHASU ?!
THAT *RŌNIN* WITH THE KID WORTH MONEY...?
HE IS. A *LOT* OF MONEY.
THAT IS, IF HE'S *REALLY* ŌGAMI ITTŌ, THE FORMER *KŌGI KAISHAKUNIN* EXECUTIONER!

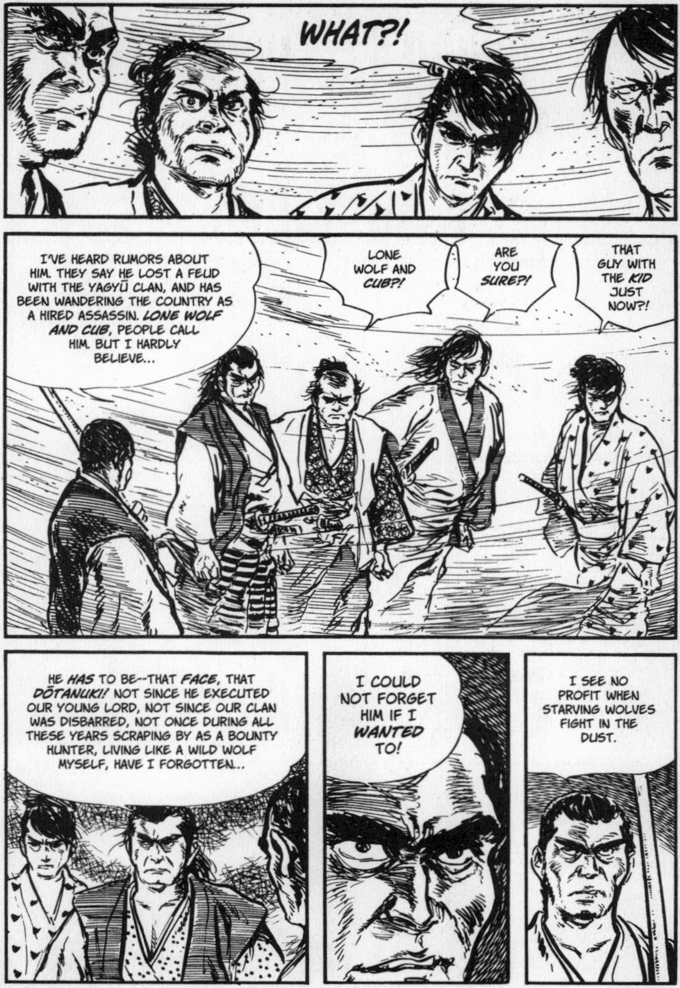
WHAT?!
I'VE HEARD RUMORS ABOUT HIM. THEY SAY HE LOST A FEUD WITH THE YAGYŪ CLAN, AND HAS BEEN WANDERING THE COUNTRY AS A HIRED ASSASSIN. LONE WOLF AND CUB, PEOPLE CALL HIM. BUT I HARDLY BELIEVE...
LONE WOLF AND CUB?!
ARE YOU SURE?!
THAT GUY WITH THE KID JUST NOW?!
HE HAS TO BE--THAT FACE, THAT DŌTANUKI! NOT SINCE HE EXECUTED OUR YOUNG LORD, NOT SINCE OUR CLAN WAS DISBARRED, NOT ONCE DURING ALL THESE YEARS SCRAPING BY AS A BOUNTY HUNTER, LIVING LIKE A WILD WOLF MYSELF, HAVE I FORGOTTEN...
I COULD NOT FORGET HIM IF I WANTED TO!
I SEE NO PROFIT WHEN STARVING WOLVES FIGHT IN THE DUST.

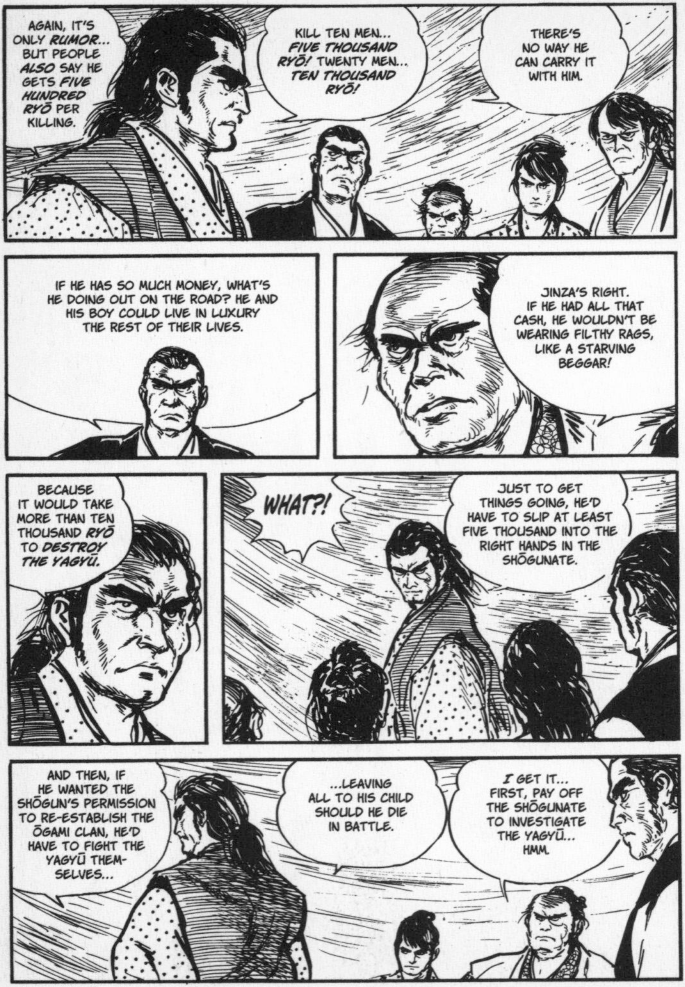
AGAIN, IT'S ONLY *RUMOR*... BUT PEOPLE *ALSO* SAY HE GETS *FIVE HUNDRED RYŌ* PER KILLING.
KILL TEN MEN... *FIVE THOUSAND RYŌ!* TWENTY MEN... *TEN THOUSAND RYŌ!*
THERE'S NO WAY HE CAN CARRY IT WITH HIM.
IF HE HAS SO MUCH MONEY, WHAT'S HE DOING OUT ON THE ROAD? HE AND HIS BOY COULD LIVE IN LUXURY THE REST OF THEIR LIVES.
JINZA'S RIGHT. IF HE HAD ALL THAT CASH, HE WOULDN'T BE WEARING FILTHY RAGS, LIKE A STARVING BEGGAR!
BECAUSE IT WOULD TAKE MORE THAN TEN THOUSAND *RYŌ* TO *DESTROY THE YAGYŪ.*
WHAT?!
JUST TO GET THINGS GOING, HE'D HAVE TO SLIP AT LEAST FIVE THOUSAND INTO THE RIGHT HANDS IN THE SHŌGUNATE.
AND THEN, IF HE WANTED THE SHŌGUN'S PERMISSION TO RE-ESTABLISH THE ŌGAMI CLAN, HE'D HAVE TO FIGHT THE YAGYŪ THEMSELVES...
...LEAVING ALL TO HIS CHILD SHOULD HE DIE IN BATTLE.
I GET IT... FIRST, PAY OFF THE SHŌGUNATE TO INVESTIGATE THE YAGYŪ... HMM.

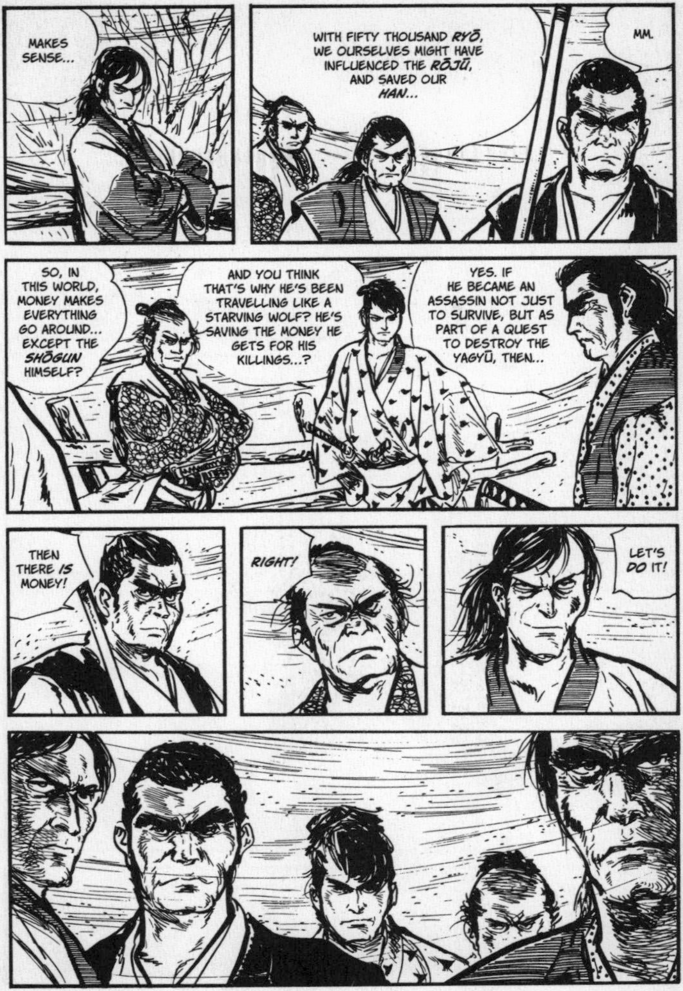
MAKES SENSE...
WITH FIFTY THOUSAND RYŌ, WE OURSELVES MIGHT HAVE INFLUENCED THE RŌJŪ, AND SAVED OUR HAN...
MM.
SO, IN THIS WORLD, MONEY MAKES EVERYTHING GO AROUND... EXCEPT THE SHŌGUN HIMSELF?
AND YOU THINK THAT'S WHY HE'S BEEN TRAVELLING LIKE A STARVING WOLF? HE'S SAVING THE MONEY HE GETS FOR HIS KILLINGS...?
YES. IF HE BECAME AN ASSASSIN NOT JUST TO SURVIVE, BUT AS PART OF A QUEST TO DESTROY THE YAGYŪ, THEN...
THEN THERE IS MONEY!
RIGHT!
LET'S DO IT!

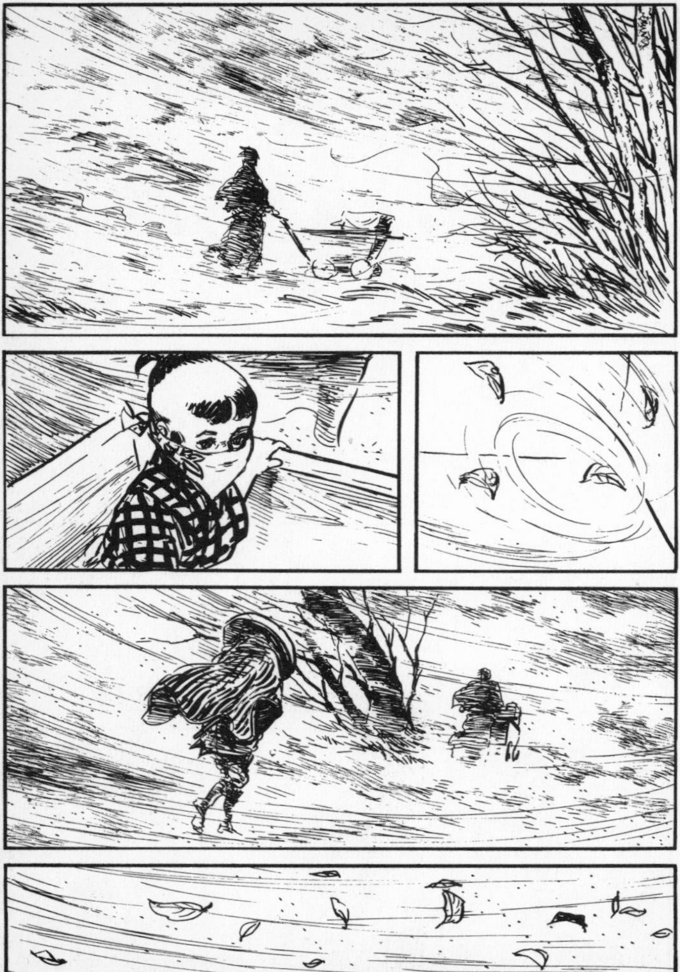

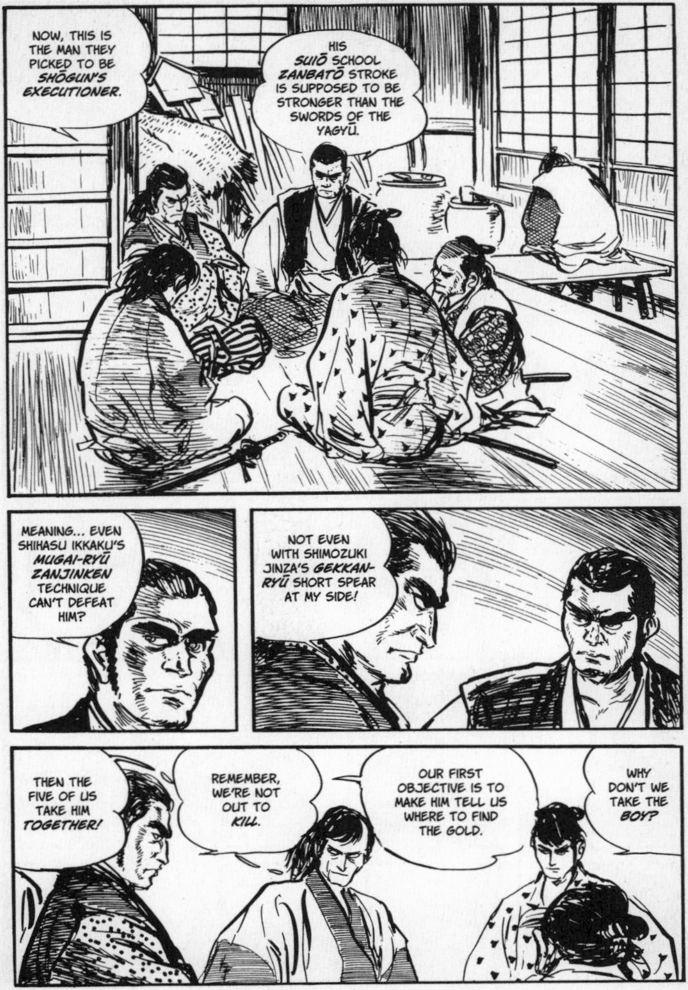
NOW, THIS IS THE MAN THEY PICKED TO BE SHŌGUN'S EXECUTIONER.
HIS SUIŌ SCHOOL ZANBATŌ STROKE IS SUPPOSED TO BE STRONGER THAN THE SWORDS OF THE YAGYŪ.
MEANING... EVEN SHIHASU IKKAKU'S MUGAI-RYŪ ZANJINKEN TECHNIQUE CAN'T DEFEAT HIM?
NOT EVEN WITH SHIMOZUKI JINZA'S GEKKAN-RYŪ SHORT SPEAR AT MY SIDE!
THEN THE FIVE OF US TAKE HIM TOGETHER!
REMEMBER, WE'RE NOT OUT TO KILL.
OUR FIRST OBJECTIVE IS TO MAKE HIM TELL US WHERE TO FIND THE GOLD.
WHY DON'T WE TAKE THE BOY?

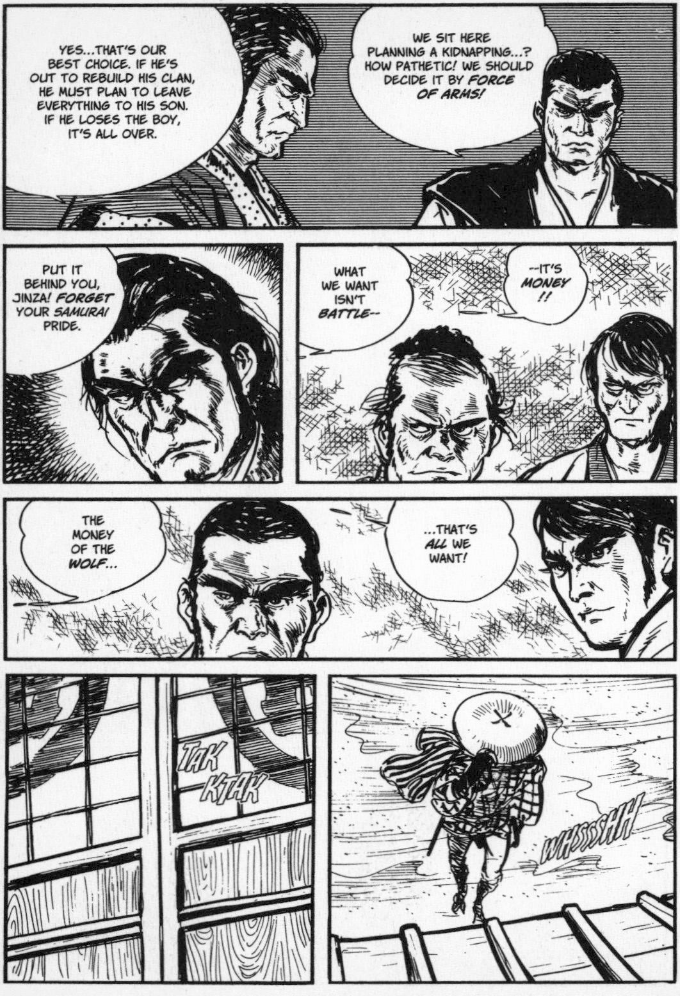
YES...THAT'S OUR BEST CHOICE. IF HE'S OUT TO REBUILD HIS CLAN, HE MUST PLAN TO LEAVE EVERYTHING TO HIS SON. IF HE LOSES THE BOY, IT'S ALL OVER.
WE SIT HERE PLANNING A KIDNAPPING...? HOW PATHETIC! WE SHOULD DECIDE IT BY FORCE OF ARMS!
PUT IT BEHIND YOU, JINZA! FORGET YOUR SAMURAI PRIDE.
WHAT WE WANT ISN'T BATTLE--
--IT'S MONEY !!
THE MONEY OF THE WOLF...
...THAT'S ALL WE WANT!
TAK KTAK
WHSSSSHH

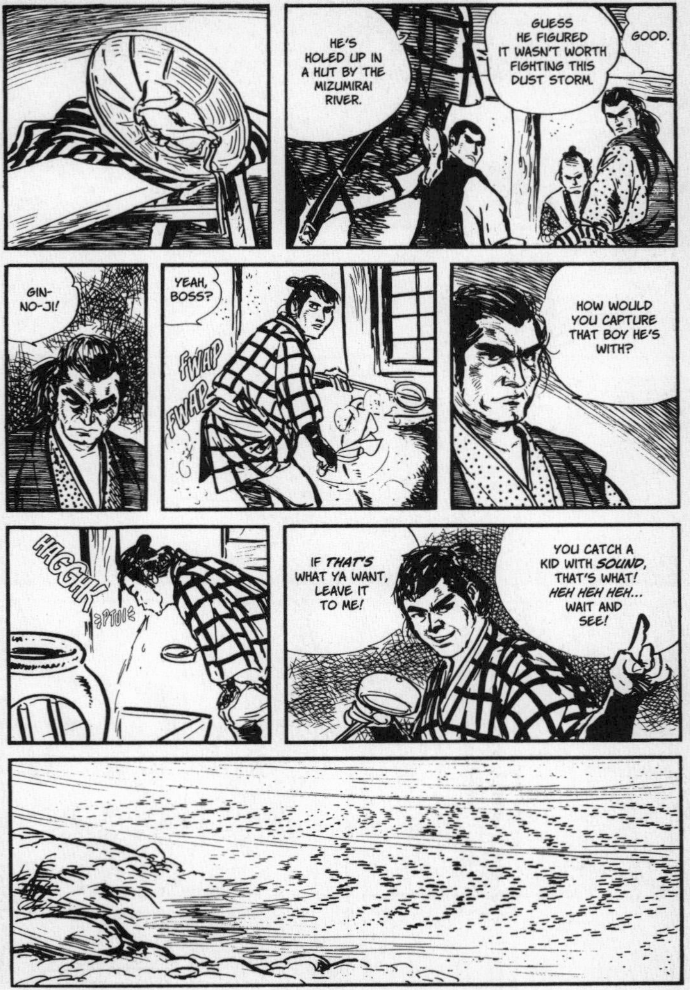

HE'S HOLED UP IN A HUT BY THE MIZUMIRAI RIVER.
GUESS HE FIGURED IT WASN'T WORTH FIGHTING THIS DUST STORM.
GOOD.
GIN-NO-JI!
YEAH, BOSS?
FWAP
FWAP
HOW WOULD YOU CAPTURE THAT BOY HE'S WITH?
HAGGHK
PTUI
IF *THAT'S* WHAT YA WANT, LEAVE IT TO ME!
YOU CATCH A KID WITH *SOUND*, THAT'S WHAT! *HEH HEH HEH...* WAIT AND SEE!

WHSSSHHH

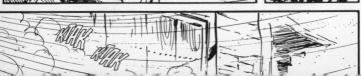

KIAK
KIAK

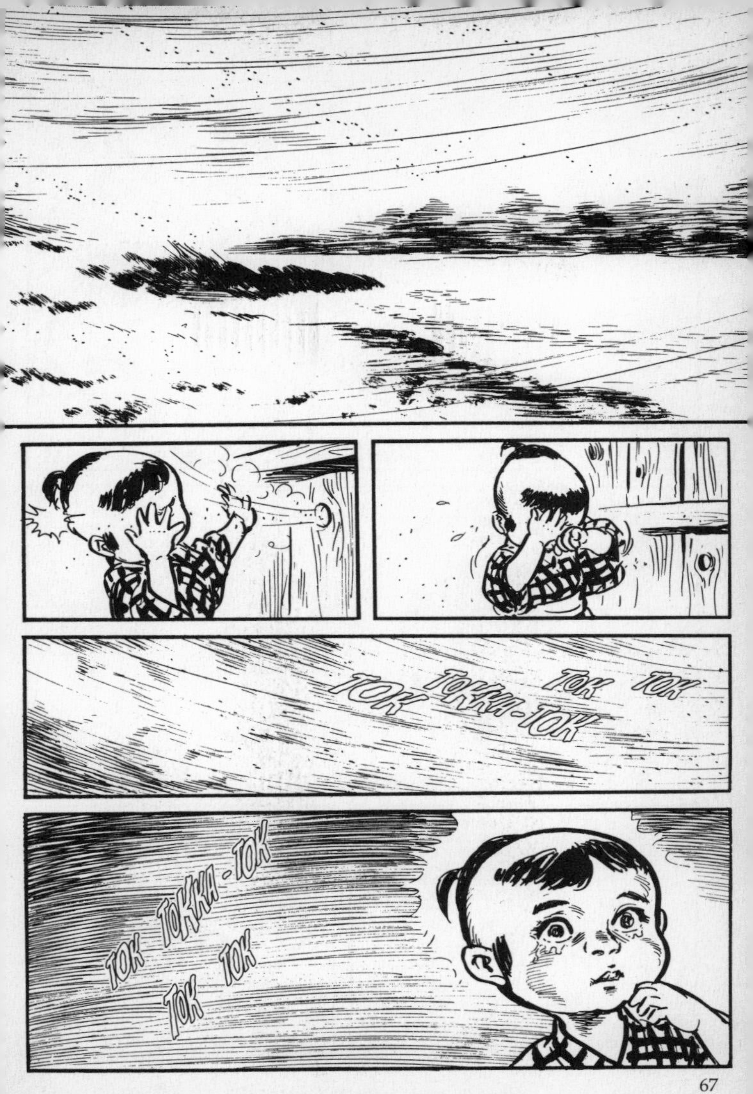
TOK TOKKA-TOK TOK TOK
TOK TOKKA-TOK TOK TOK

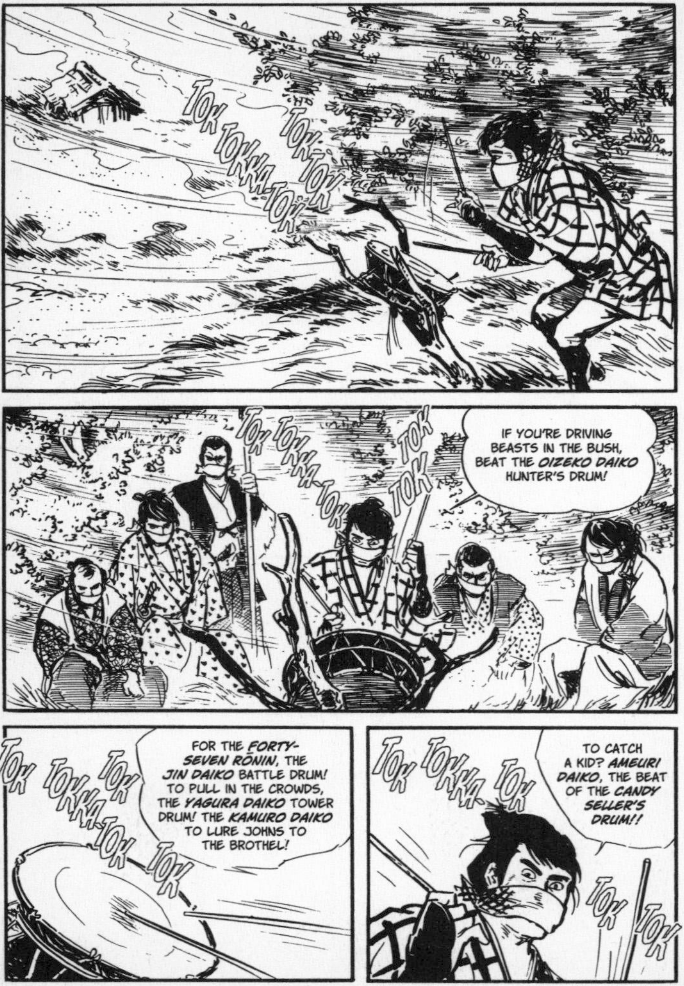
TOK TOKKA-TOK
TOK-TOK TOK
TOK TOKKA-TOK
TOK TOK
IF YOU'RE DRIVING BEASTS IN THE BUSH, BEAT THE *OIZEKO DAIKO* HUNTER'S DRUM!
TOK TOKKA-TOK TOK TOK
FOR THE *FORTY-SEVEN RŌNIN*, THE *JIN DAIKO* BATTLE DRUM! TO PULL IN THE CROWDS, THE *YAGURA DAIKO* TOWER DRUM! THE *KAMURO DAIKO* TO LURE JOHNS TO THE BROTHEL!
TOK TOKKA TOK
TO CATCH A KID? *AMEURI DAIKO*, THE BEAT OF THE *CANDY SELLER'S DRUM!!*
TOK TOK

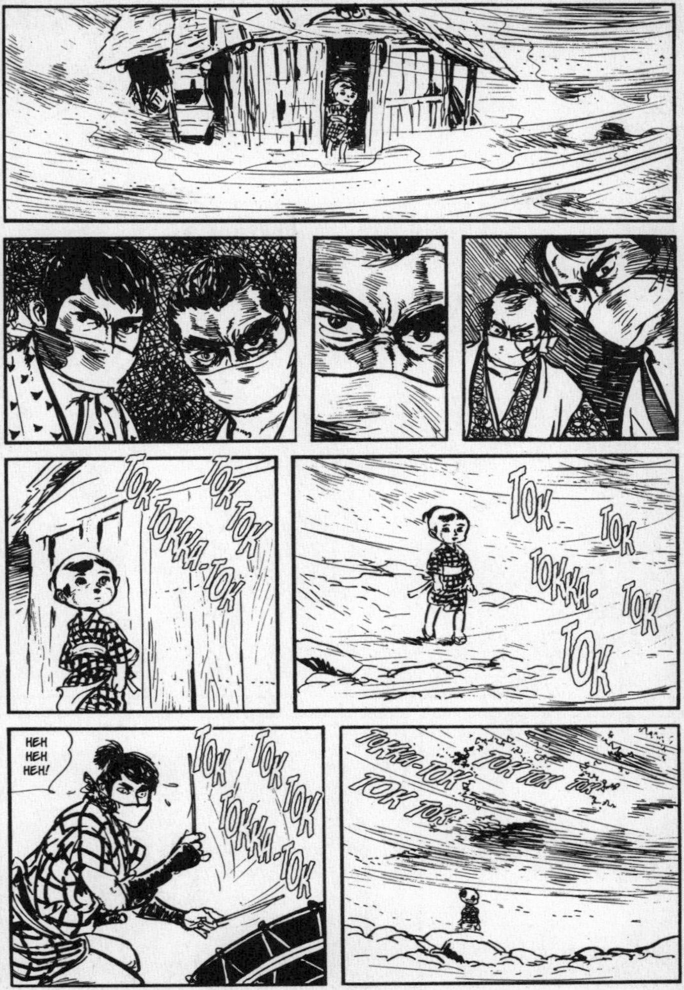
TOK TOKKA-TOK
TOK TOK
TOK TOK TOKKA-TOK TOK
HEH HEH HEH!
TOK TOK TOKKA-TOK TOK
TOKKA-TOK TOK TOK TOK
TOK TOK

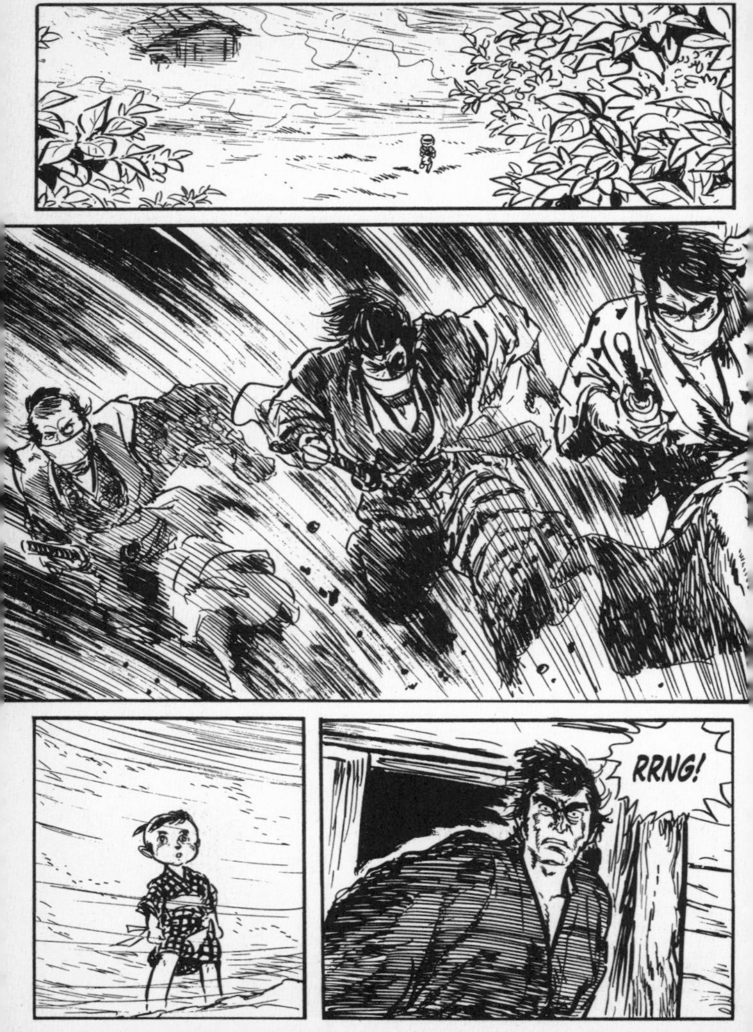
RRNG!

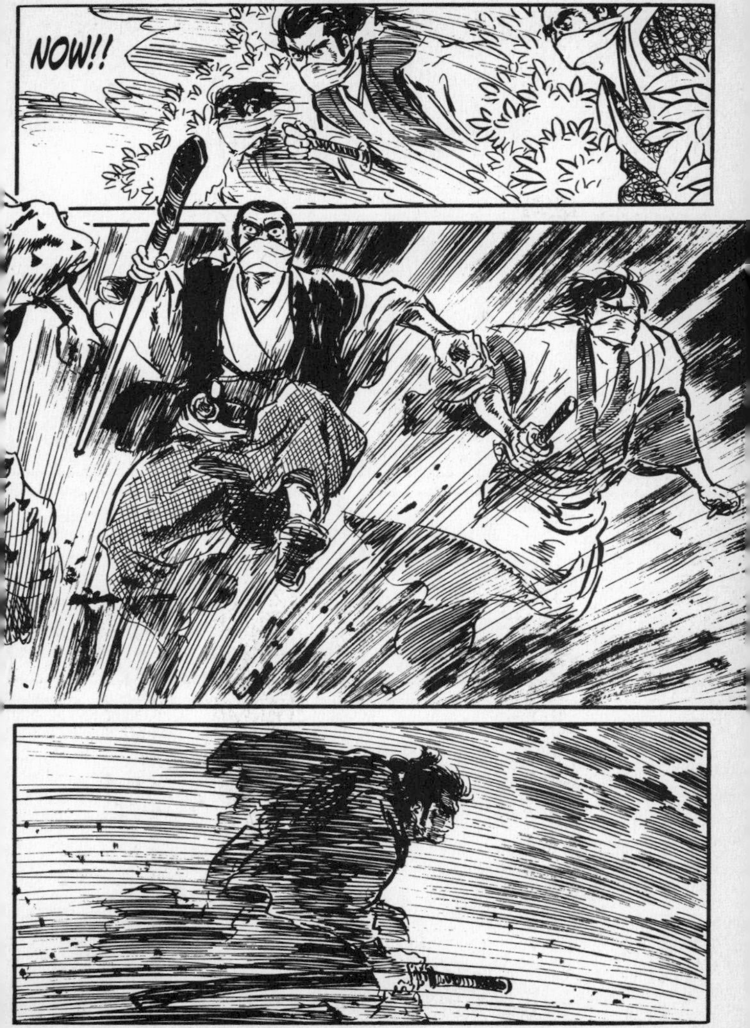
NOW!!

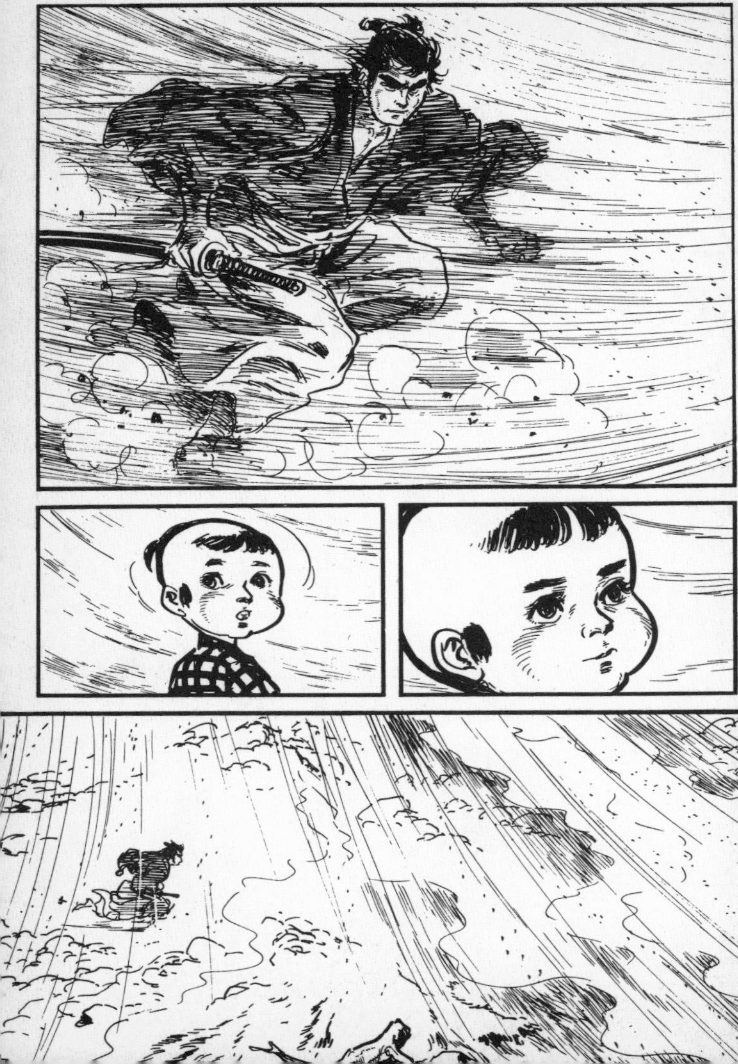

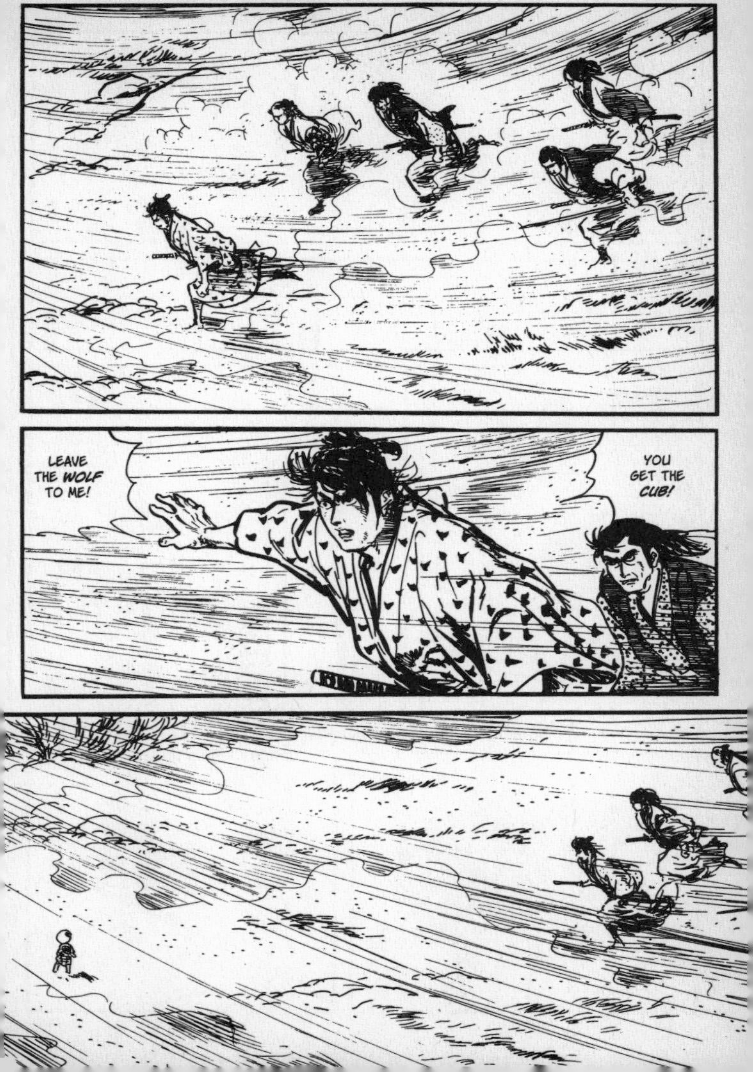
LEAVE THE WOLF TO ME!
YOU GET THE CUB!

RYAA!!
FWHTT
HYAH!
WHTT

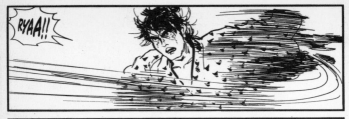

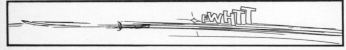

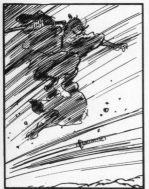

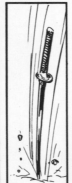

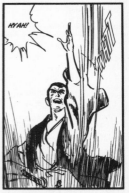

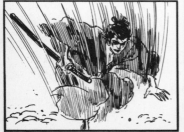

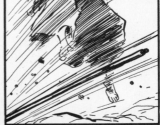

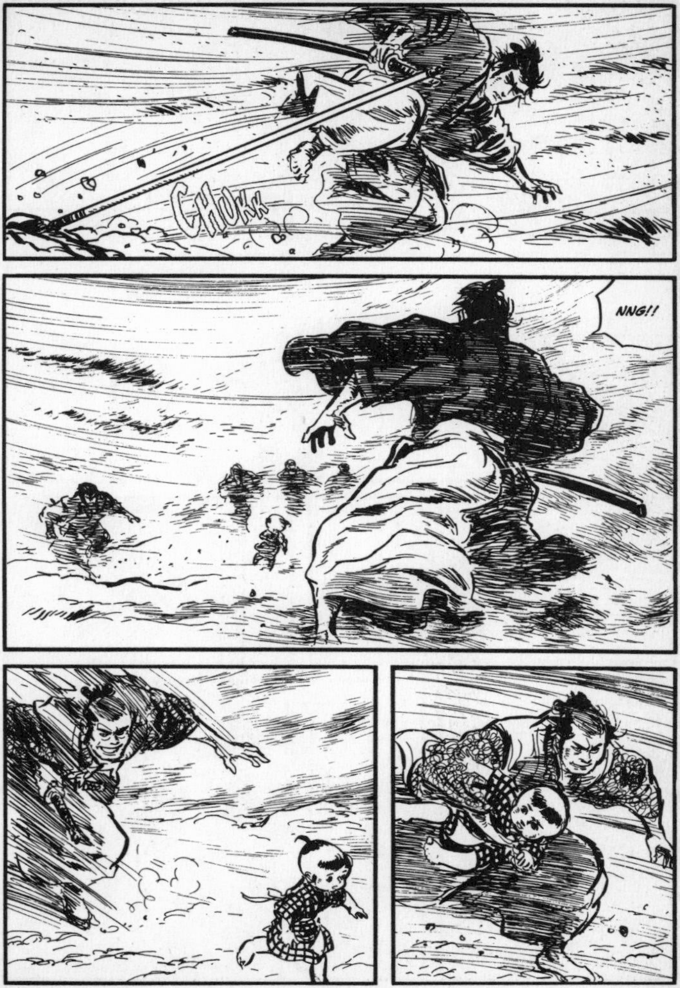
CHUKK
NNG!!

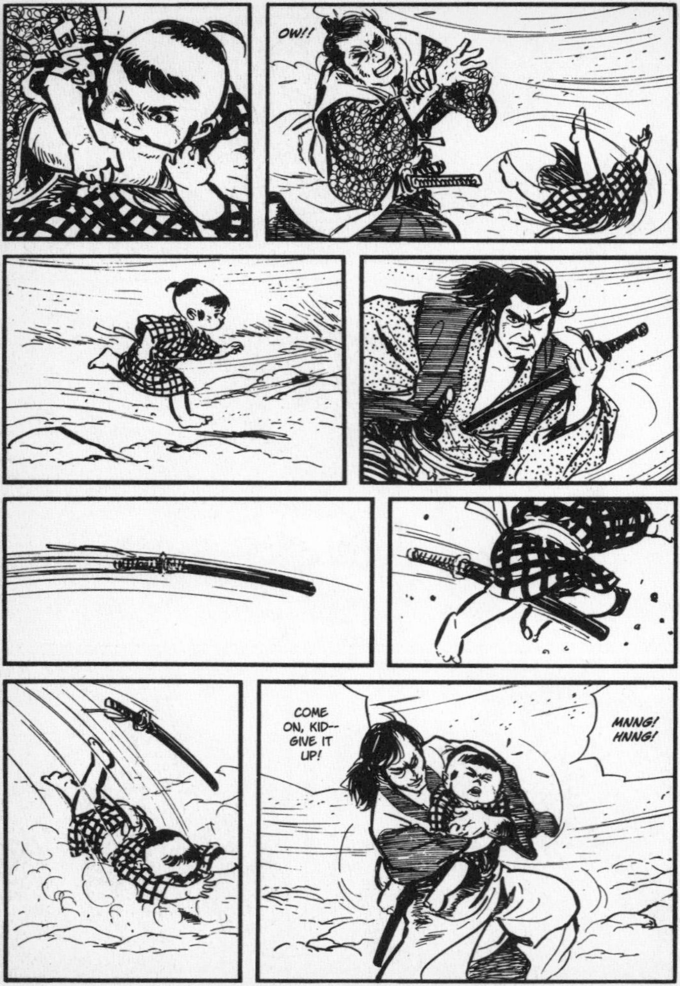
OW!!
COME ON, KID-- GIVE IT UP!
MNNG! HNNG!

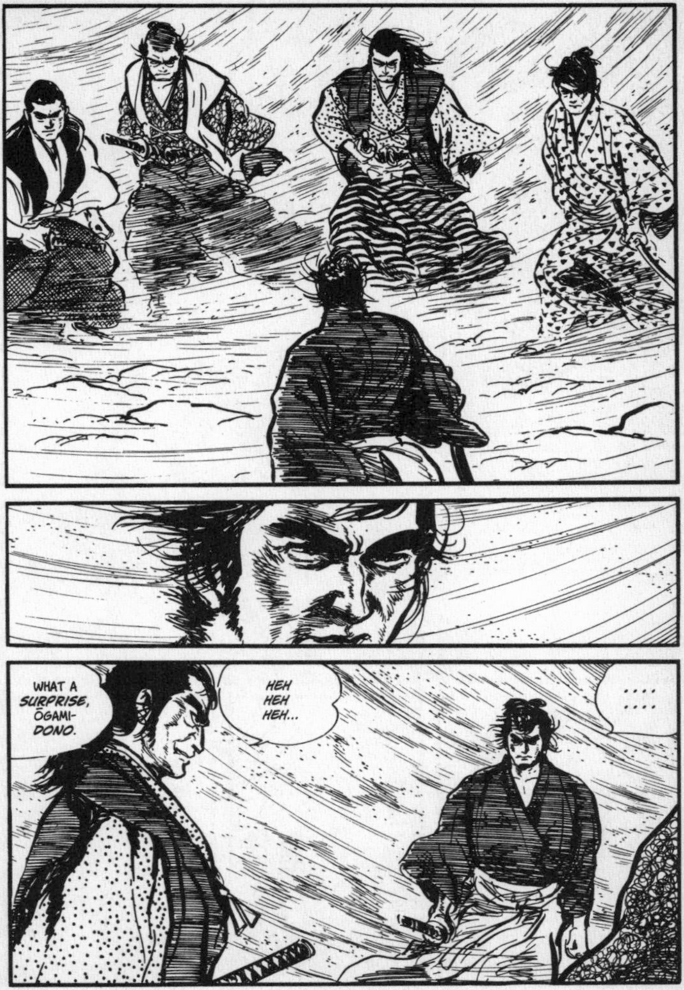
WHAT A SURPRISE, ŌGAMI-DONO.
HEH HEH HEH...
....
....

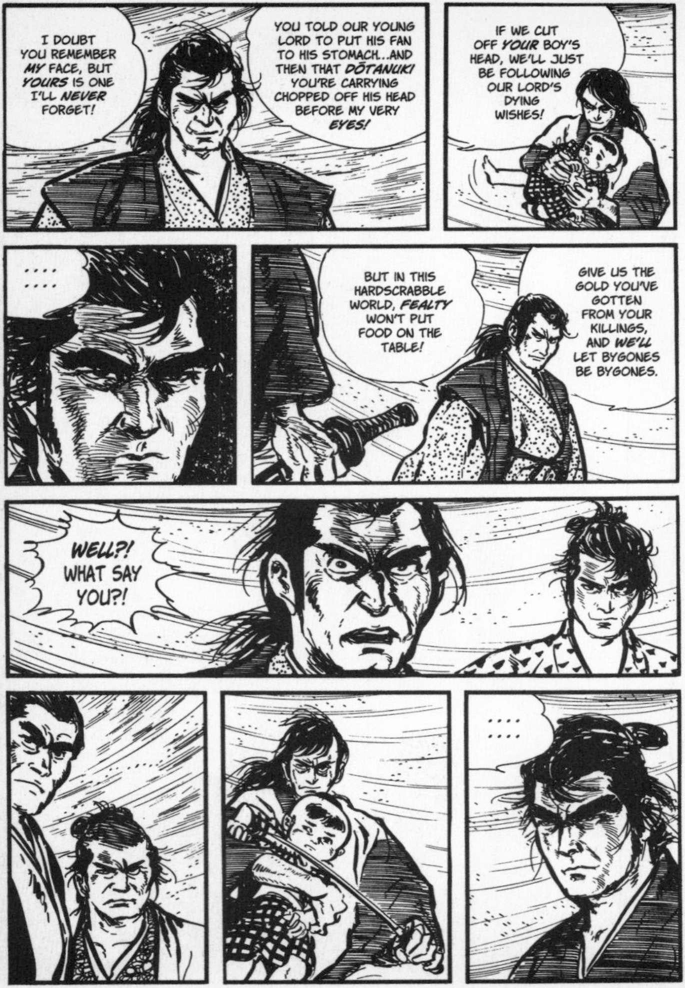
I DOUBT YOU REMEMBER MY FACE, BUT YOURS IS ONE I'LL NEVER FORGET!
YOU TOLD OUR YOUNG LORD TO PUT HIS FAN TO HIS STOMACH...AND THEN THAT DŌTANUKI YOU'RE CARRYING CHOPPED OFF HIS HEAD BEFORE MY VERY EYES!
IF WE CUT OFF YOUR BOY'S HEAD, WE'LL JUST BE FOLLOWING OUR LORD'S DYING WISHES!
....
....
BUT IN THIS HARDSCRABBLE WORLD, FEALTY WON'T PUT FOOD ON THE TABLE!
GIVE US THE GOLD YOU'VE GOTTEN FROM YOUR KILLINGS, AND WE'LL LET BYGONES BE BYGONES.
WELL?! WHAT SAY YOU?!
....
....

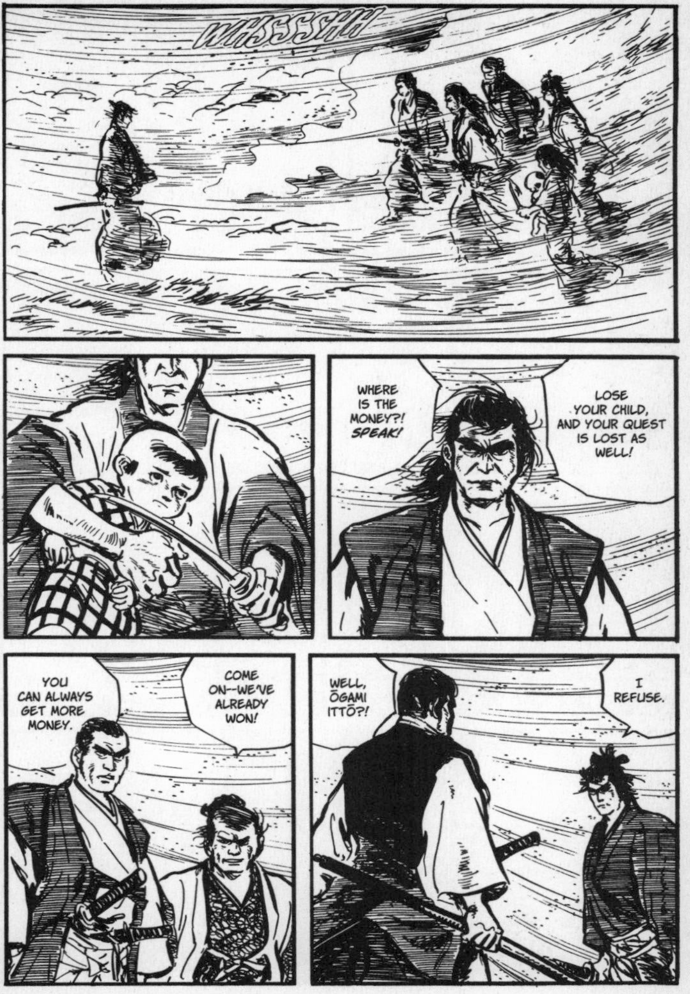
WHSSSHH
WHERE IS THE MONEY?! *SPEAK!*
LOSE YOUR CHILD, AND YOUR QUEST IS LOST AS WELL!
YOU CAN ALWAYS GET MORE MONEY.
COME ON--WE'VE ALREADY WON!
WELL, ŌGAMI ITTŌ?!
I REFUSE.

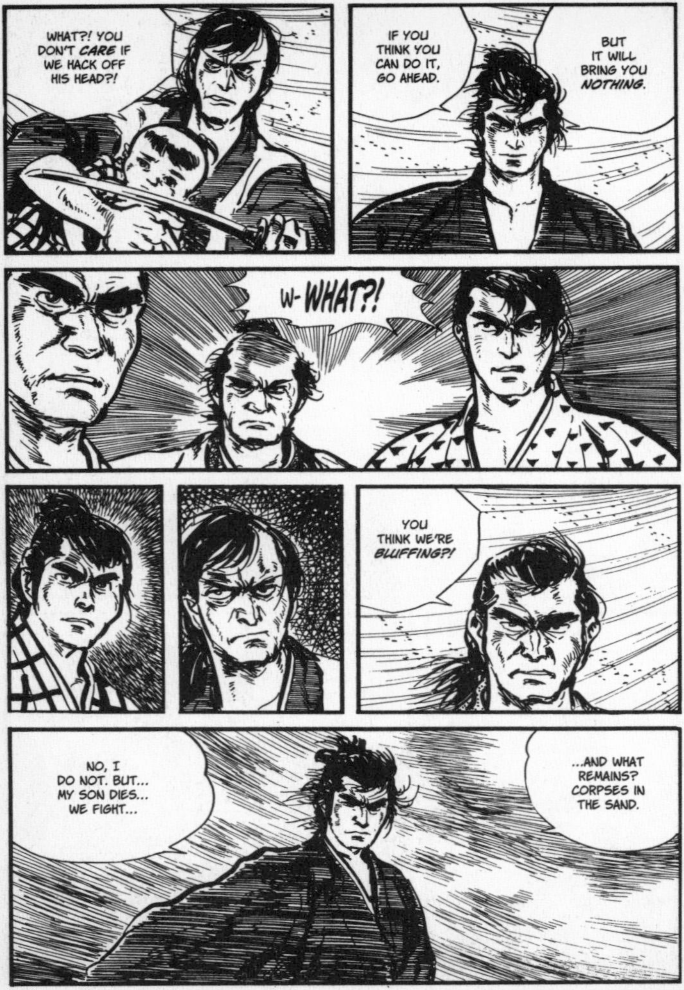
WHAT?! YOU DON'T *CARE* IF WE HACK OFF HIS HEAD?!
IF YOU THINK YOU CAN DO IT, GO AHEAD.
BUT IT WILL BRING YOU *NOTHING*.
W-WHAT?!
YOU THINK WE'RE *BLUFFING?!*
NO, I DO NOT. BUT... MY SON DIES... WE FIGHT...
...AND WHAT REMAINS? CORPSES IN THE SAND.

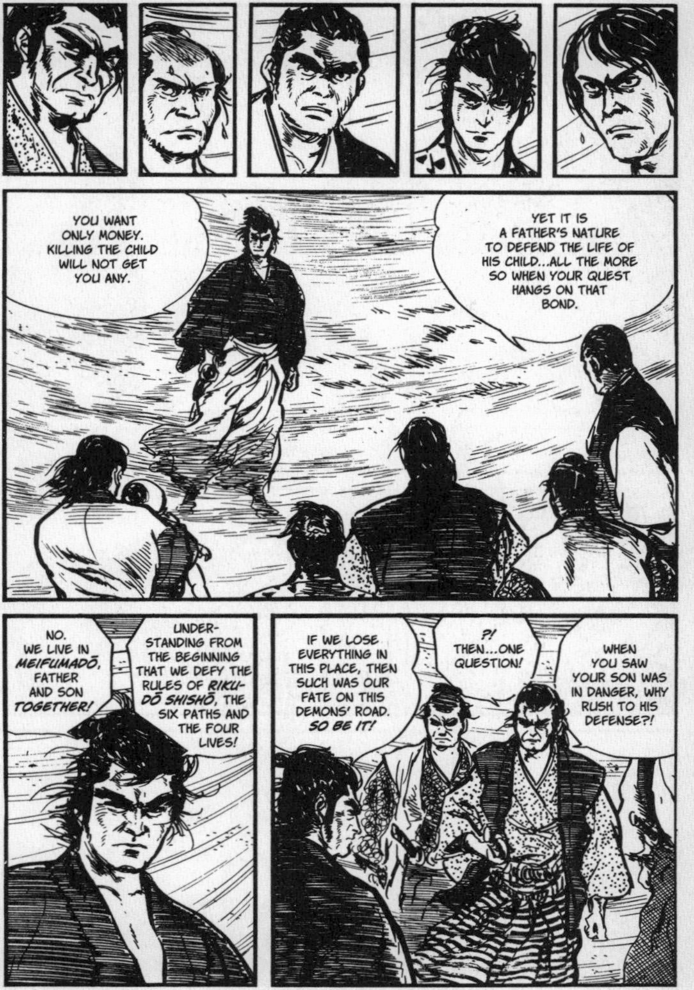
YOU WANT ONLY MONEY. KILLING THE CHILD WILL NOT GET YOU ANY.
YET IT IS A FATHER'S NATURE TO DEFEND THE LIFE OF HIS CHILD...ALL THE MORE SO WHEN YOUR QUEST HANGS ON THAT BOND.
NO. WE LIVE IN *MEIFUMADŌ*, FATHER AND SON *TOGETHER!*
UNDER-STANDING FROM THE BEGINNING THAT WE DEFY THE RULES OF *RIKU-DŌ SHISHŌ*, THE SIX PATHS AND THE FOUR LIVES!
IF WE LOSE EVERYTHING IN THIS PLACE, THEN SUCH WAS OUR FATE ON THIS DEMONS' ROAD. *SO BE IT!*
?! THEN...ONE QUESTION!
WHEN YOU SAW YOUR SON WAS IN DANGER, WHY RUSH TO HIS DEFENSE?!

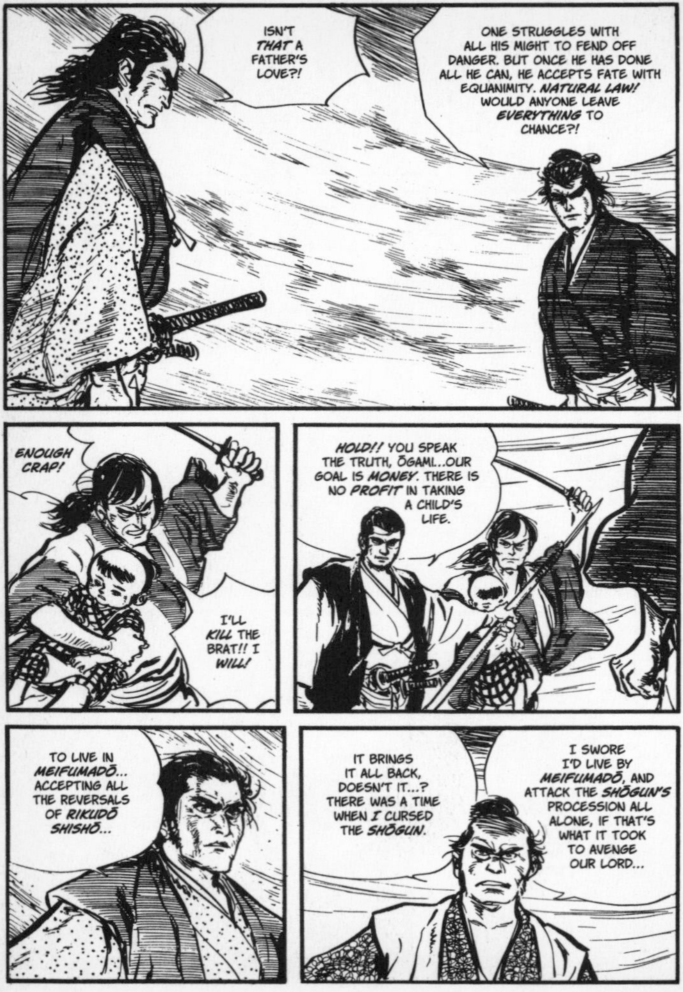
ISN'T THAT A FATHER'S LOVE?!
ONE STRUGGLES WITH ALL HIS MIGHT TO FEND OFF DANGER. BUT ONCE HE HAS DONE ALL HE CAN, HE ACCEPTS FATE WITH EQUANIMITY. NATURAL LAW! WOULD ANYONE LEAVE EVERYTHING TO CHANCE?!
ENOUGH CRAP!
I'LL KILL THE BRAT!! I WILL!
HOLD!! YOU SPEAK THE TRUTH, ŌGAMI...OUR GOAL IS MONEY. THERE IS NO PROFIT IN TAKING A CHILD'S LIFE.
TO LIVE IN MEIFUMADŌ... ACCEPTING ALL THE REVERSALS OF RIKUDŌ SHISHŌ...
IT BRINGS IT ALL BACK, DOESN'T IT...? THERE WAS A TIME WHEN I CURSED THE SHŌGUN.
I SWORE I'D LIVE BY MEIFUMADŌ, AND ATTACK THE SHŌGUN'S PROCESSION ALL ALONE, IF THAT'S WHAT IT TOOK TO AVENGE OUR LORD...

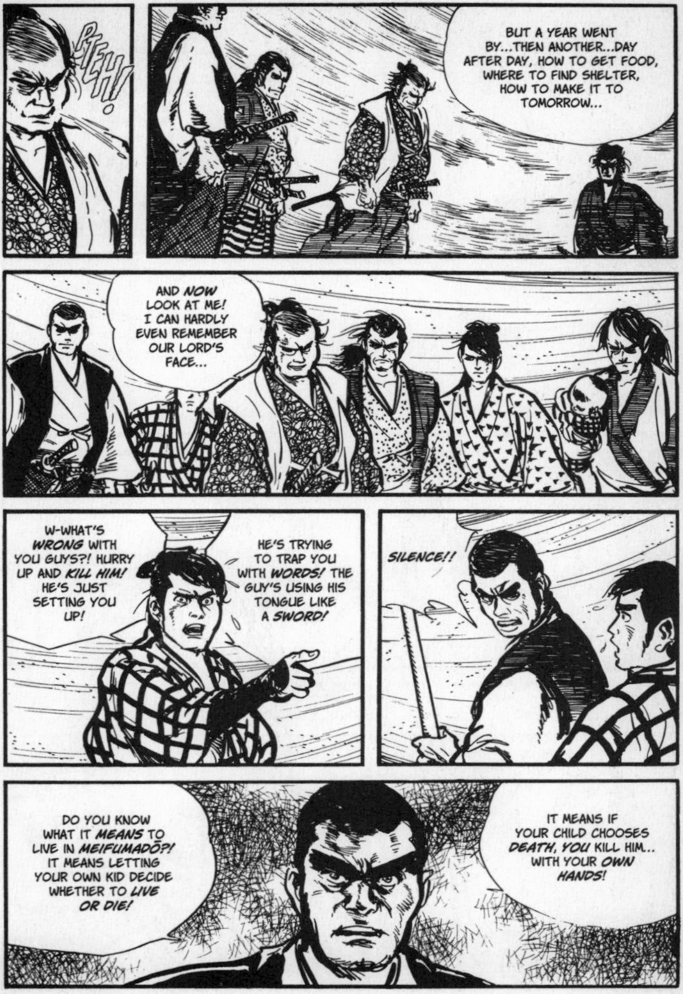
PTEH!
BUT A YEAR WENT BY...THEN ANOTHER...DAY AFTER DAY, HOW TO GET FOOD, WHERE TO FIND SHELTER, HOW TO MAKE IT TO TOMORROW...
AND NOW LOOK AT ME! I CAN HARDLY EVEN REMEMBER OUR LORD'S FACE...
W-WHAT'S WRONG WITH YOU GUYS?! HURRY UP AND KILL HIM! HE'S JUST SETTING YOU UP!
HE'S TRYING TO TRAP YOU WITH WORDS! THE GUY'S USING HIS TONGUE LIKE A SWORD!
SILENCE!!
DO YOU KNOW WHAT IT MEANS TO LIVE IN MEIFUMADŌ?! IT MEANS LETTING YOUR OWN KID DECIDE WHETHER TO LIVE OR DIE!
IT MEANS IF YOUR CHILD CHOOSES DEATH, YOU KILL HIM... WITH YOUR OWN HANDS!

IT'S MORE PAINFUL TO LIVE THAN TO *DIE!* HOW MUCH EASIER TO SLEEP *FOREVER...*

YOU'RE A *YAKUZA!* DON'T TELL ME *YOU'VE* NEVER FELT THAT WAY! EH?!

· · · ·

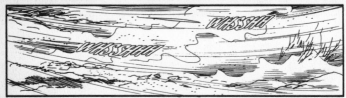

AN ASSASSIN WITH A CHILD.

IT MUST BE LIKE HAVING SHACKLES ON YOUR ARMS AND LEGS. BUT IF YOU *ALREADY* WALK IN *MEIFUMADŌ,* IT ALL MAKES SENSE.

BUT... IT'S TOO LATE TO TURN BACK.

RELEASE THE BOY!

B- BUT...

84

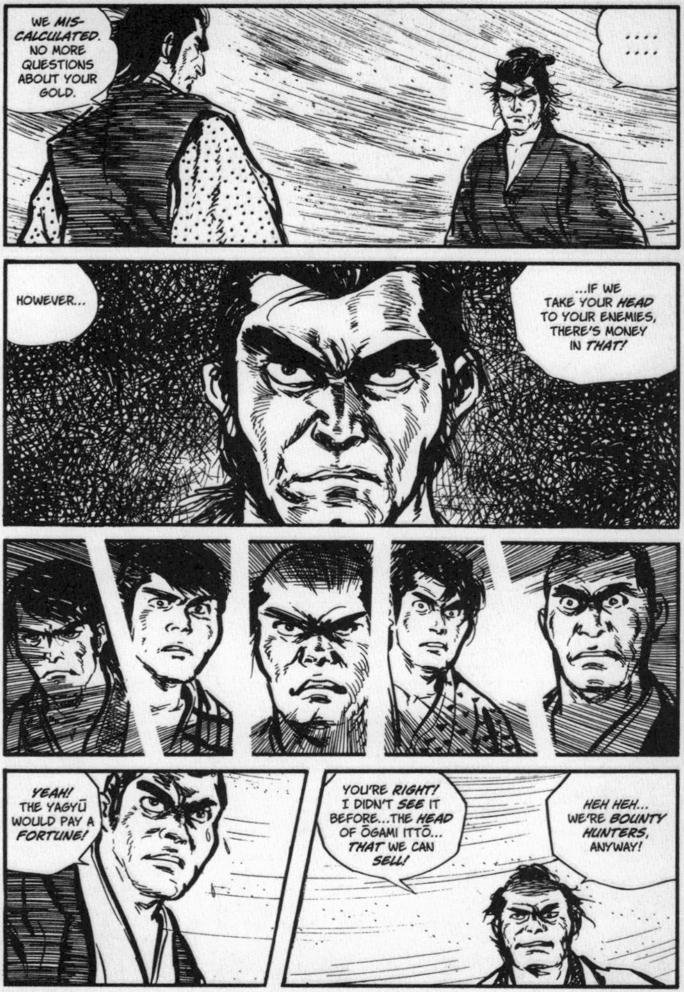
WE MIS-CALCULATED. NO MORE QUESTIONS ABOUT YOUR GOLD.
....
....
HOWEVER...
...IF WE TAKE YOUR HEAD TO YOUR ENEMIES, THERE'S MONEY IN THAT!
YEAH! THE YAGYŪ WOULD PAY A FORTUNE!
YOU'RE RIGHT! I DIDN'T SEE IT BEFORE...THE HEAD OF ŌGAMI ITTŌ... THAT WE CAN SELL!
HEH HEH... WE'RE BOUNTY HUNTERS, ANYWAY!

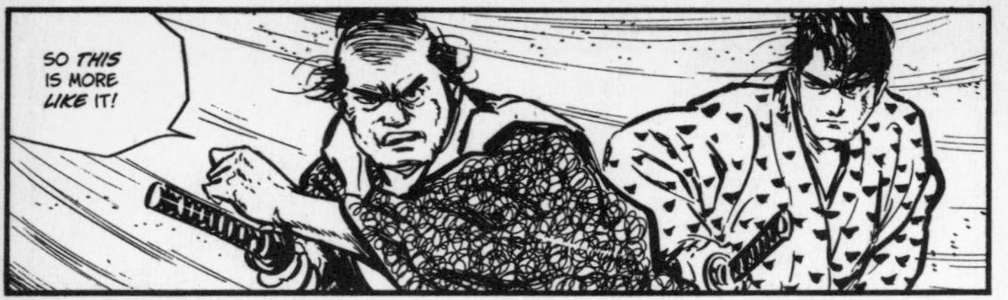
SO *THIS* IS MORE *LIKE* IT!

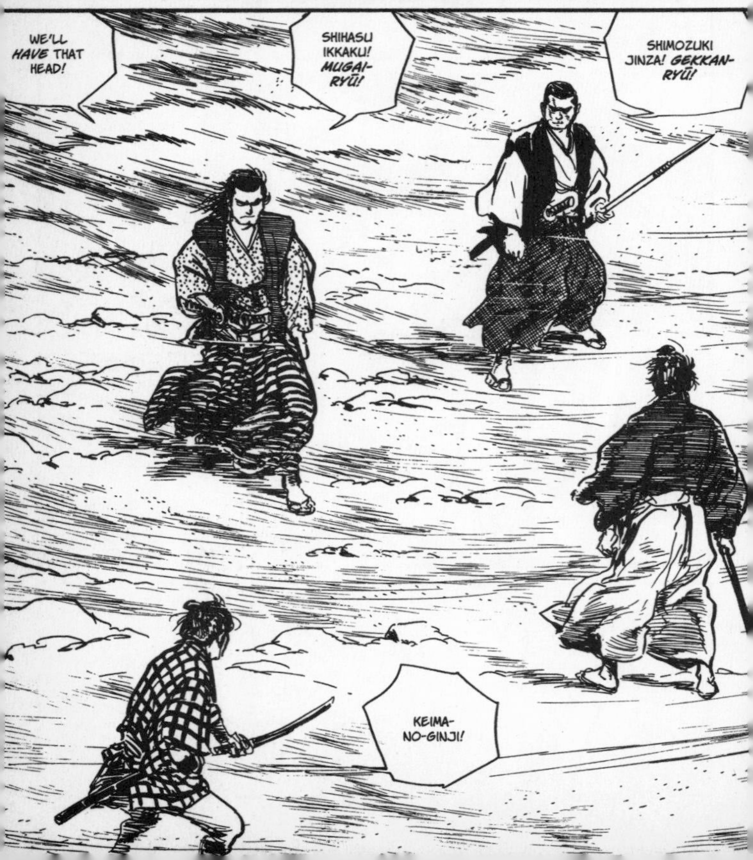
WE'LL *HAVE* THAT HEAD!
SHIHASU IKKAKU! *MUGAI-RYŪ!*
SHIMOZUKI JINZA! *GEKKAN-RYŪ!*
KEIMA-NO-GINJI!

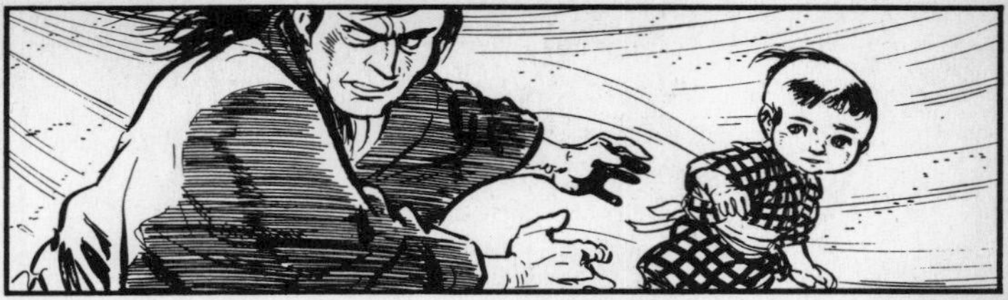

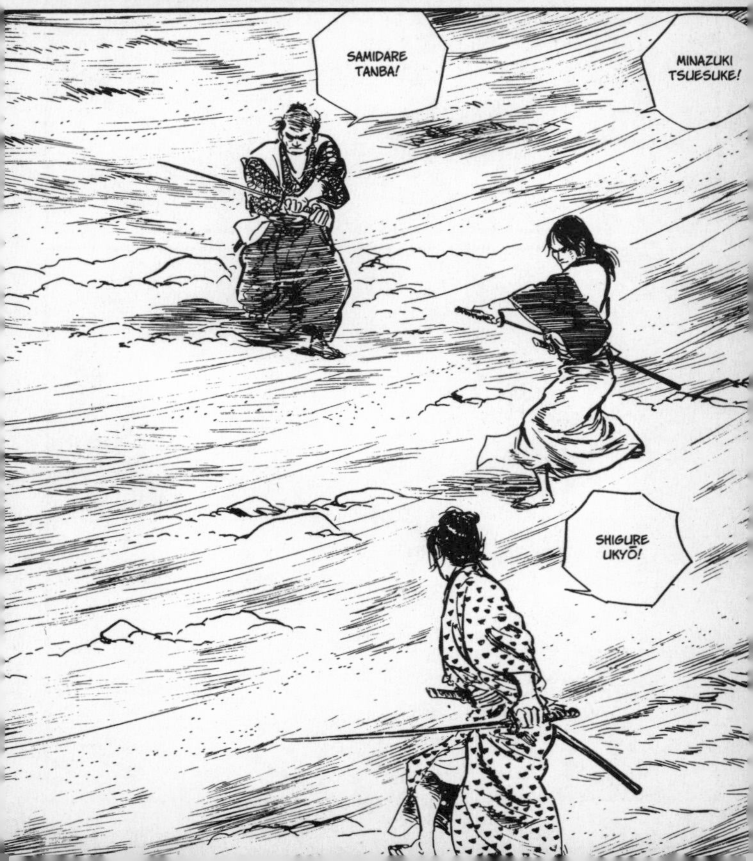
SAMIDARE TANBA!
MINAZUKI TSUESUKE!
SHIGURE UKYŌ!

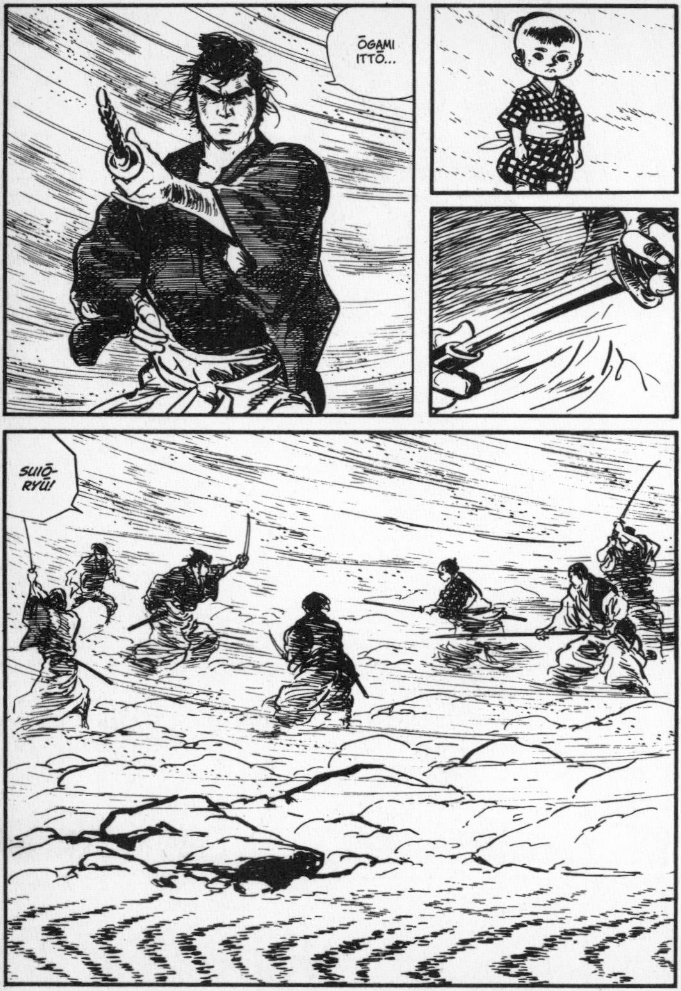
ŌGAMI ITTŌ...
SUIŌ-RYŪ!

KAWW　KAWW

WASSSSHH

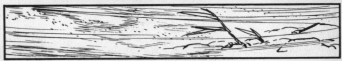

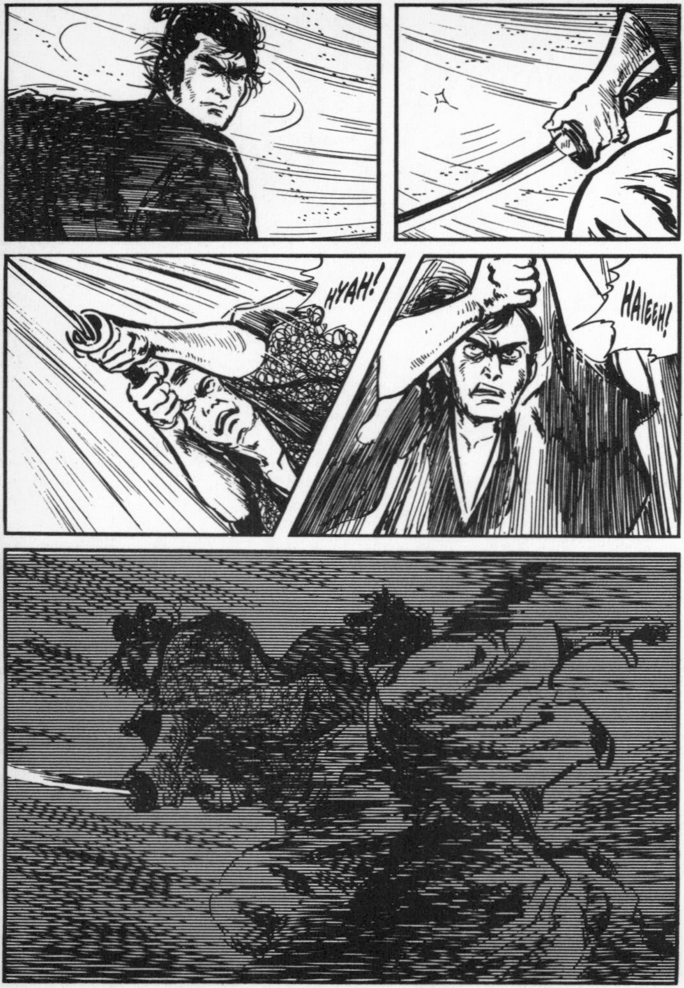
HYAH!
HAIEEH!

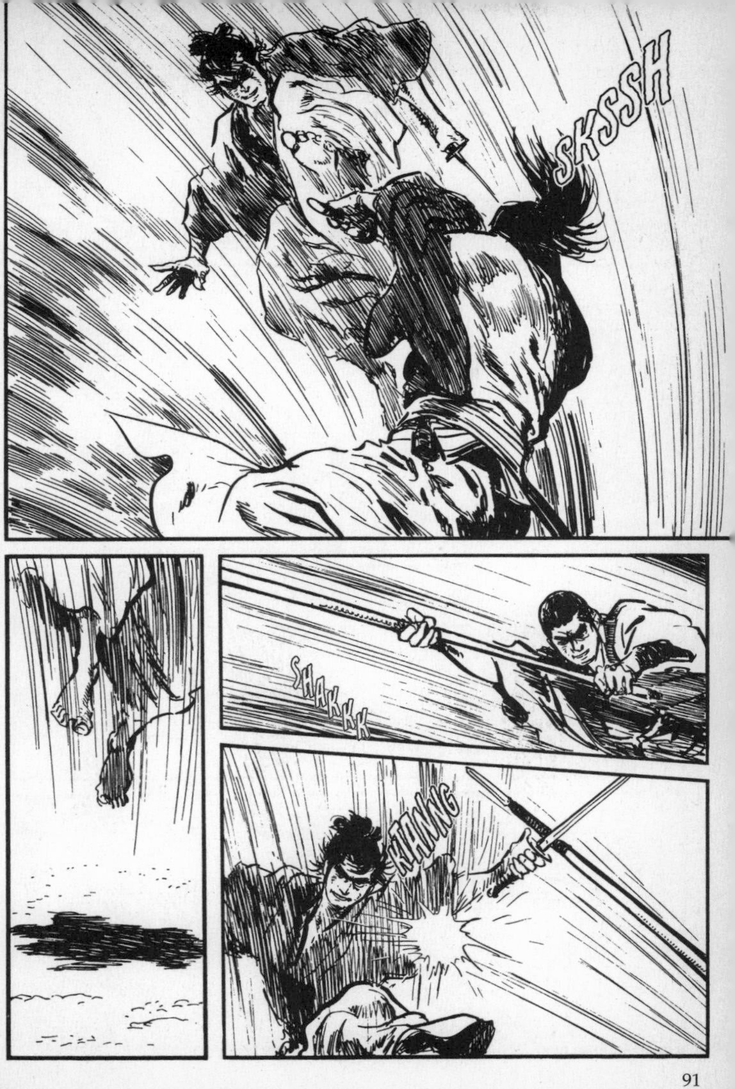
SKSSH
SHAKKK
KTANNG

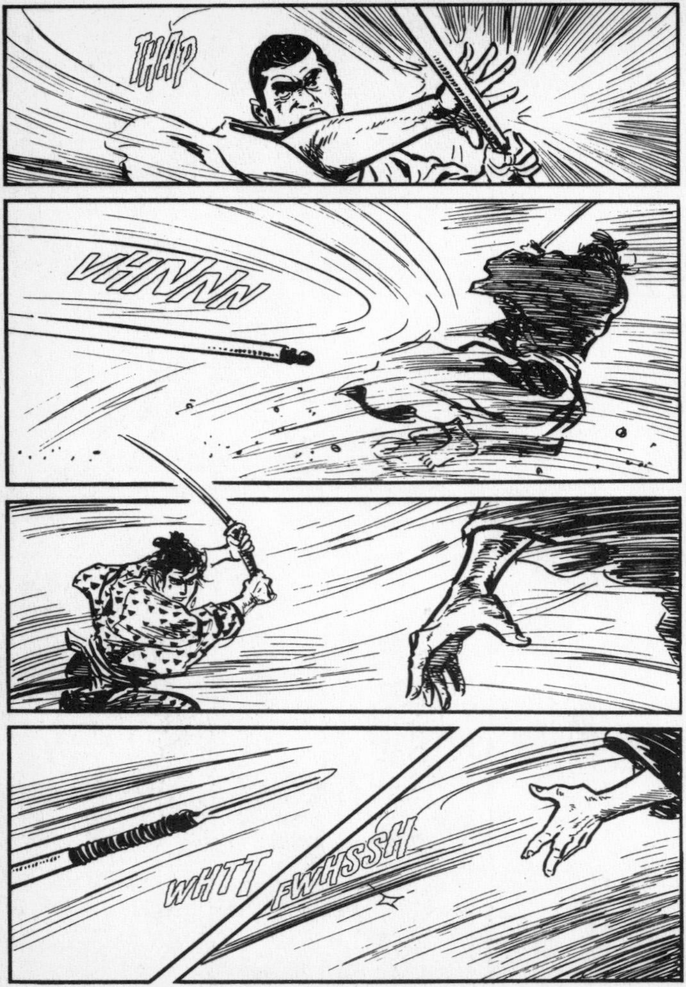
THAP
VHNNN
WHTT
FWHSSH

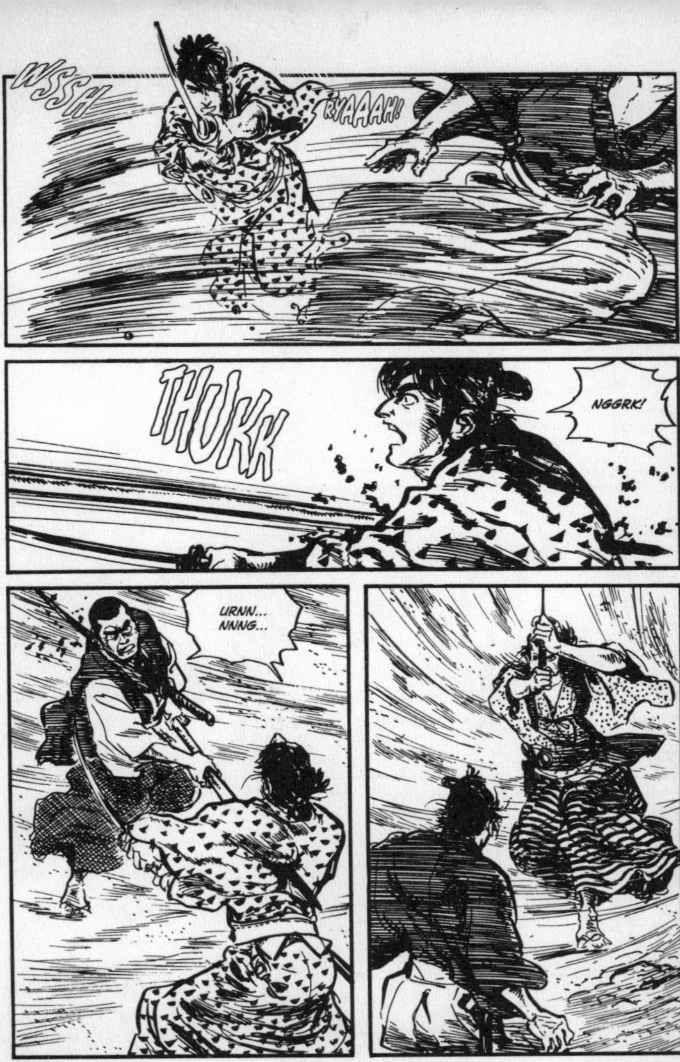
WSSH
RYAAAH!
THUKK
NGGRK!
URNN...
NNNG...

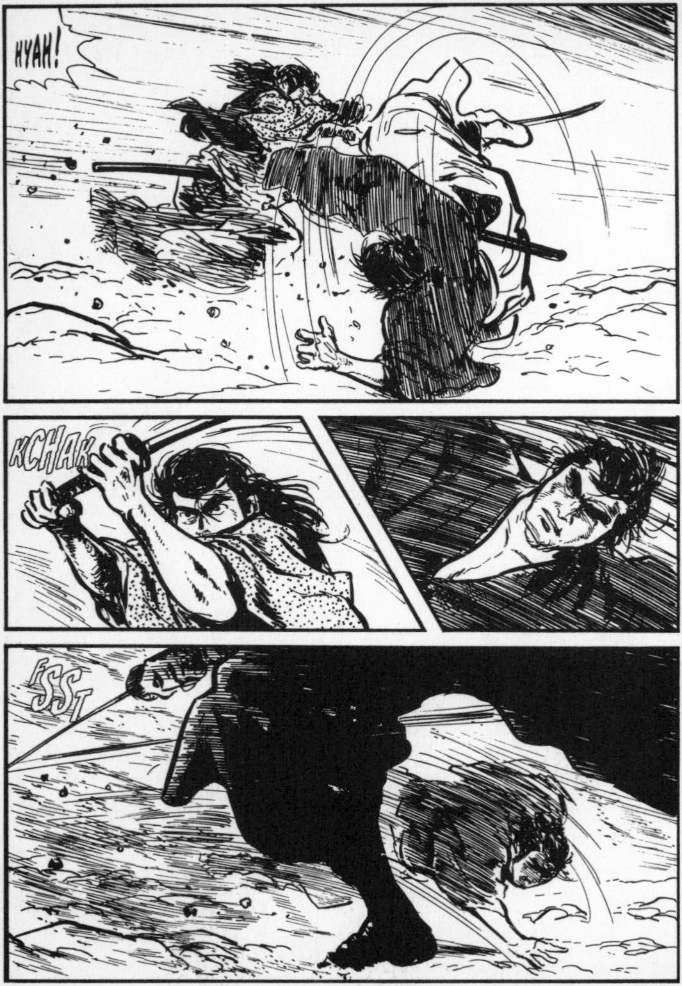
HYAH!
KCHAK
FSST

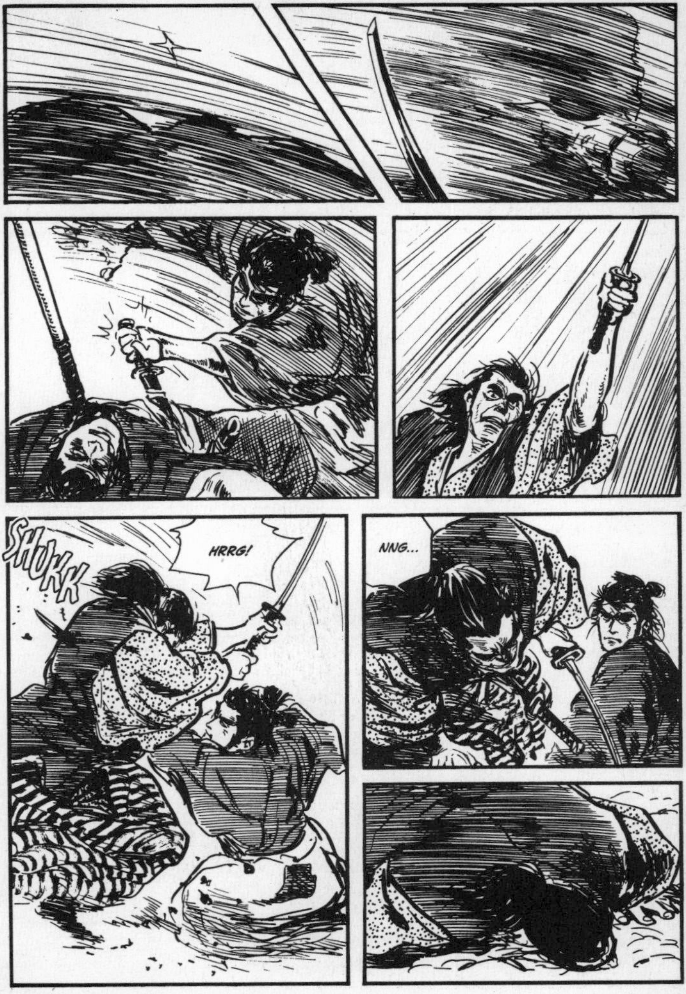
SHUKK
HRRG!
NNG...

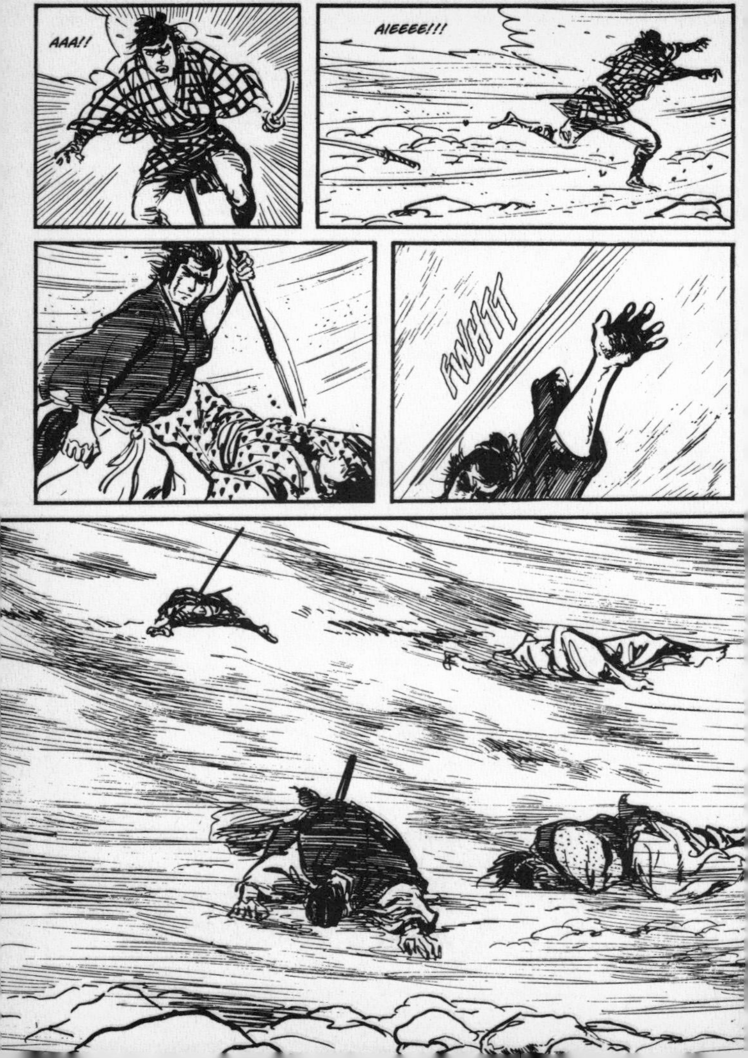
AAA!!
AIEEEE!!!
FWHTT

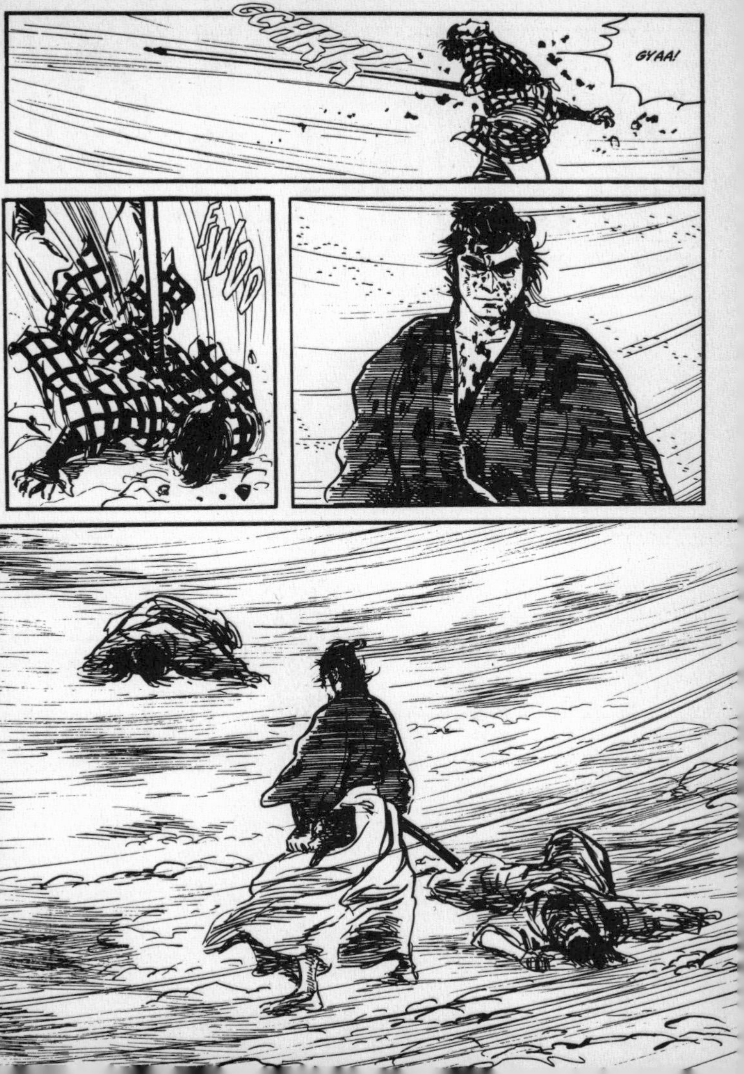
GCHKK
GYAA!
FWOO

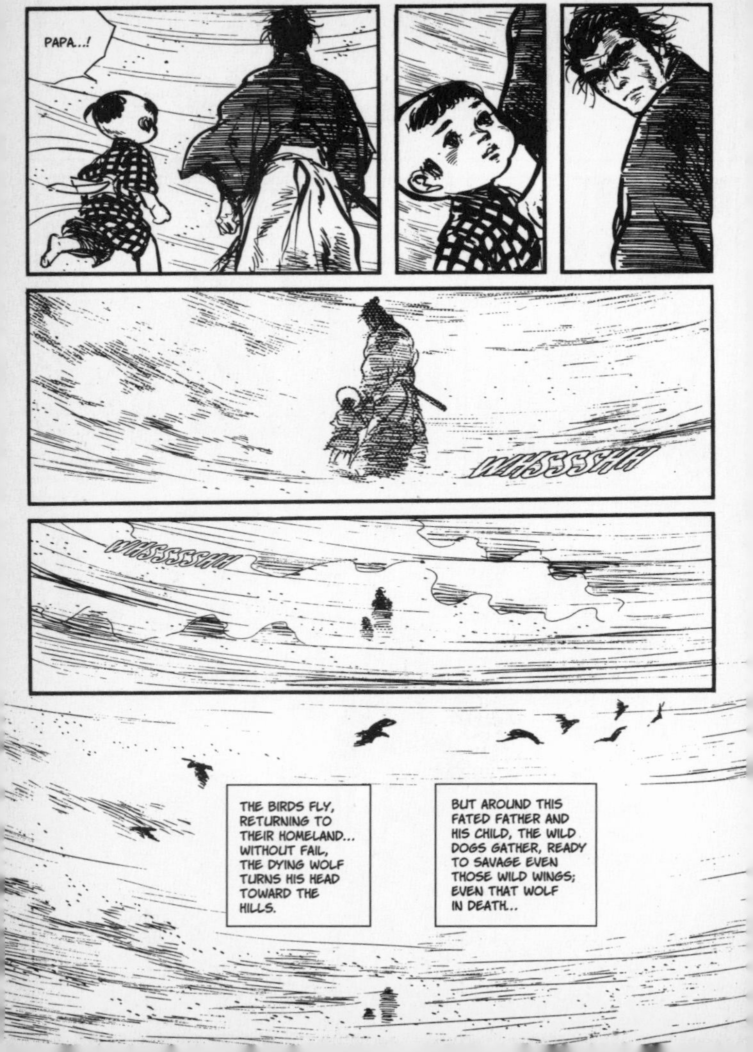
PAPA..!
WHSSSSHH
WHSSSSHH
THE BIRDS FLY, RETURNING TO THEIR HOMELAND... WITHOUT FAIL, THE DYING WOLF TURNS HIS HEAD TOWARD THE HILLS.
BUT AROUND THIS FATED FATHER AND HIS CHILD, THE WILD DOGS GATHER, READY TO SAVAGE EVEN THOSE WILD WINGS; EVEN THAT WOLF IN DEATH..

the twenty-sixth

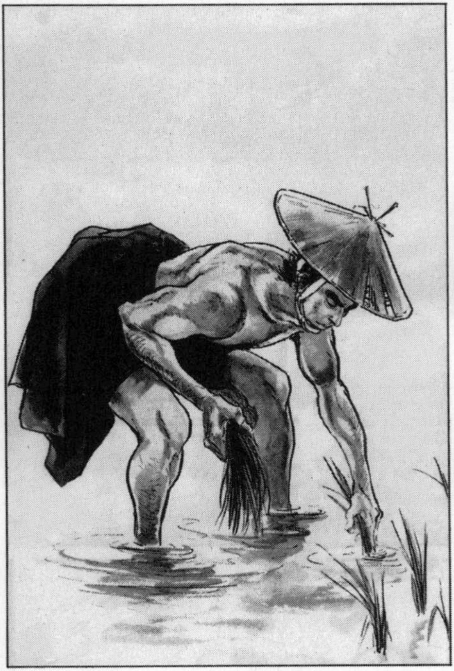

Black Wind

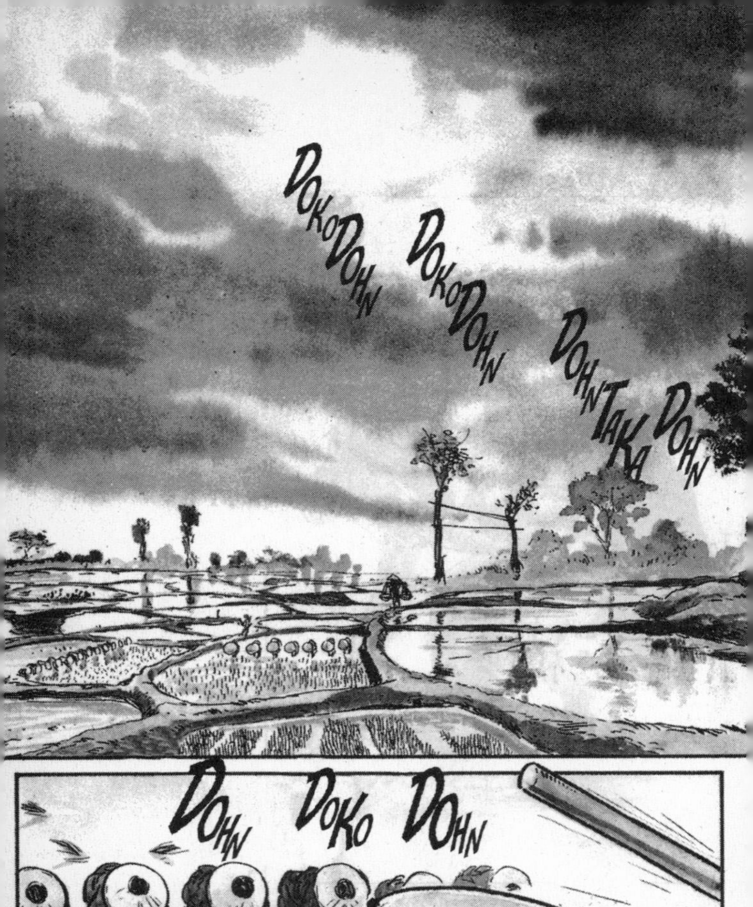
DOKODOHN
DOKODOHN
DOHNTAKADOHN
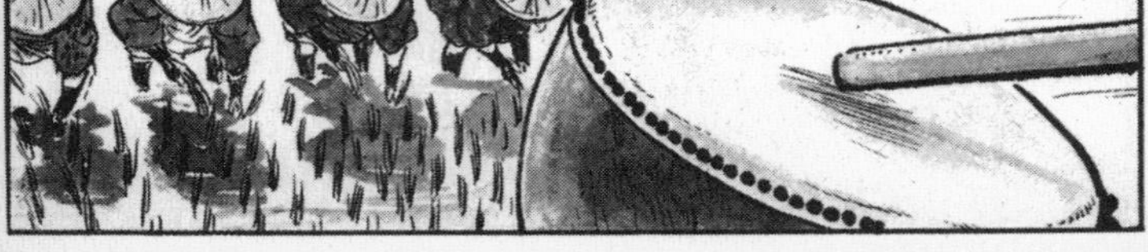
DOHN
DOKO
DOHN

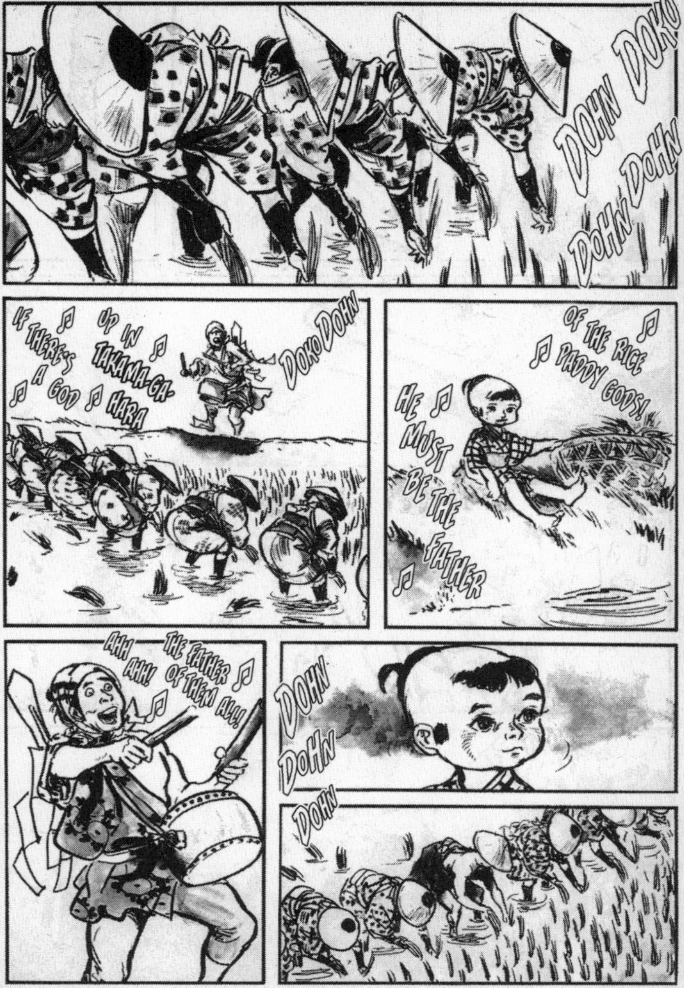

DOHN DOKO
DOHN DOHN
IF THERE'S ♫ A GOD ♫ UP IN TAKAMA-GA-HARA ♫
DOKO DOHN
OF THE RICE PADDY GODS! ♫
HE ♫ MUST BE THE FATHER ♫
AHH AHH! THE FATHER ♫ OF THEM ALL! ♫
DOHN DOHN
DOHN

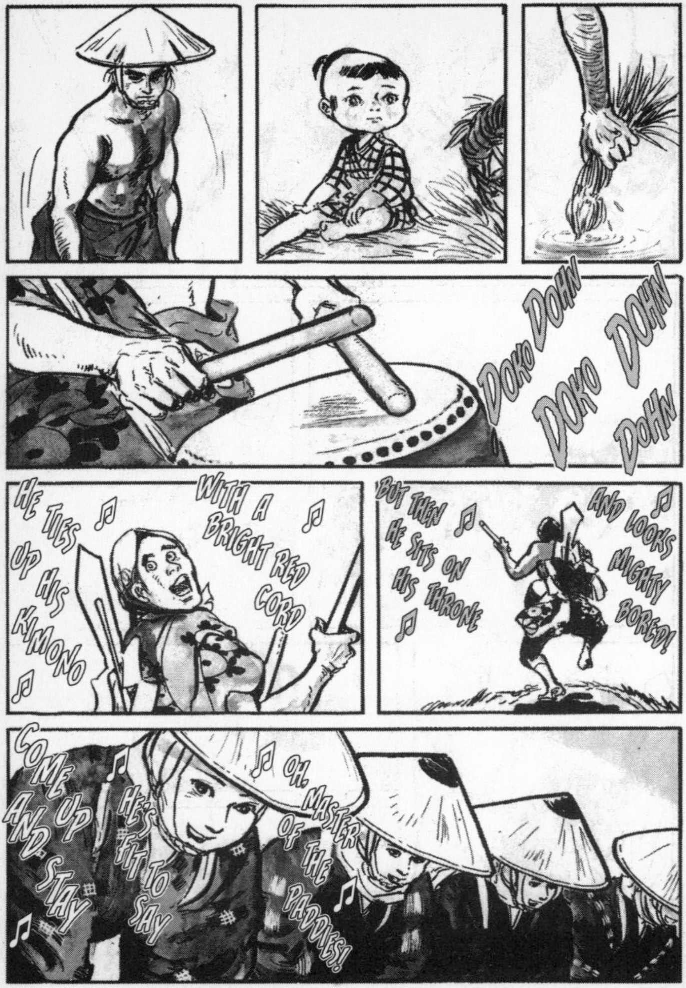
DOKO DOHN
DOKO DOHN
DOHN
HE TIES UP HIS KIMONO ♫
WITH A BRIGHT RED CORD ♫
BUT THEN ♫ HE SITS ON HIS THRONE ♫
AND LOOKS MIGHTY BORED!
COME UP AND STAY ♫
HE'S FIT TO SAY
OH, MASTER OF THE PADDIES! ♫

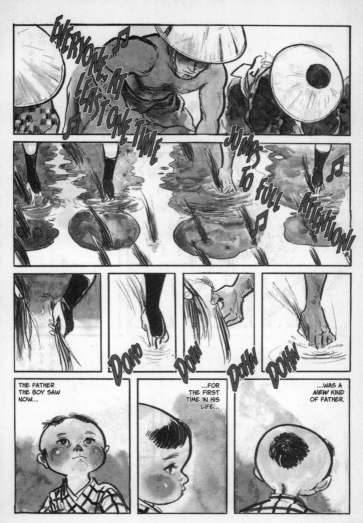

EVERYONE...AT LEAST ONE TIME ♪ ♪ JUMPS TO FULL ATTENTION! ♪

DOKO DOON DOON DOON

THE FATHER THE BOY SAW NOW...

...FOR THE FIRST TIME IN HIS LIFE...

...WAS A *NEW* KIND OF FATHER.

103

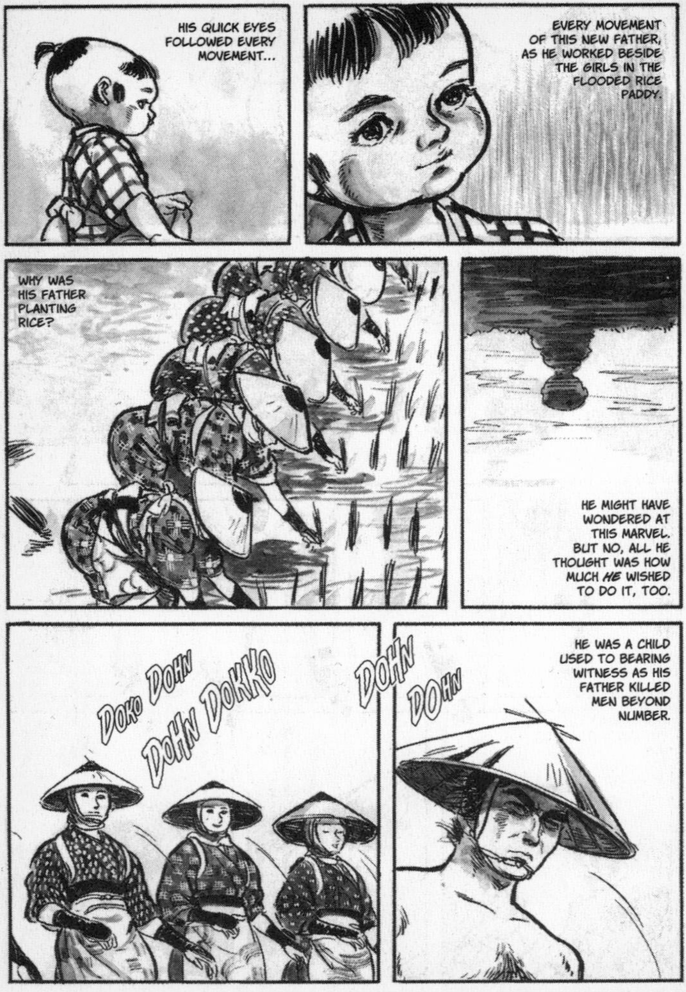
HIS QUICK EYES FOLLOWED EVERY MOVEMENT...
EVERY MOVEMENT OF THIS NEW FATHER, AS HE WORKED BESIDE THE GIRLS IN THE FLOODED RICE PADDY.
WHY WAS HIS FATHER PLANTING RICE?
HE MIGHT HAVE WONDERED AT THIS MARVEL. BUT NO, ALL HE THOUGHT WAS HOW MUCH *HE* WISHED TO DO IT, TOO.
DOKO DOHN
DOHN DOKKO
DOHN
DOHN
HE WAS A CHILD USED TO BEARING WITNESS AS HIS FATHER KILLED MEN BEYOND NUMBER.

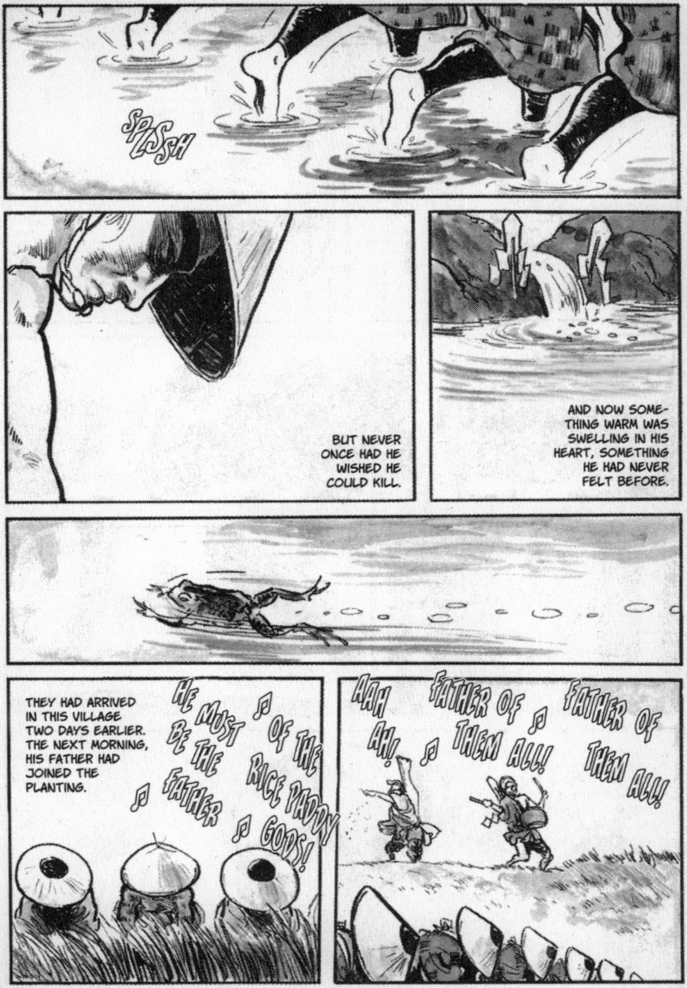
SPZSSH
BUT NEVER ONCE HAD HE WISHED HE COULD KILL.
AND NOW SOMETHING WARM WAS SWELLING IN HIS HEART, SOMETHING HE HAD NEVER FELT BEFORE.
THEY HAD ARRIVED IN THIS VILLAGE TWO DAYS EARLIER. THE NEXT MORNING, HIS FATHER HAD JOINED THE PLANTING.
HE MUST BE THE ♫ FATHER ♫ OF THE RICE PADDY ♫ GODS!
AAH AH! ♫ FATHER OF ♫ THEM ALL! FATHER OF THEM ALL!

DAIGORO NEEDED NO REASONS. HE ONLY KNEW THIS MUCH—FOR HIS FATHER TO STAY IN ONE PLACE FOR LONGER THAN A SINGLE DAY...

...FOR HIS FATHER TO BEND HIMSELF TO SUCH SIMPLE WORK...THESE THINGS FILLED HIS HEART WITH A LIGHTNESS HE HAD NEVER KNOWN BEFORE.

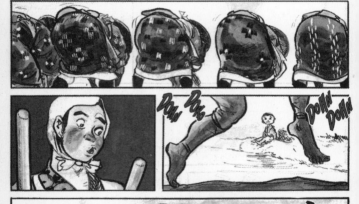

DOHN DOKO

DOHN DOHN

HE WAS A CHILD WITH SHISHŌGAN EYES, A DESTINY WRITTEN BENEATH STRANGE STARS, FORCED BY FATE TO WANDER WITHOUT A HOME. FOR SUCH A CHILD, THIS MOMENT BY THE RICE PADDIES, ALL SO ORDINARY, WAS A FLEETING OASIS OF PEACE...

DOHN DOKO DOHN

106

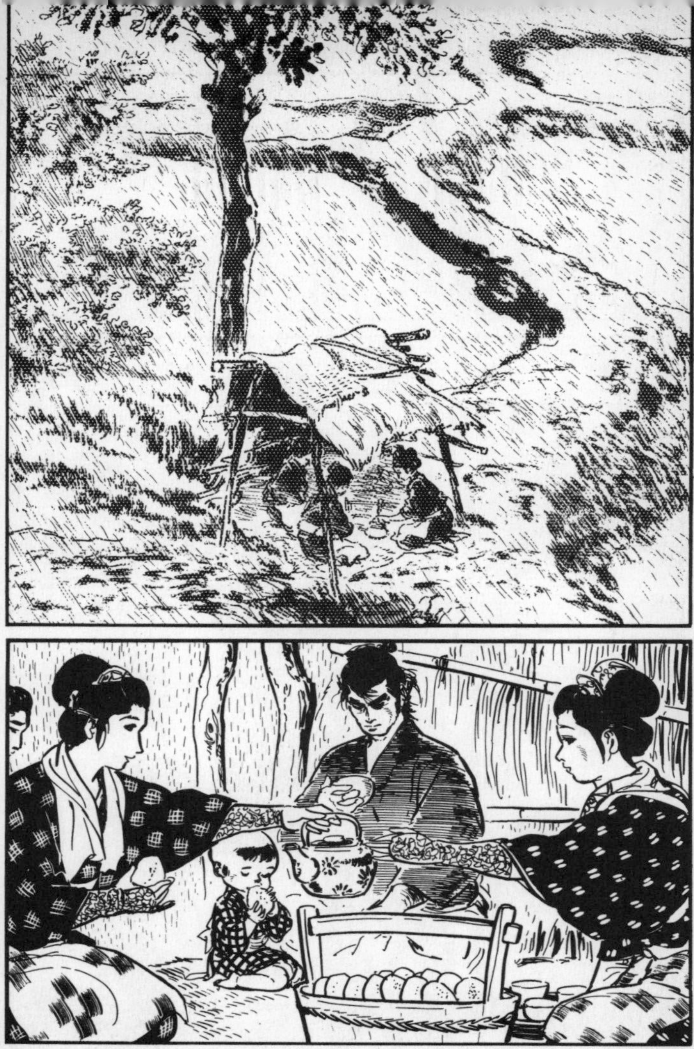

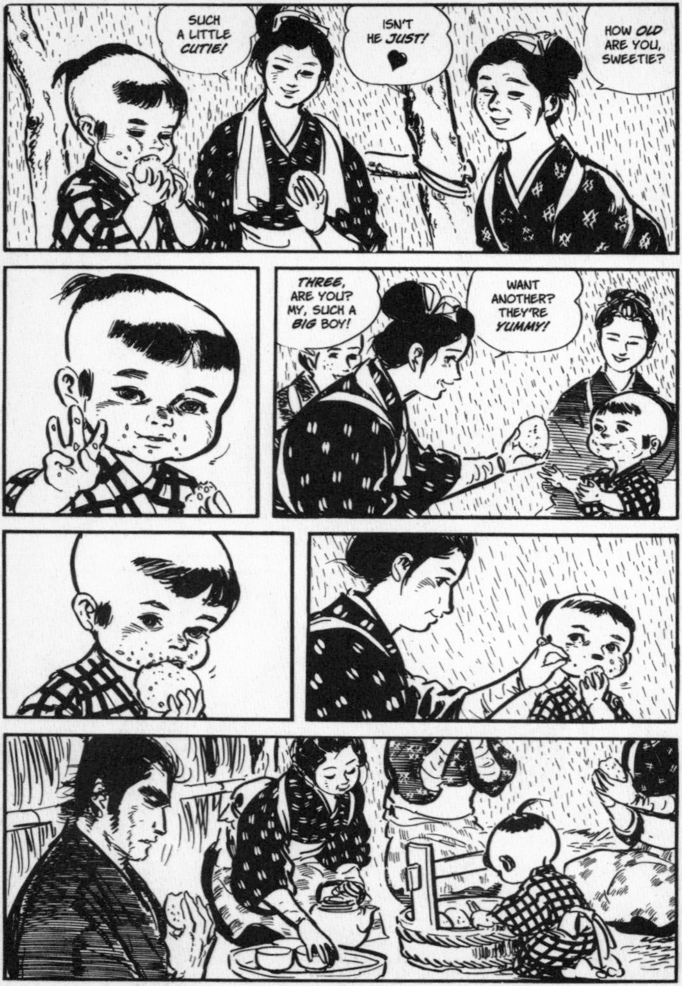
SUCH A LITTLE CUTIE!
ISN'T HE JUST! ♥
HOW OLD ARE YOU, SWEETIE?
THREE, ARE YOU? MY, SUCH A BIG BOY!
WANT ANOTHER? THEY'RE YUMMY!

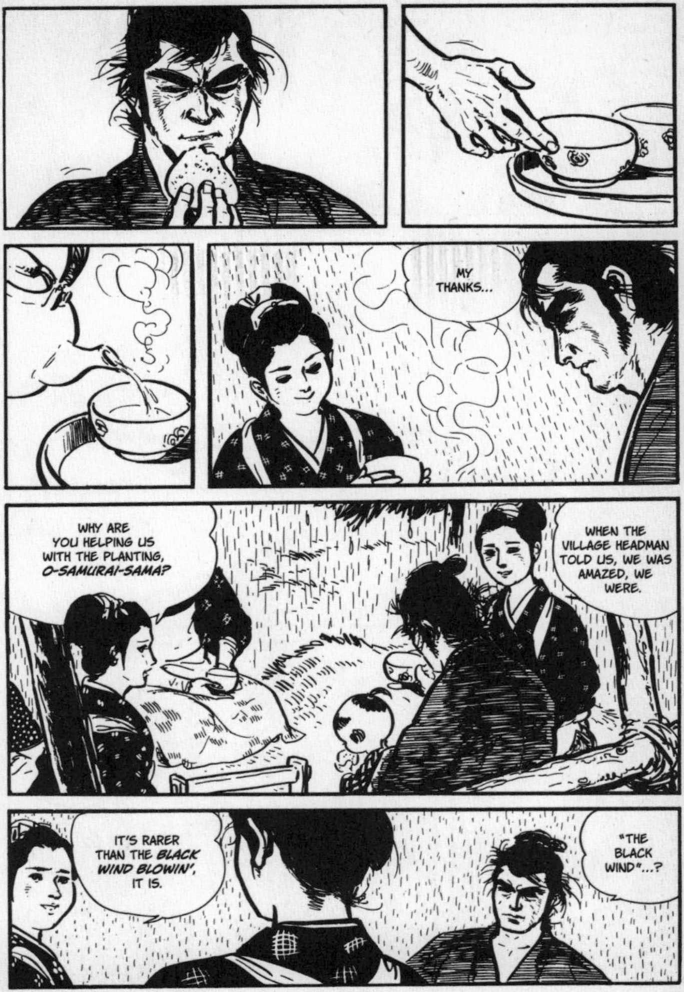
MY THANKS...
WHY ARE YOU HELPING US WITH THE PLANTING, *O-SAMURAI-SAMA?*
WHEN THE VILLAGE HEADMAN TOLD US, WE WAS AMAZED, WE WERE.
IT'S RARER THAN THE *BLACK WIND BLOWIN'*, IT IS.
"THE BLACK WIND"...?

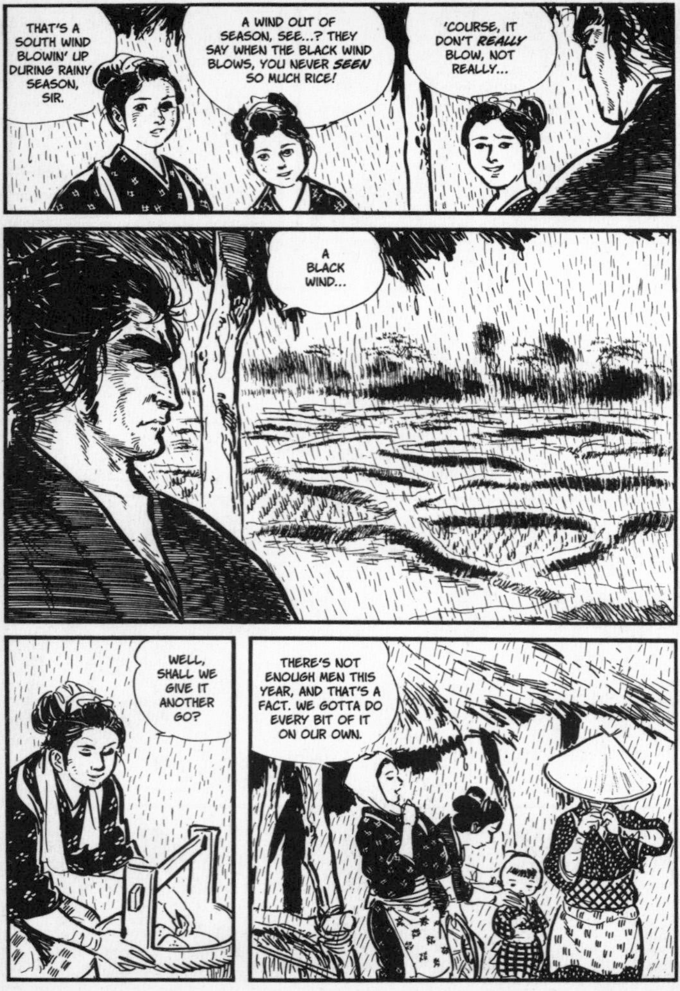
THAT'S A SOUTH WIND BLOWIN' UP DURING RAINY SEASON, SIR.
A WIND OUT OF SEASON, SEE...? THEY SAY WHEN THE BLACK WIND BLOWS, YOU NEVER *SEEN* SO MUCH RICE!
'COURSE, IT DON'T *REALLY* BLOW, NOT REALLY...
A BLACK WIND...
WELL, SHALL WE GIVE IT ANOTHER GO?
THERE'S NOT ENOUGH MEN THIS YEAR, AND THAT'S A FACT. WE GOTTA DO EVERY BIT OF IT ON OUR OWN.

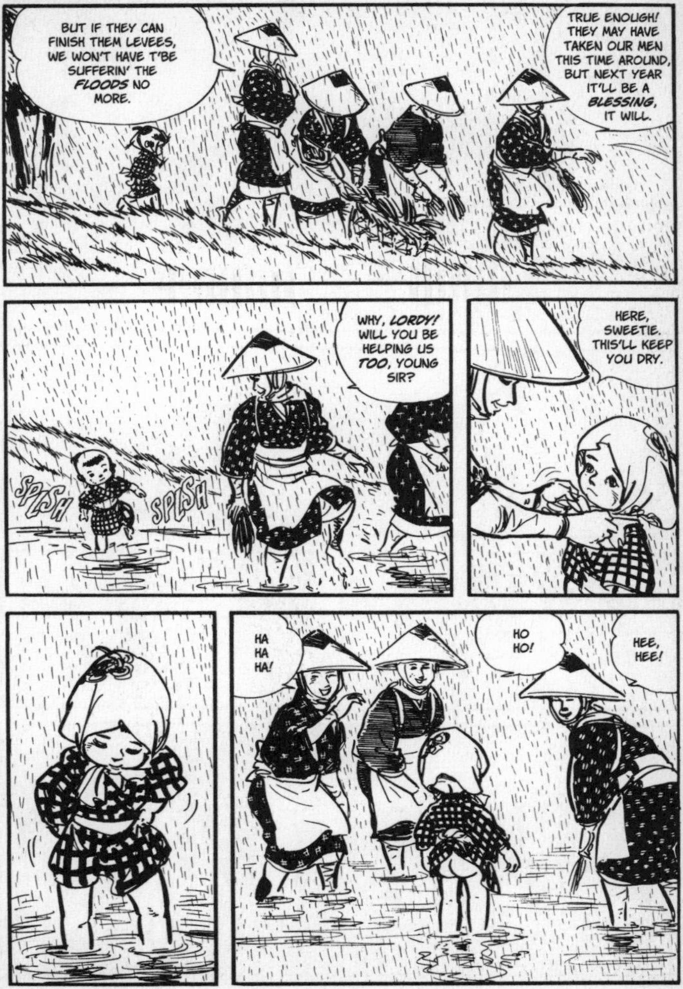
BUT IF THEY CAN FINISH THEM LEVEES, WE WON'T HAVE T'BE SUFFERIN' THE FLOODS NO MORE.
TRUE ENOUGH! THEY MAY HAVE TAKEN OUR MEN THIS TIME AROUND, BUT NEXT YEAR IT'LL BE A BLESSING, IT WILL.
SPLSH
SPLSH
WHY, LORDY! WILL YOU BE HELPING US TOO, YOUNG SIR?
HERE, SWEETIE. THIS'LL KEEP YOU DRY.
HA HA HA!
HO HO!
HEE, HEE!

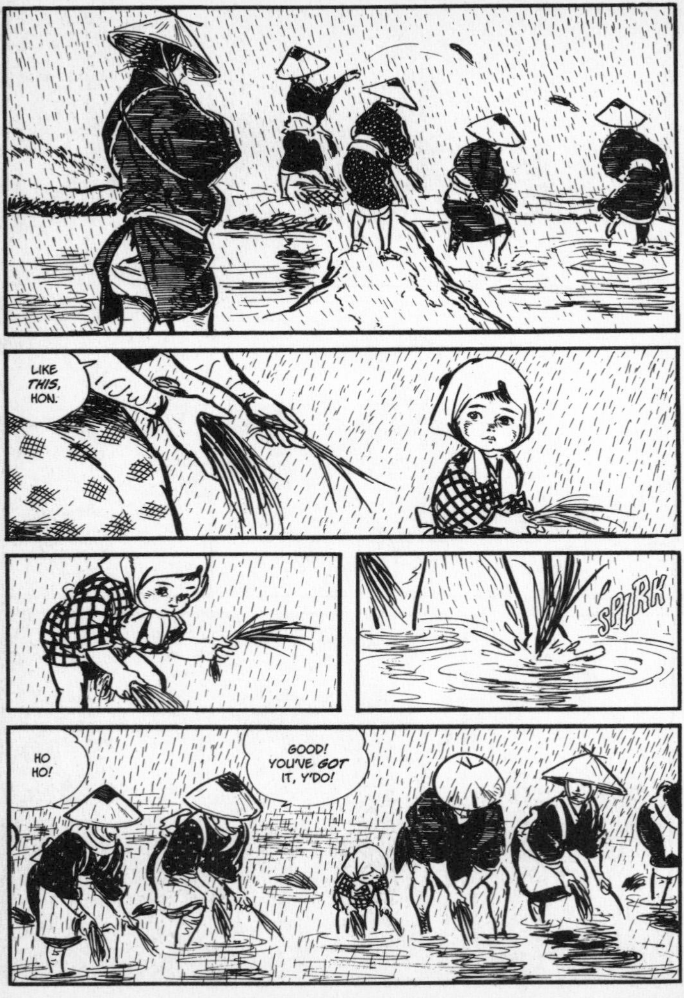
LIKE *THIS*, HON.
SPLRK
HO HO!
GOOD! YOU'VE *GOT* IT, Y'DO!

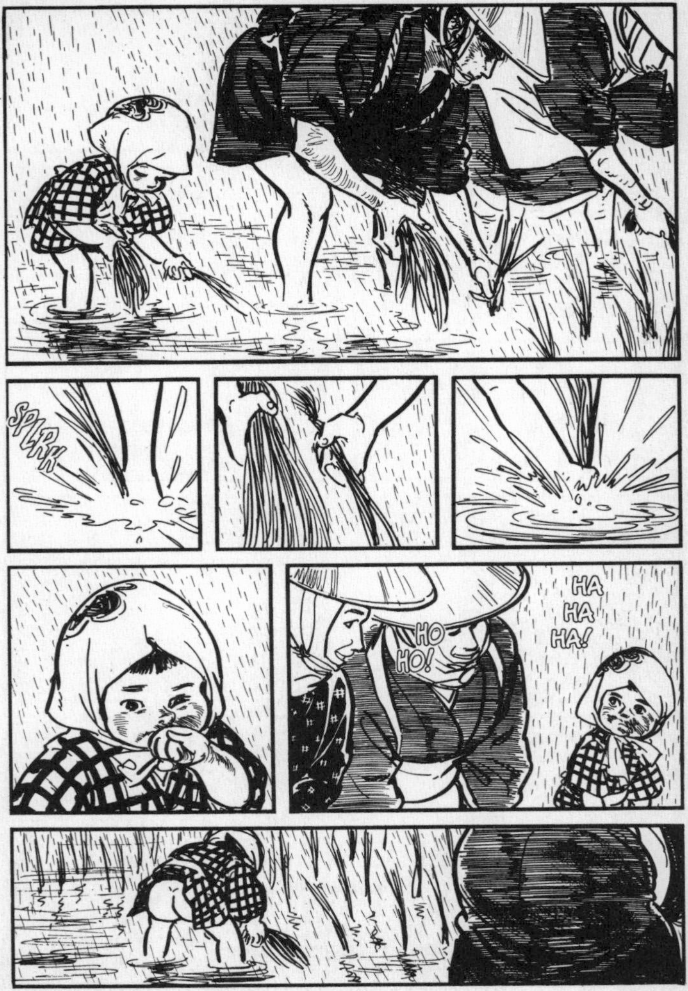
SPLRK
HO HO!
HA HA HA!

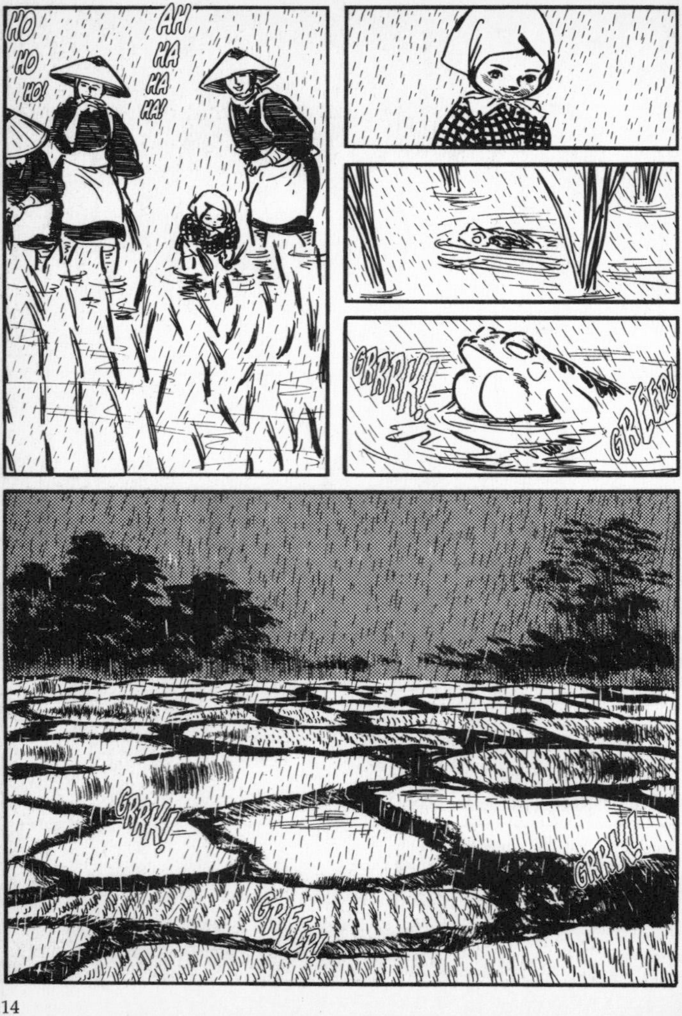
HO HO HO!
AH HA HA HA!
GRRRK!
GREEP!
GRRK!
GRRK!
GREEP!

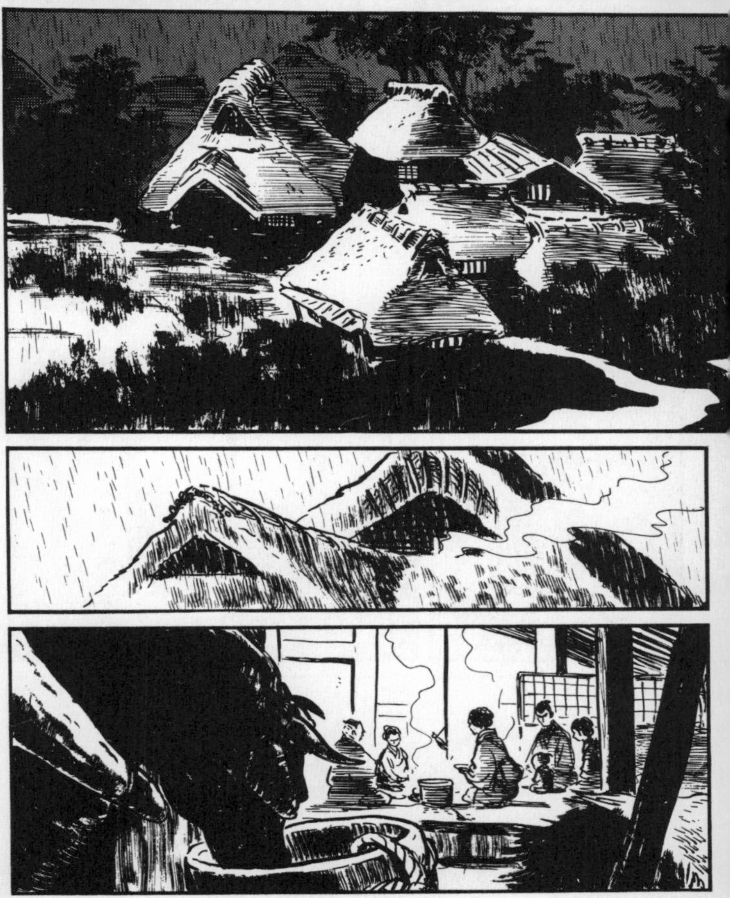

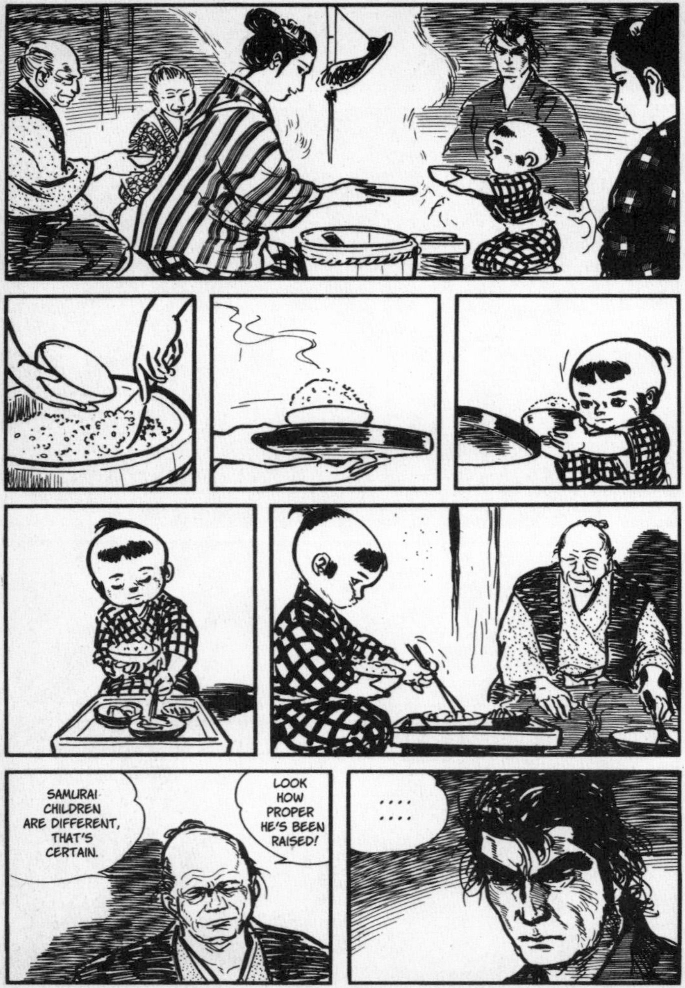
SAMURAI CHILDREN ARE DIFFERENT, THAT'S CERTAIN.
LOOK HOW PROPER HE'S BEEN RAISED!
....
....

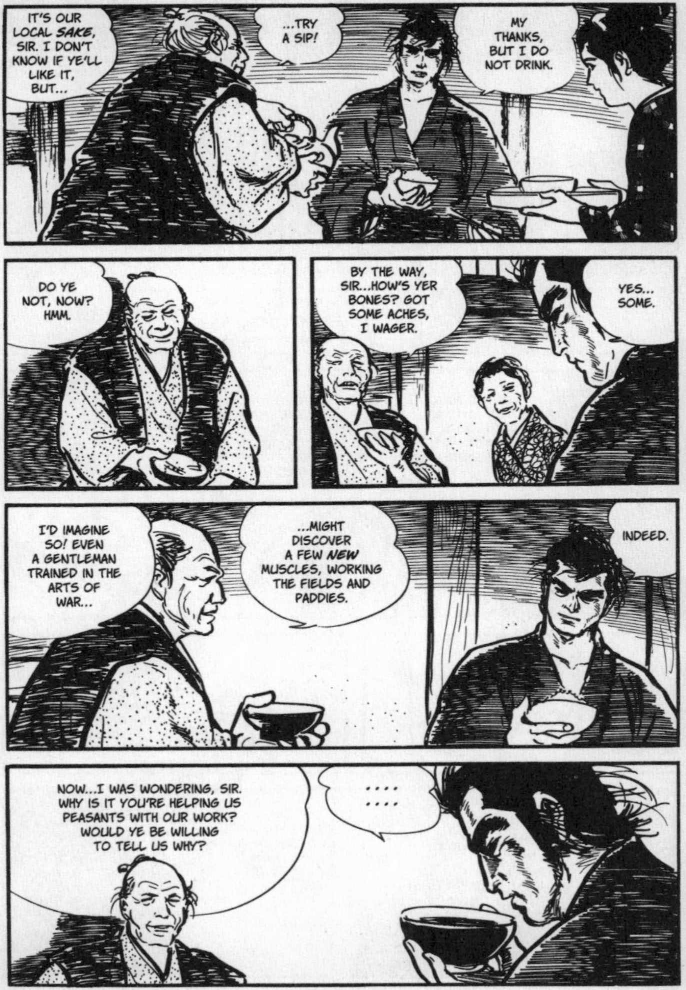
IT'S OUR LOCAL SAKE, SIR. I DON'T KNOW IF YE'LL LIKE IT, BUT...
...TRY A SIP!
MY THANKS, BUT I DO NOT DRINK.
DO YE NOT, NOW? HMM.
BY THE WAY, SIR...HOW'S YER BONES? GOT SOME ACHES, I WAGER.
YES... SOME.
I'D IMAGINE SO! EVEN A GENTLEMAN TRAINED IN THE ARTS OF WAR...
...MIGHT DISCOVER A FEW NEW MUSCLES, WORKING THE FIELDS AND PADDIES.
INDEED.
NOW...I WAS WONDERING, SIR. WHY IS IT YOU'RE HELPING US PEASANTS WITH OUR WORK? WOULD YE BE WILLING TO TELL US WHY?
....
....

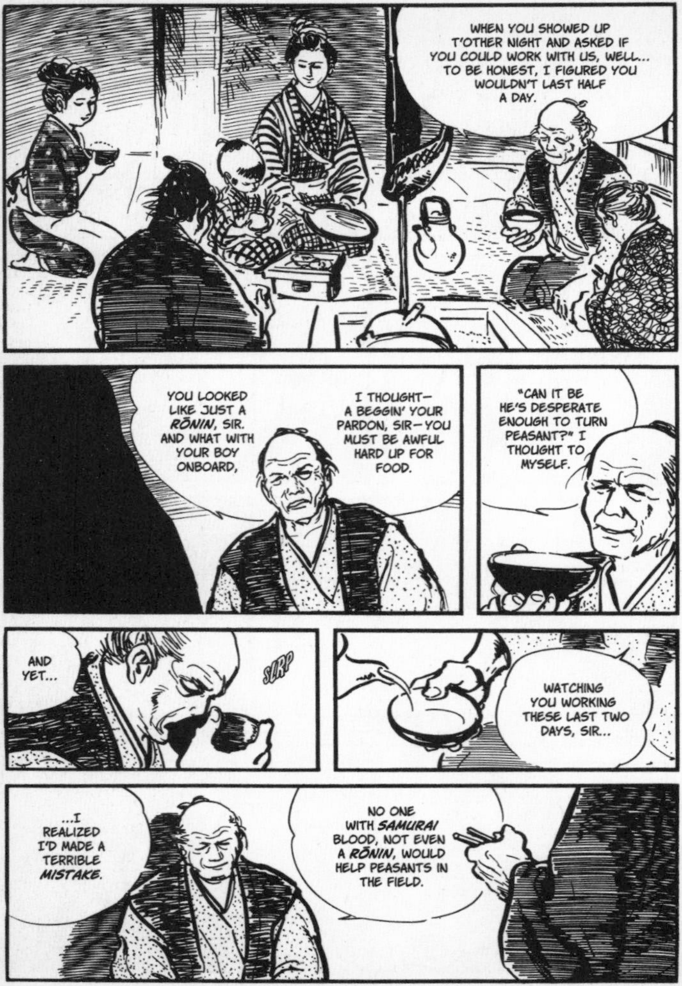
WHEN YOU SHOWED UP T'OTHER NIGHT AND ASKED IF YOU COULD WORK WITH US, WELL... TO BE HONEST, I FIGURED YOU WOULDN'T LAST HALF A DAY.
YOU LOOKED LIKE JUST A *RŌNIN*, SIR. AND WHAT WITH YOUR BOY ONBOARD,
I THOUGHT— A BEGGIN' YOUR PARDON, SIR—YOU MUST BE AWFUL HARD UP FOR FOOD.
"CAN IT BE HE'S DESPERATE ENOUGH TO TURN PEASANT?" I THOUGHT TO MYSELF.
AND YET...
SLRP
WATCHING YOU WORKING THESE LAST TWO DAYS, SIR...
NO ONE WITH *SAMURAI* BLOOD, NOT EVEN A *RŌNIN*, WOULD HELP PEASANTS IN THE FIELD.
...I REALIZED I'D MADE A TERRIBLE *MISTAKE*.

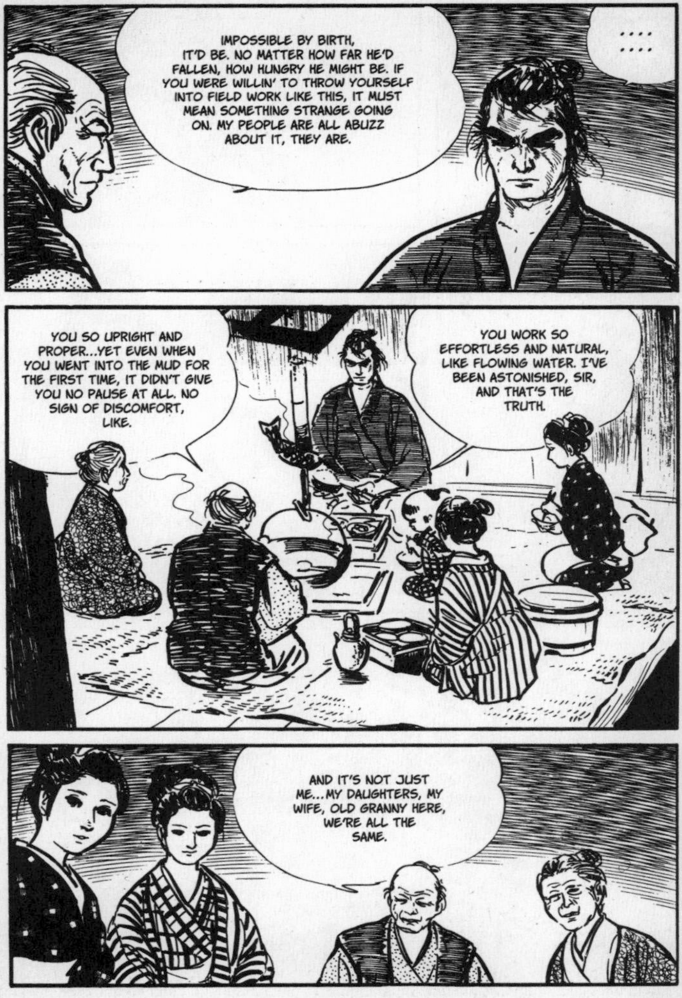
IMPOSSIBLE BY BIRTH, IT'D BE. NO MATTER HOW FAR HE'D FALLEN, HOW HUNGRY HE MIGHT BE. IF YOU WERE WILLIN' TO THROW YOURSELF INTO FIELD WORK LIKE THIS, IT MUST MEAN SOMETHING STRANGE GOING ON. MY PEOPLE ARE ALL ABUZZ ABOUT IT, THEY ARE.
....
YOU SO UPRIGHT AND PROPER...YET EVEN WHEN YOU WENT INTO THE MUD FOR THE FIRST TIME, IT DIDN'T GIVE YOU NO PAUSE AT ALL. NO SIGN OF DISCOMFORT, LIKE.
YOU WORK SO EFFORTLESS AND NATURAL, LIKE FLOWING WATER. I'VE BEEN ASTONISHED, SIR, AND THAT'S THE TRUTH.
AND IT'S NOT JUST ME...MY DAUGHTERS, MY WIFE, OLD GRANNY HERE, WE'RE ALL THE SAME.

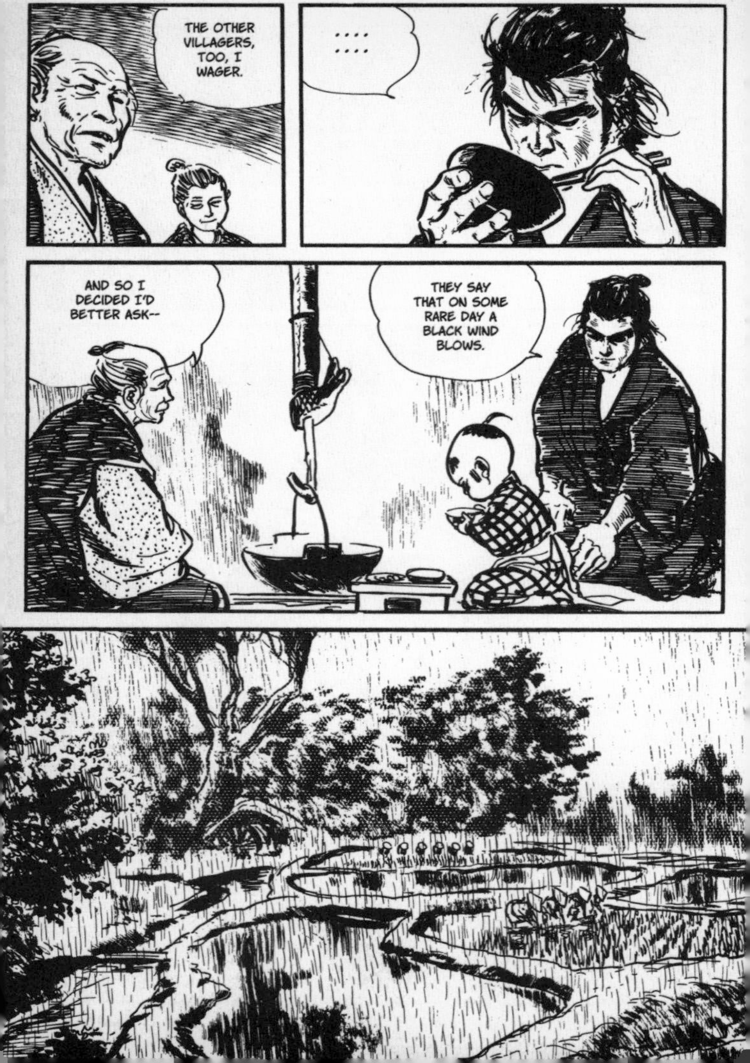
THE OTHER VILLAGERS, TOO, I WAGER.
....
....
AND SO I DECIDED I'D BETTER ASK--
THEY SAY THAT ON SOME RARE DAY A BLACK WIND BLOWS.

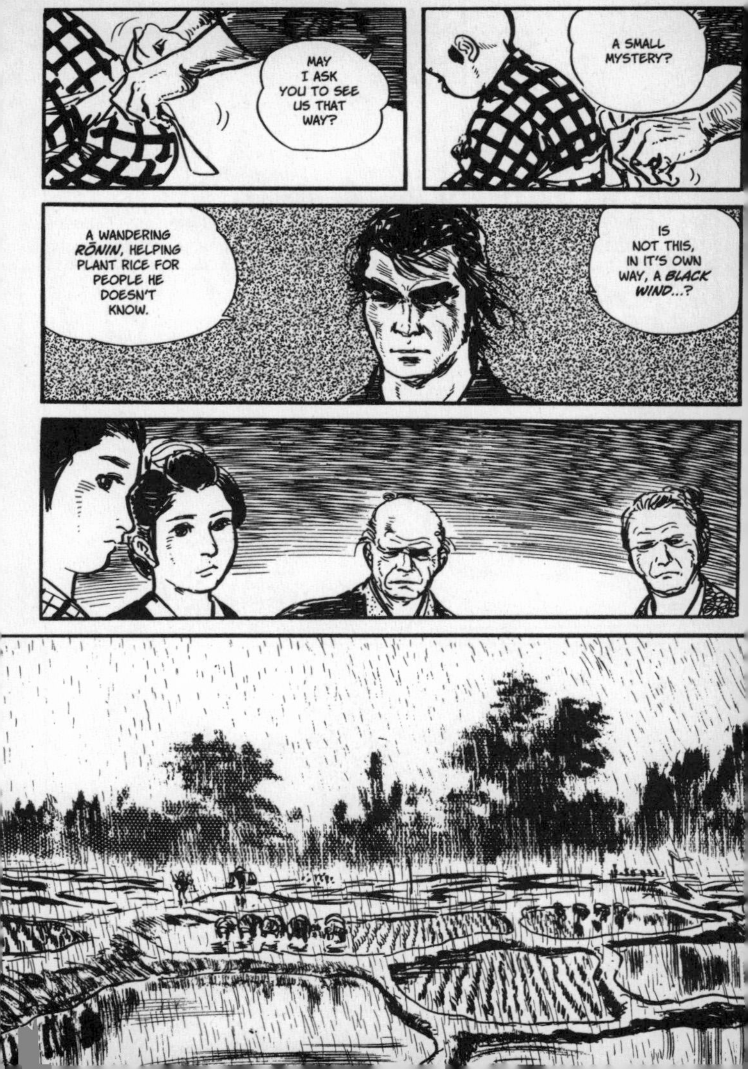
MAY I ASK YOU TO SEE US THAT WAY?
A SMALL MYSTERY?
A WANDERING *RŌNIN*, HELPING PLANT RICE FOR PEOPLE HE DOESN'T KNOW.
IS NOT THIS, IN IT'S OWN WAY, A *BLACK WIND*...?

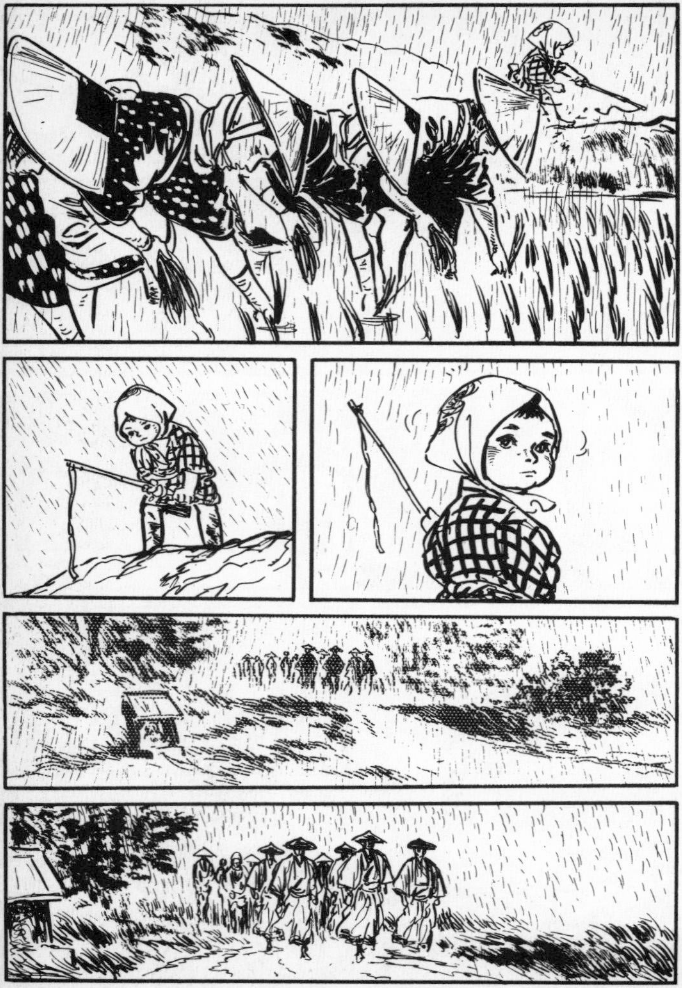

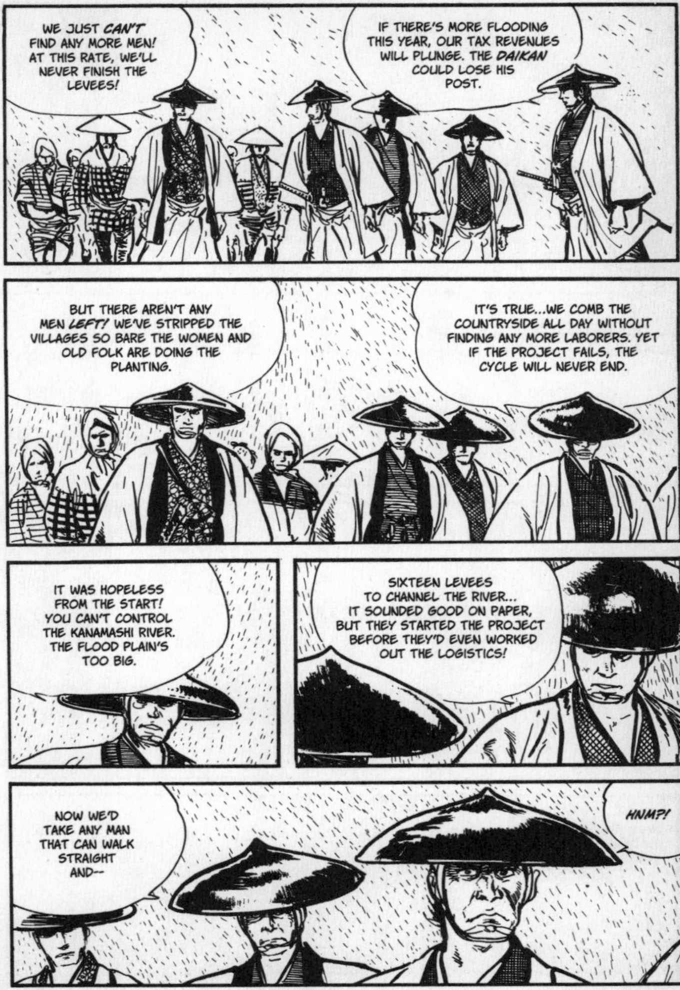
WE JUST CAN'T FIND ANY MORE MEN! AT THIS RATE, WE'LL NEVER FINISH THE LEVEES!
IF THERE'S MORE FLOODING THIS YEAR, OUR TAX REVENUES WILL PLUNGE. THE DAIKAN COULD LOSE HIS POST.
BUT THERE AREN'T ANY MEN LEFT! WE'VE STRIPPED THE VILLAGES SO BARE THE WOMEN AND OLD FOLK ARE DOING THE PLANTING.
IT'S TRUE...WE COMB THE COUNTRYSIDE ALL DAY WITHOUT FINDING ANY MORE LABORERS. YET IF THE PROJECT FAILS, THE CYCLE WILL NEVER END.
IT WAS HOPELESS FROM THE START! YOU CAN'T CONTROL THE KANAMASHI RIVER. THE FLOOD PLAIN'S TOO BIG.
SIXTEEN LEVEES TO CHANNEL THE RIVER... IT SOUNDED GOOD ON PAPER, BUT THEY STARTED THE PROJECT BEFORE THEY'D EVEN WORKED OUT THE LOGISTICS!
NOW WE'D TAKE ANY MAN THAT CAN WALK STRAIGHT AND--
HNM?!

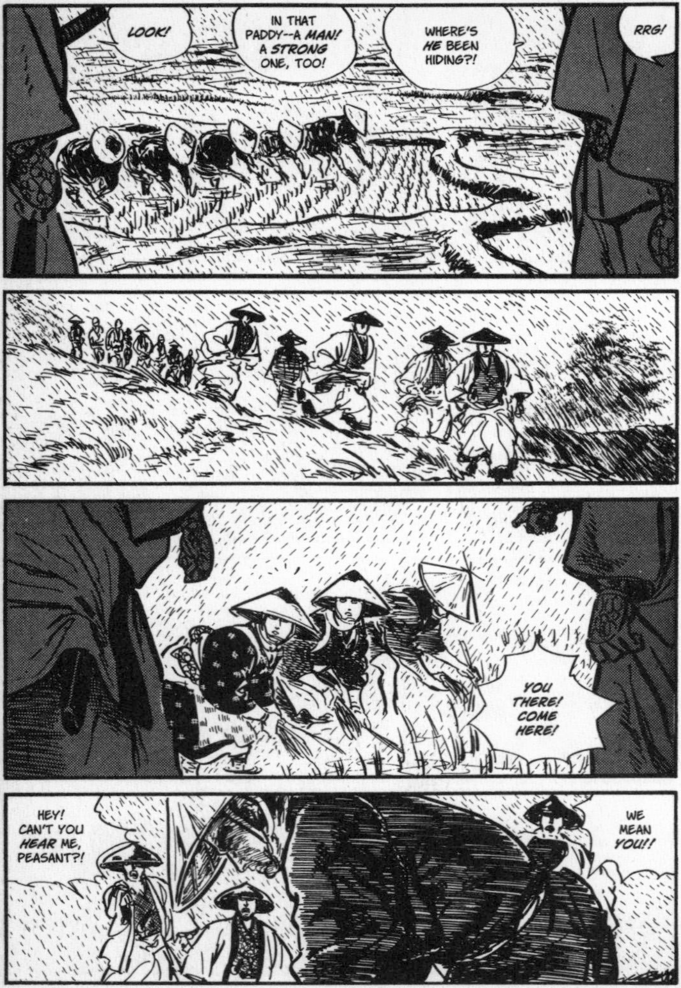
LOOK!
IN THAT PADDY--A MAN! A STRONG ONE, TOO!
WHERE'S HE BEEN HIDING?!
RRG!
YOU THERE! COME HERE!
HEY! CAN'T YOU HEAR ME, PEASANT?!
WE MEAN YOU!!

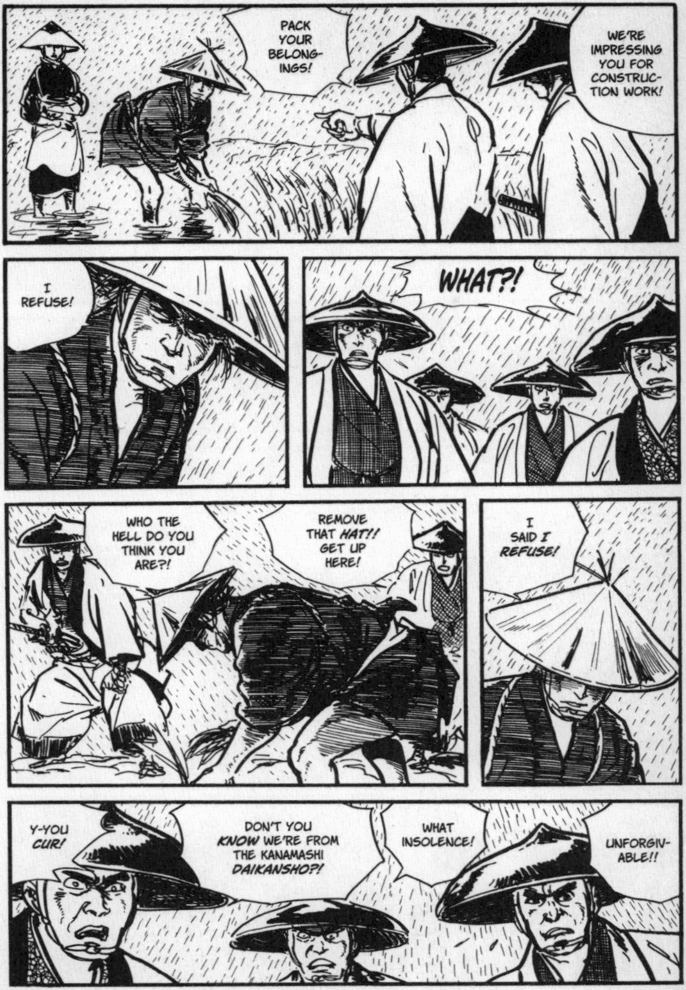
PACK YOUR BELONG-INGS!
WE'RE IMPRESSING YOU FOR CONSTRUC-TION WORK!
I REFUSE!
WHAT?!
WHO THE HELL DO YOU THINK YOU ARE?!
REMOVE THAT HAT!! GET UP HERE!
I SAID I REFUSE!
Y-YOU CUR!
DON'T YOU KNOW WE'RE FROM THE KANAMASHI DAIKANSHO?!
WHAT INSOLENCE!
UNFORGIV-ABLE!!

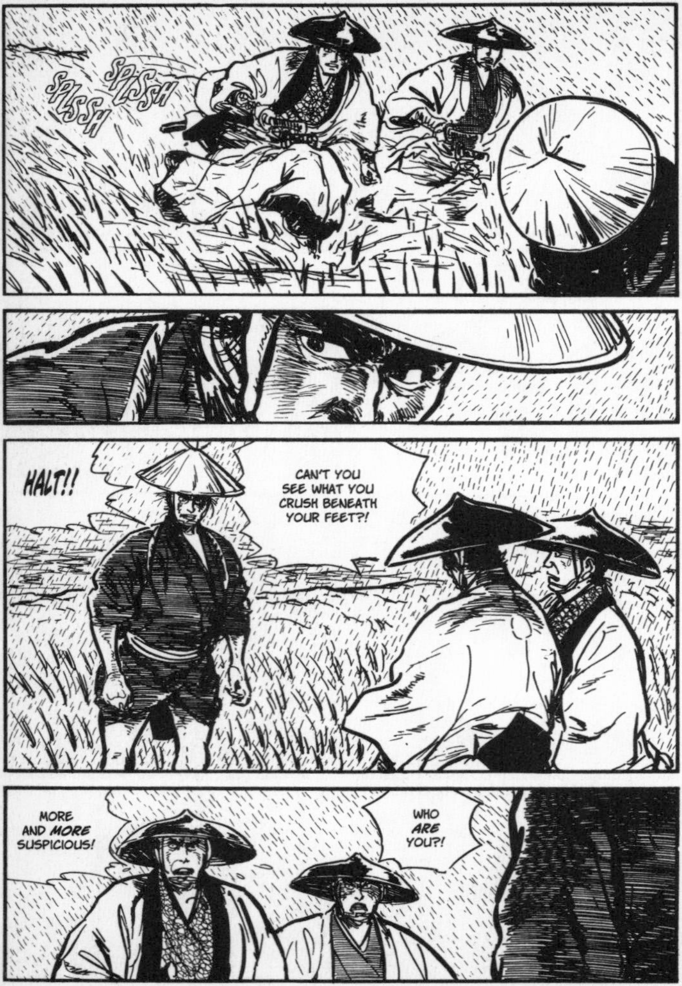
SPLSSH
SPLSSH
HALT!!
CAN'T YOU SEE WHAT YOU CRUSH BENEATH YOUR FEET?!
MORE AND MORE SUSPICIOUS!
WHO ARE YOU?!

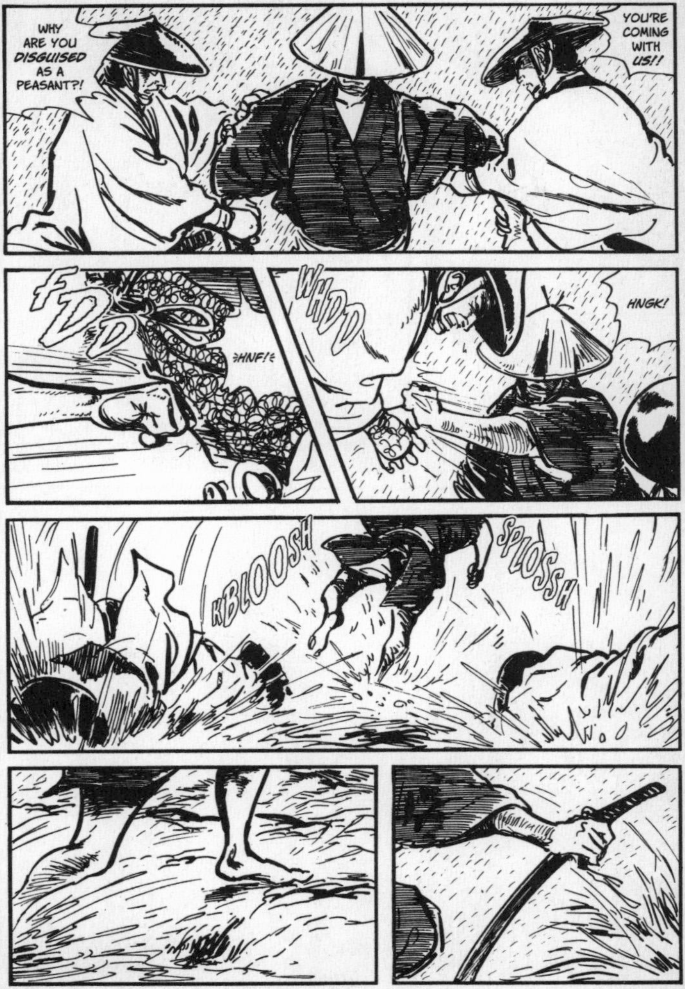
WHY ARE YOU DISGUISED AS A PEASANT?!
YOU'RE COMING WITH US!!
FDD
HNF!
WHDD
HNGK!
KBLOOSH
SPLOSSH

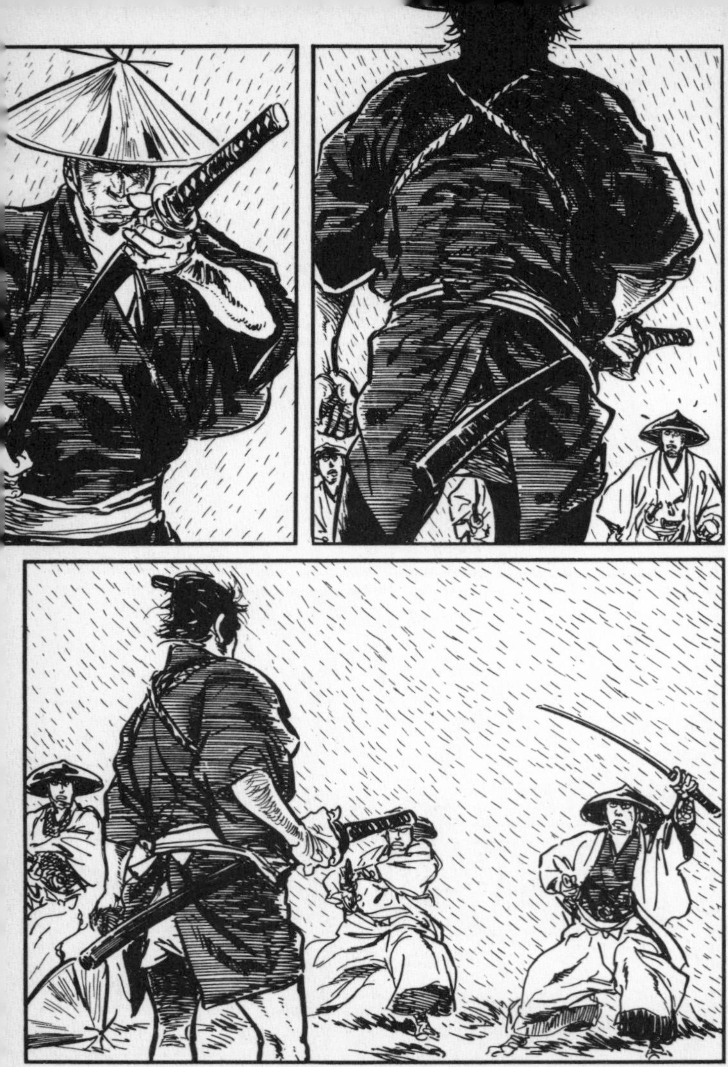

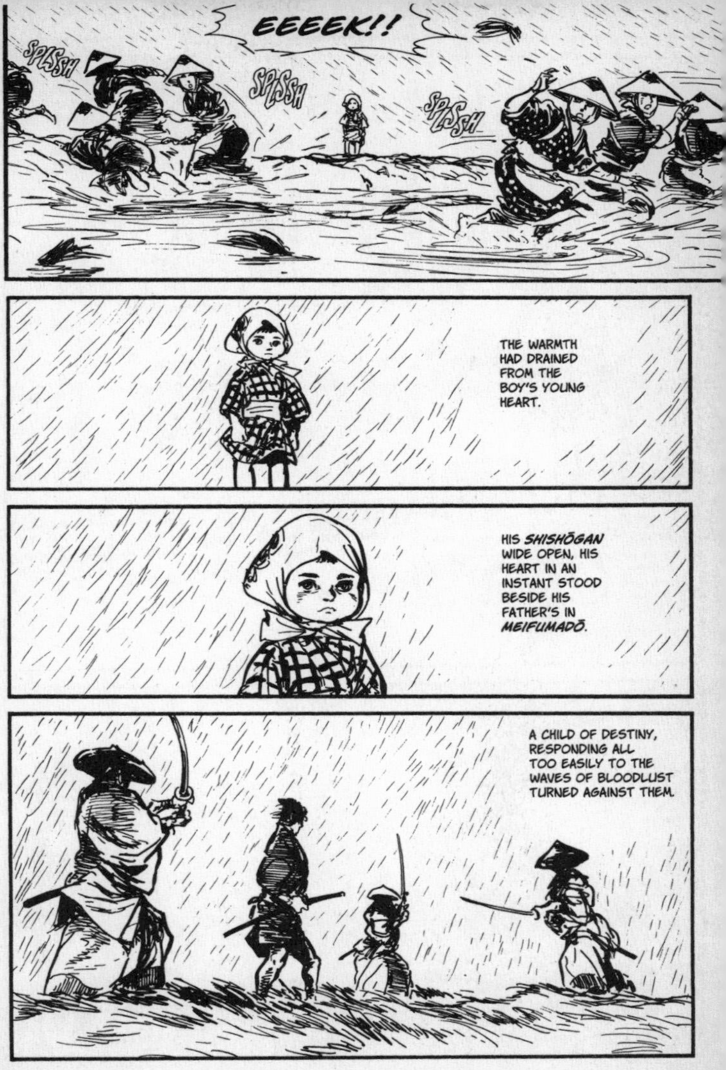
EEEEK!!
SPLSSH
SPLSSH
SPLSSH
THE WARMTH HAD DRAINED FROM THE BOY'S YOUNG HEART.
HIS *SHISHŌGAN* WIDE OPEN, HIS HEART IN AN INSTANT STOOD BESIDE HIS FATHER'S IN *MEIFUMADŌ*.
A CHILD OF DESTINY, RESPONDING ALL TOO EASILY TO THE WAVES OF BLOODLUST TURNED AGAINST THEM.

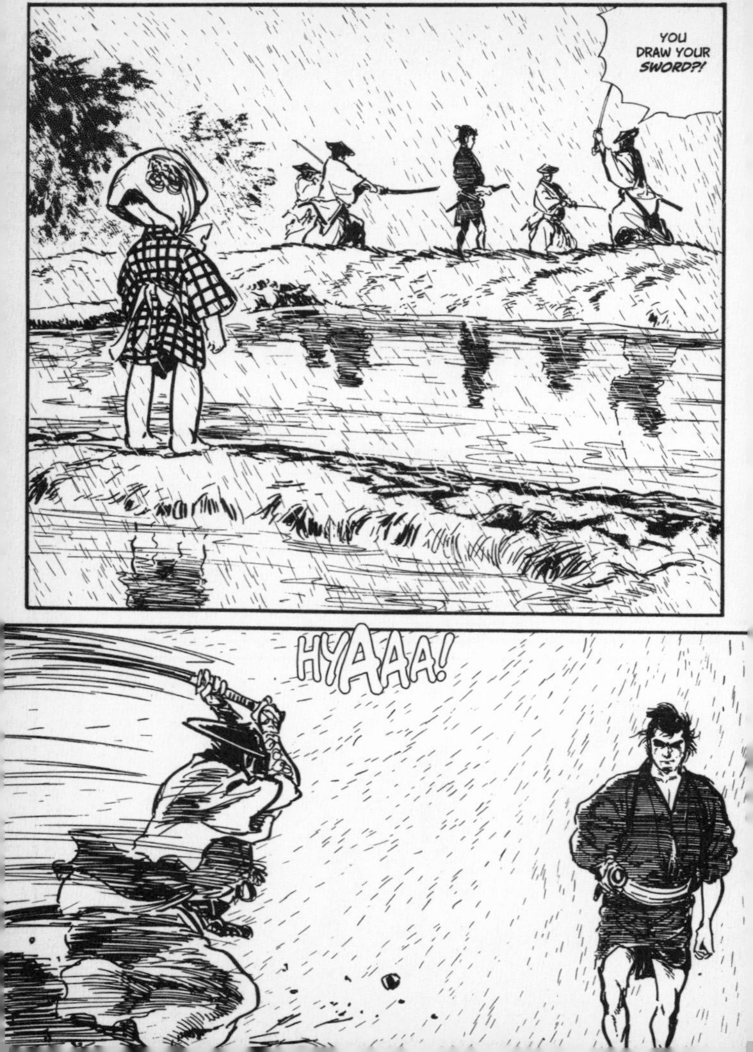
YOU DRAW YOUR SWORD?!
HYAAAA!

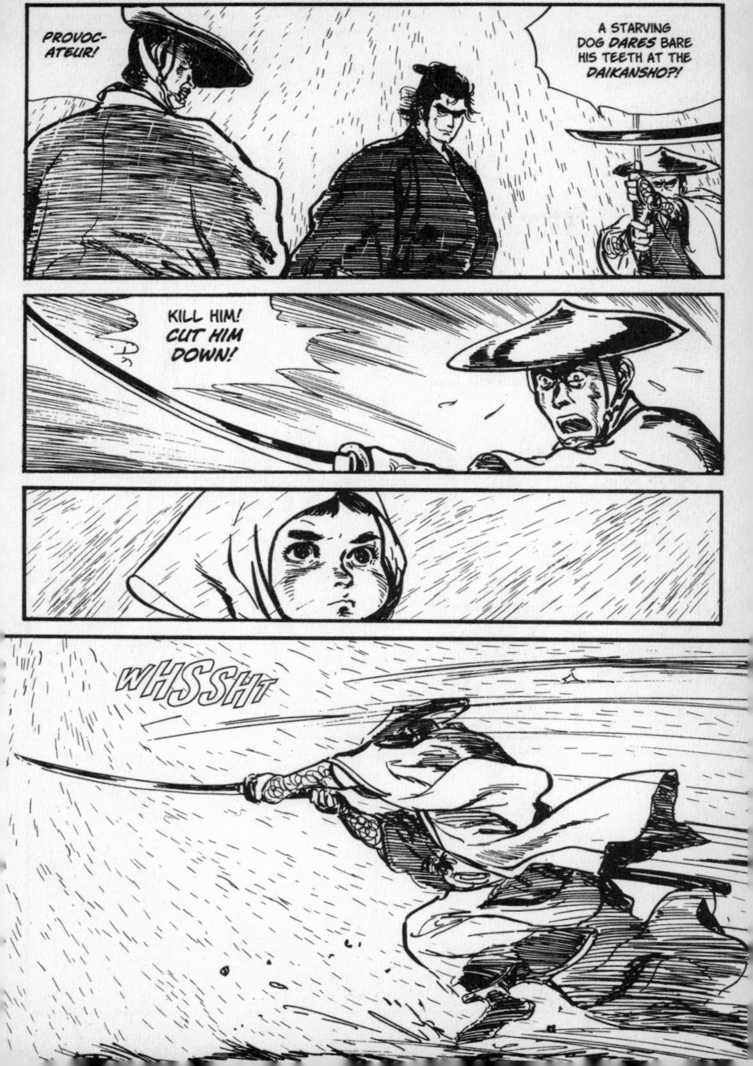
A STARVING DOG DARES BARE HIS TEETH AT THE DAIKANSHO?!
PROVOC-ATEUR!
KILL HIM! CUT HIM DOWN!
WHSSHT

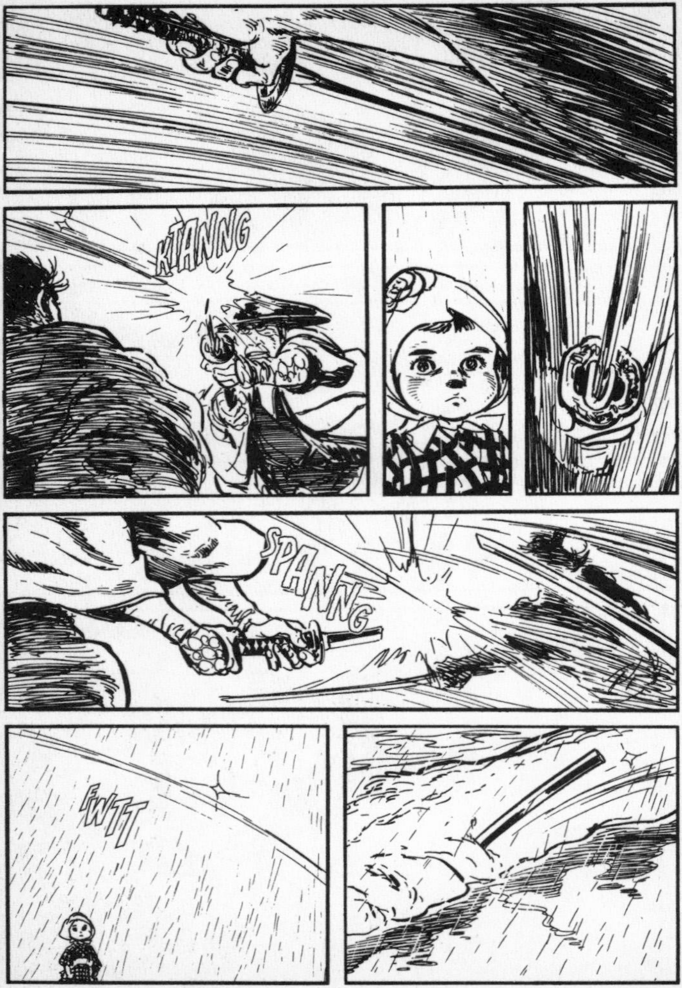
KTANNG
SPANNG
FWTT

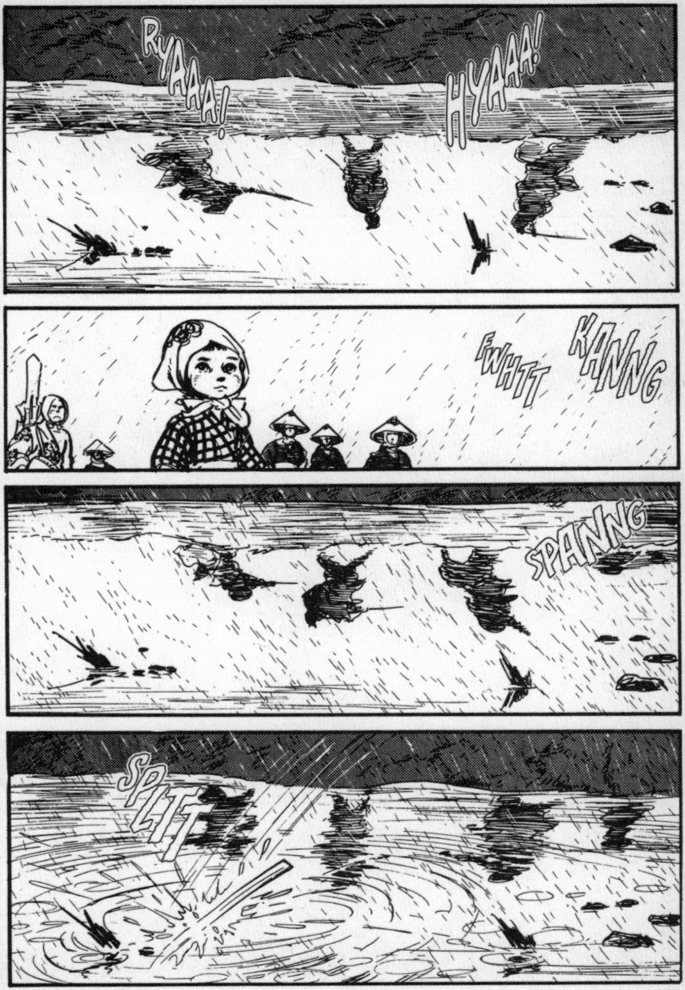
RYAAA!
HYAAA!
FWHTT
KANNG
SPANNG
SPLITT

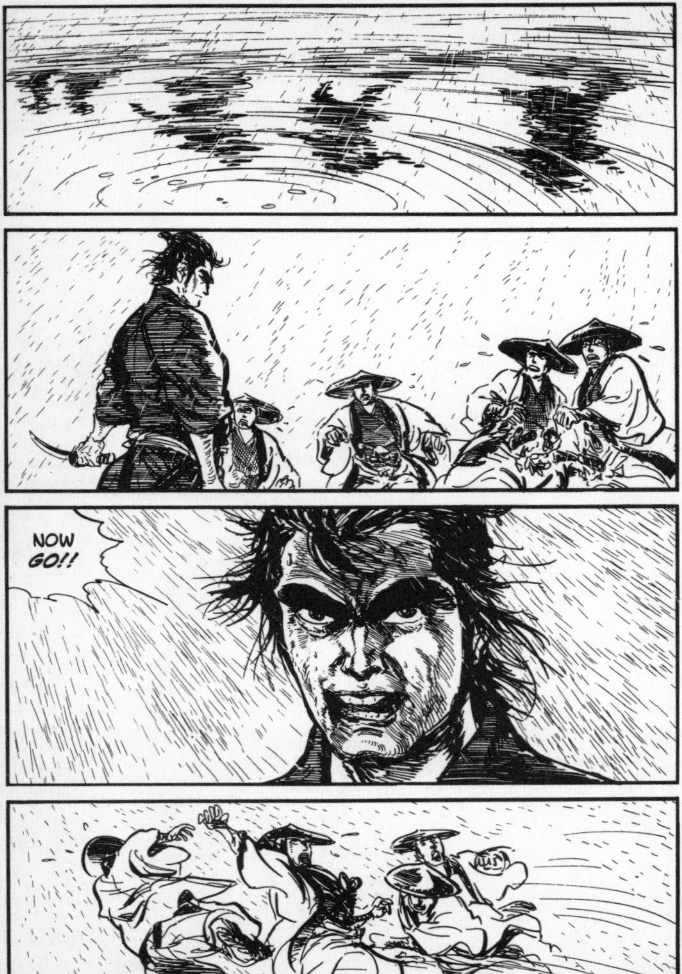
NOW GO!!

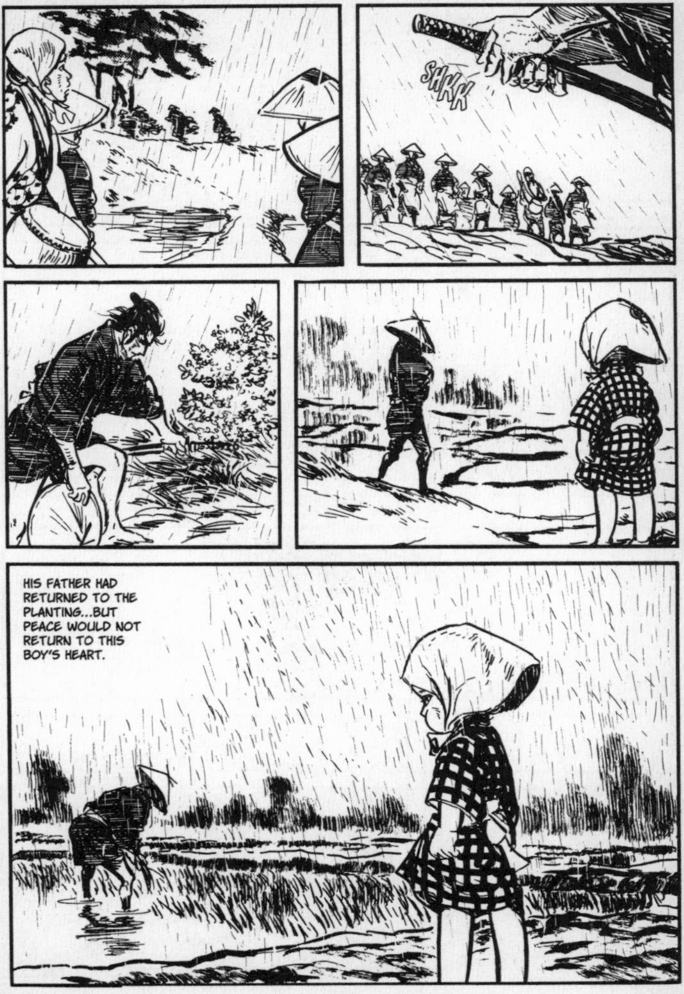
SHKK
HIS FATHER HAD RETURNED TO THE PLANTING...BUT PEACE WOULD NOT RETURN TO THIS BOY'S HEART.

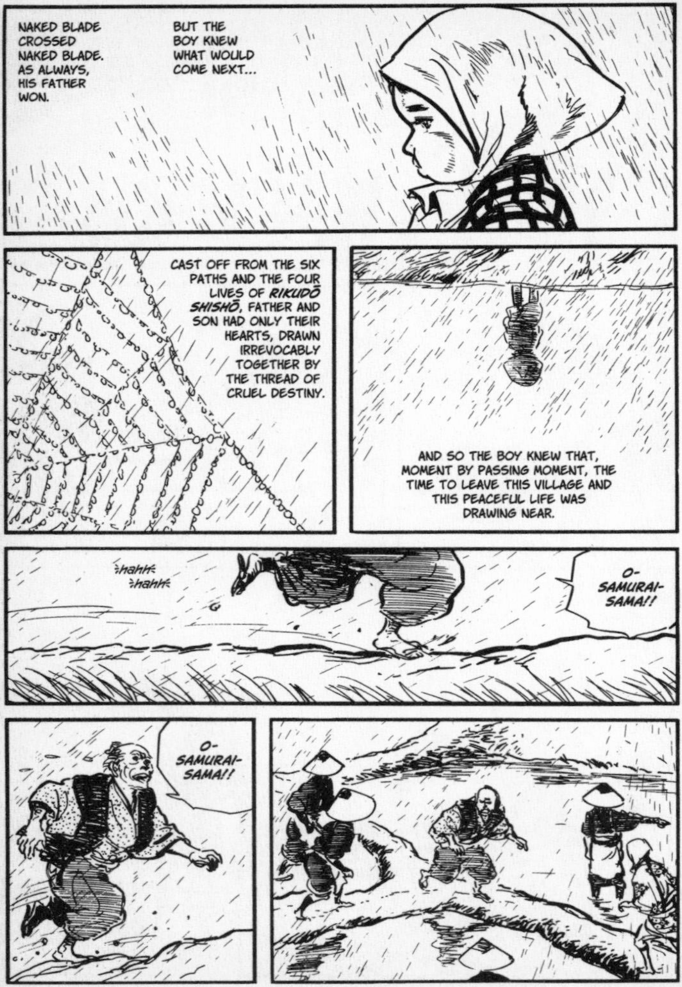
NAKED BLADE CROSSED NAKED BLADE. AS ALWAYS, HIS FATHER WON.
BUT THE BOY KNEW WHAT WOULD COME NEXT...
CAST OFF FROM THE SIX PATHS AND THE FOUR LIVES OF *RIKUDŌ SHISHŌ*, FATHER AND SON HAD ONLY THEIR HEARTS, DRAWN IRREVOCABLY TOGETHER BY THE THREAD OF CRUEL DESTINY.
AND SO THE BOY KNEW THAT, MOMENT BY PASSING MOMENT, THE TIME TO LEAVE THIS VILLAGE AND THIS PEACEFUL LIFE WAS DRAWING NEAR.
O-SAMURAI-SAMA!!
hahh *hahh*
O-SAMURAI-SAMA!!

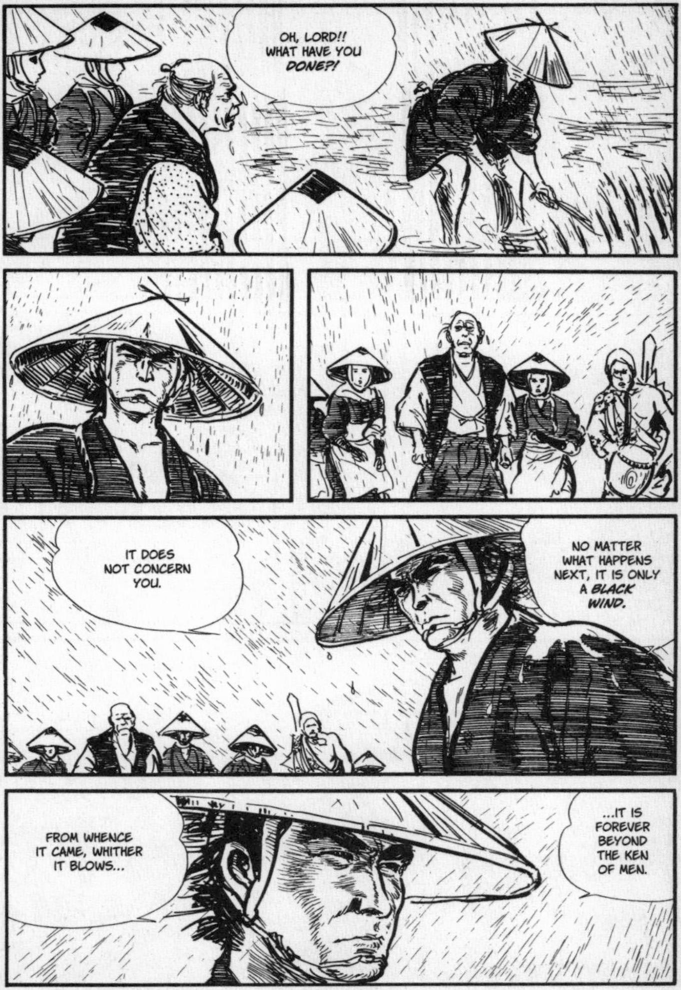

OH, LORD!! WHAT HAVE YOU DONE?!
IT DOES NOT CONCERN YOU.
NO MATTER WHAT HAPPENS NEXT, IT IS ONLY A BLACK WIND.
FROM WHENCE IT CAME, WHITHER IT BLOWS...
...IT IS FOREVER BEYOND THE KEN OF MEN.

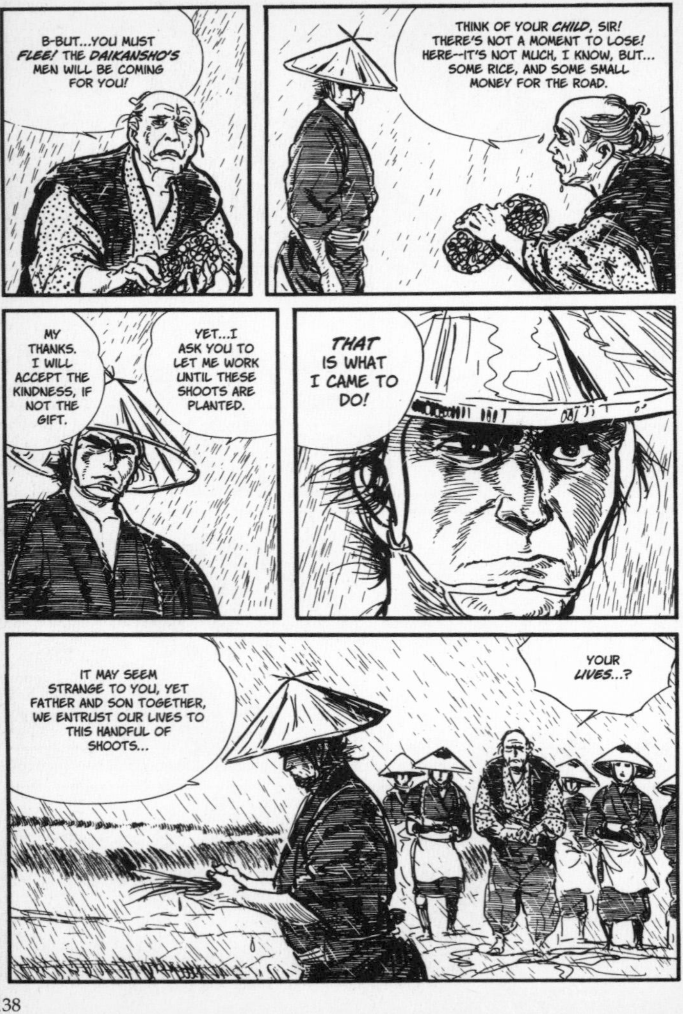
B-BUT...YOU MUST FLEE! THE DAIKANSHO'S MEN WILL BE COMING FOR YOU!
THINK OF YOUR CHILD, SIR! THERE'S NOT A MOMENT TO LOSE! HERE--IT'S NOT MUCH, I KNOW, BUT... SOME RICE, AND SOME SMALL MONEY FOR THE ROAD.
MY THANKS. I WILL ACCEPT THE KINDNESS, IF NOT THE GIFT.
YET...I ASK YOU TO LET ME WORK UNTIL THESE SHOOTS ARE PLANTED.
THAT IS WHAT I CAME TO DO!
IT MAY SEEM STRANGE TO YOU, YET FATHER AND SON TOGETHER, WE ENTRUST OUR LIVES TO THIS HANDFUL OF SHOOTS...
YOUR LIVES...?

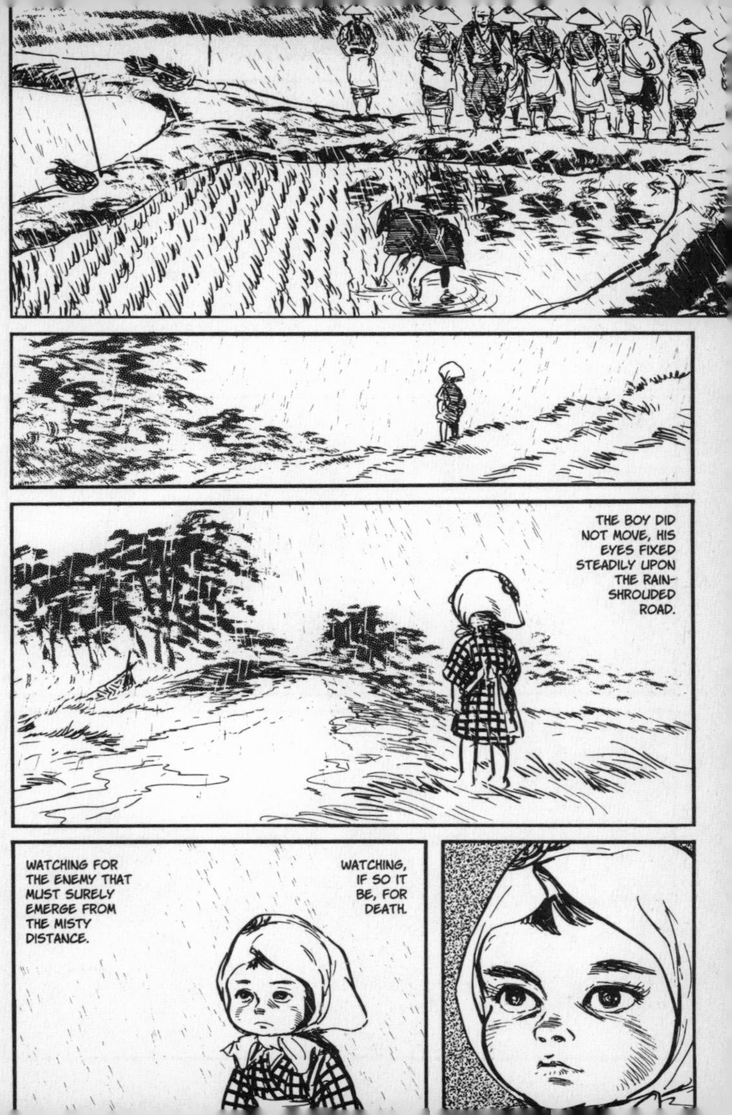
THE BOY DID NOT MOVE, HIS EYES FIXED STEADILY UPON THE RAIN-SHROUDED ROAD.
WATCHING FOR THE ENEMY THAT MUST SURELY EMERGE FROM THE MISTY DISTANCE.
WATCHING, IF SO IT BE, FOR DEATH.

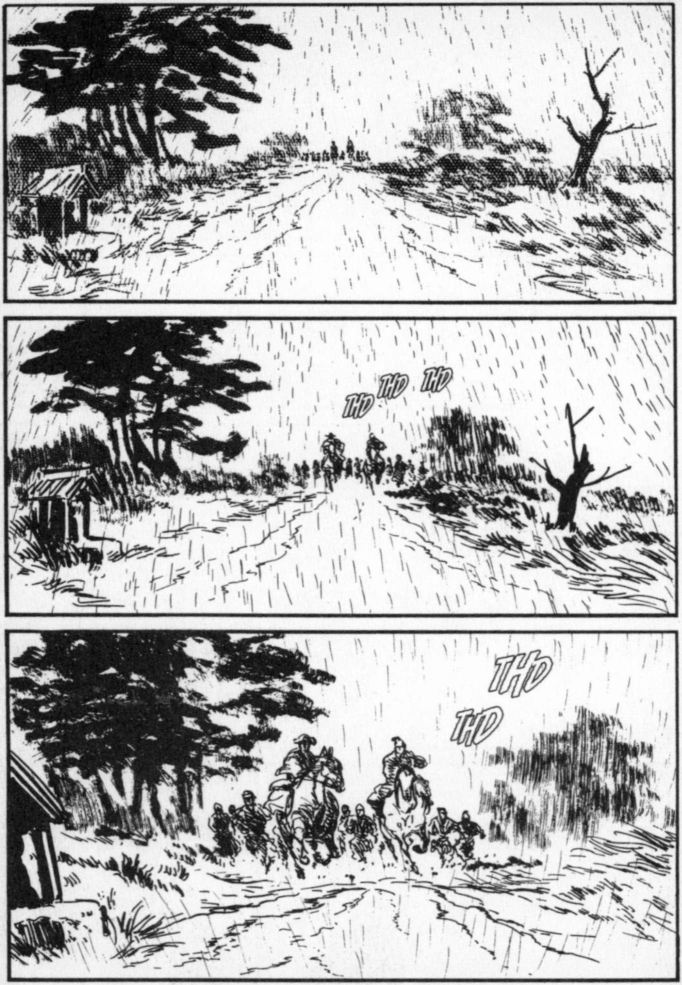
THD THD THD
THD
THD

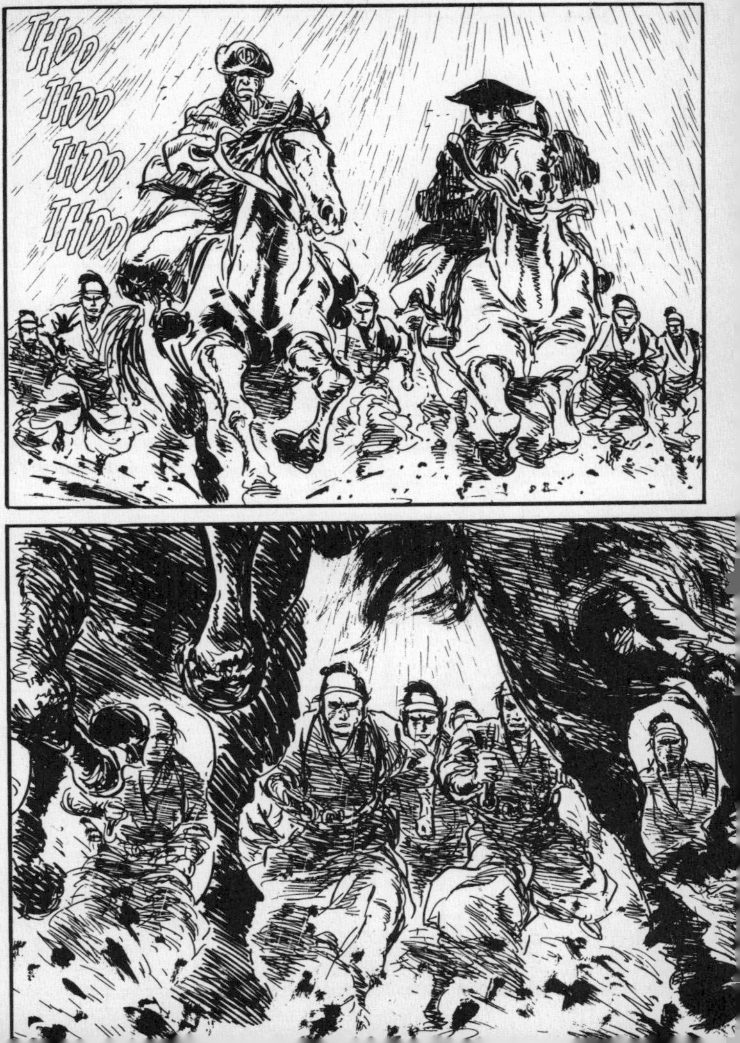
THDD
THDD
THDD
THDD

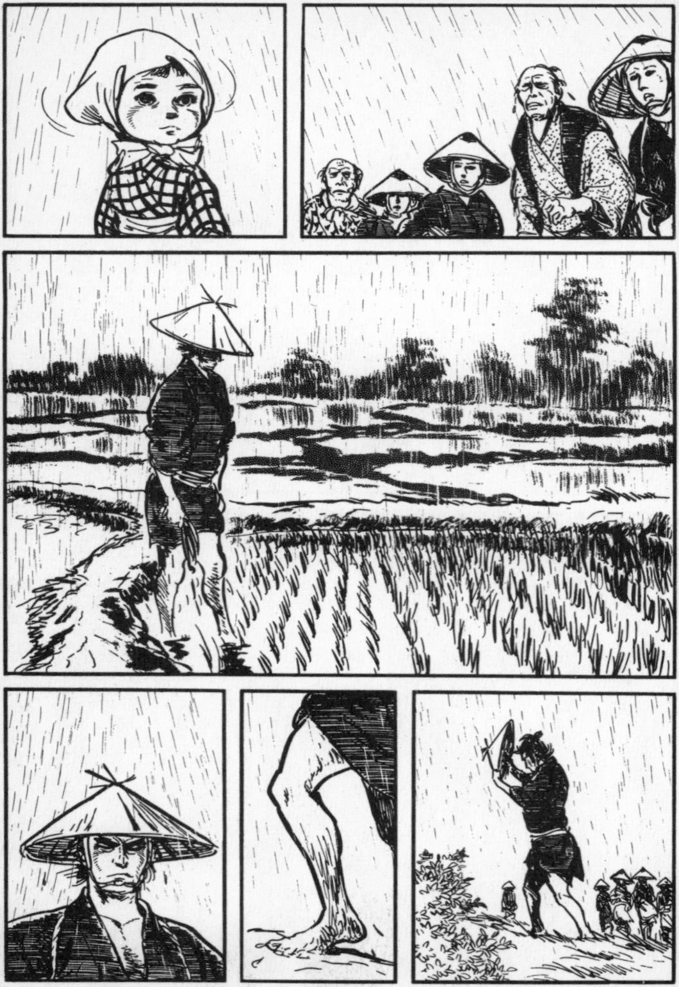

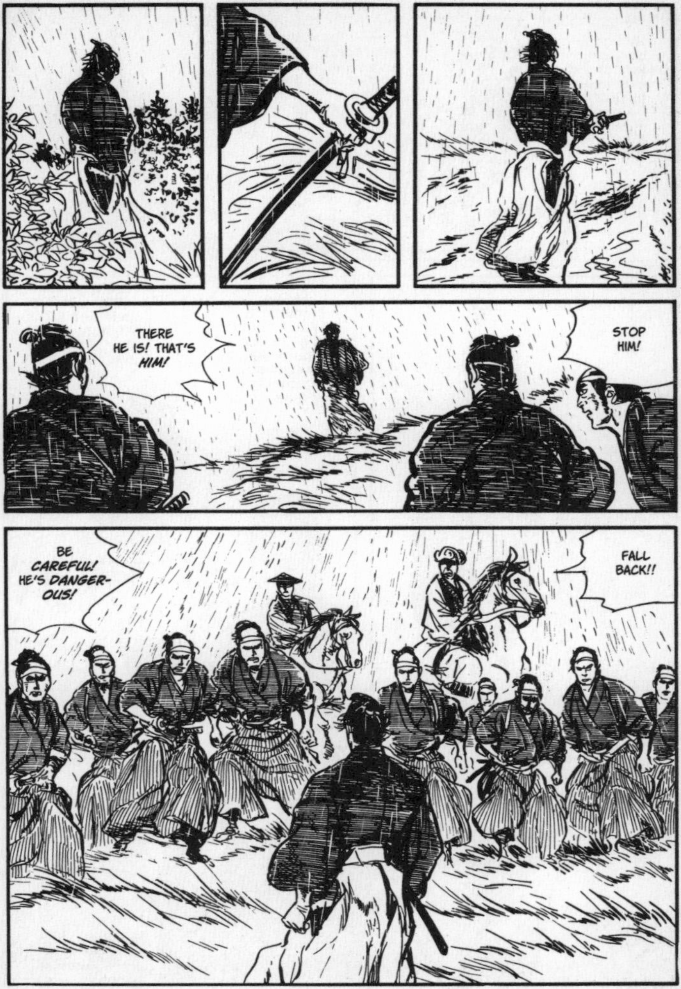
THERE HE IS! THAT'S HIM!
STOP HIM!
BE CAREFUL! HE'S DANGER-OUS!
FALL BACK!!

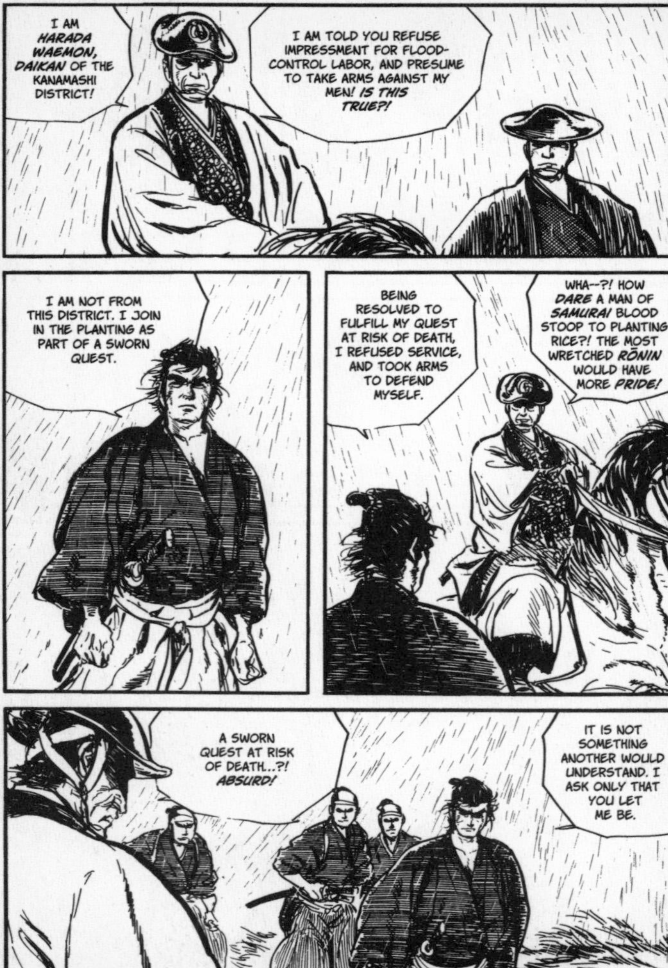
I AM *HARADA WAEMON, DAIKAN* OF THE KANAMASHI DISTRICT!
I AM TOLD YOU REFUSE IMPRESSMENT FOR FLOOD-CONTROL LABOR, AND PRESUME TO TAKE ARMS AGAINST MY MEN! *IS THIS TRUE?!*
I AM NOT FROM THIS DISTRICT. I JOIN IN THE PLANTING AS PART OF A SWORN QUEST.
BEING RESOLVED TO FULFILL MY QUEST AT RISK OF DEATH, I REFUSED SERVICE, AND TOOK ARMS TO DEFEND MYSELF.
WHA--?! HOW *DARE* A MAN OF *SAMURAI* BLOOD STOOP TO PLANTING RICE?! THE MOST WRETCHED *RŌNIN* WOULD HAVE MORE *PRIDE!*
A SWORN QUEST AT RISK OF DEATH...?! *ABSURD!*
IT IS NOT SOMETHING ANOTHER WOULD UNDERSTAND. I ASK ONLY THAT YOU LET ME BE.

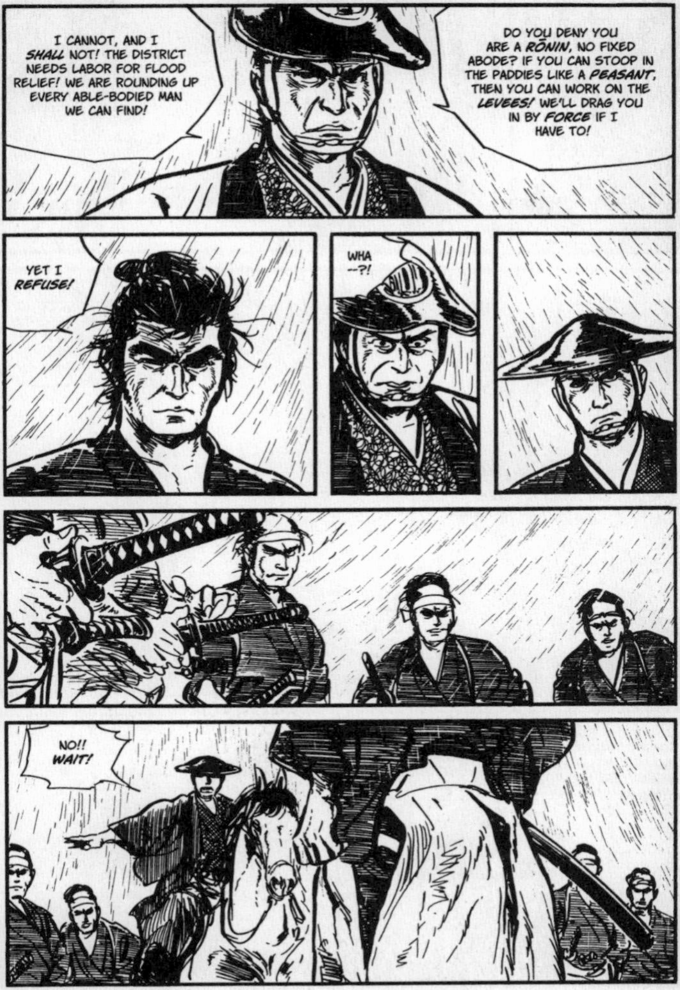
I CANNOT, AND I SHALL NOT! THE DISTRICT NEEDS LABOR FOR FLOOD RELIEF! WE ARE ROUNDING UP EVERY ABLE-BODIED MAN WE CAN FIND!
DO YOU DENY YOU ARE A RŌNIN, NO FIXED ABODE? IF YOU CAN STOOP IN THE PADDIES LIKE A PEASANT, THEN YOU CAN WORK ON THE LEVEES! WE'LL DRAG YOU IN BY FORCE IF I HAVE TO!
YET I REFUSE!
WHA --?!
NO!! WAIT!

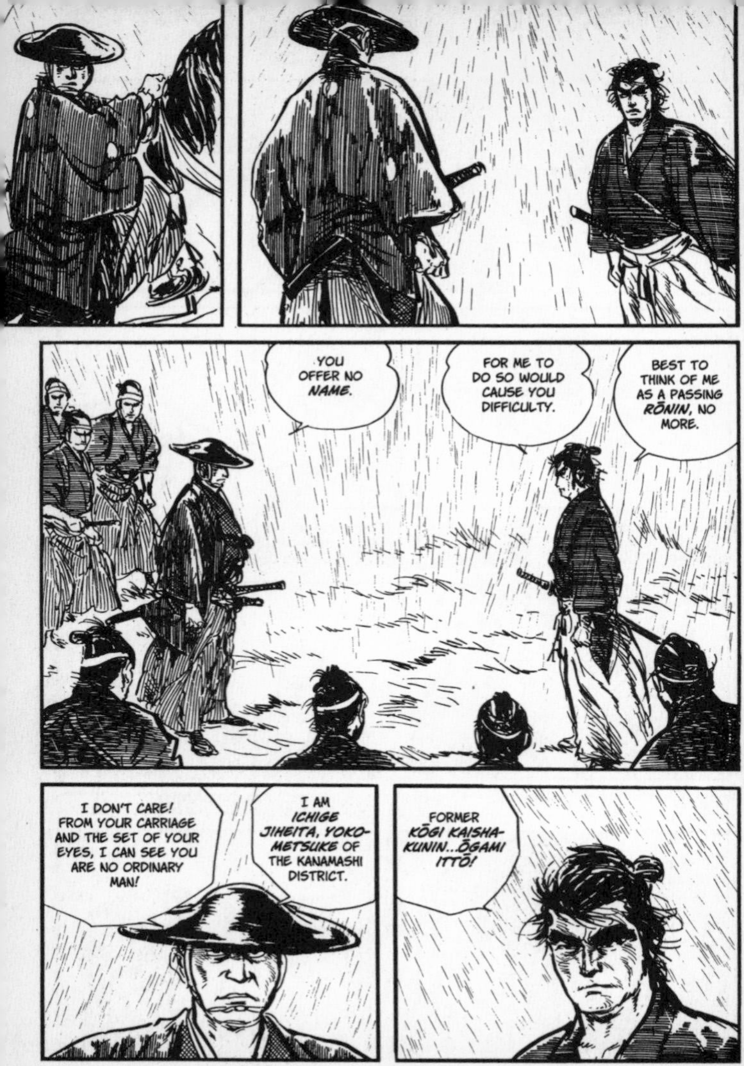
YOU OFFER NO NAME.
FOR ME TO DO SO WOULD CAUSE YOU DIFFICULTY.
BEST TO THINK OF ME AS A PASSING RŌNIN, NO MORE.
I DON'T CARE! FROM YOUR CARRIAGE AND THE SET OF YOUR EYES, I CAN SEE YOU ARE NO ORDINARY MAN!
I AM ICHIGE JIHEITA, YOKO-METSUKE OF THE KANAMASHI DISTRICT.
FORMER KŌGI KAISHA-KUNIN...ŌGAMI ITTŌ!

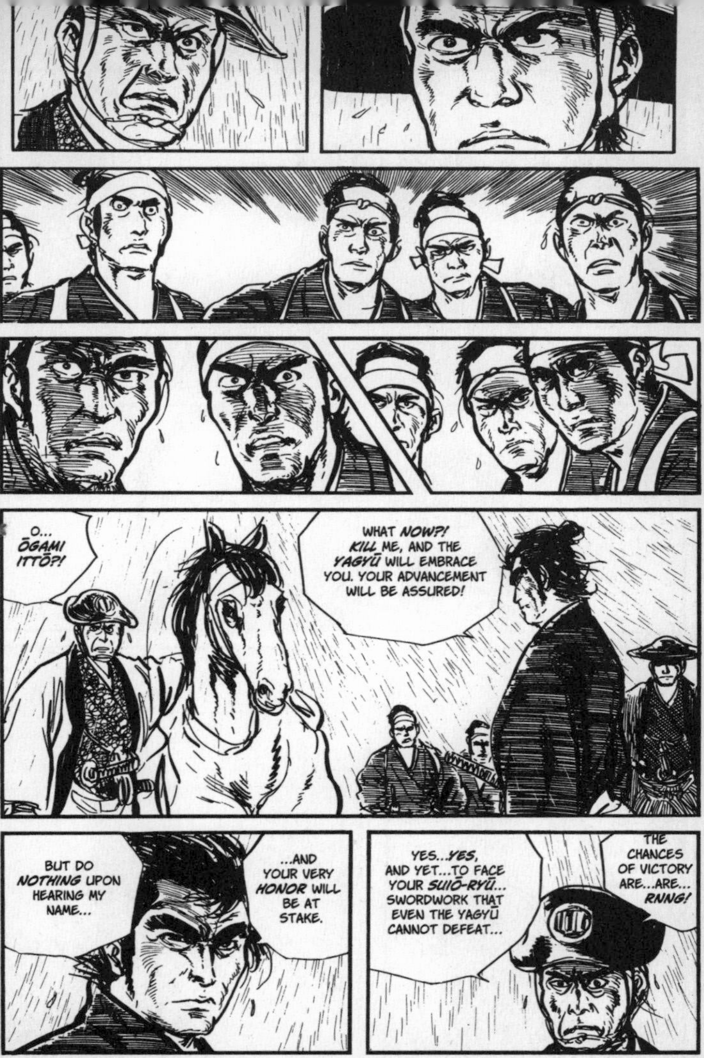
O... ŌGAMI ITTŌ?!
WHAT NOW?! KILL ME, AND THE YAGYŪ WILL EMBRACE YOU. YOUR ADVANCEMENT WILL BE ASSURED!
BUT DO NOTHING UPON HEARING MY NAME...
...AND YOUR VERY HONOR WILL BE AT STAKE.
YES...YES, AND YET...TO FACE YOUR SUIŌ-RYŪ... SWORDWORK THAT EVEN THE YAGYŪ CANNOT DEFEAT...
THE CHANCES OF VICTORY ARE...ARE... RNNG!

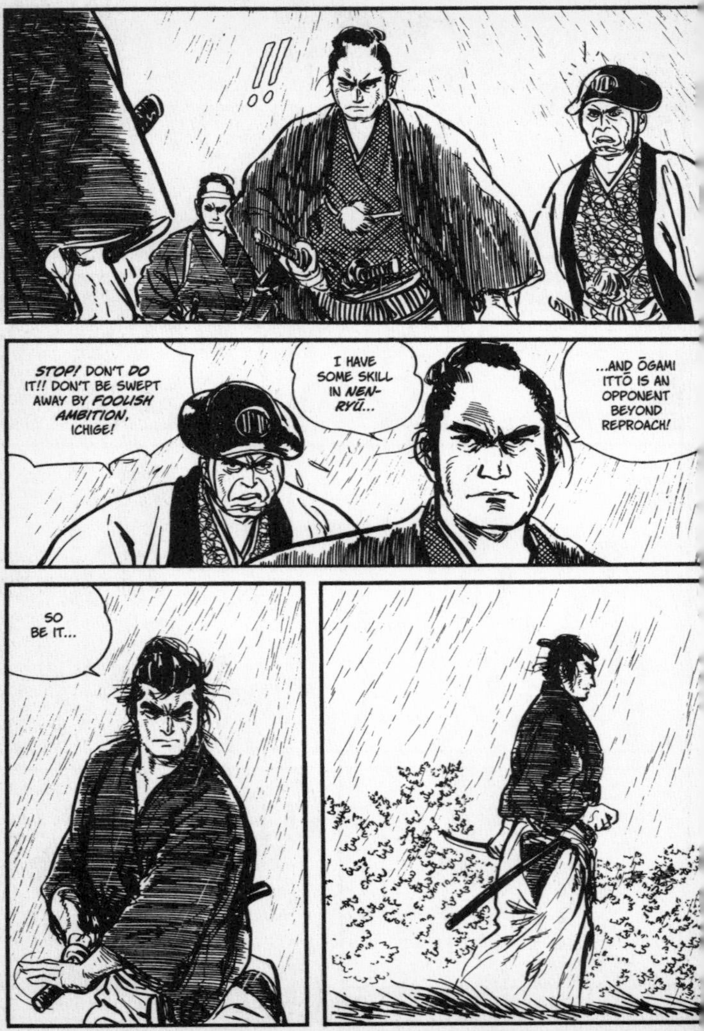

!!
STOP! DON'T DO IT!! DON'T BE SWEPT AWAY BY FOOLISH AMBITION, ICHIGE!
I HAVE SOME SKILL IN NEN-RYŪ...
...AND ŌGAMI ITTŌ IS AN OPPONENT BEYOND REPROACH!
SO BE IT...

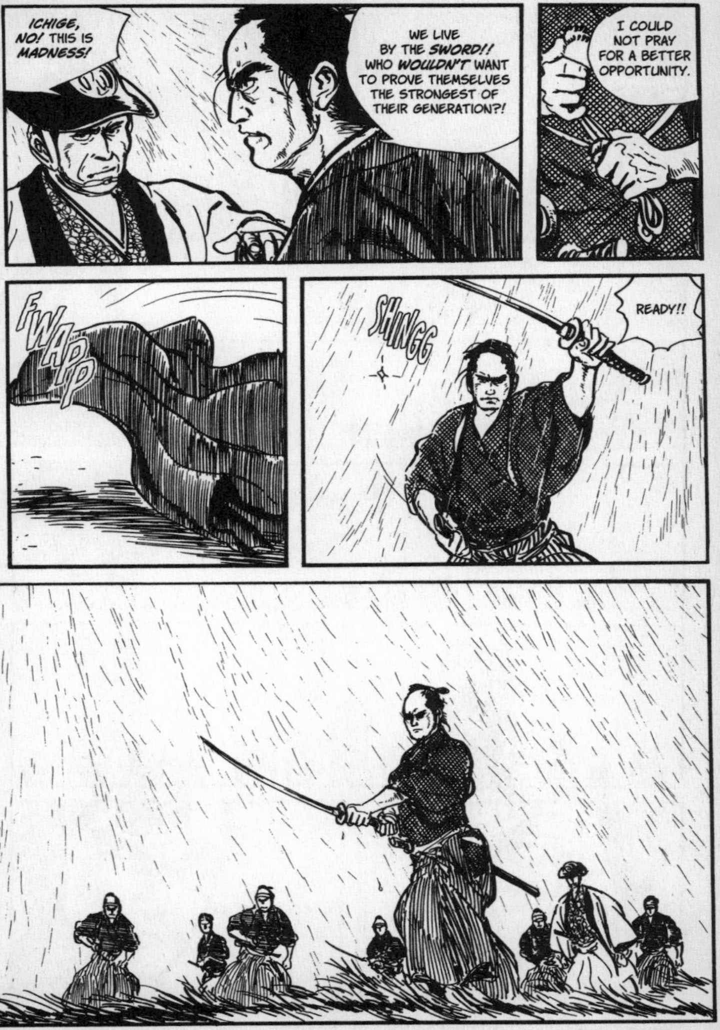
ICHIGE, NO! THIS IS MADNESS!
WE LIVE BY THE SWORD!! WHO WOULDN'T WANT TO PROVE THEMSELVES THE STRONGEST OF THEIR GENERATION?!
I COULD NOT PRAY FOR A BETTER OPPORTUNITY.
FWAPP
SHINGG
READY!!

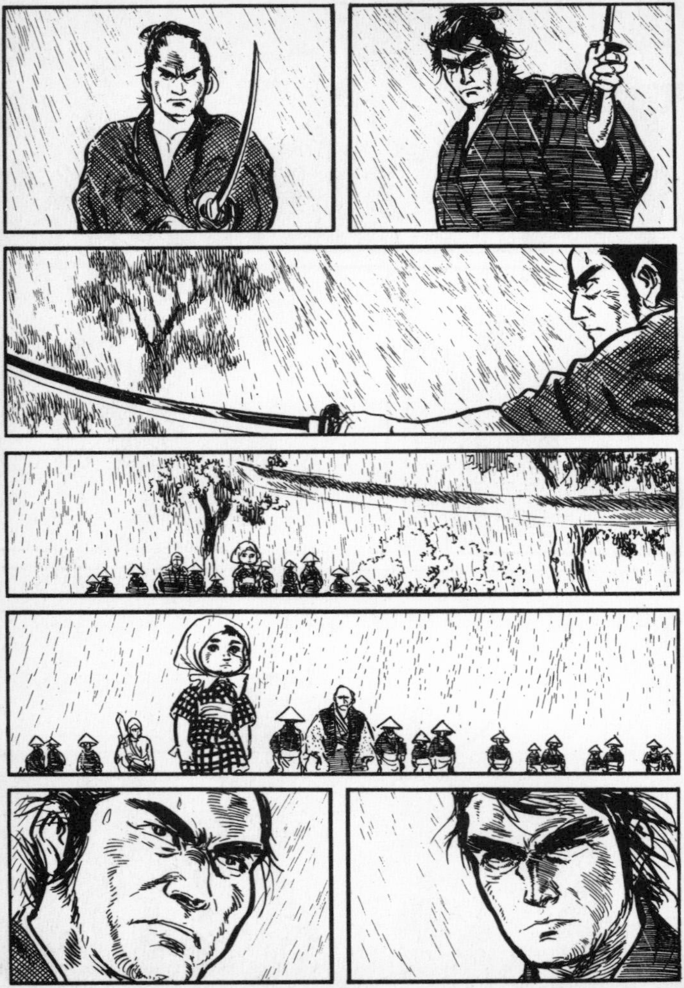

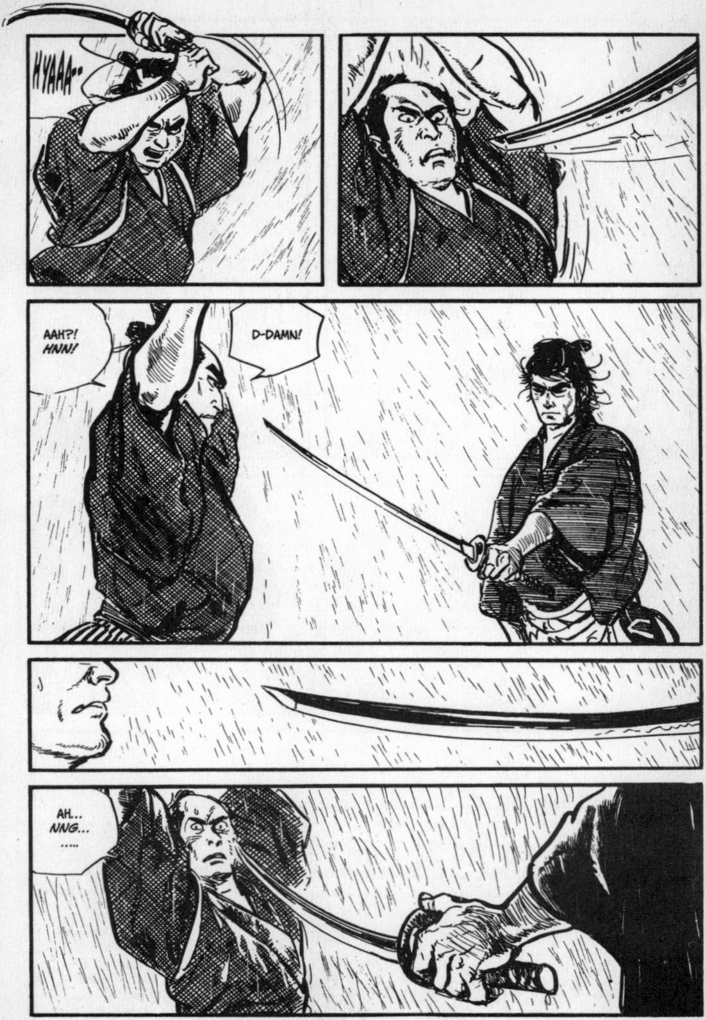
HYAAA--
AAH?! HNN!
D-DAMN!
AH... NNG... .....

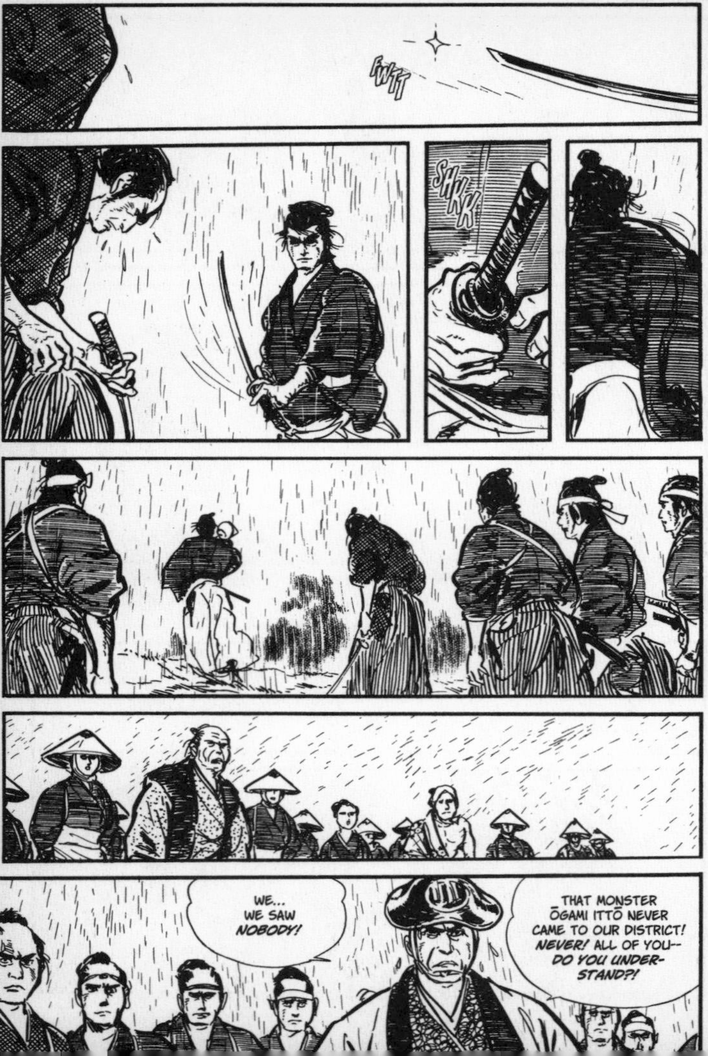
FWTT
SHKK
WE... WE SAW NOBODY!
THAT MONSTER ŌGAMI ITTŌ NEVER CAME TO OUR DISTRICT! NEVER! ALL OF YOU-- DO YOU UNDERSTAND?!

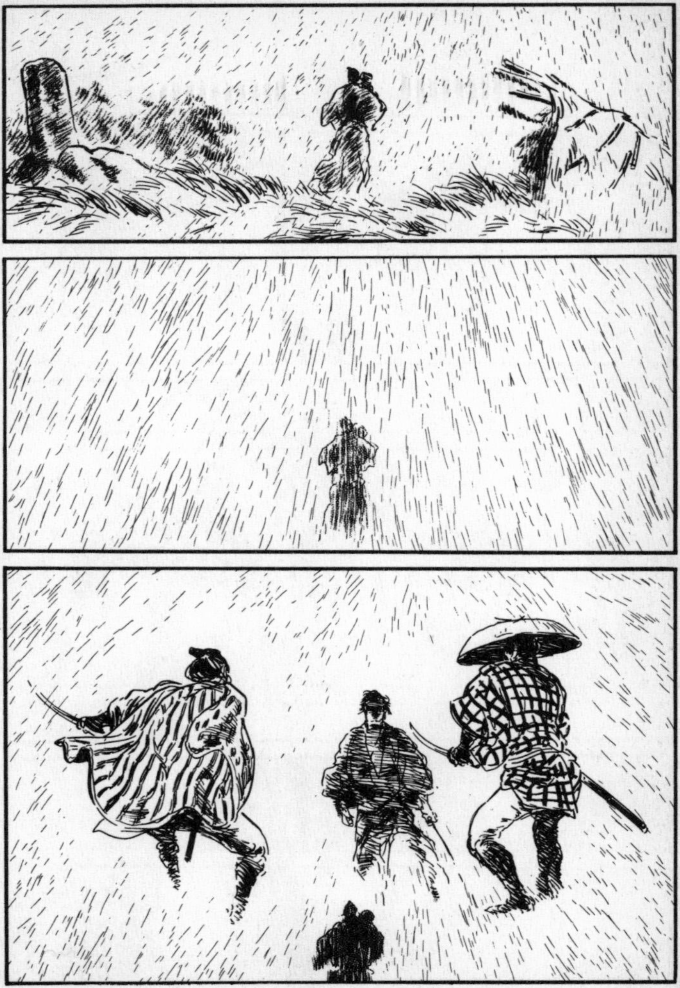

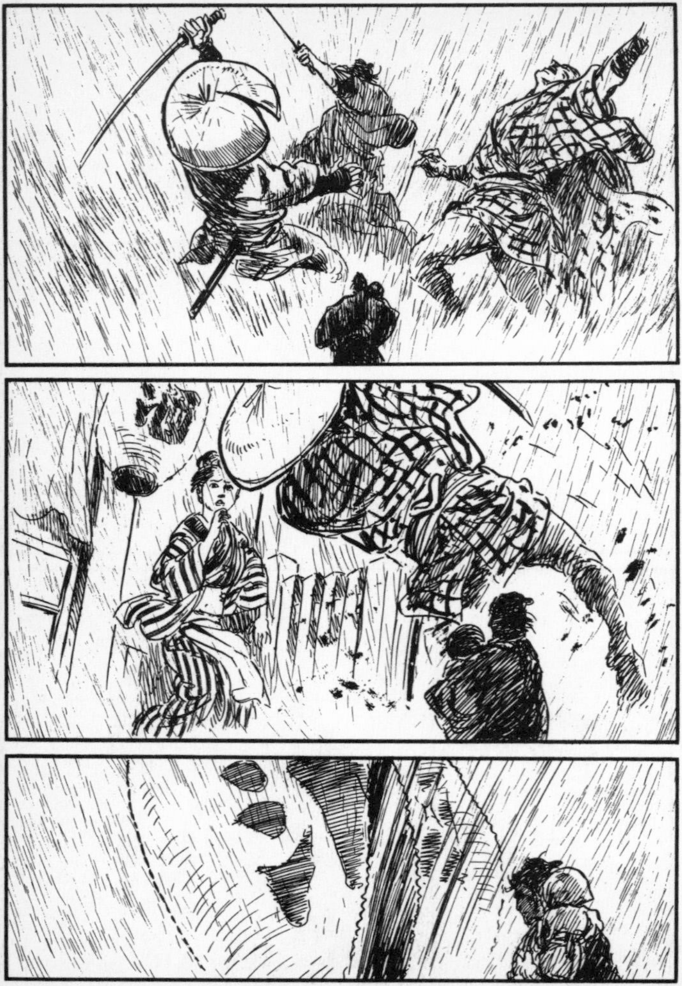

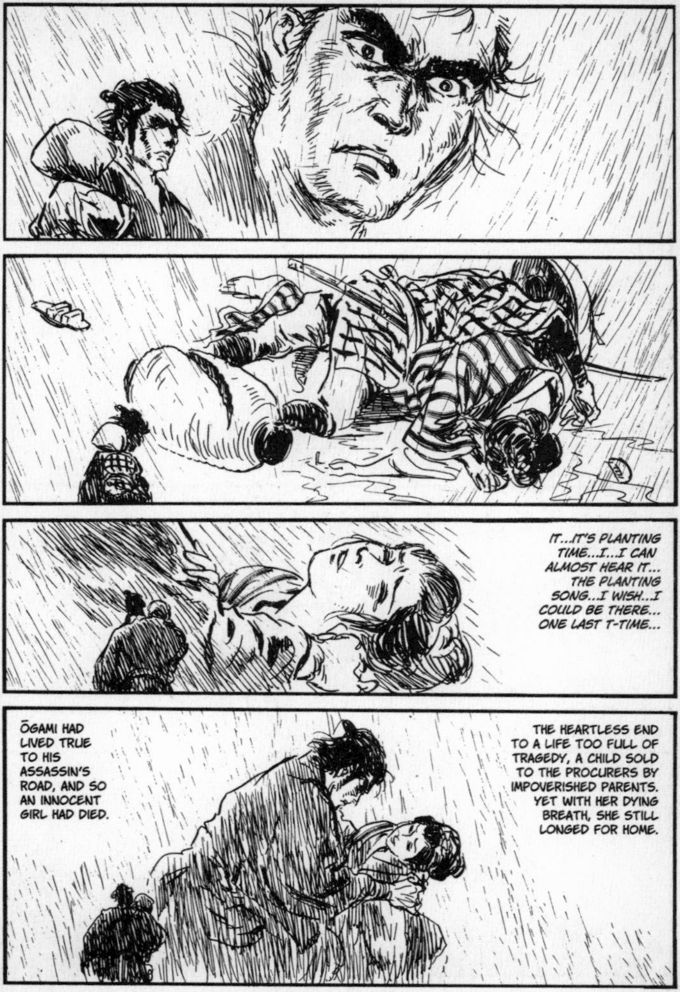
IT...IT'S PLANTING TIME...I...I CAN ALMOST HEAR IT... THE PLANTING SONG...I WISH...I COULD BE THERE... ONE LAST T-TIME...
ŌGAMI HAD LIVED TRUE TO HIS ASSASSIN'S ROAD, AND SO AN INNOCENT GIRL HAD DIED.
THE HEARTLESS END TO A LIFE TOO FULL OF TRAGEDY, A CHILD SOLD TO THE PROCURERS BY IMPOVERISHED PARENTS. YET WITH HER DYING BREATH, SHE STILL LONGED FOR HOME.

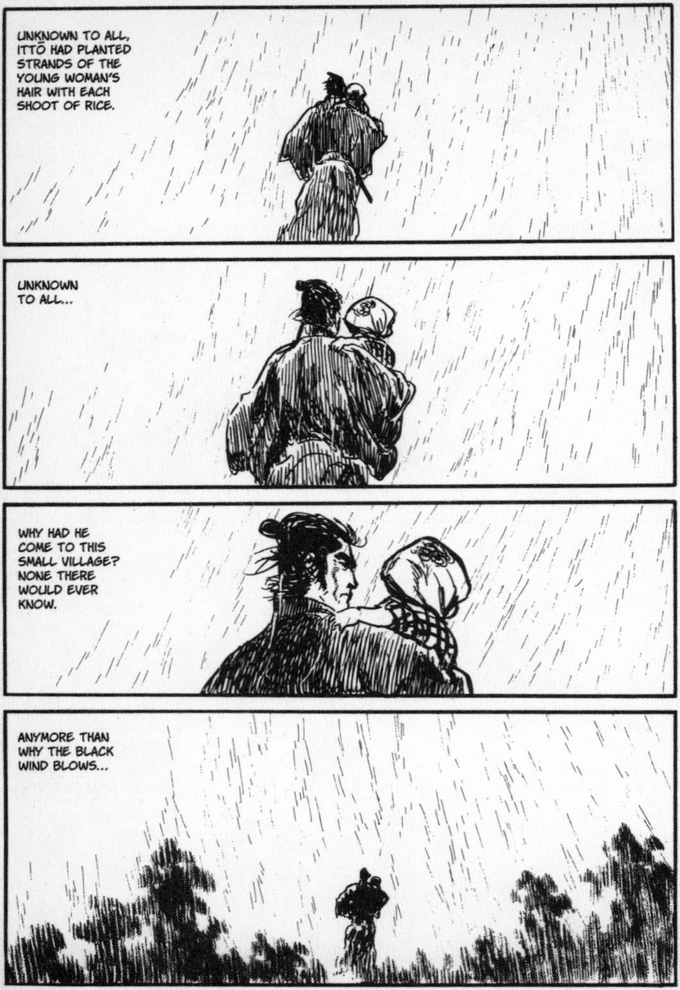
UNKNOWN TO ALL, ITTŌ HAD PLANTED STRANDS OF THE YOUNG WOMAN'S HAIR WITH EACH SHOOT OF RICE.
UNKNOWN TO ALL...
WHY HAD HE COME TO THIS SMALL VILLAGE? NONE THERE WOULD EVER KNOW.
ANYMORE THAN WHY THE BLACK WIND BLOWS...

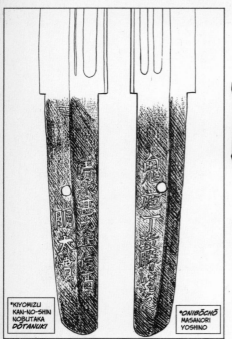

*KIYOMIZU
KAN-NO-SHIN
NOBUTAKA
DŌTANUKI

*ONIBŌCHŌ
MASANORI
YOSHINO*

Decapitato Asaemon

YAMADA ASAEMON

THE FIRST, SADATOKI. DIED DECEMBER 18, THE FIRST YEAR OF *KYŌHŌ*, 1716.

THE SECOND, YOSHITOKI. DIED APRIL 19, THE FIRST YEAR OF *ENKYŌ*, 1744.

THE THIRD, YOSHITSUGU. DIED MAY 22, THE SEVENTH YEAR OF MEIWA, 1770.

THE FOURTH, YOSHITOMO. DIED SEPTEMEBER 17, THE FIRST YEAR OF *TENMEI*, 1786.

THE FIFTH, YOSHIMUTSU. DIED FEBRUARY 9, THE SIXTH YEAR OF *BUNSEI*, 1823.

THE SIXTH, YOSHIMASA. DIED JUNE 17, THE FIFTH YEAR OF *KAEI*, 1852.

THE SEVENTH, YOSHITOSHI. DIED DECEMBER 29, THE SEVENTEENTH YEAR OF *MEIJI*, 1882.

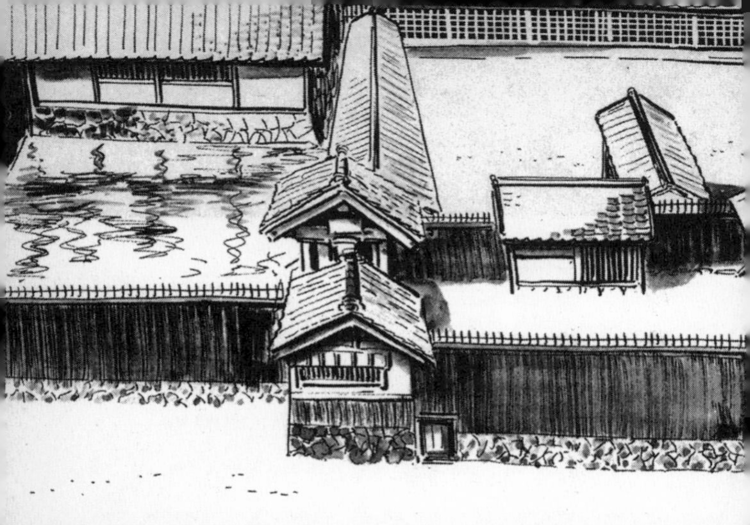

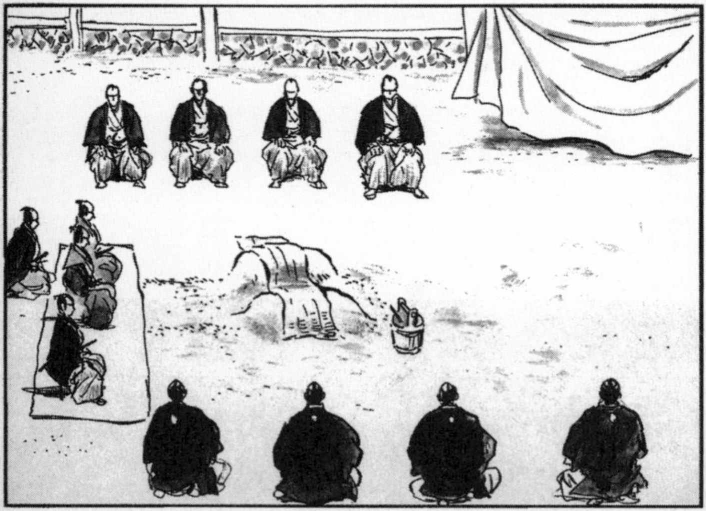

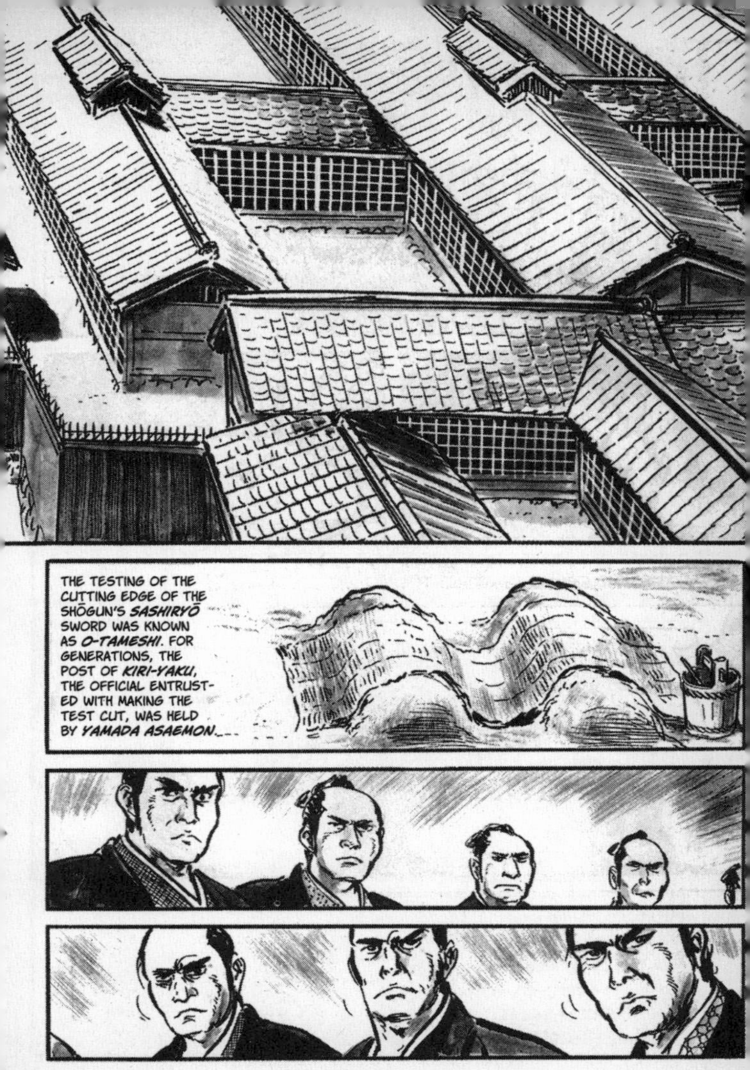
THE TESTING OF THE CUTTING EDGE OF THE SHŌGUN'S *SASHIRYŌ* SWORD WAS KNOWN AS *O-TAMESHI*. FOR GENERATIONS, THE POST OF *KIRI-YAKU*, THE OFFICIAL ENTRUSTED WITH MAKING THE TEST CUT, WAS HELD BY *YAMADA ASAEMON*...

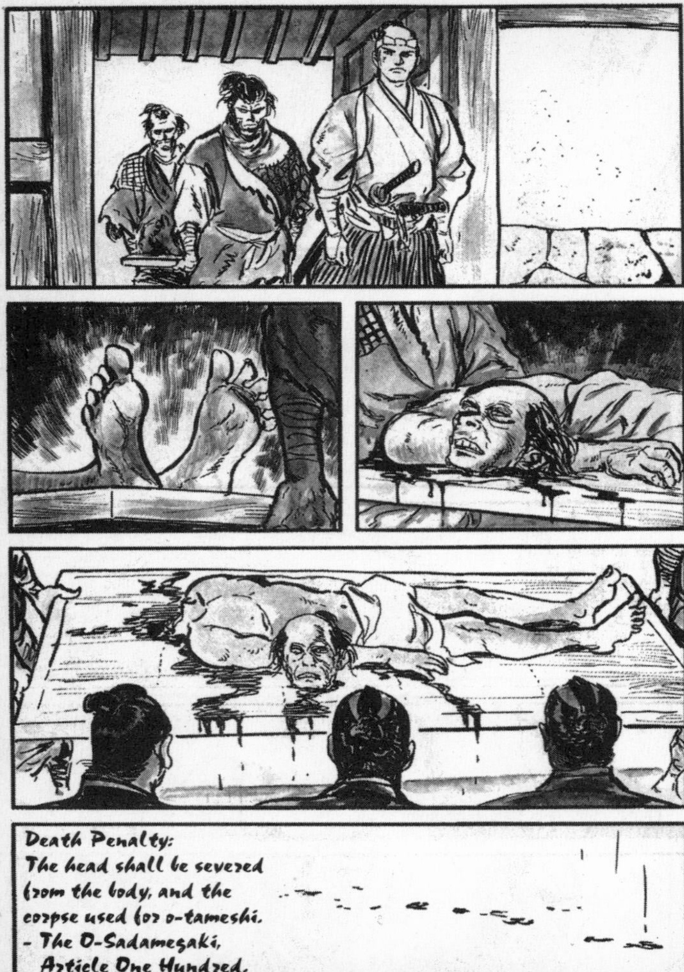
Death Penalty:
The head shall be severed from the body, and the corpse used for o-tameshi.
- The O-Sadamegaki, Article One Hundred.

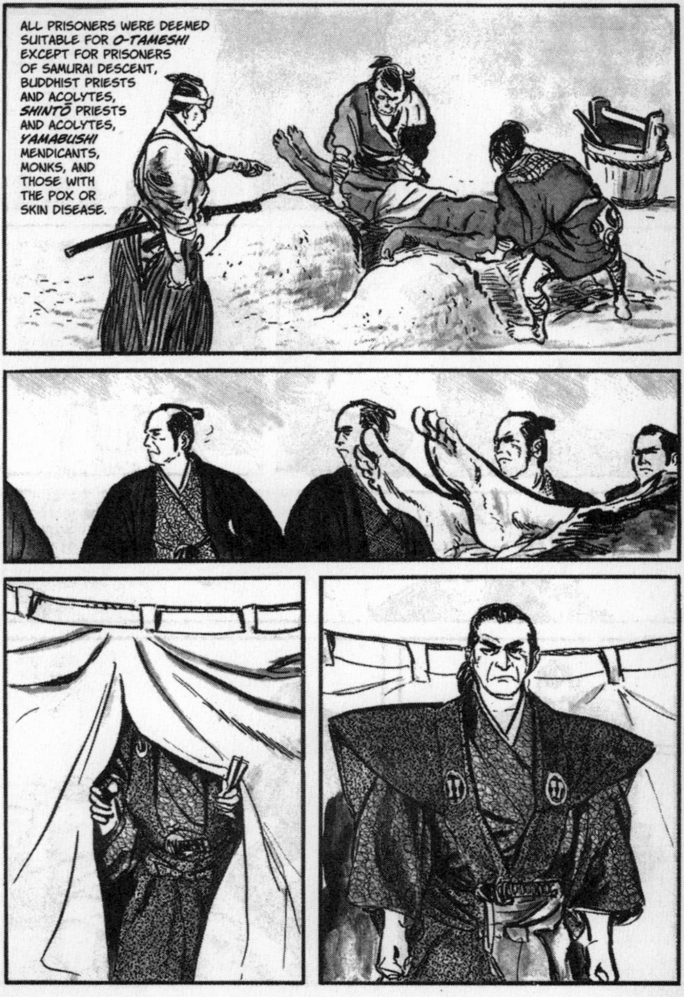
ALL PRISONERS WERE DEEMED SUITABLE FOR *O-TAMESHI* EXCEPT FOR PRISONERS OF SAMURAI DESCENT, BUDDHIST PRIESTS AND ACOLYTES, *SHINTŌ* PRIESTS AND ACOLYTES, *YAMABUSHI* MENDICANTS, MONKS, AND THOSE WITH THE POX OR SKIN DISEASE.

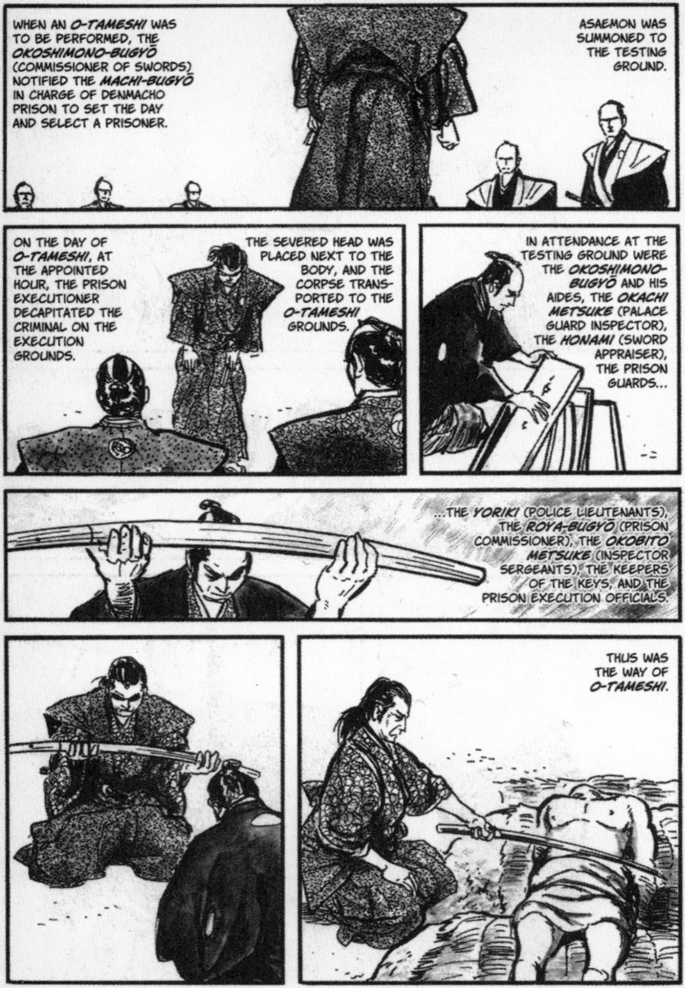

WHEN AN *O-TAMESHI* WAS TO BE PERFORMED, THE *OKOSHIMONO-BUGYŌ* (COMMISSIONER OF SWORDS) NOTIFIED THE *MACHI-BUGYŌ* IN CHARGE OF DENMACHO PRISON TO SET THE DAY AND SELECT A PRISONER.
ASAEMON WAS SUMMONED TO THE TESTING GROUND.
ON THE DAY OF *O-TAMESHI*, AT THE APPOINTED HOUR, THE PRISON EXECUTIONER DECAPITATED THE CRIMINAL ON THE EXECUTION GROUNDS.
THE SEVERED HEAD WAS PLACED NEXT TO THE BODY, AND THE CORPSE TRANS-PORTED TO THE *O-TAMESHI* GROUNDS.
IN ATTENDANCE AT THE TESTING GROUND WERE THE *OKOSHIMONO-BUGYŌ* AND HIS AIDES, THE *OKACHI METSUKE* (PALACE GUARD INSPECTOR), THE *HONAMI* (SWORD APPRAISER), THE PRISON GUARDS...
...THE *YORIKI* (POLICE LIEUTENANTS), THE *ROYA-BUGYŌ* (PRISON COMMISSIONER), THE *OKOBITO METSUKE* (INSPECTOR SERGEANTS), THE KEEPERS OF THE KEYS, AND THE PRISON EXECUTION OFFICIALS.
THUS WAS THE WAY OF *O-TAMESHI*.

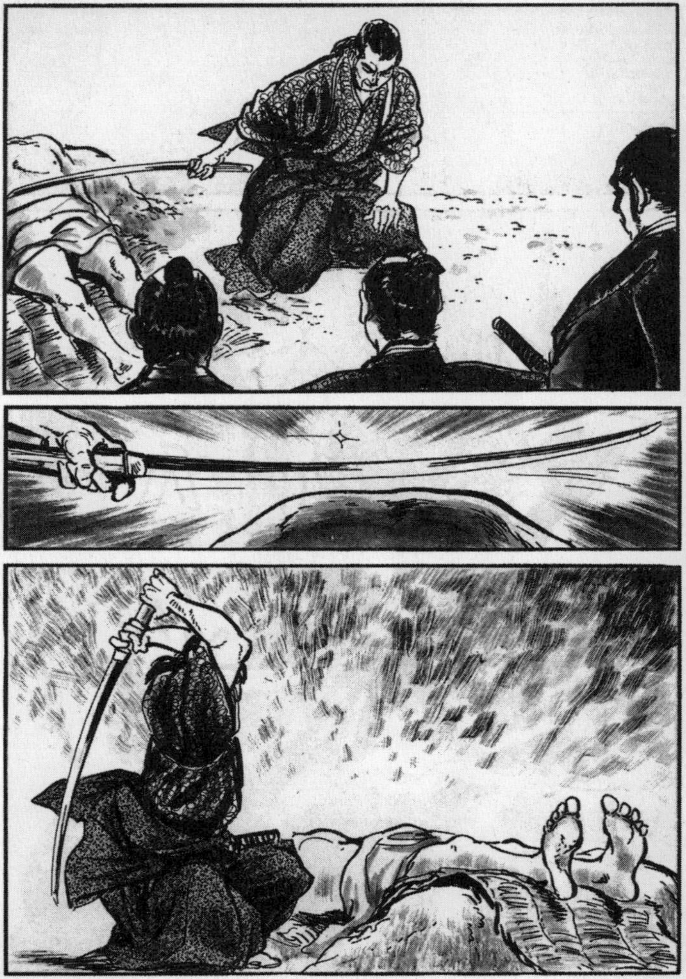

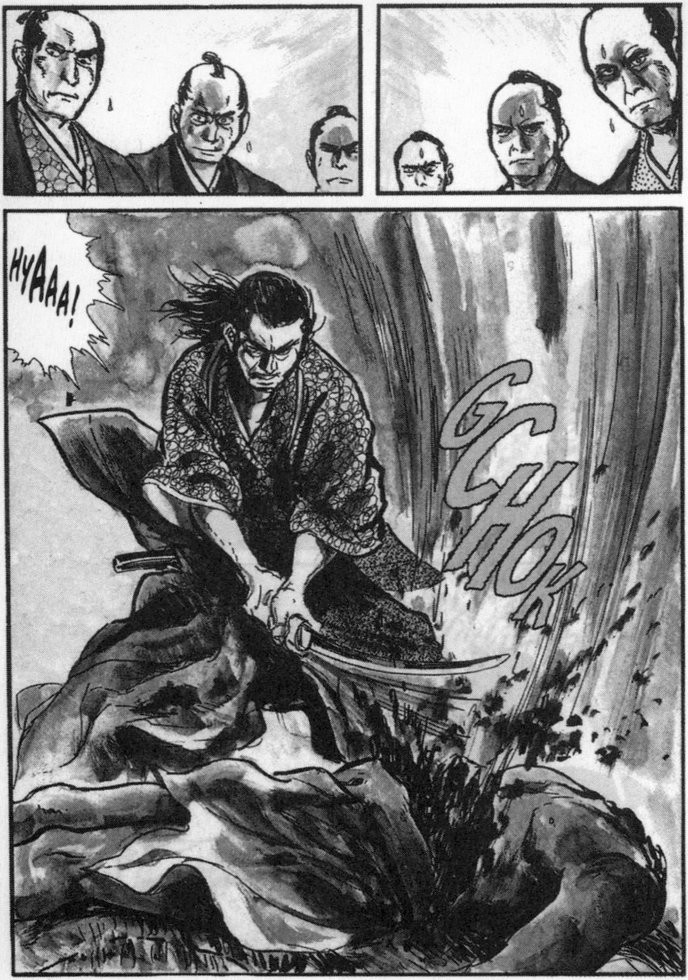
HYAAAA!
GCHOK!

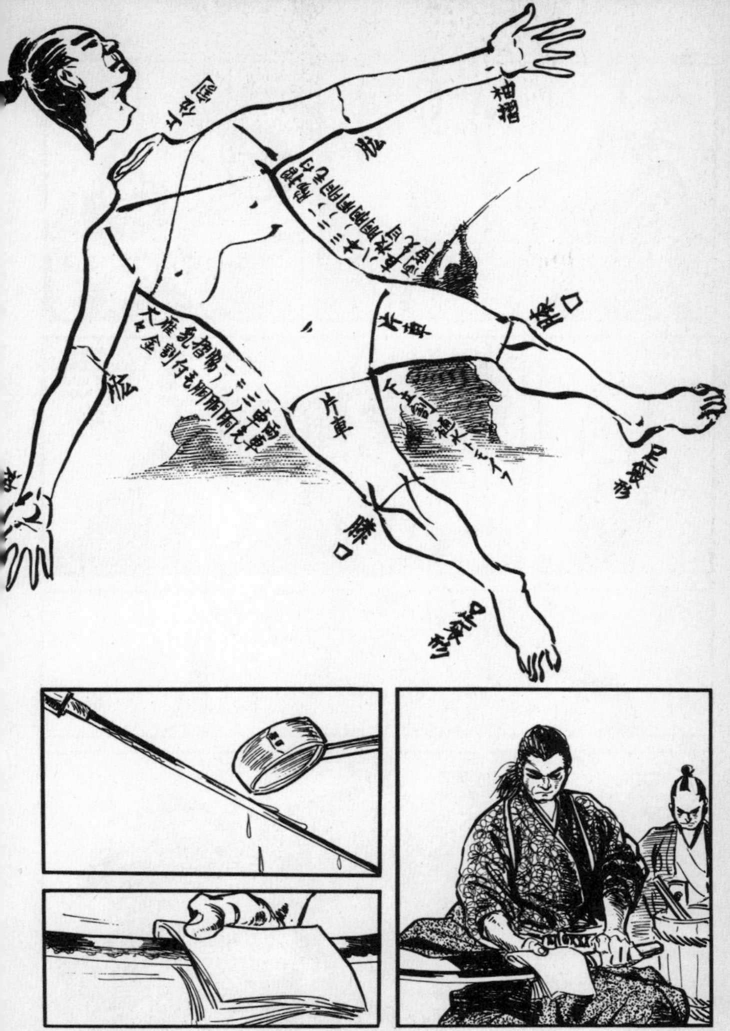
片車
片車
膝口

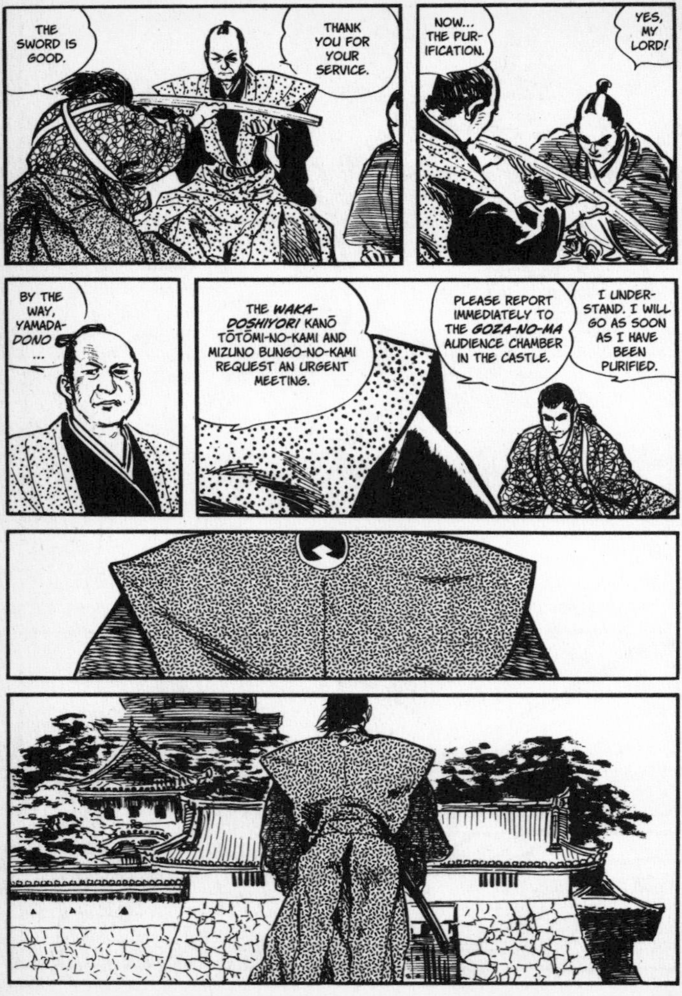
THE SWORD IS GOOD.
THANK YOU FOR YOUR SERVICE.
NOW... THE PURIFICATION.
YES, MY LORD!
BY THE WAY, YAMADA-DONO ...
THE *WAKA-DOSHIYORI* KANŌ TŌTŌMI-NO-KAMI AND MIZUNO BUNGO-NO-KAMI REQUEST AN URGENT MEETING.
PLEASE REPORT IMMEDIATELY TO THE *GOZA-NO-MA* AUDIENCE CHAMBER IN THE CASTLE.
I UNDERSTAND. I WILL GO AS SOON AS I HAVE BEEN PURIFIED.

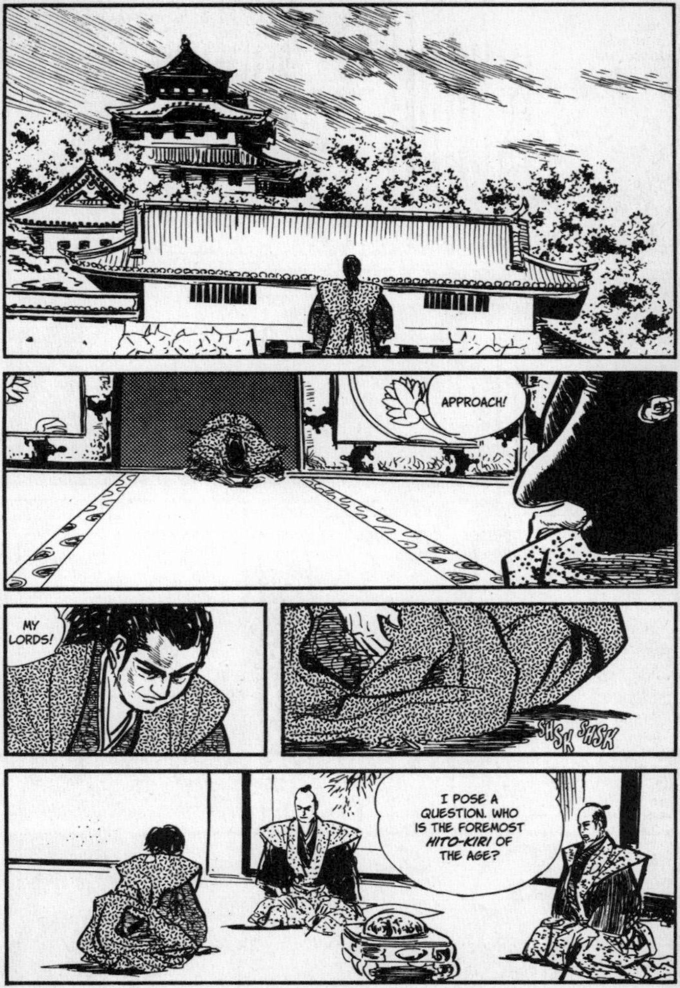
APPROACH!
MY LORDS!
SHSK SHSK
I POSE A QUESTION. WHO IS THE FOREMOST *HITO-KIRI* OF THE AGE?

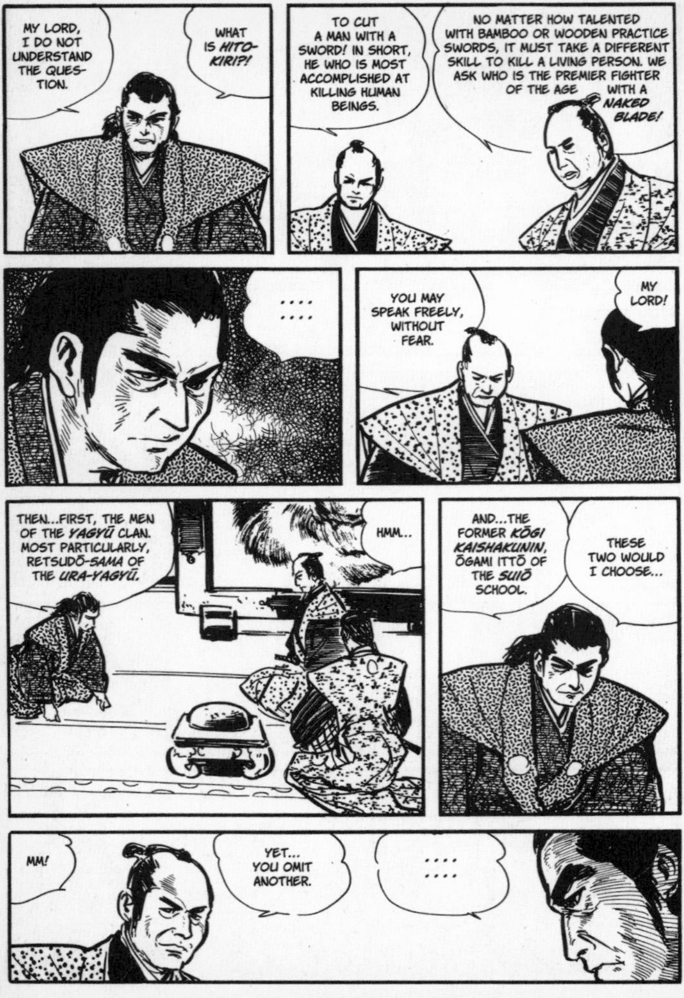
MY LORD, I DO NOT UNDERSTAND THE QUES- TION.
WHAT IS HITO- KIRI?!
TO CUT A MAN WITH A SWORD! IN SHORT, HE WHO IS MOST ACCOMPLISHED AT KILLING HUMAN BEINGS.
NO MATTER HOW TALENTED WITH BAMBOO OR WOODEN PRACTICE SWORDS, IT MUST TAKE A DIFFERENT SKILL TO KILL A LIVING PERSON. WE ASK WHO IS THE PREMIER FIGHTER OF THE AGE WITH A NAKED BLADE!
....
....
MY LORD!
YOU MAY SPEAK FREELY, WITHOUT FEAR.
THEN...FIRST, THE MEN OF THE YAGYŪ CLAN. MOST PARTICULARLY, RETSUDŌ-SAMA OF THE URA-YAGYŪ.
HMM...
THESE TWO WOULD I CHOOSE...
AND...THE FORMER KŌGI KAISHAKUNIN, ŌGAMI ITTŌ OF THE SUIŌ SCHOOL.
....
....
YET... YOU OMIT ANOTHER.
MM!

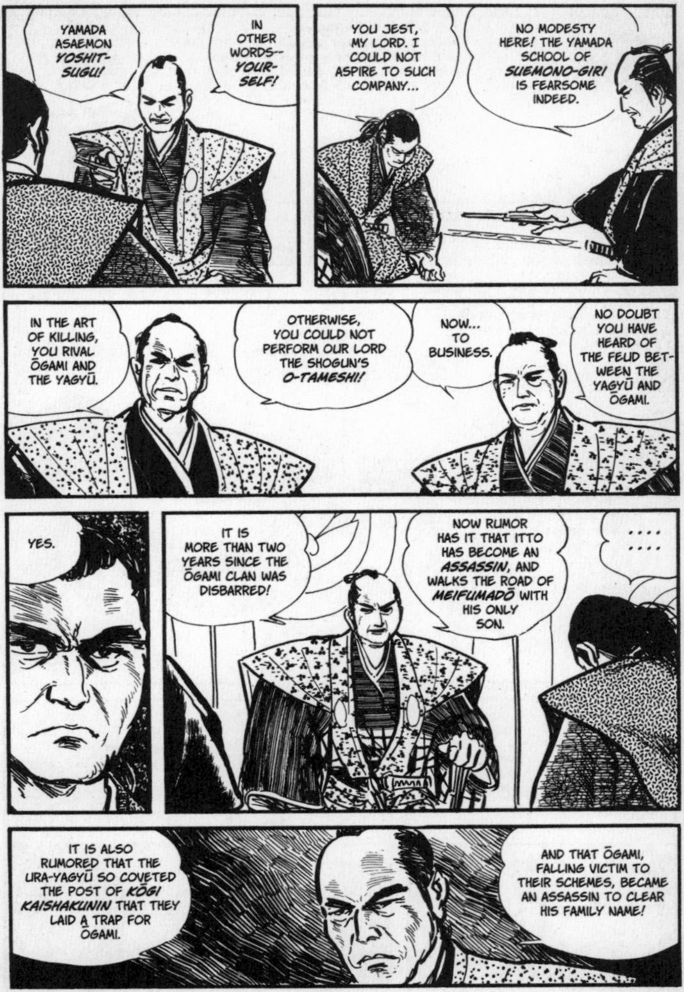
YAMADA ASAEMON YOSHIT-SUGU!
IN OTHER WORDS-- YOUR-SELF!
YOU JEST, MY LORD. I COULD NOT ASPIRE TO SUCH COMPANY...
NO MODESTY HERE! THE YAMADA SCHOOL OF SUEMONO-GIRI IS FEARSOME INDEED.
IN THE ART OF KILLING, YOU RIVAL ŌGAMI AND THE YAGYŪ.
OTHERWISE, YOU COULD NOT PERFORM OUR LORD THE SHOGUN'S O-TAMESHI!
NOW... TO BUSINESS.
NO DOUBT YOU HAVE HEARD OF THE FEUD BETWEEN THE YAGYŪ AND ŌGAMI.
YES.
IT IS MORE THAN TWO YEARS SINCE THE ŌGAMI CLAN WAS DISBARRED!
NOW RUMOR HAS IT THAT ITTO HAS BECOME AN ASSASSIN, AND WALKS THE ROAD OF MEIFUMADŌ WITH HIS ONLY SON.
....
IT IS ALSO RUMORED THAT THE URA-YAGYŪ SO COVETED THE POST OF KŌGI KAISHAKUNIN THAT THEY LAID A TRAP FOR ŌGAMI.
AND THAT ŌGAMI, FALLING VICTIM TO THEIR SCHEMES, BECAME AN ASSASSIN TO CLEAR HIS FAMILY NAME!

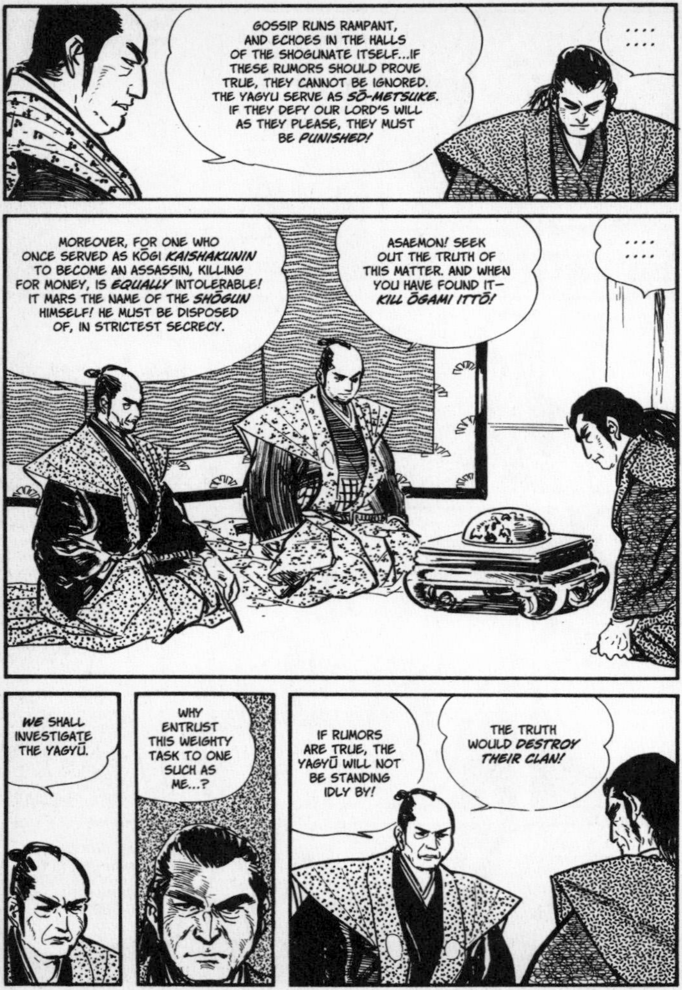
GOSSIP RUNS RAMPANT, AND ECHOES IN THE HALLS OF THE SHOGUNATE ITSELF...IF THESE RUMORS SHOULD PROVE TRUE, THEY CANNOT BE IGNORED. THE YAGYU SERVE AS *SŌ-METSUKE*. IF THEY DEFY OUR LORD'S WILL AS THEY PLEASE, THEY MUST BE *PUNISHED!*
....
MOREOVER, FOR ONE WHO ONCE SERVED AS KŌGI *KAISHAKUNIN* TO BECOME AN ASSASSIN, KILLING FOR MONEY, IS *EQUALLY* INTOLERABLE! IT MARS THE NAME OF THE *SHŌGUN* HIMSELF! HE MUST BE DISPOSED OF, IN STRICTEST SECRECY.
ASAEMON! SEEK OUT THE TRUTH OF THIS MATTER. AND WHEN YOU HAVE FOUND IT— *KILL ŌGAMI ITTŌ!*
....
WE SHALL INVESTIGATE THE YAGYŪ.
WHY ENTRUST THIS WEIGHTY TASK TO ONE SUCH AS ME...?
IF RUMORS ARE TRUE, THE YAGYŪ WILL NOT BE STANDING IDLY BY!
THE TRUTH WOULD *DESTROY THEIR CLAN!*

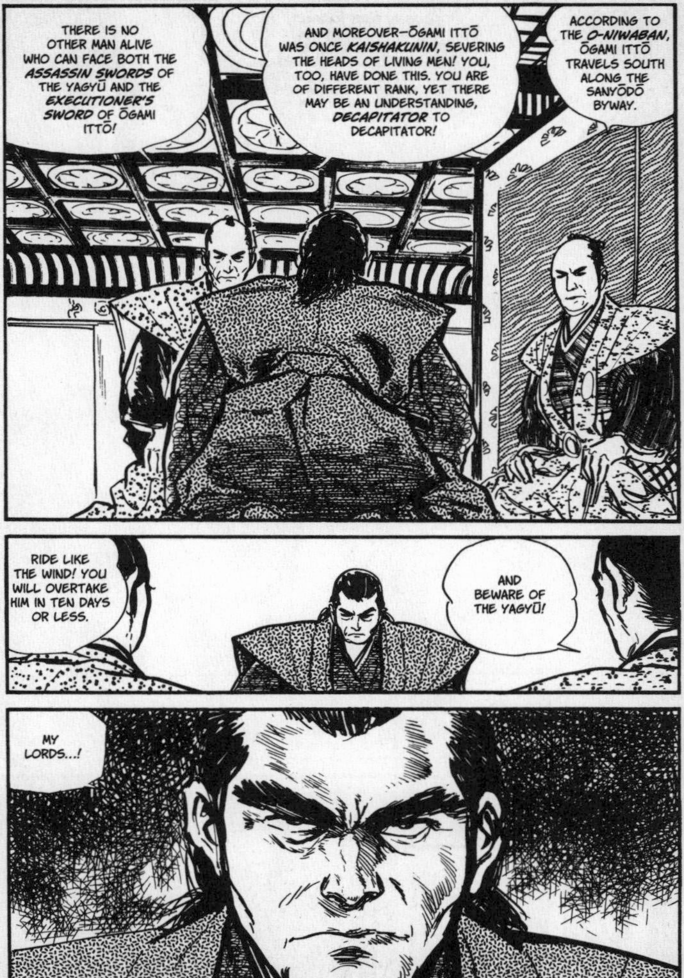
THERE IS NO OTHER MAN ALIVE WHO CAN FACE BOTH THE ASSASSIN SWORDS OF THE YAGYŪ AND THE EXECUTIONER'S SWORD OF ŌGAMI ITTŌ!
AND MOREOVER—ŌGAMI ITTŌ WAS ONCE KAISHAKUNIN, SEVERING THE HEADS OF LIVING MEN! YOU, TOO, HAVE DONE THIS. YOU ARE OF DIFFERENT RANK, YET THERE MAY BE AN UNDERSTANDING, DECAPITATOR TO DECAPITATOR!
ACCORDING TO THE O-NIWABAN, ŌGAMI ITTŌ TRAVELS SOUTH ALONG THE SANYŌDŌ BYWAY.
RIDE LIKE THE WIND! YOU WILL OVERTAKE HIM IN TEN DAYS OR LESS.
AND BEWARE OF THE YAGYŪ!
MY LORDS...!

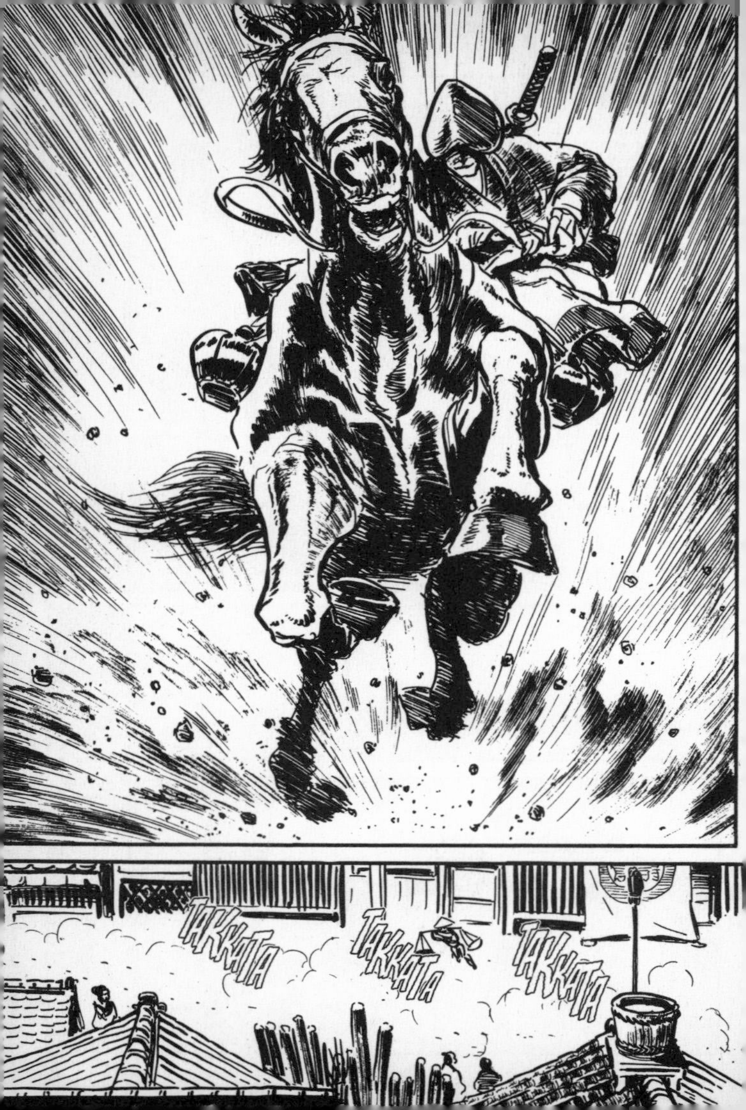
TAKKATA
TAKKATA
TAKKATA

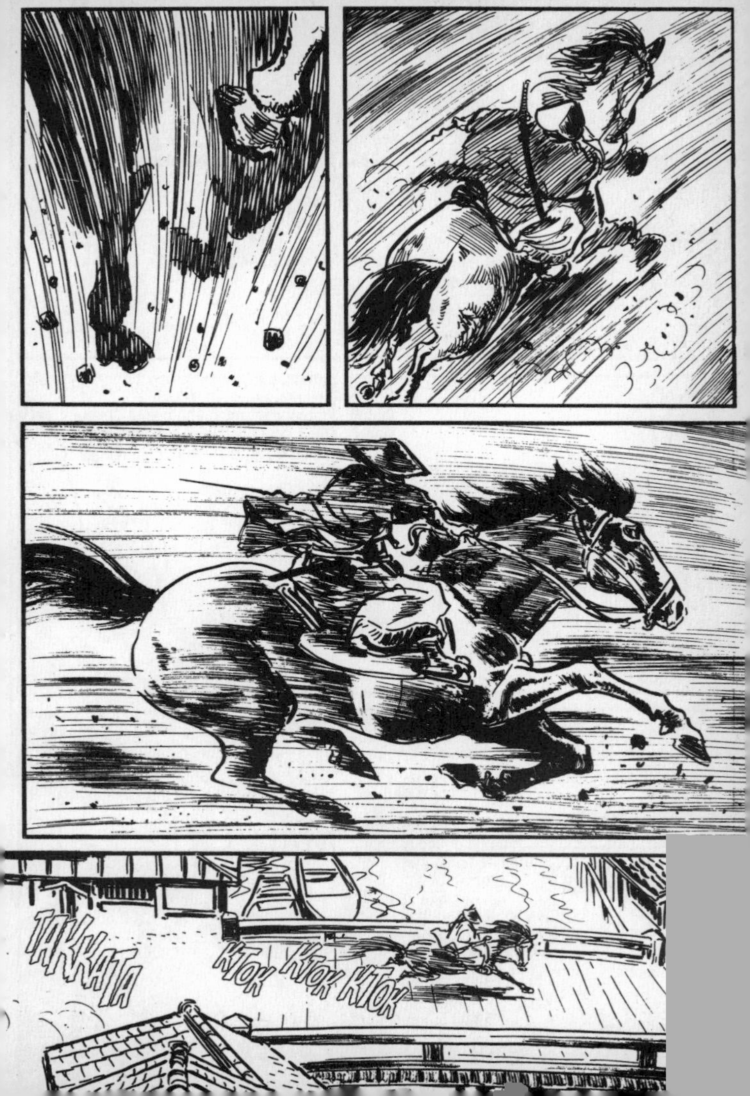
TAKKATA
KTOK KTOK KTOK

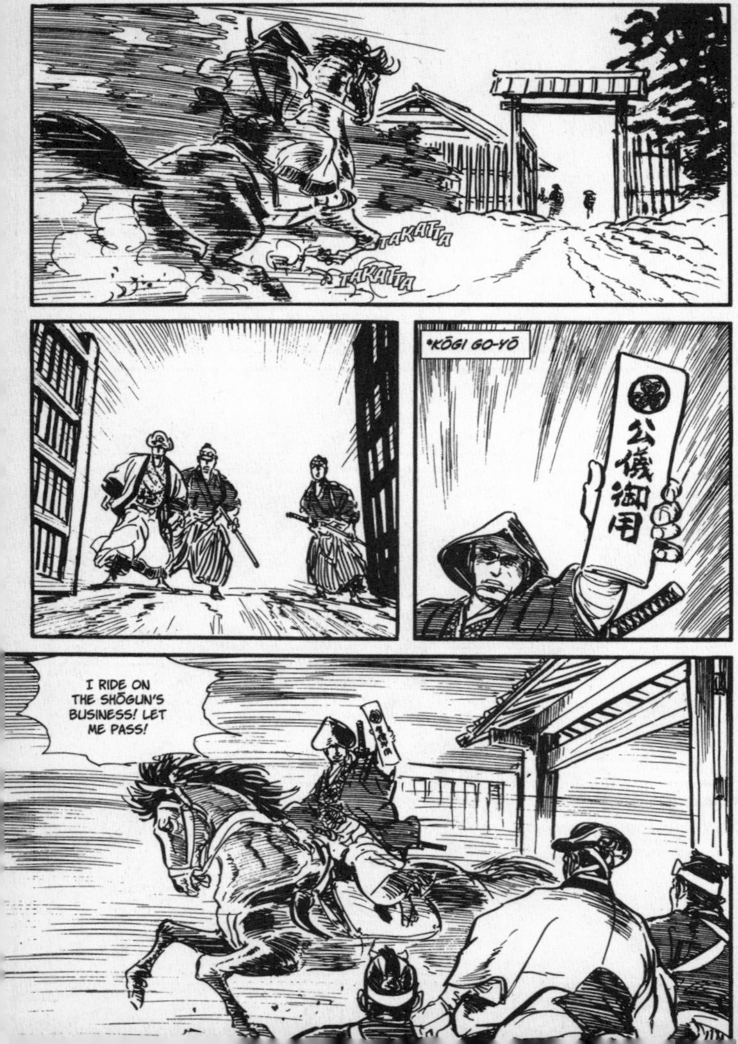
TAKATTA
TAKATTA
*KŌGI GO-YŌ
公儀御用
I RIDE ON THE SHŌGUN'S BUSINESS! LET ME PASS!

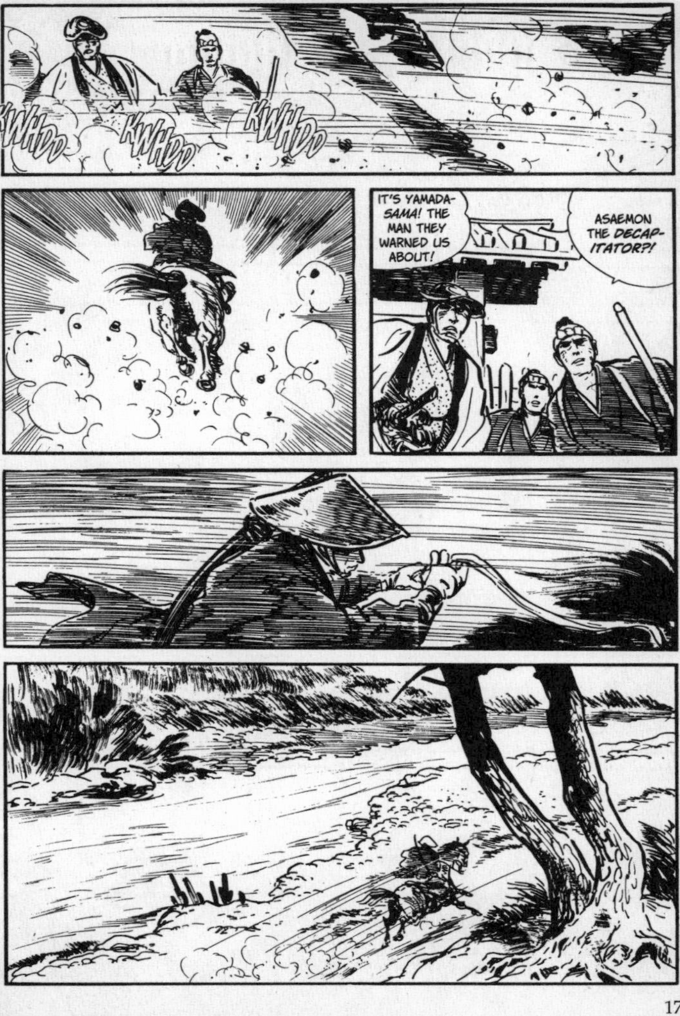
KWHDD
KWHDD
KWHDD
IT'S YAMADA-SAMA! THE MAN THEY WARNED US ABOUT!
ASAEMON THE *DECAPITATOR?!*

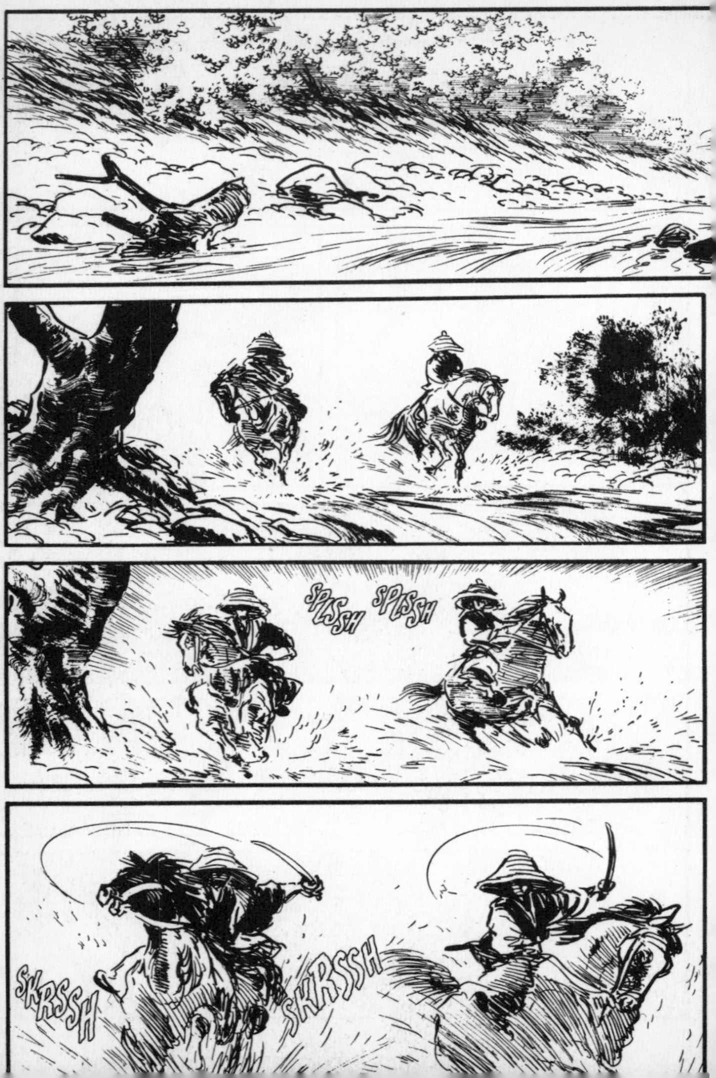
SPLSSH
SPLSSH
SKRSSH
SKRSSH

SPLSSSH

URA-
YAGYU
...?!

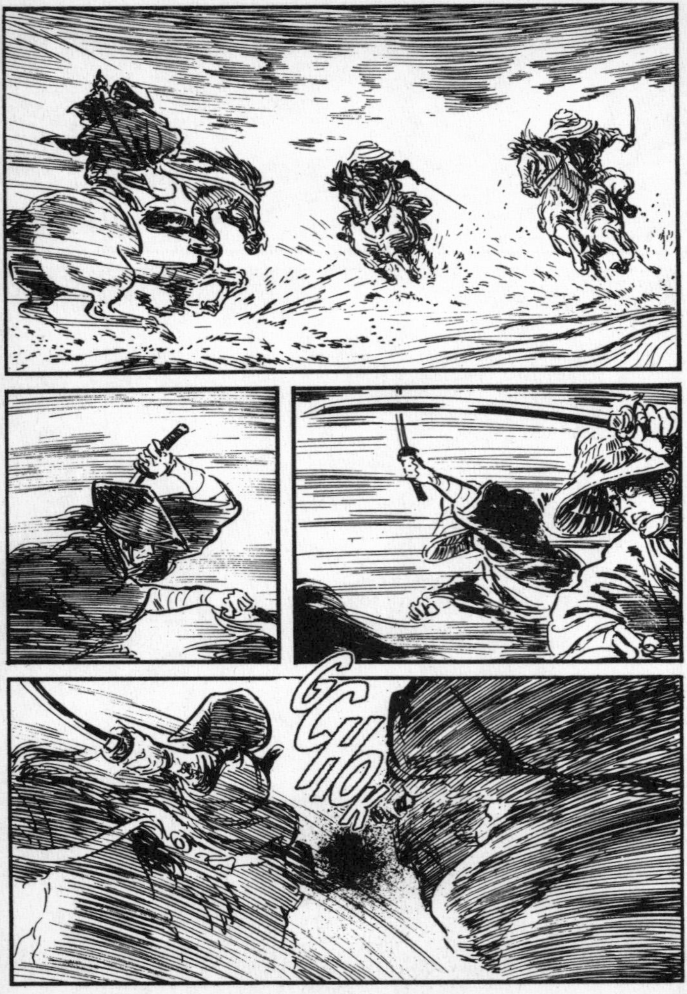
GCHOK

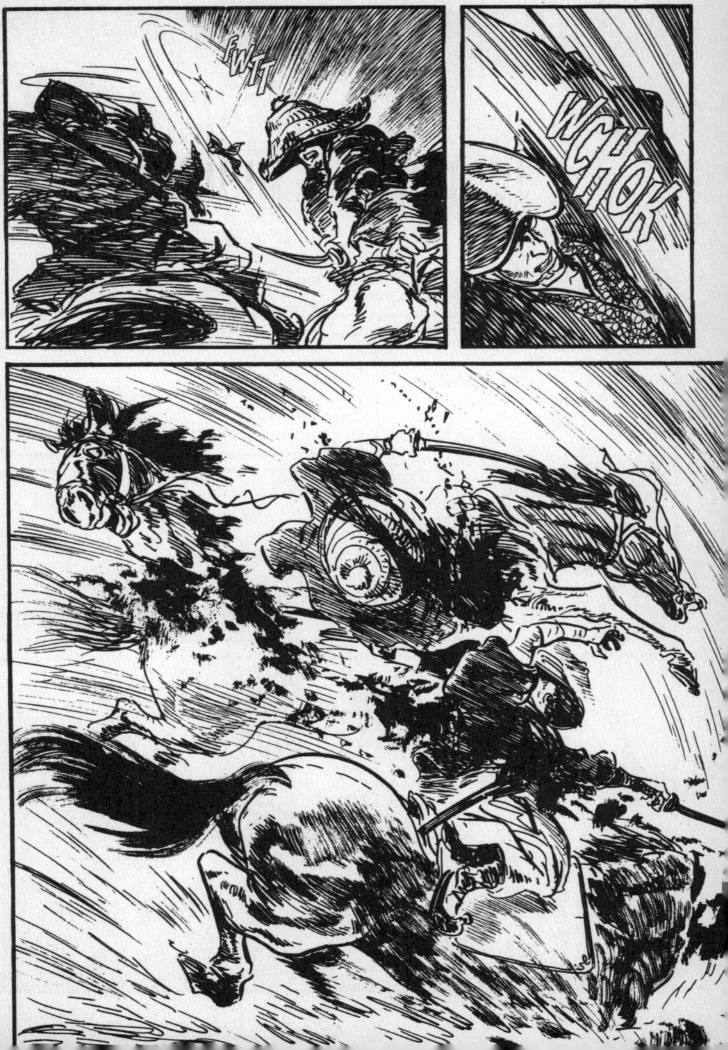
FWTT
WCHOK

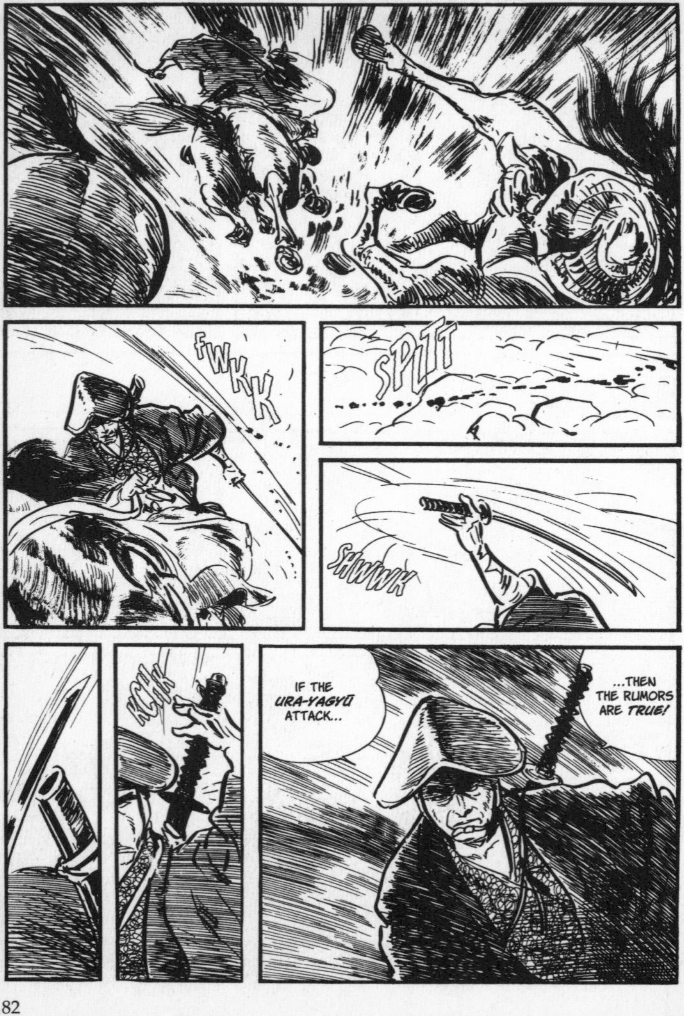
FWKKK
SPLTT
SHWWK
KCHK
IF THE URA-YAGYŪ ATTACK...
...THEN THE RUMORS ARE TRUE!

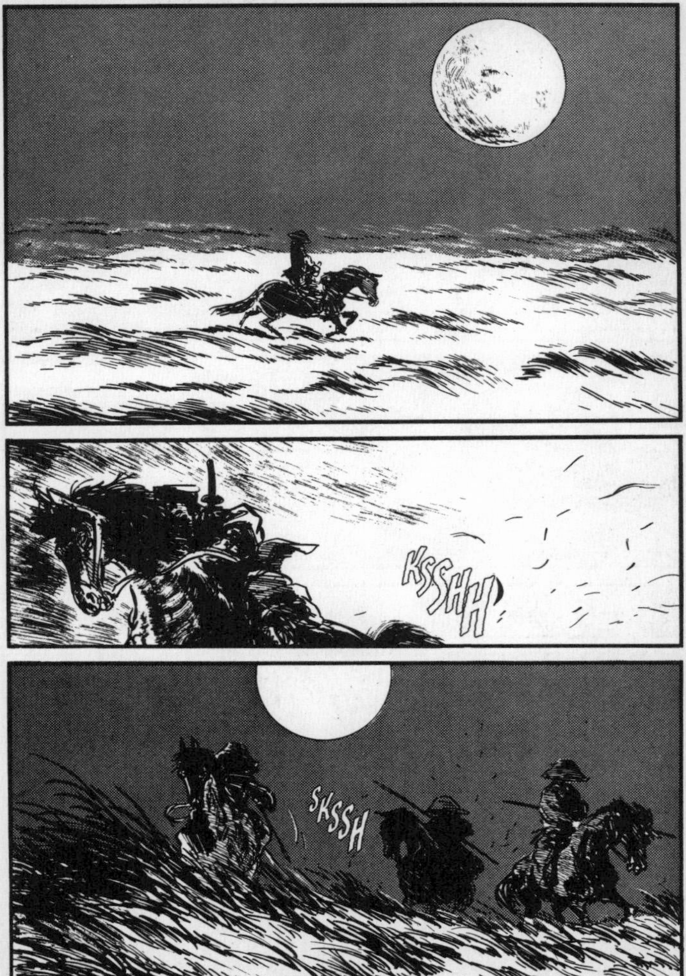
KSSHH
SKSSH

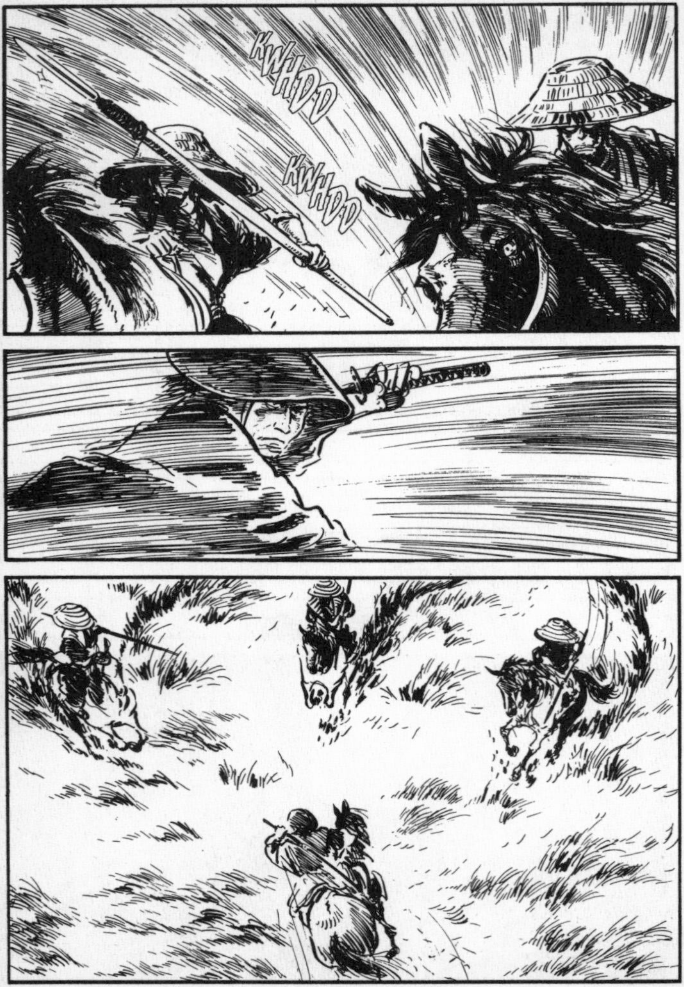
KWHOO
KWHOO

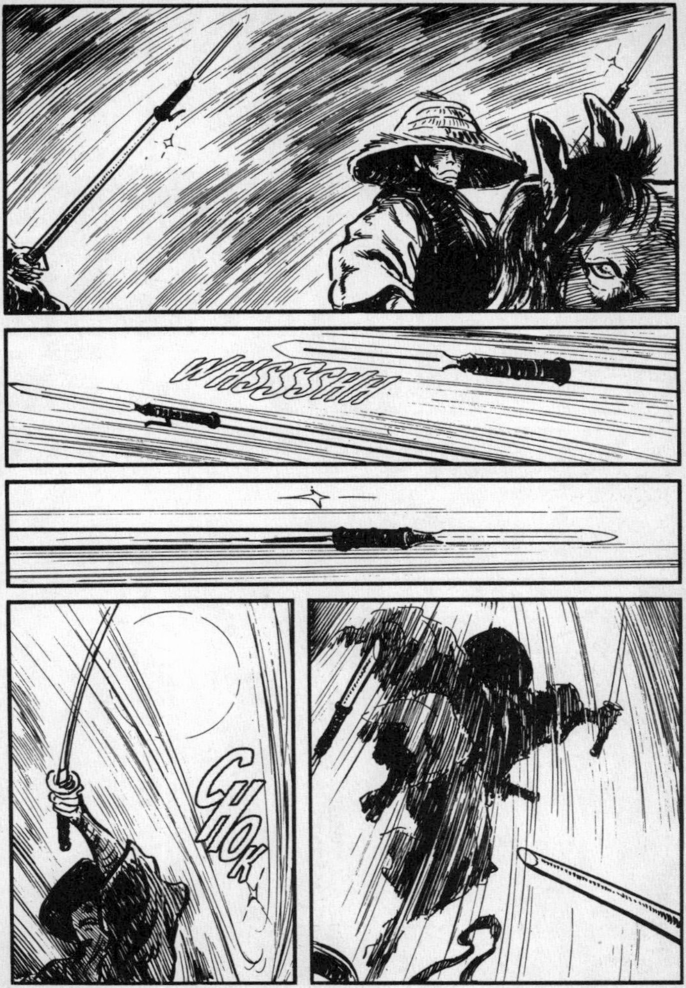
WHSSSHH
CHOK

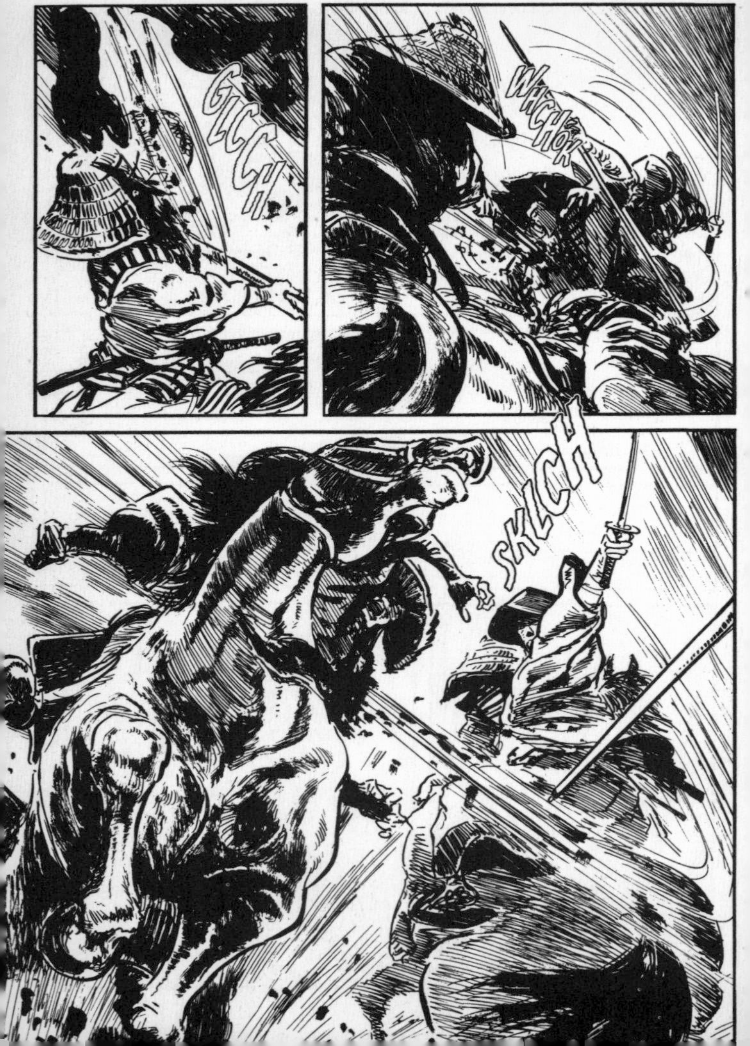
GICCH
WHCHOK
SKLCH

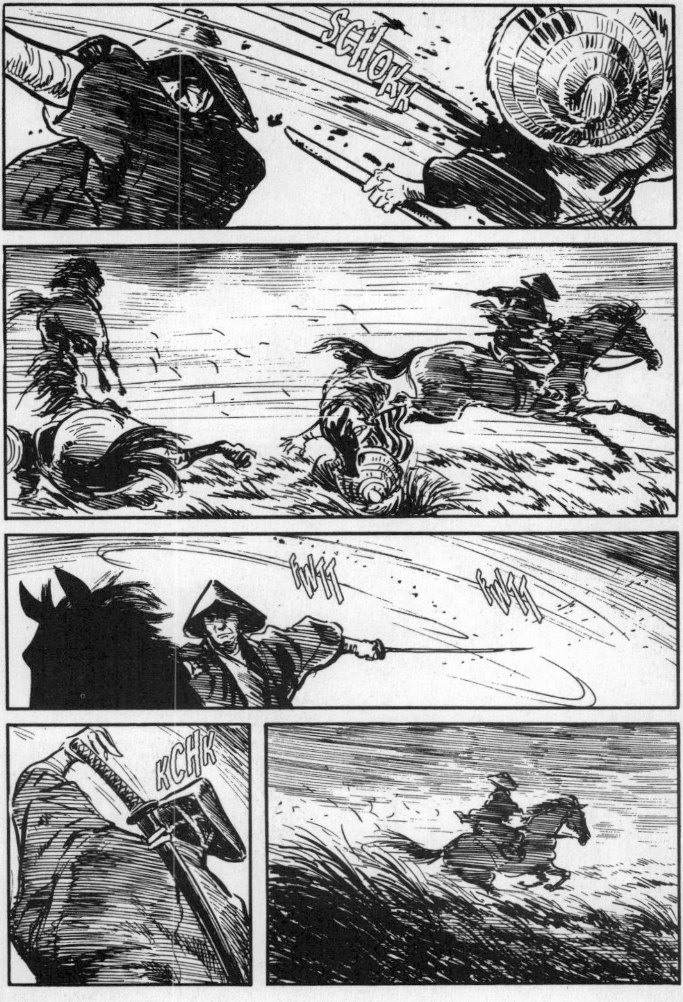
SCHOKK
FWTT
FWTT
KCHK

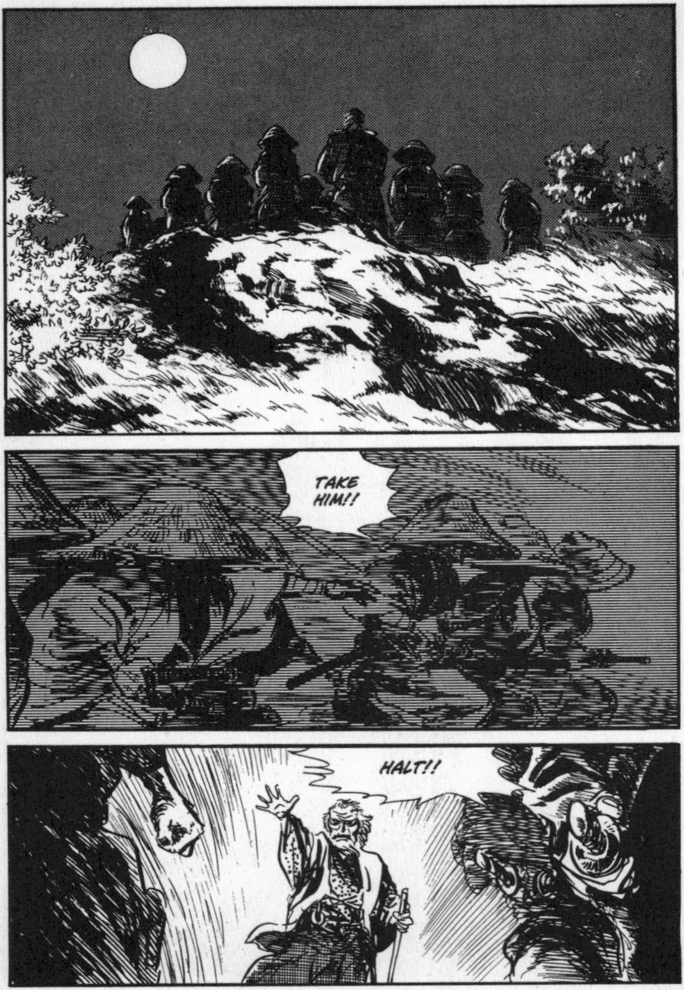
TAKE HIM!!
HALT!!

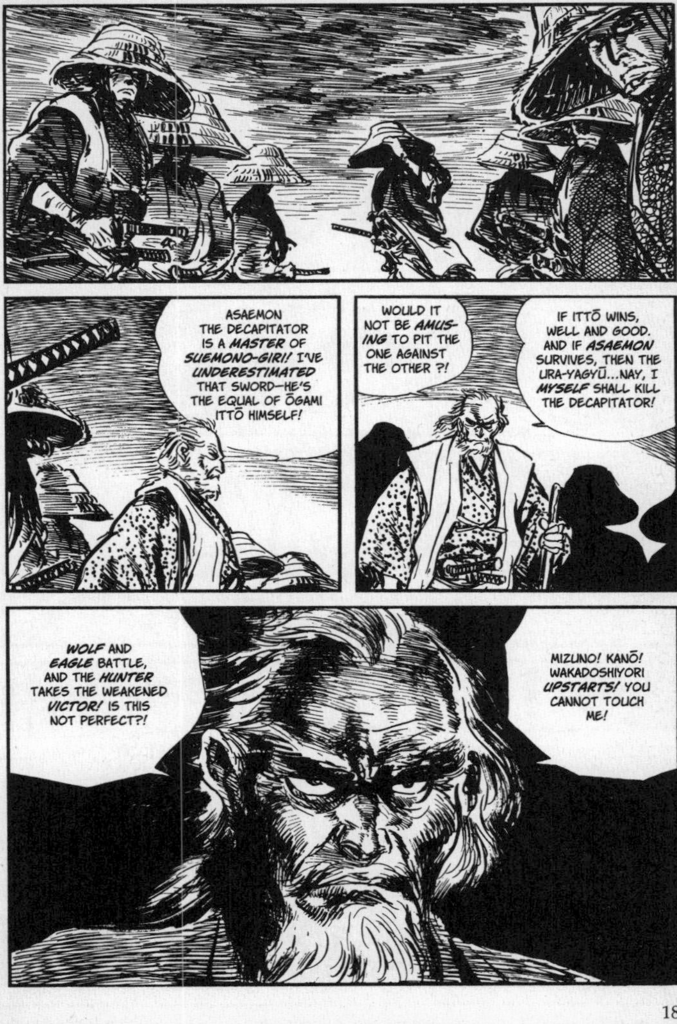
ASAEMON THE DECAPITATOR IS A MASTER OF SUEMONO-GIRI! I'VE UNDERESTIMATED THAT SWORD—HE'S THE EQUAL OF ŌGAMI ITTŌ HIMSELF!
WOULD IT NOT BE AMUSING TO PIT THE ONE AGAINST THE OTHER ?!
IF ITTŌ WINS, WELL AND GOOD. AND IF ASAEMON SURVIVES, THEN THE URA-YAGYŪ...NAY, I MYSELF SHALL KILL THE DECAPITATOR!
WOLF AND EAGLE BATTLE, AND THE HUNTER TAKES THE WEAKENED VICTOR! IS THIS NOT PERFECT?!
MIZUNO! KANŌ! WAKADOSHIYORI UPSTARTS! YOU CANNOT TOUCH ME!

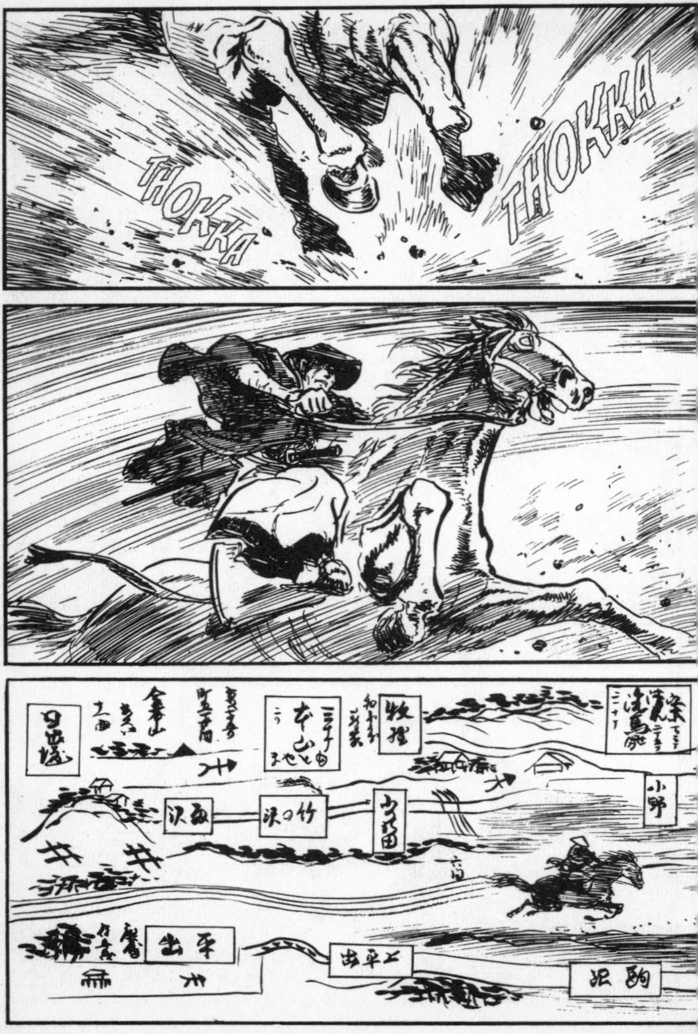
THOKKA
THOKKA
小野

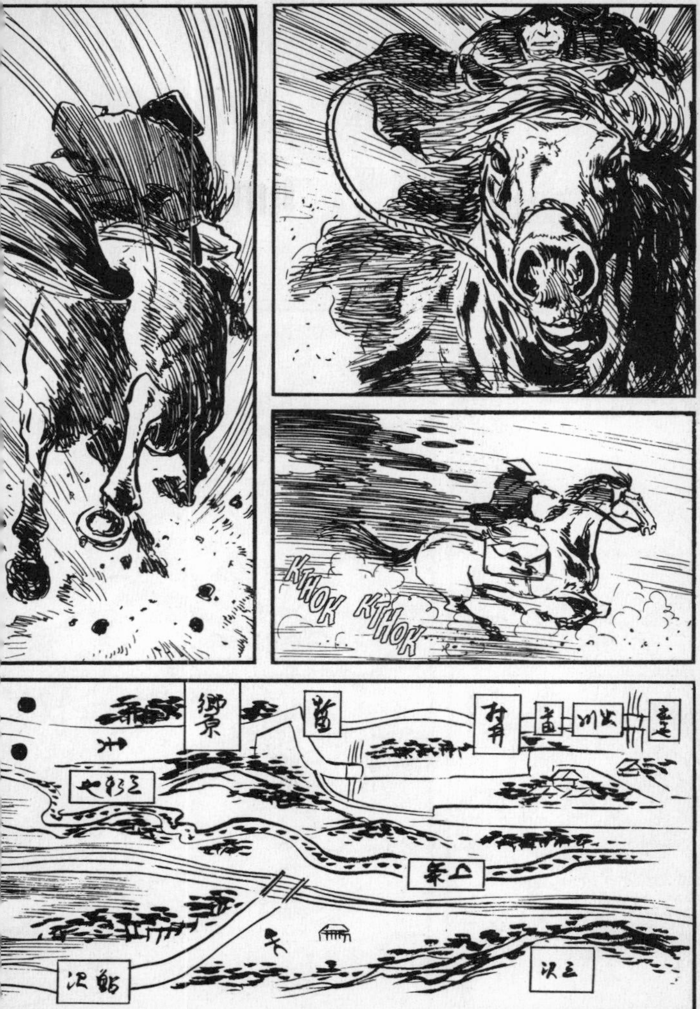
KTHOK KTHOK

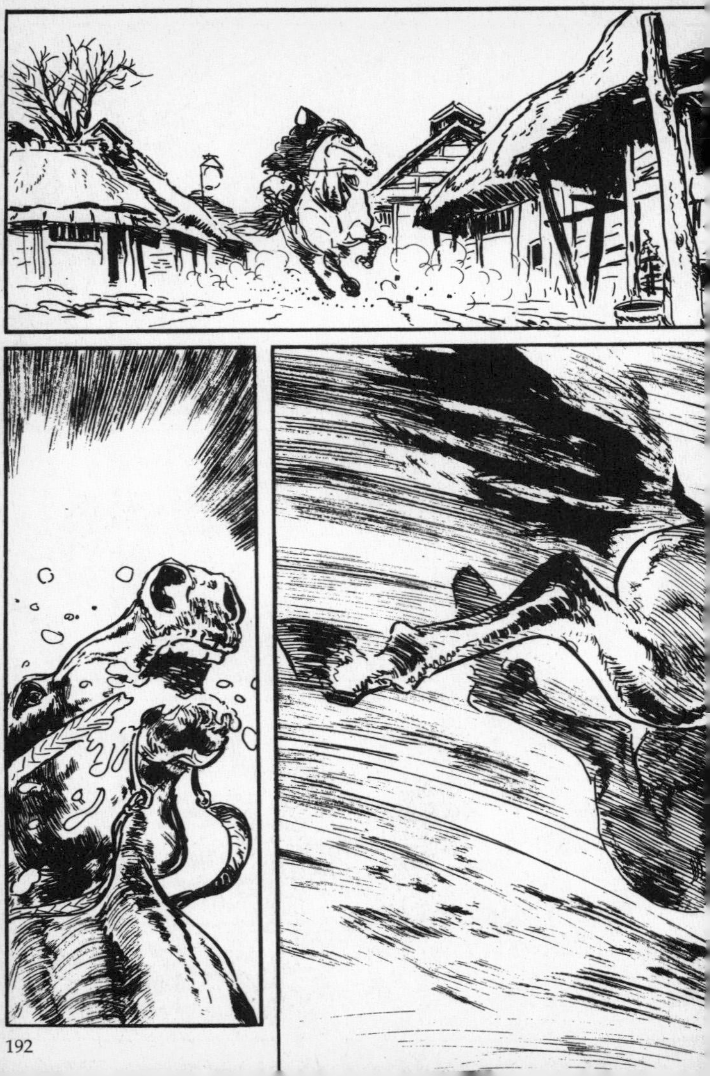

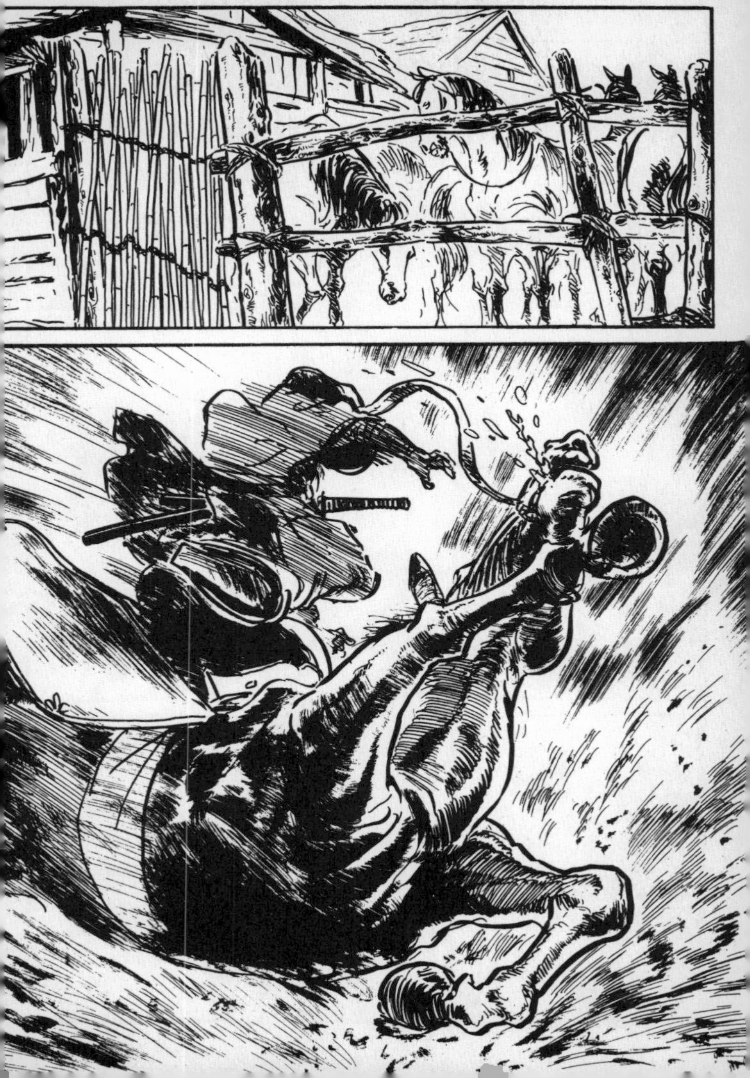

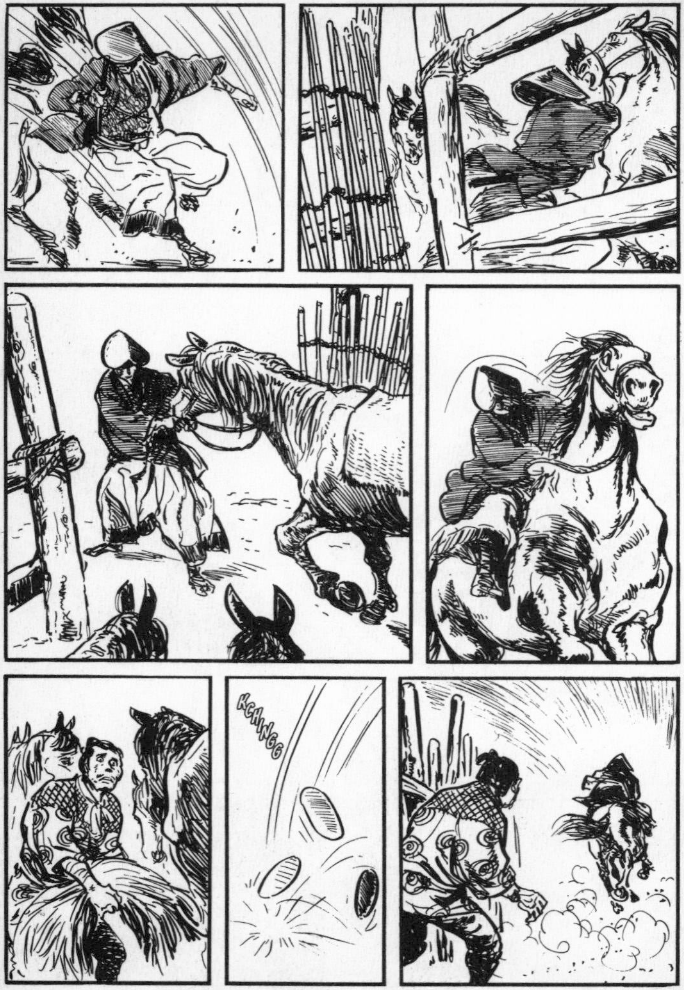
KCHINGG

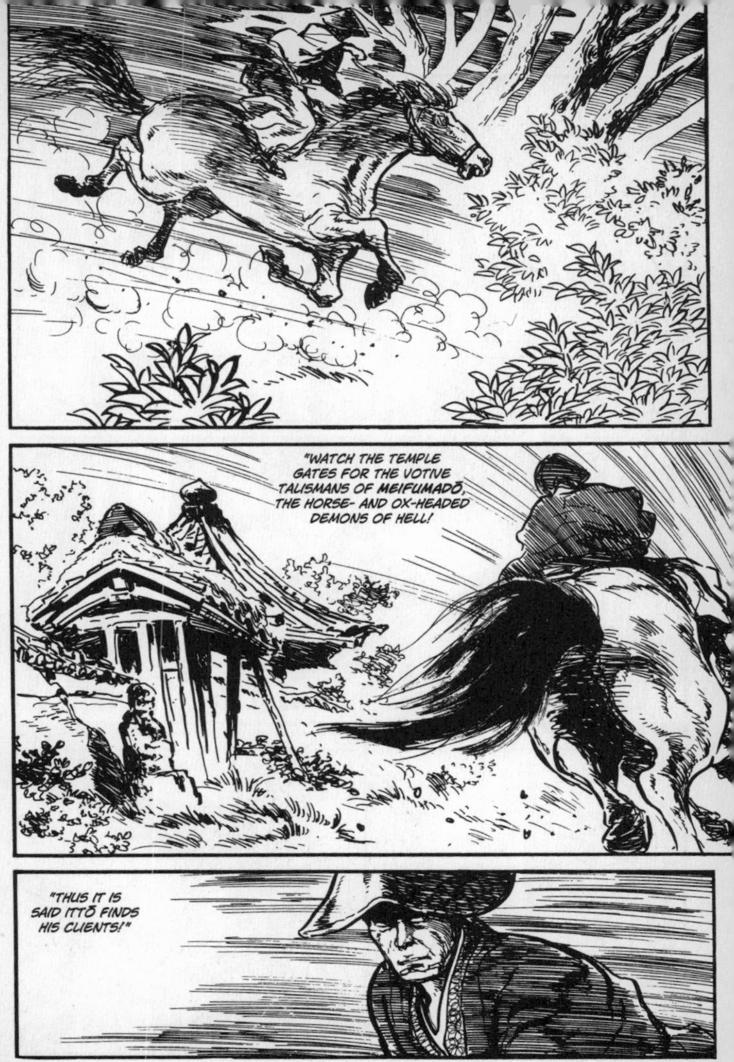
"WATCH THE TEMPLE GATES FOR THE VOTIVE TALISMANS OF MEIFUMADŌ, THE HORSE- AND OX-HEADED DEMONS OF HELL!
"THUS IT IS SAID ITTŌ FINDS HIS CLIENTS!"

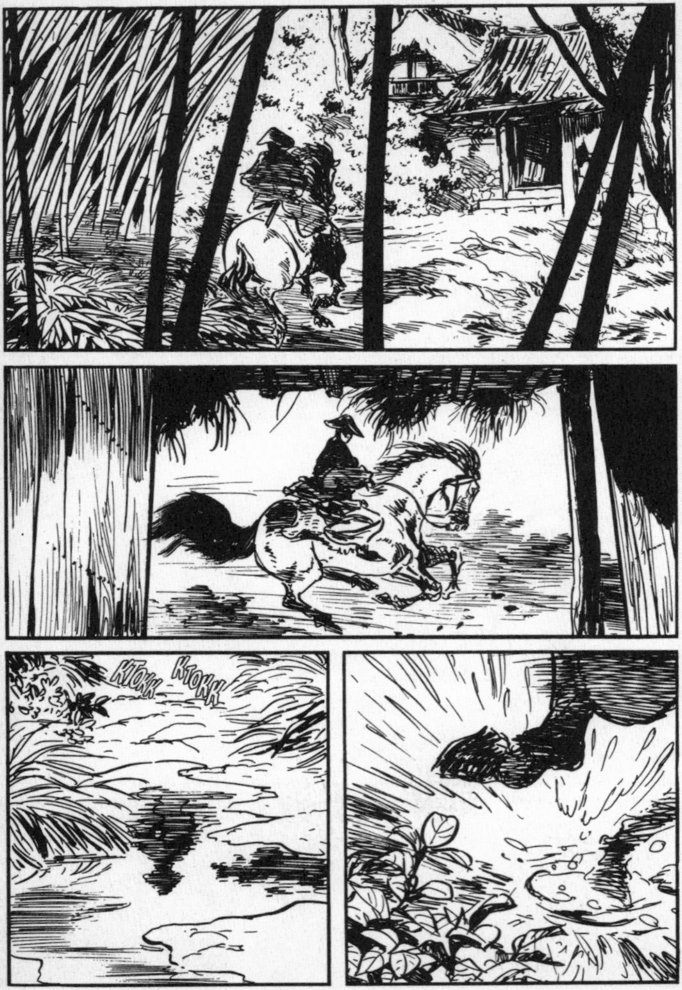
KTOKK
KTOKK

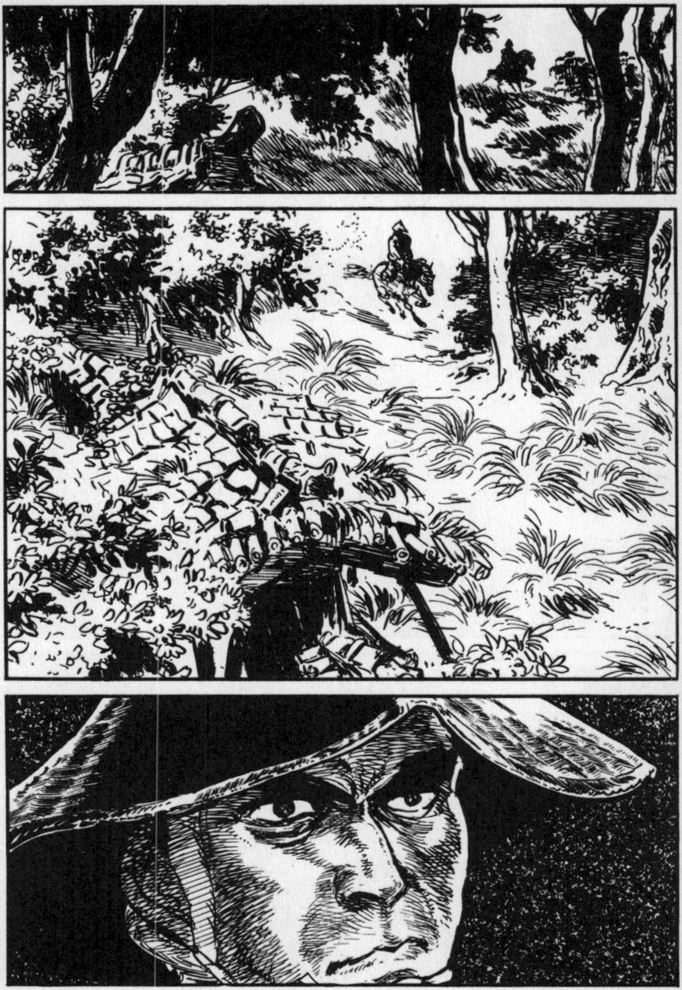

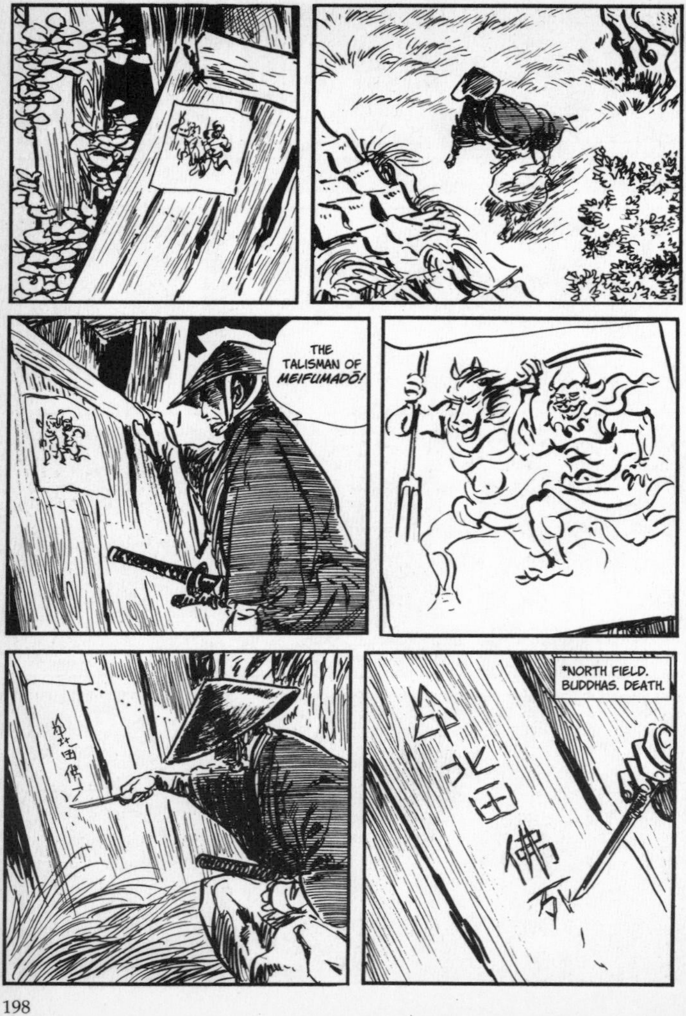
THE TALISMAN OF MEIFUMADŌ!
北田佛死
*NORTH FIELD. BUDDHAS. DEATH.

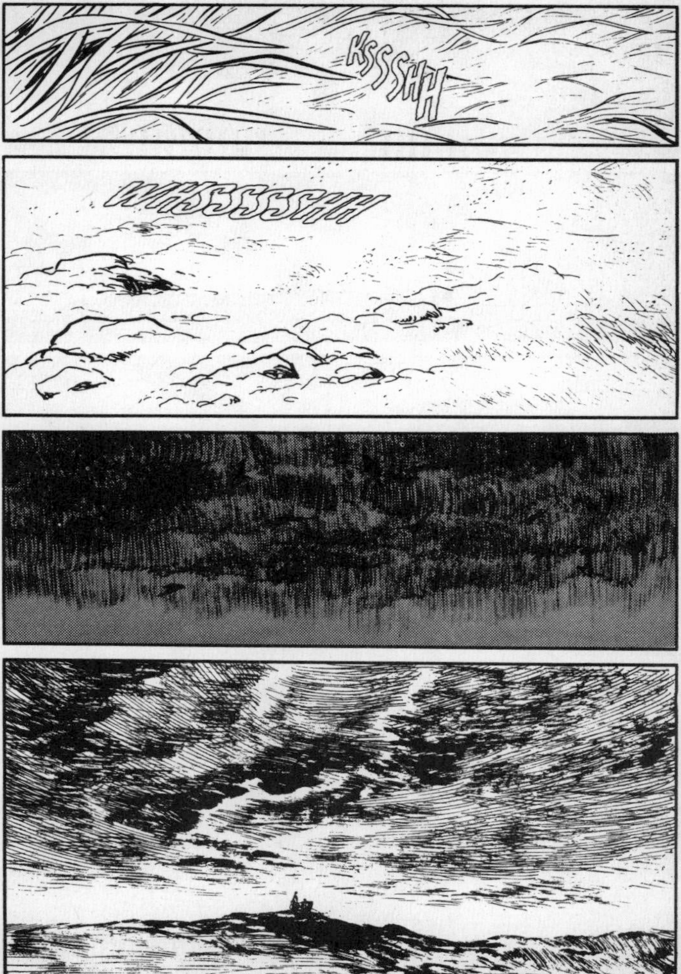
KSSSHH
WHSSSSSHH

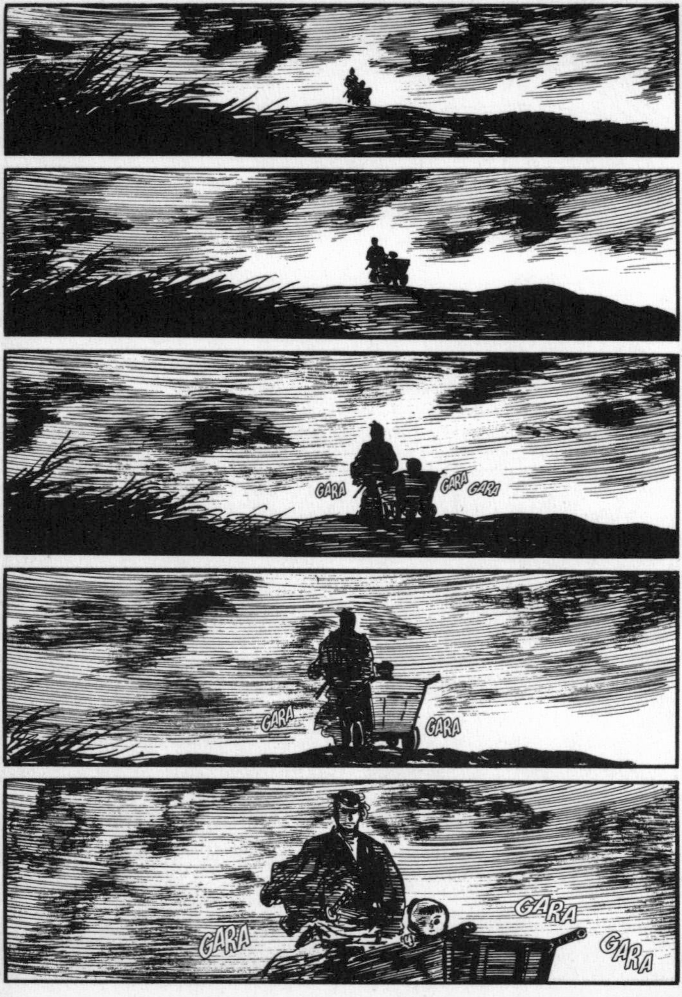
GARA
GARA
GARA
GARA
GARA
GARA
GARA
GARA

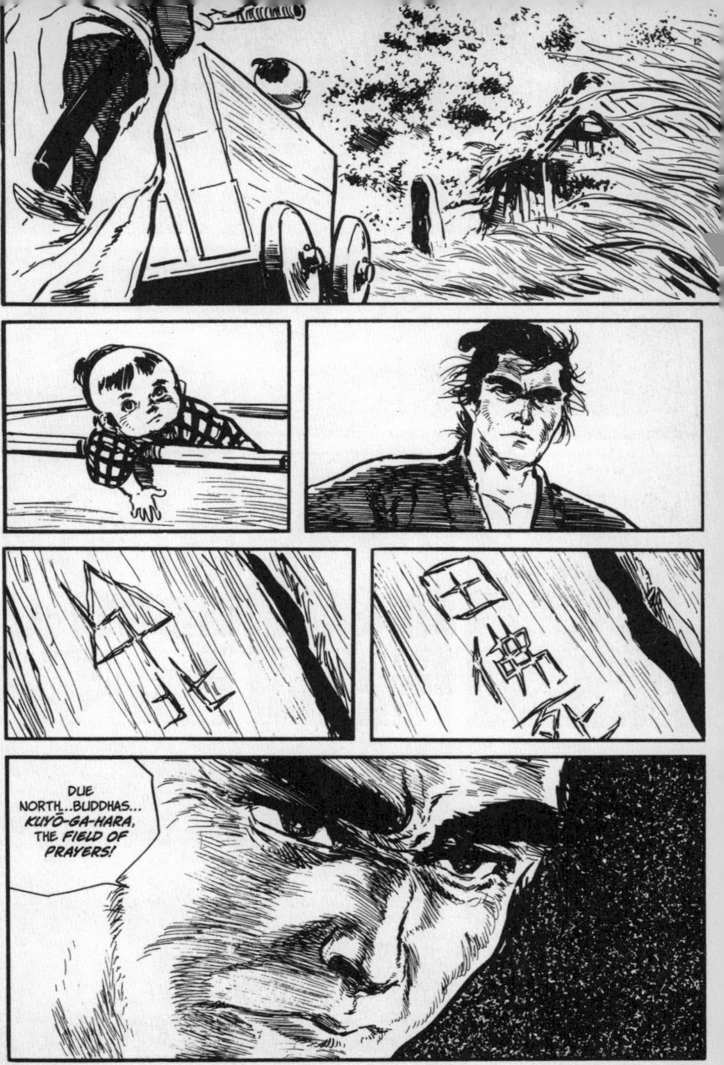
DUE NORTH...BUDDHAS... KUYŌ-GA-HARA, THE FIELD OF PRAYERS!

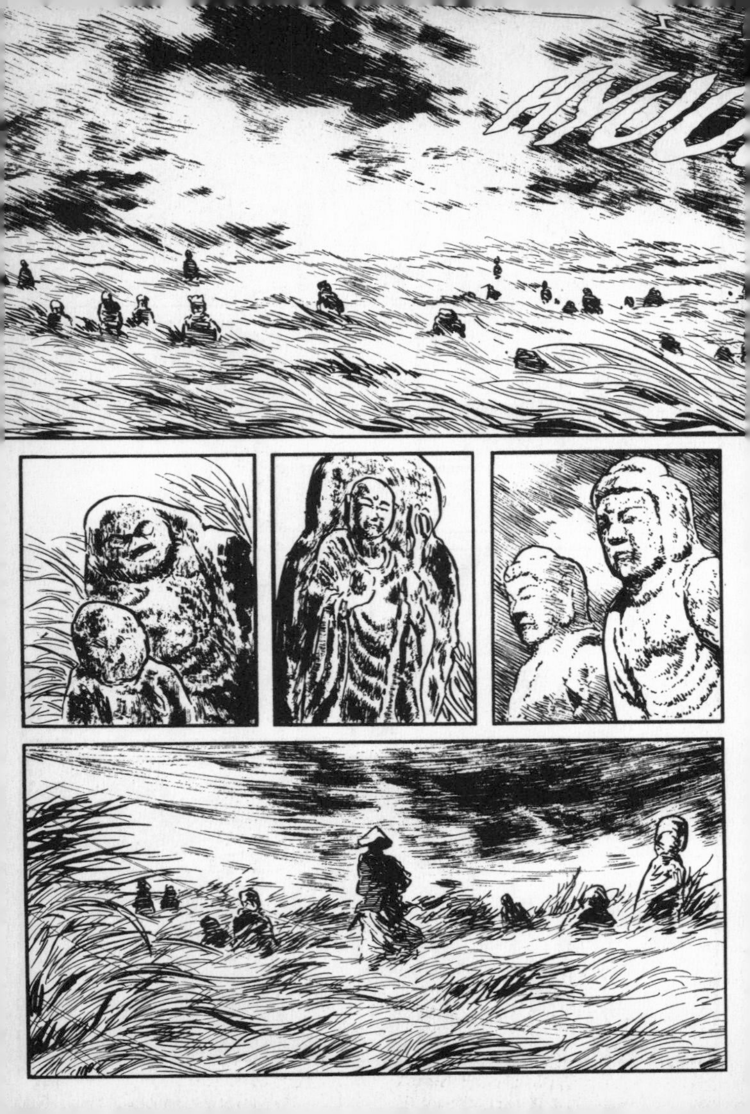
HYUU

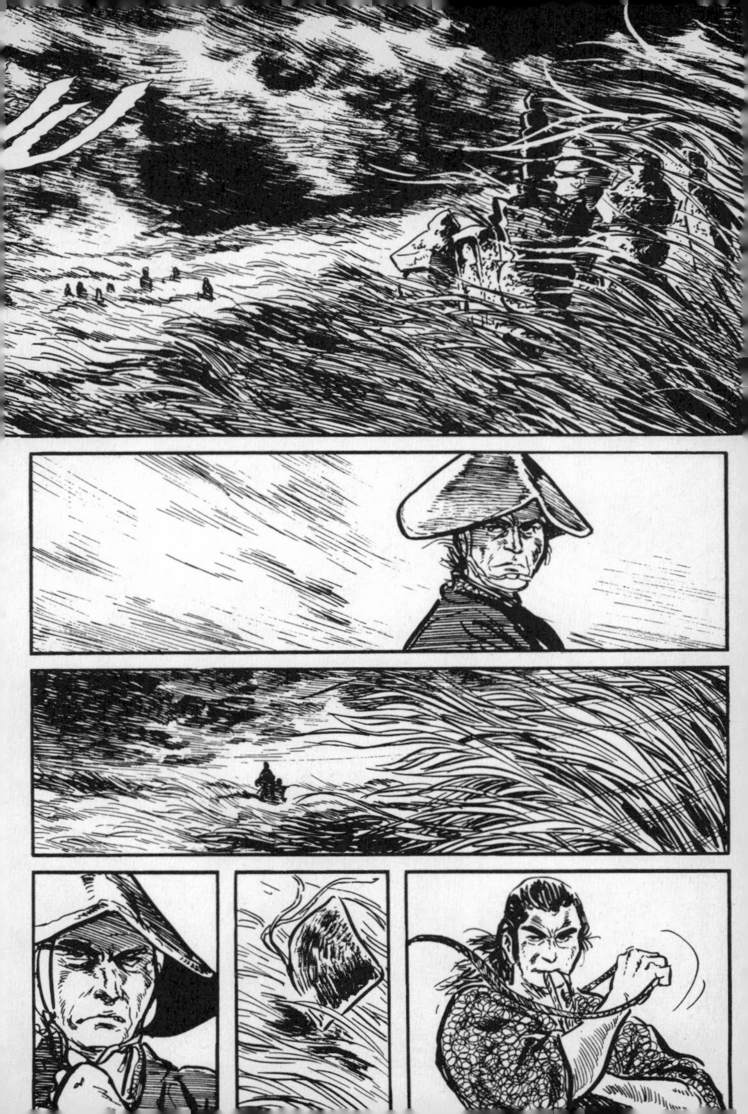

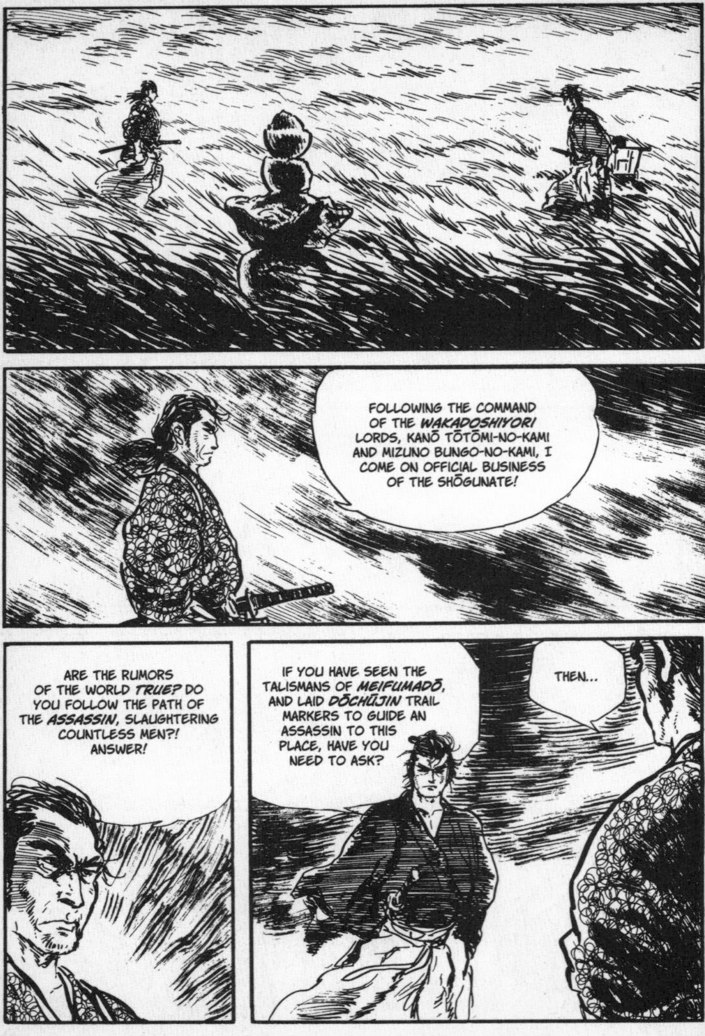

FOLLOWING THE COMMAND OF THE WAKADOSHIYORI LORDS, KANŌ TŌTŌMI-NO-KAMI AND MIZUNO BUNGO-NO-KAMI, I COME ON OFFICIAL BUSINESS OF THE SHŌGUNATE!
ARE THE RUMORS OF THE WORLD TRUE? DO YOU FOLLOW THE PATH OF THE ASSASSIN, SLAUGHTERING COUNTLESS MEN?! ANSWER!
IF YOU HAVE SEEN THE TALISMANS OF MEIFUMADŌ, AND LAID DŌCHŪJIN TRAIL MARKERS TO GUIDE AN ASSASSIN TO THIS PLACE, HAVE YOU NEED TO ASK?
THEN...

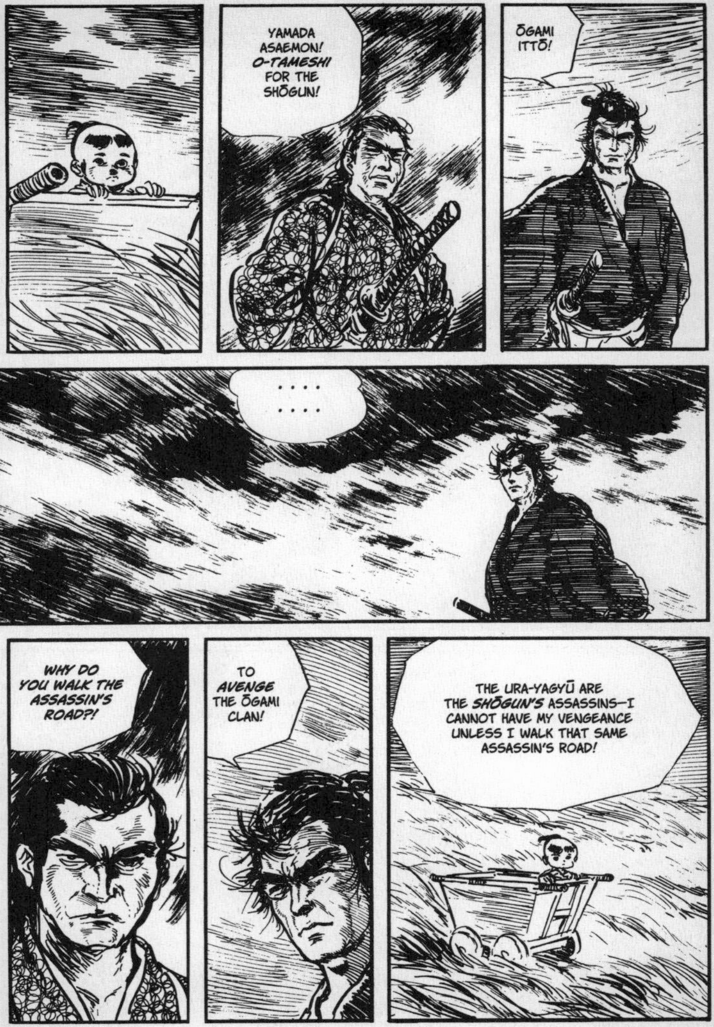
YAMADA ASAEMON! *O-TAMESHI* FOR THE SHŌGUN!
ŌGAMI ITTŌ!
. . . .
. . . .
WHY DO YOU WALK THE ASSASSIN'S ROAD?!
TO *AVENGE* THE ŌGAMI CLAN!
THE URA-YAGYŪ ARE THE *SHŌGUN'S* ASSASSINS—I CANNOT HAVE MY VENGEANCE UNLESS I WALK THAT SAME ASSASSIN'S ROAD!

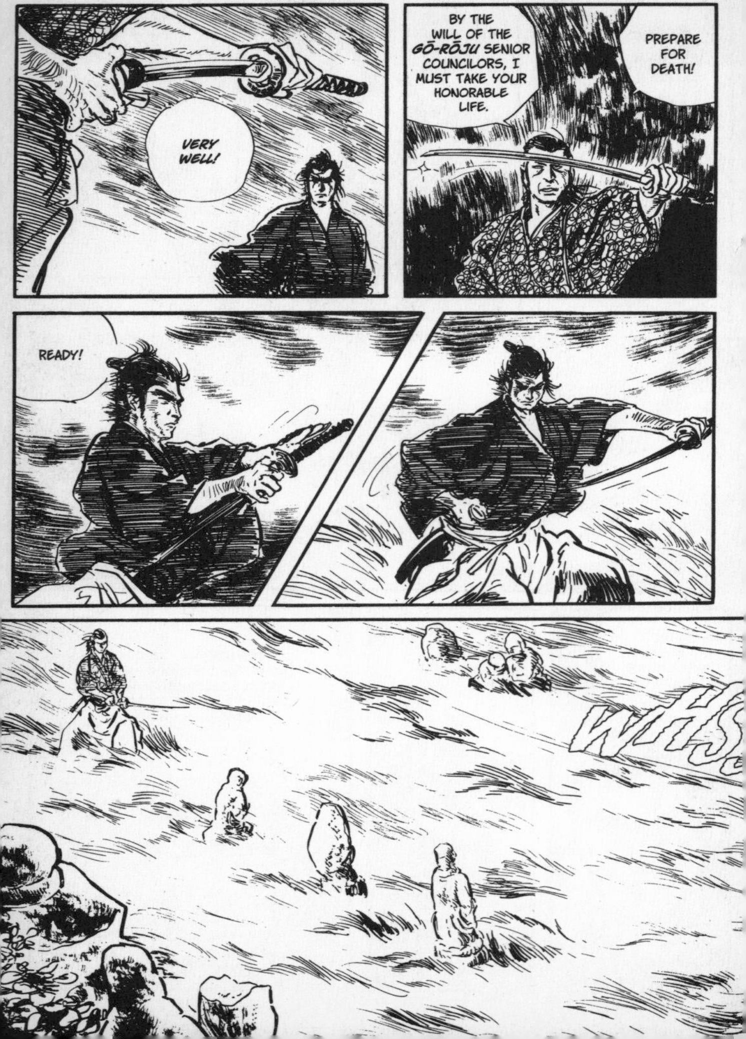
VERY WELL!
BY THE WILL OF THE GŌ-RŌJU SENIOR COUNCILORS, I MUST TAKE YOUR HONORABLE LIFE.
PREPARE FOR DEATH!
READY!
WHS

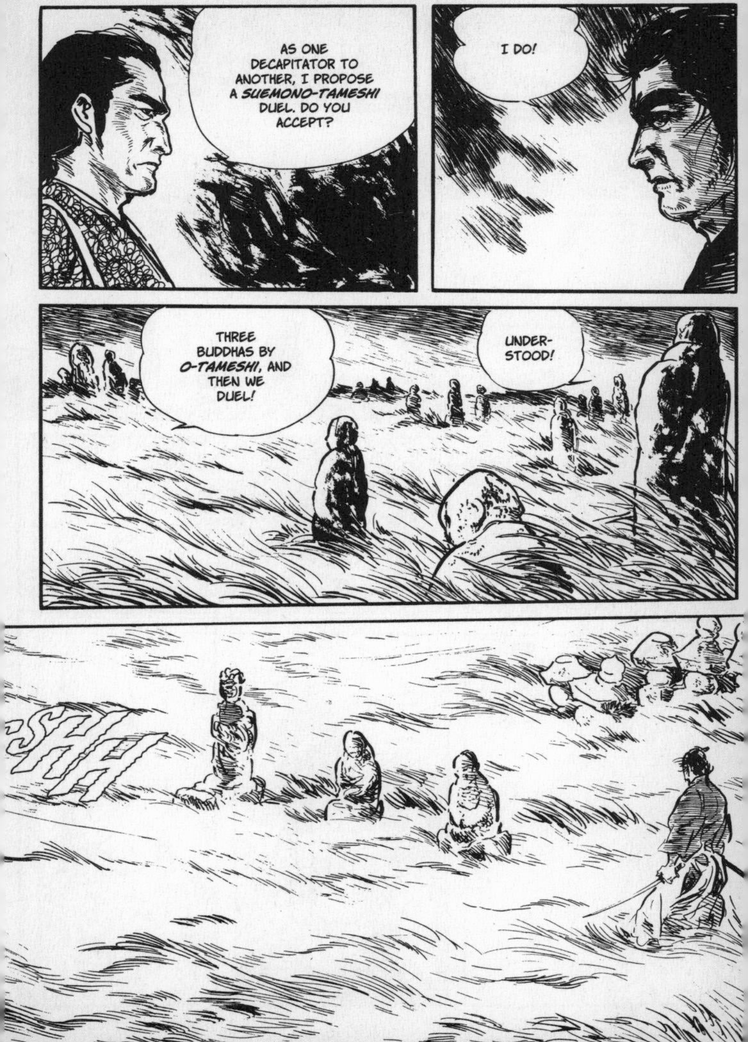
AS ONE DECAPITATOR TO ANOTHER, I PROPOSE A *SUEMONO-TAMESHI* DUEL. DO YOU ACCEPT?
I DO!
THREE BUDDHAS BY *O-TAMESHI*, AND THEN WE DUEL!
UNDER-STOOD!

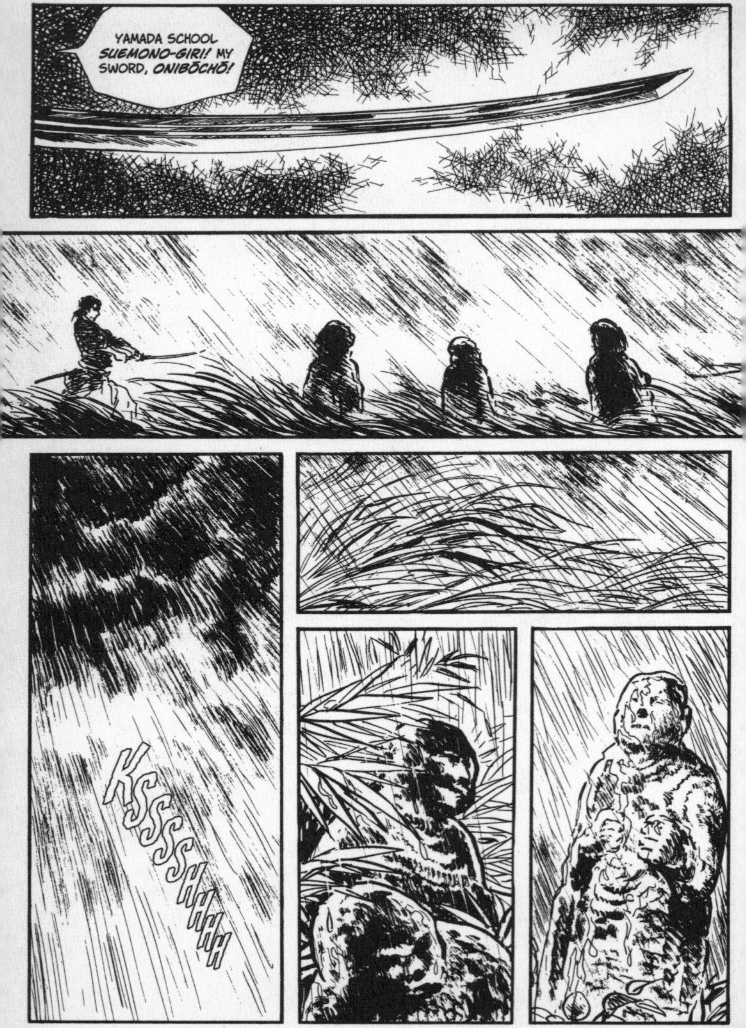
YAMADA SCHOOL SUEMONO-GIRI!! MY SWORD, ONIBŌCHŌ!
KSSSSHHHHH

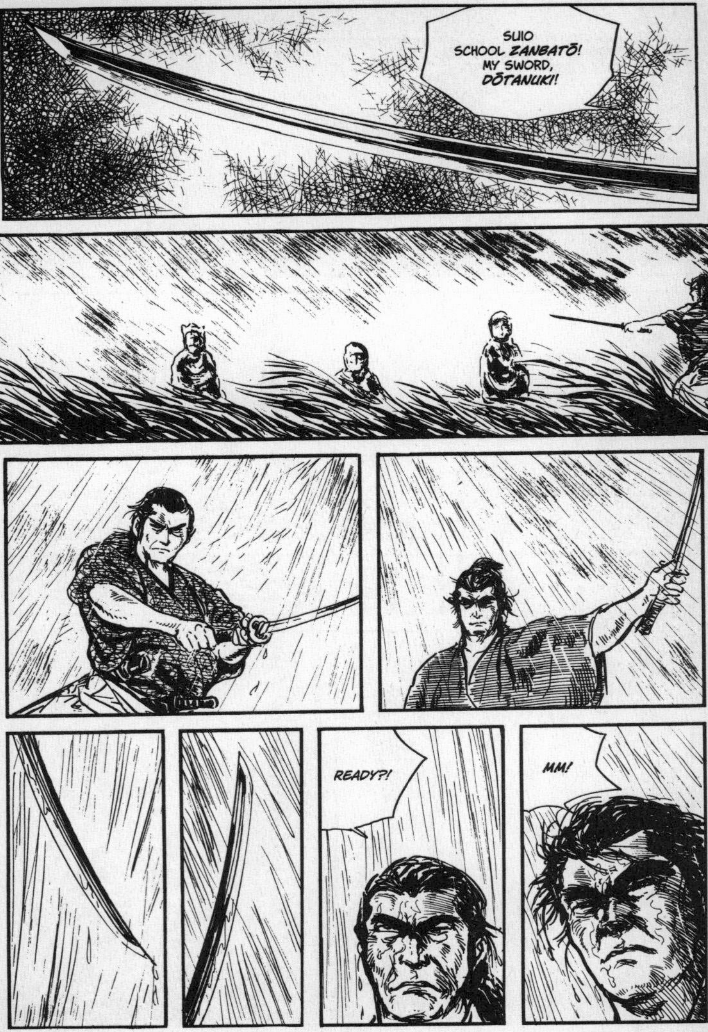
SUIO SCHOOL ZANBATŌ! MY SWORD, DŌTANUKI!
READY?!
MM!

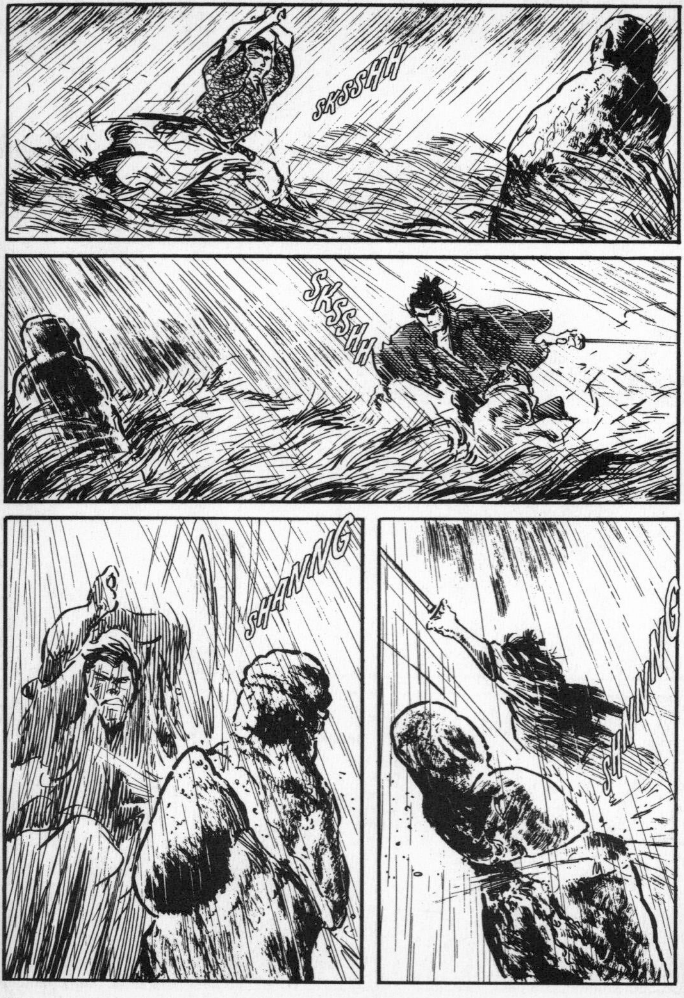
SKSSHH
SKSSHH
SHANNG
SHNNNG

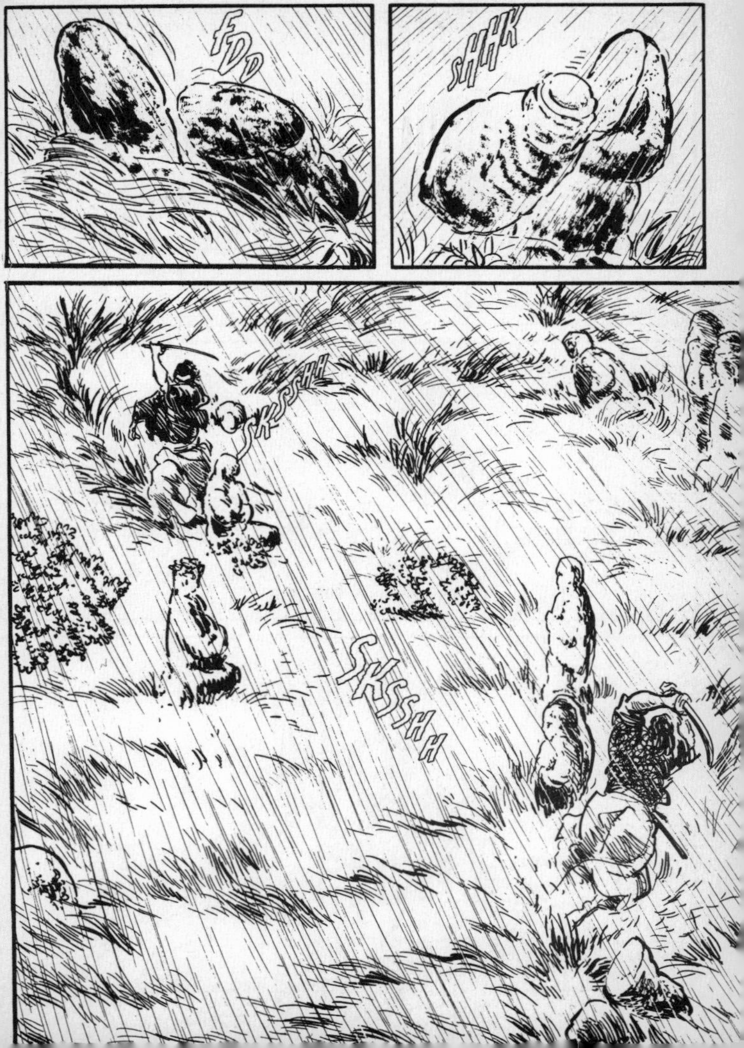
FDD
SHHK
SKSSHH
SKSSHH

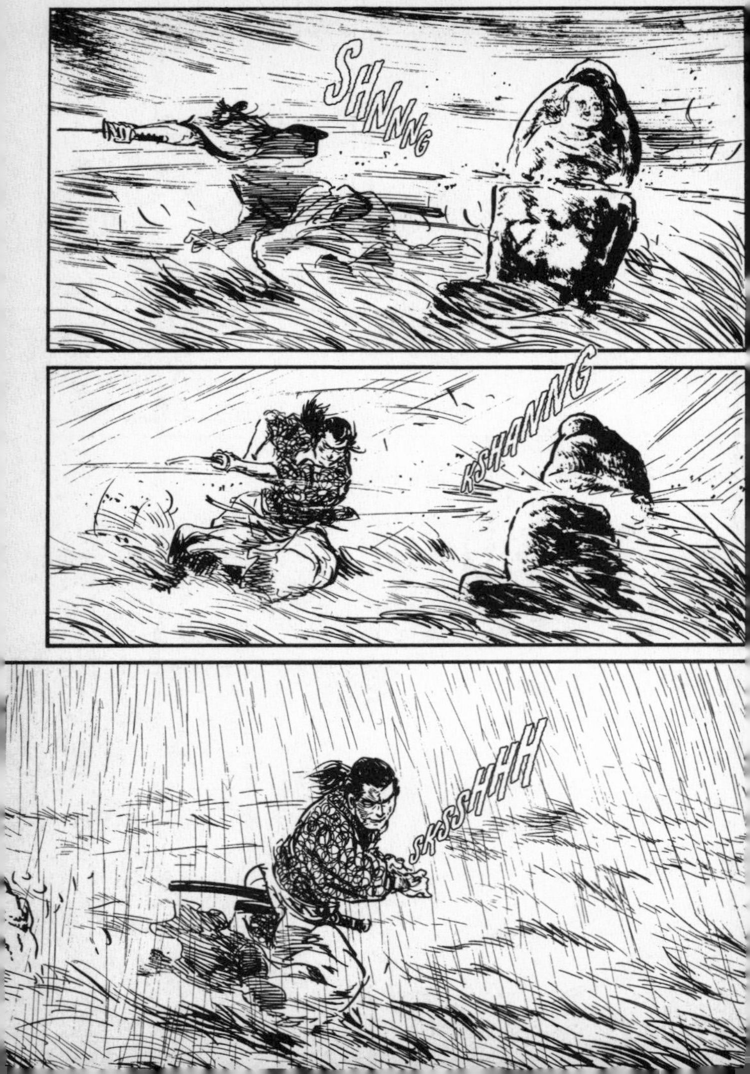
SHNNNG
KSHANNG
SKSSHHH

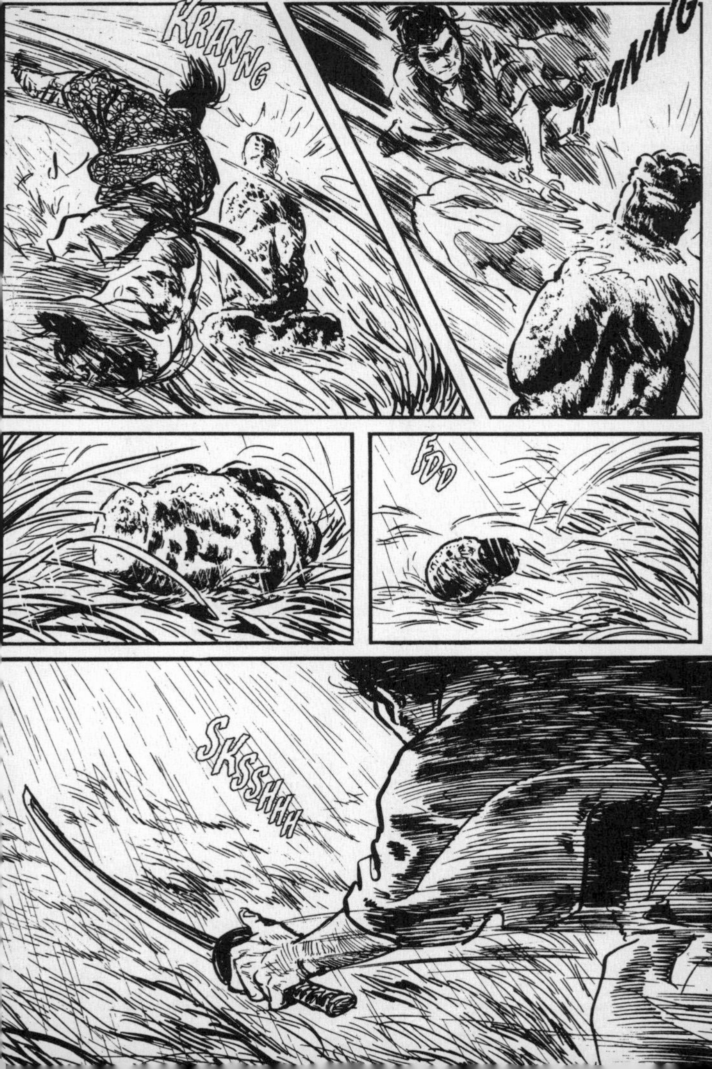
KTANNG
KRANNG
FDD
SKSSHHH

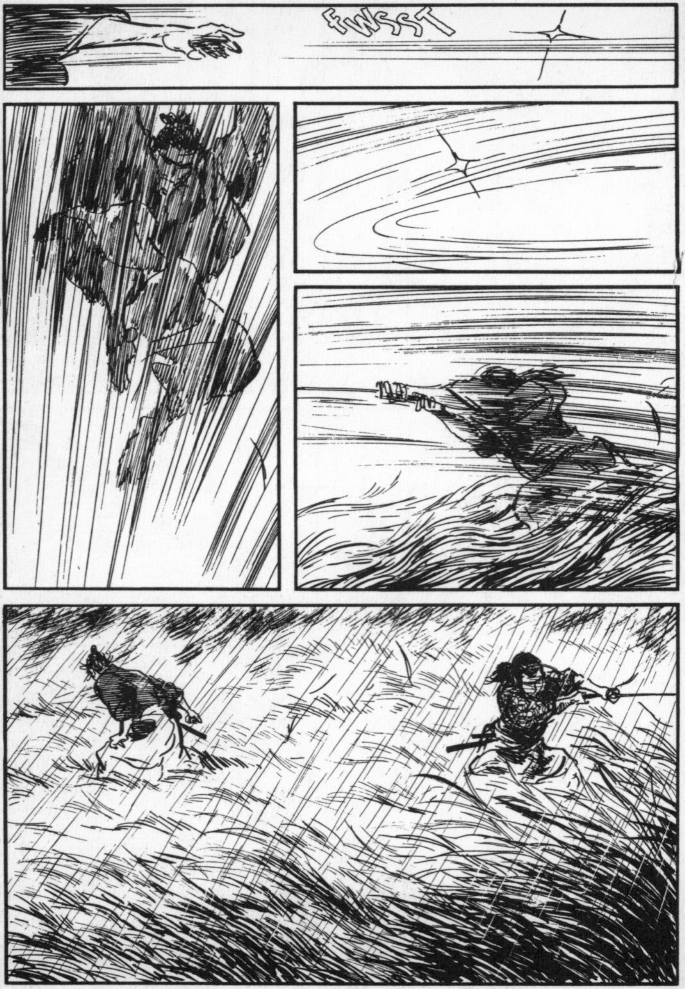
FWSST

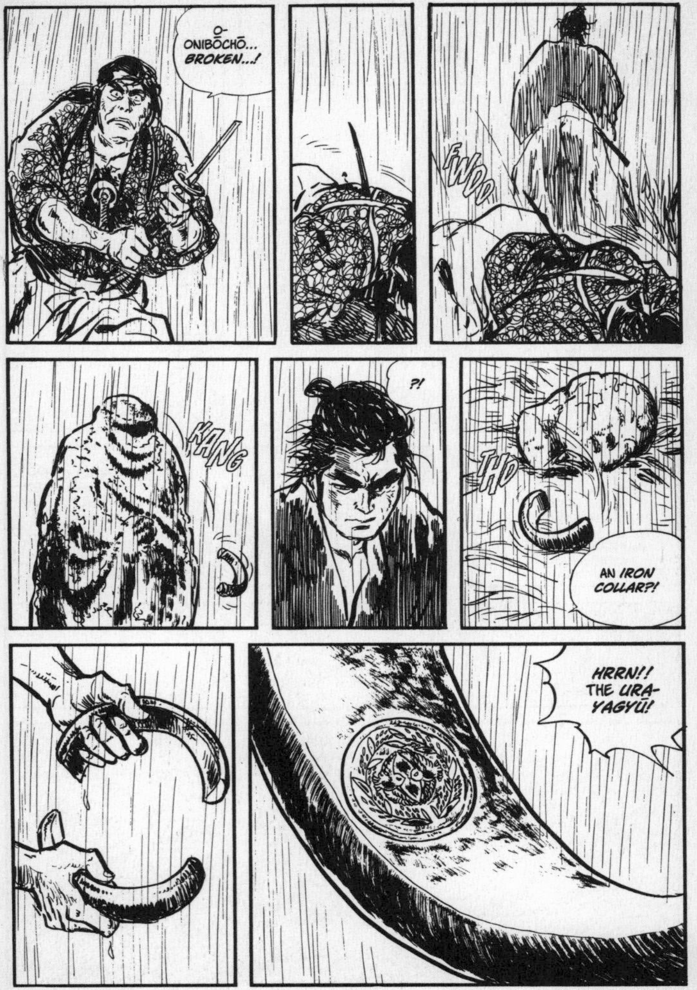
O-ONIBŌCHŌ... BROKEN...!
FWOOO
KANG
?!
THD
AN IRON COLLAR?!
HRRN!! THE URA-YAGYŪ!

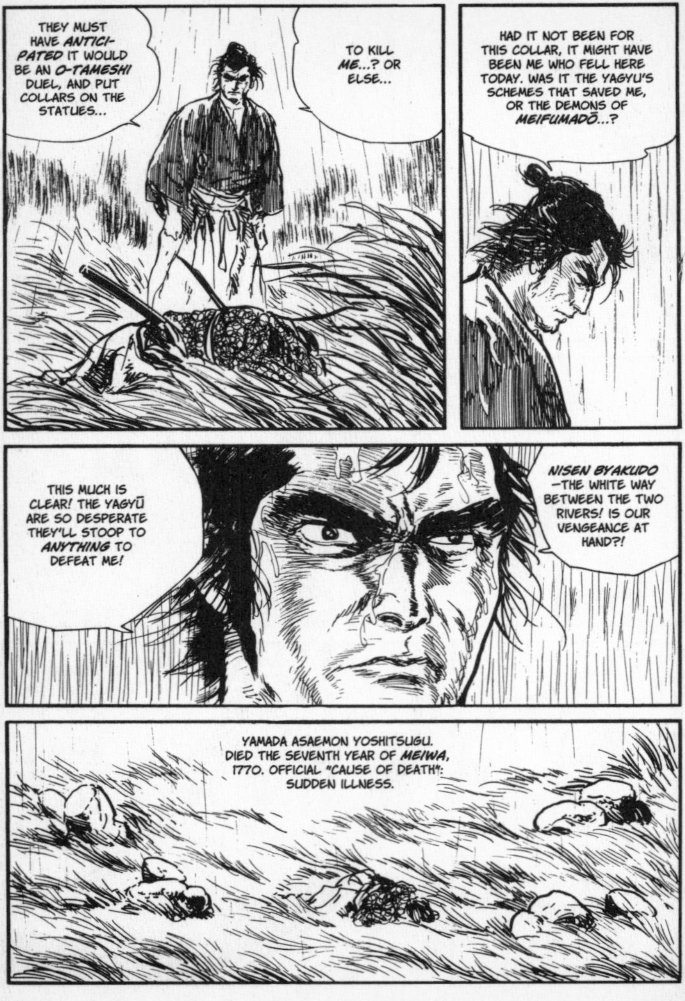
THEY MUST HAVE ANTICI-PATED IT WOULD BE AN O-TAMESHI DUEL, AND PUT COLLARS ON THE STATUES...
TO KILL ME...? OR ELSE...
HAD IT NOT BEEN FOR THIS COLLAR, IT MIGHT HAVE BEEN ME WHO FELL HERE TODAY. WAS IT THE YAGYU'S SCHEMES THAT SAVED ME, OR THE DEMONS OF MEIFUMADŌ...?
THIS MUCH IS CLEAR! THE YAGYŪ ARE SO DESPERATE THEY'LL STOOP TO ANYTHING TO DEFEAT ME!
NISEN BYAKUDO—THE WHITE WAY BETWEEN THE TWO RIVERS! IS OUR VENGEANCE AT HAND?!
YAMADA ASAEMON YOSHITSUGU. DIED THE SEVENTH YEAR OF MEIWA, 1770. OFFICIAL "CAUSE OF DEATH": SUDDEN ILLNESS.

the twenty-eighth

The Guns of Sakai

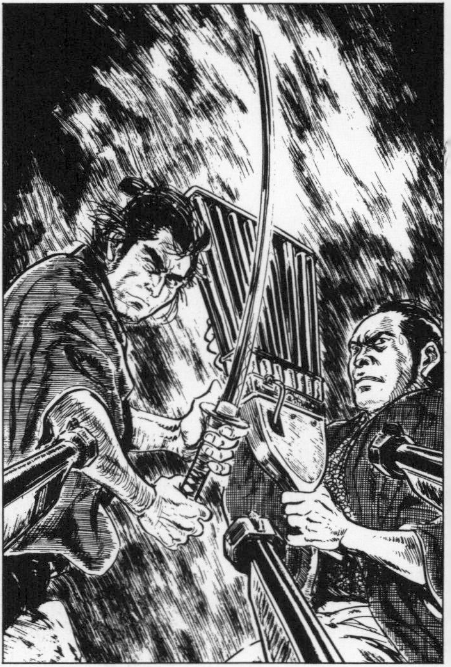

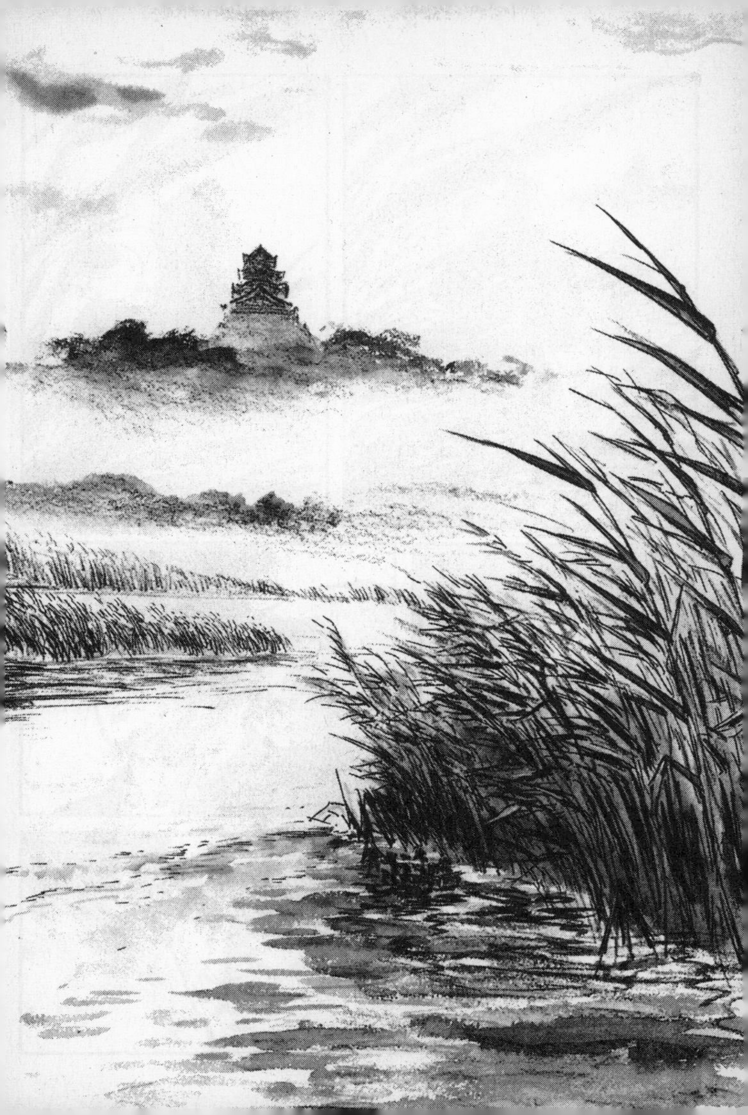

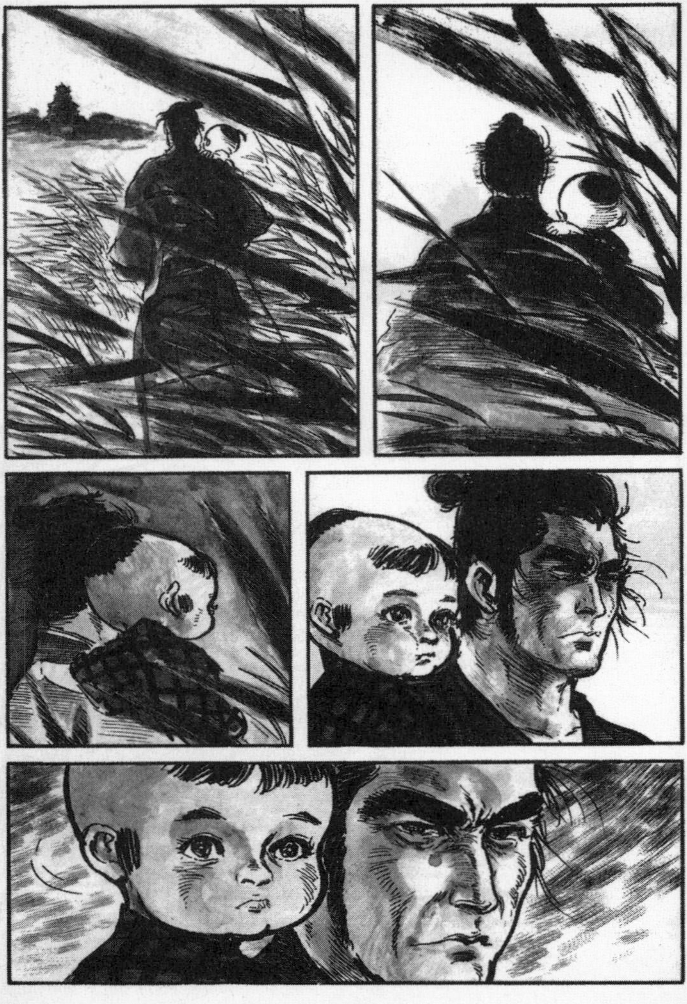

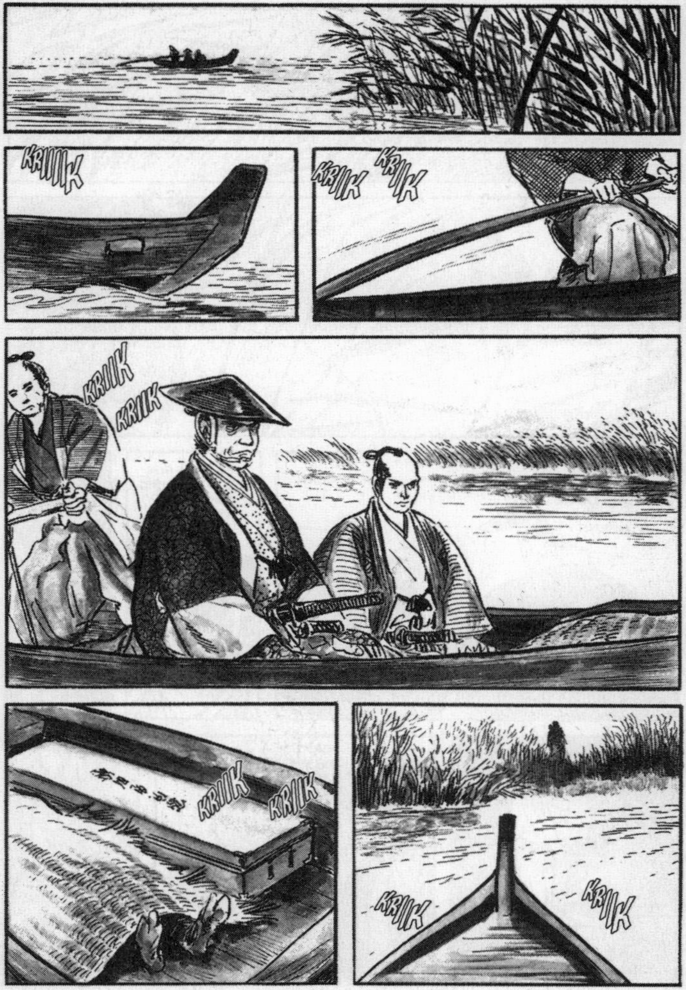
KRIIIIK
KRIIK
KRIIK
KRIIK
KRIIK
KRIIK
KRIIK
KRIIK
KRIIK

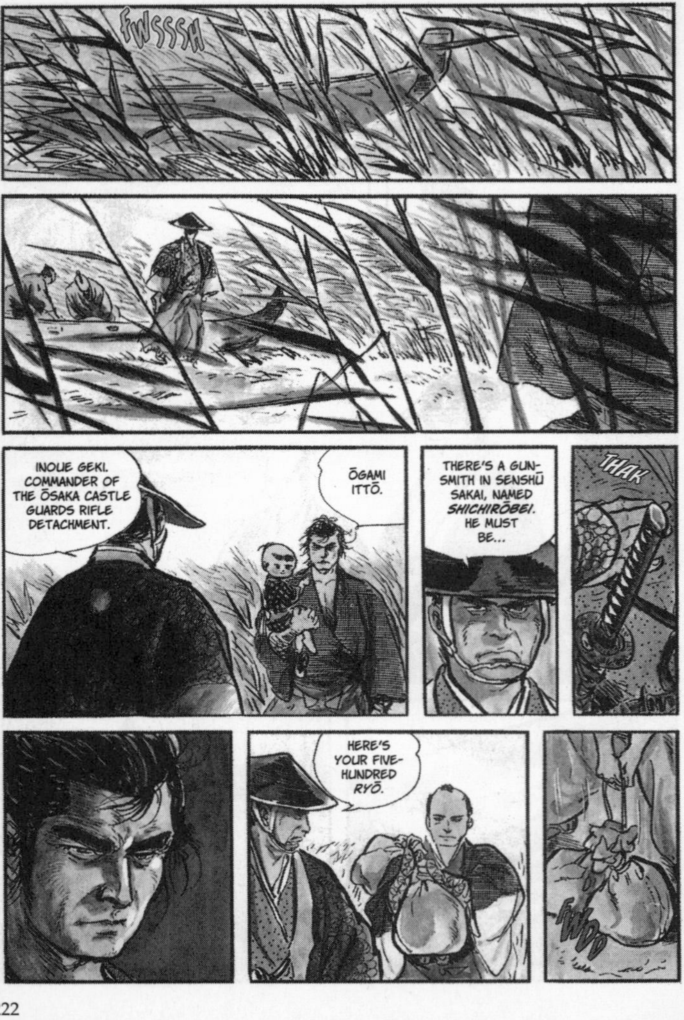
FWSSSH
INOUE GEKI. COMMANDER OF THE ŌSAKA CASTLE GUARDS RIFLE DETACHMENT.
ŌGAMI ITTŌ.
THERE'S A GUNSMITH IN SENSHŪ SAKAI, NAMED *SHICHIRŌBEI*. HE MUST BE...
THAK
HERE'S YOUR FIVE-HUNDRED *RYŌ*.

TELL ME WHY... IT'S MY ONLY CONDITION.

I KNEW DAMN WELL I'D HAVE TO TELL EVERYTHING IF I WANTED THE SERVICES OF LONE WOLF AND CUB, THE SHOGUNATE'S OWN *KAISHAKUNIN*.

I'LL KEEP IT BRIEF.

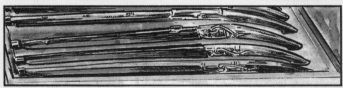

THIS IS A *SAKAI-ZUTSU*.

THE FIVE GUNSMITHS OF SAKAI WHO MAKE THEM ARE THE OFFICIAL GUNSMITHS FOR THE *SHŌGUN*. TOGETHER, THEY TURN OUT APPROXIMATELY NINE HUNDRED WEAPONS A YEAR.

BUT RECENTLY ONE OF THE GUNSMITHS UNDER THEM, THIS SHICHIROBEI, HAS BEEN MAKING GUNS IN SECRET FOR OTHER CLIENTS. HE'S SELLING THEM TO THE WESTERN *HAN*!

223

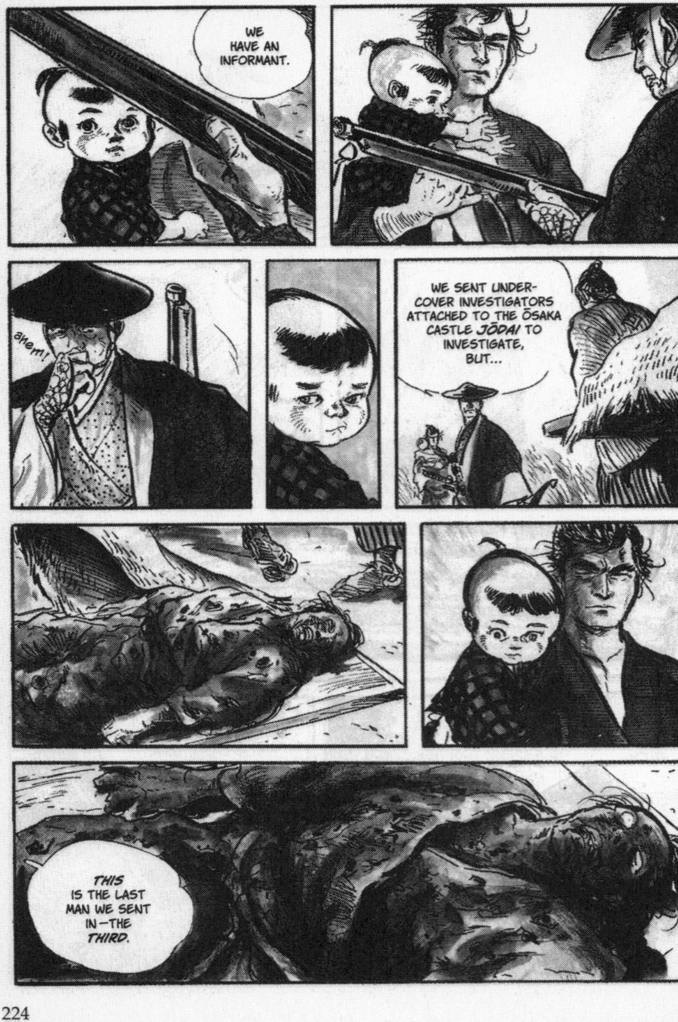
WE HAVE AN INFORMANT.
ahem!
WE SENT UNDER-COVER INVESTIGATORS ATTACHED TO THE ŌSAKA CASTLE *JŌDAI* TO INVESTIGATE, BUT...
THIS IS THE LAST MAN WE SENT IN—THE *THIRD*.

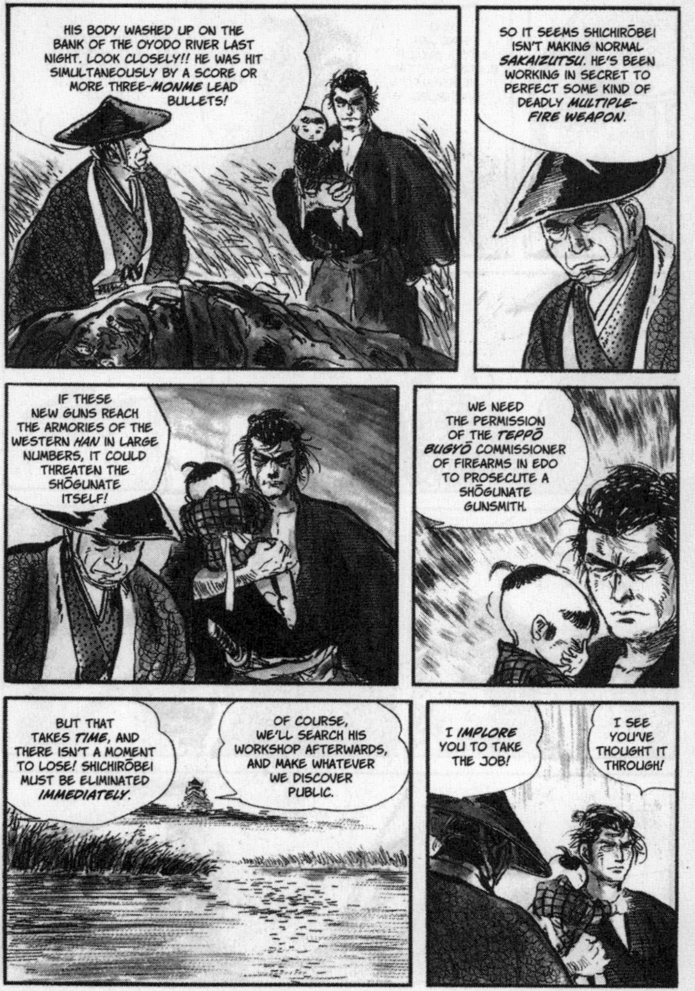
HIS BODY WASHED UP ON THE BANK OF THE OYODO RIVER LAST NIGHT. LOOK CLOSELY!! HE WAS HIT SIMULTANEOUSLY BY A SCORE OR MORE THREE-MONME LEAD BULLETS!
SO IT SEEMS SHICHIRŌBEI ISN'T MAKING NORMAL SAKAIZUTSU. HE'S BEEN WORKING IN SECRET TO PERFECT SOME KIND OF DEADLY MULTIPLE-FIRE WEAPON.
IF THESE NEW GUNS REACH THE ARMORIES OF THE WESTERN HAN IN LARGE NUMBERS, IT COULD THREATEN THE SHŌGUNATE ITSELF!
WE NEED THE PERMISSION OF THE TEPPŌ BUGYŌ COMMISSIONER OF FIREARMS IN EDO TO PROSECUTE A SHŌGUNATE GUNSMITH.
BUT THAT TAKES TIME, AND THERE ISN'T A MOMENT TO LOSE! SHICHIRŌBEI MUST BE ELIMINATED IMMEDIATELY.
OF COURSE, WE'LL SEARCH HIS WORKSHOP AFTERWARDS, AND MAKE WHATEVER WE DISCOVER PUBLIC.
I IMPLORE YOU TO TAKE THE JOB!
I SEE YOU'VE THOUGHT IT THROUGH!

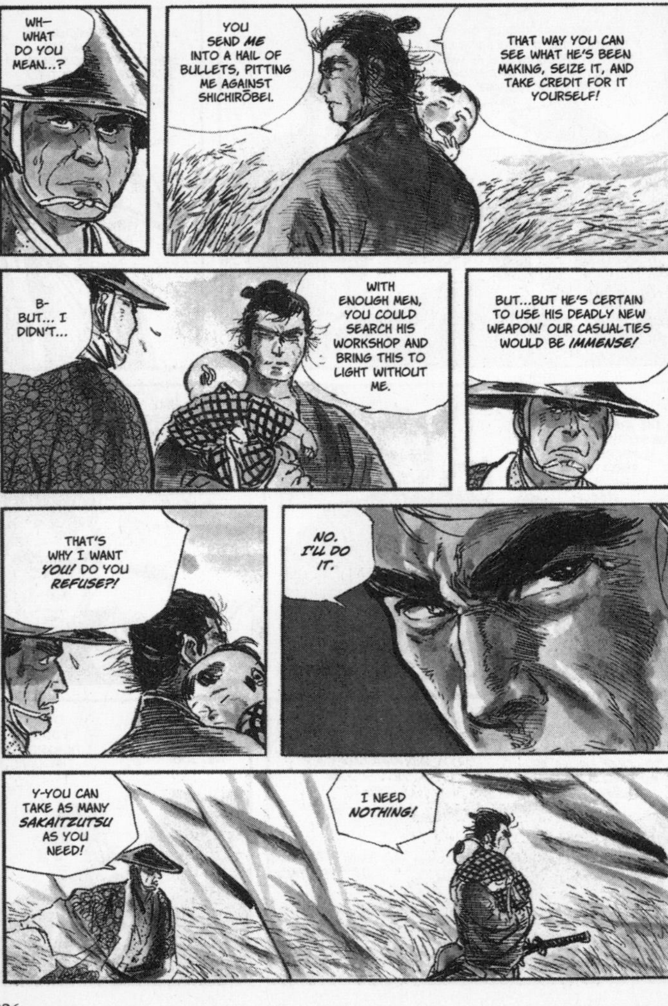
WH— WHAT DO YOU MEAN...?
YOU SEND *ME* INTO A HAIL OF BULLETS, PITTING ME AGAINST SHICHIRŌBEI.
THAT WAY YOU CAN SEE WHAT HE'S BEEN MAKING, SEIZE IT, AND TAKE CREDIT FOR IT YOURSELF!
B- BUT... I DIDN'T...
WITH ENOUGH MEN, YOU COULD SEARCH HIS WORKSHOP AND BRING THIS TO LIGHT WITHOUT ME.
BUT...BUT HE'S CERTAIN TO USE HIS DEADLY NEW WEAPON! OUR CASUALTIES WOULD BE *IMMENSE!*
THAT'S WHY I WANT *YOU!* DO YOU *REFUSE?!*
NO. I'LL DO IT.
Y-YOU CAN TAKE AS MANY *SAKAITZUTSU* AS YOU NEED!
I NEED *NOTHING!*

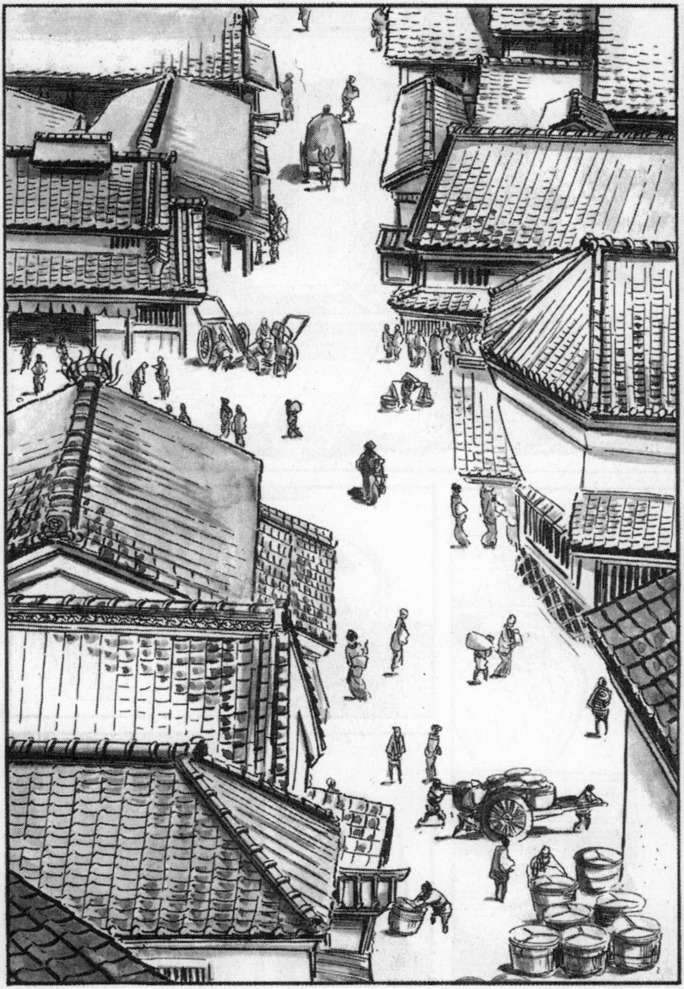

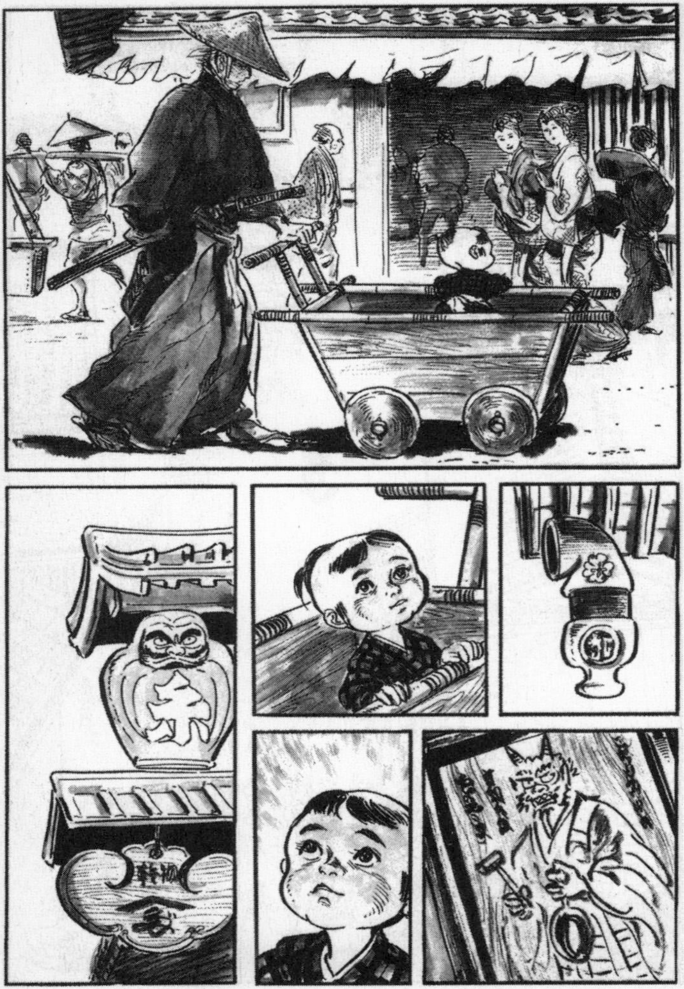

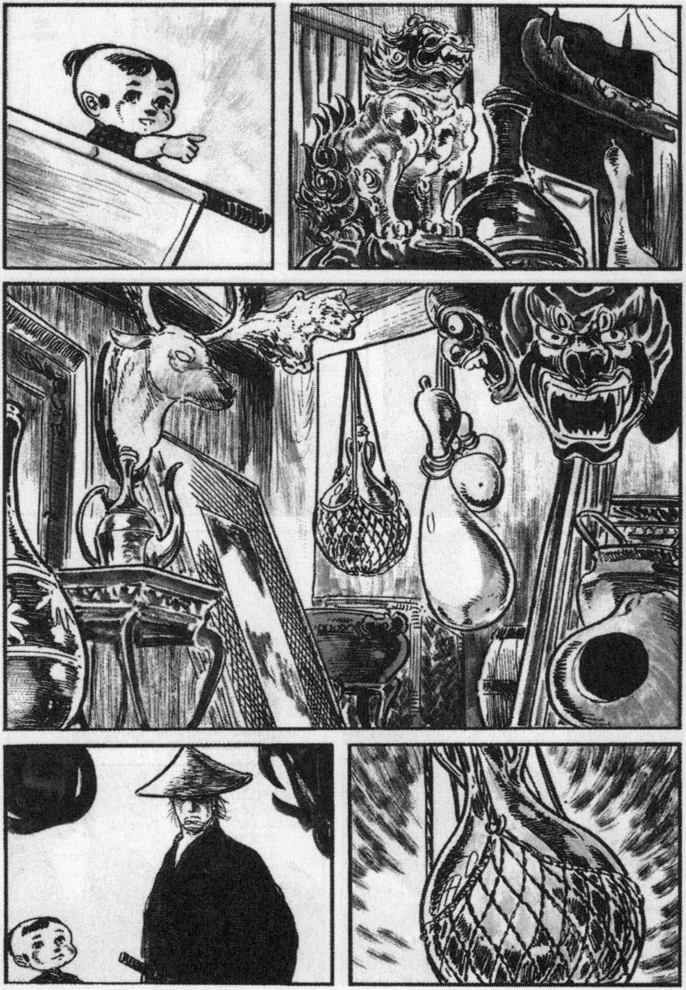

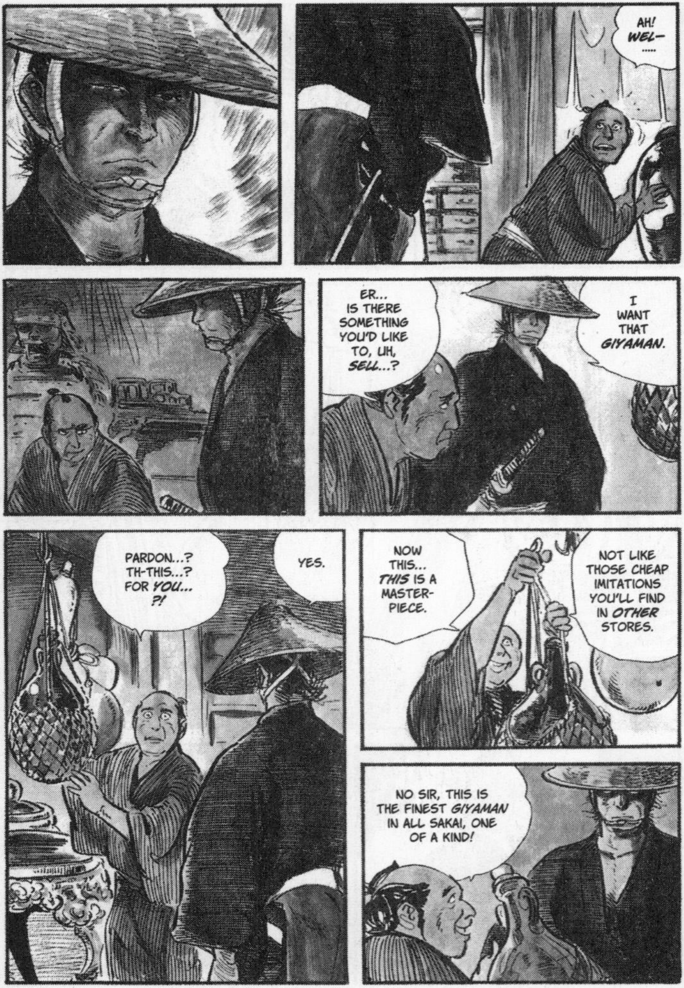
AH! WEL- .....
ER... IS THERE SOMETHING YOU'D LIKE TO, UH, SELL...?
I WANT THAT GIYAMAN.
PARDON...? TH-THIS...? FOR YOU...?!
YES.
NOW THIS... THIS IS A MASTERPIECE.
NOT LIKE THOSE CHEAP IMITATIONS YOU'LL FIND IN OTHER STORES.
NO SIR, THIS IS THE FINEST GIYAMAN IN ALL SAKAI, ONE OF A KIND!

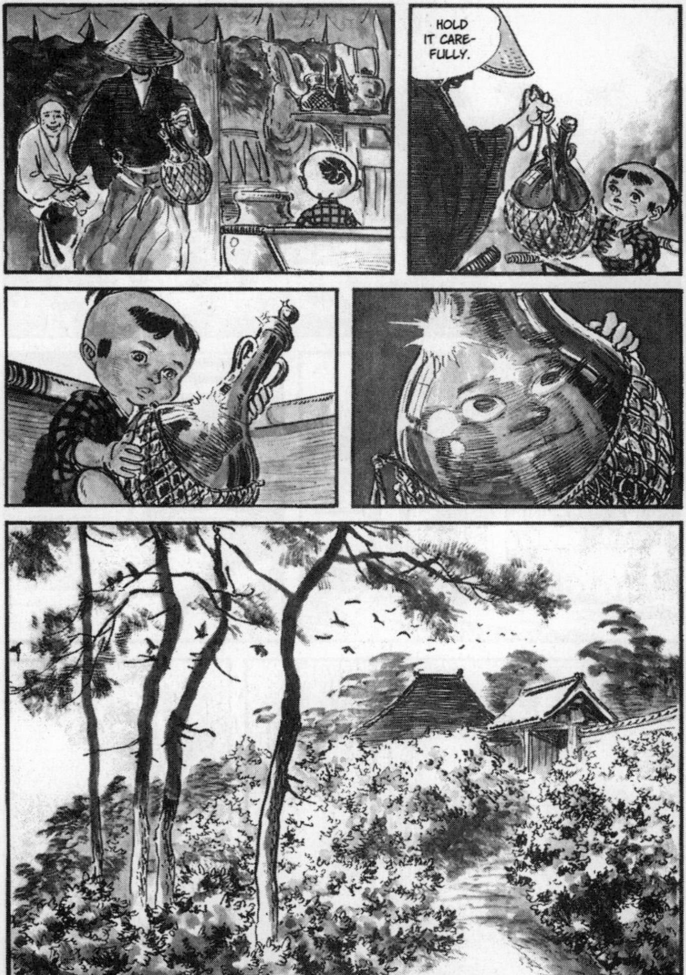
HOLD IT CARE-FULLY.

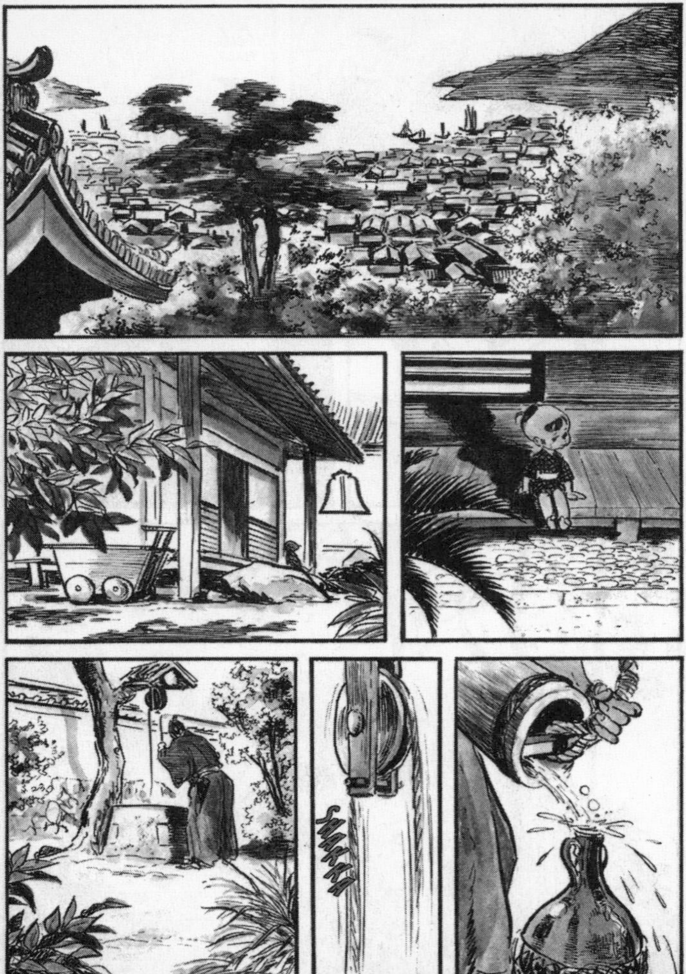

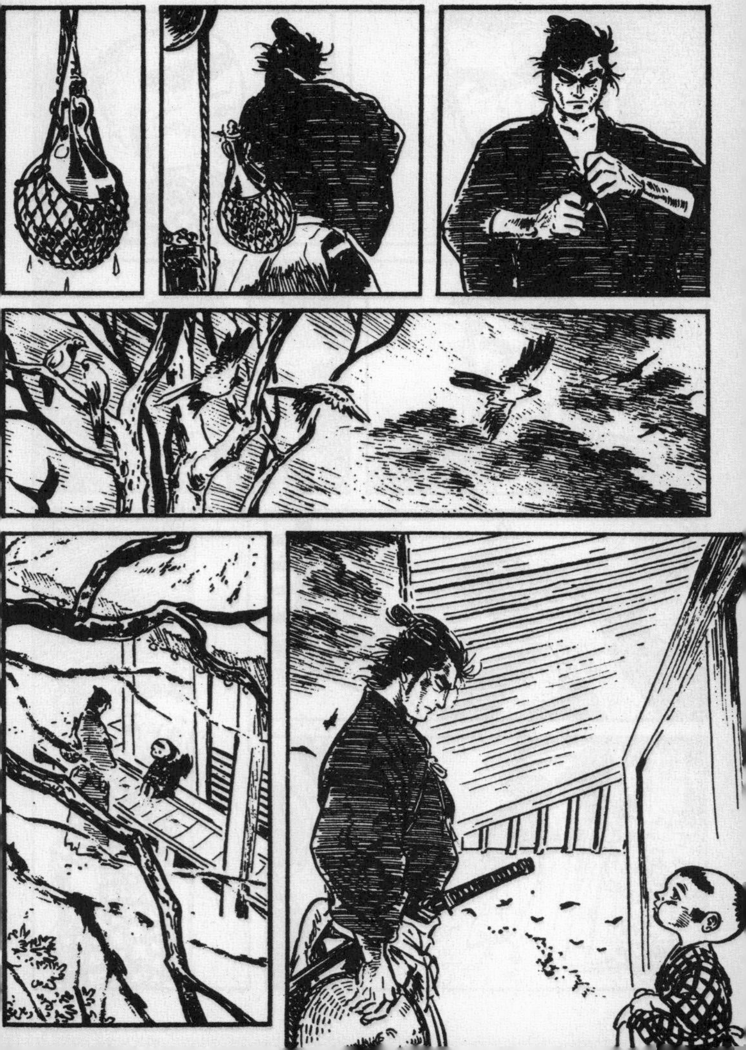

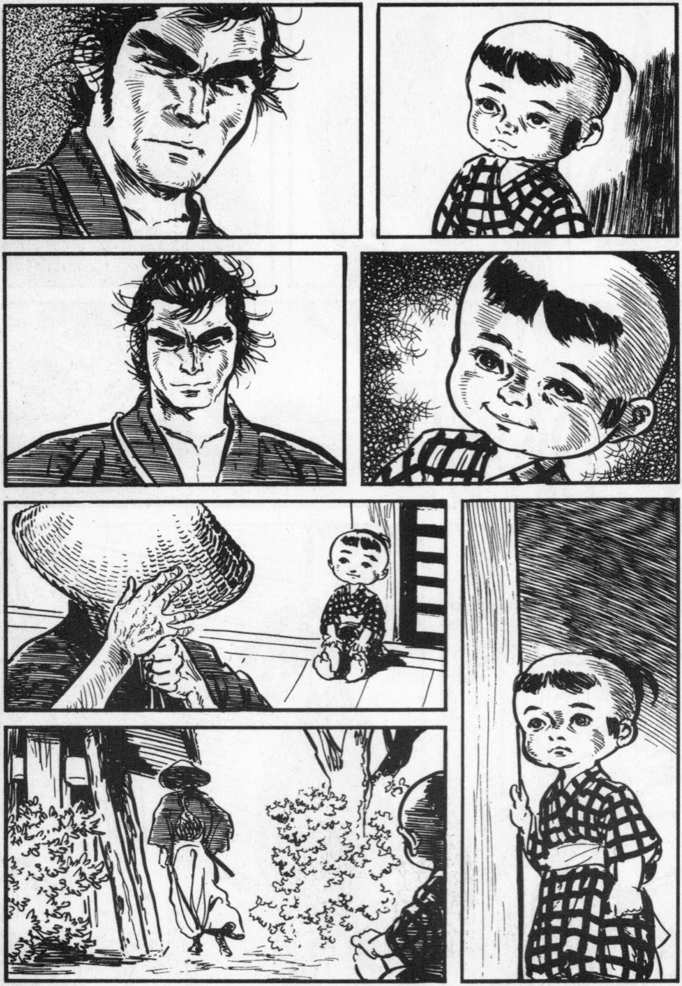

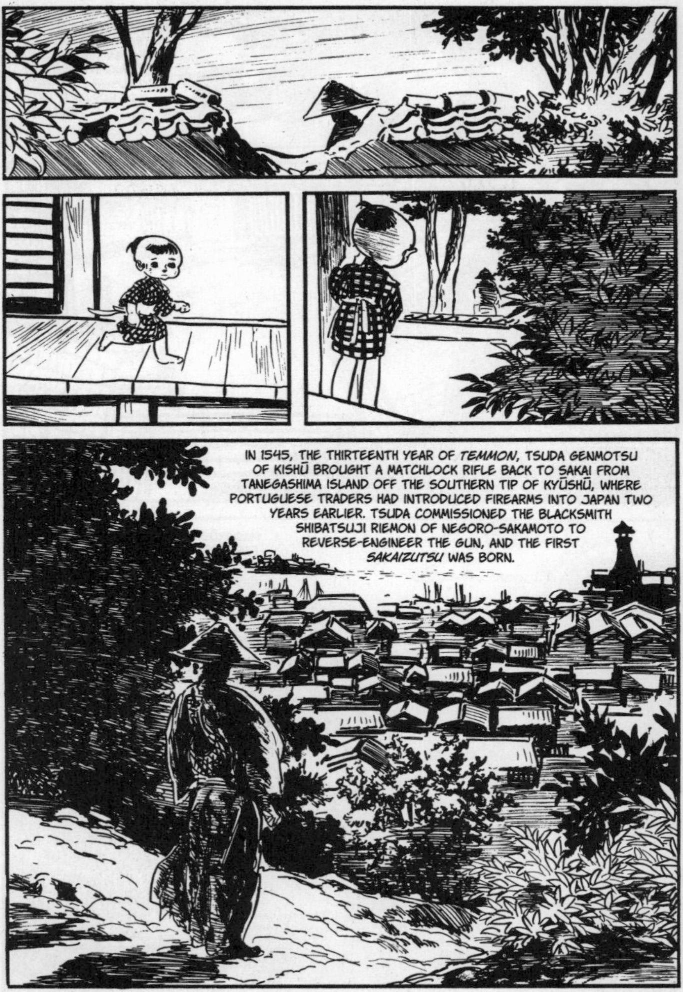
IN 1545, THE THIRTEENTH YEAR OF *TEMMON*, TSUDA GENMOTSU OF KISHŪ BROUGHT A MATCHLOCK RIFLE BACK TO SAKAI FROM TANEGASHIMA ISLAND OFF THE SOUTHERN TIP OF KYŪSHŪ, WHERE PORTUGUESE TRADERS HAD INTRODUCED FIREARMS INTO JAPAN TWO YEARS EARLIER. TSUDA COMMISSIONED THE BLACKSMITH SHIBATSUJI RIEMON OF NEGORO-SAKAMOTO TO REVERSE-ENGINEER THE GUN, AND THE FIRST *SAKAIZUTSU* WAS BORN.

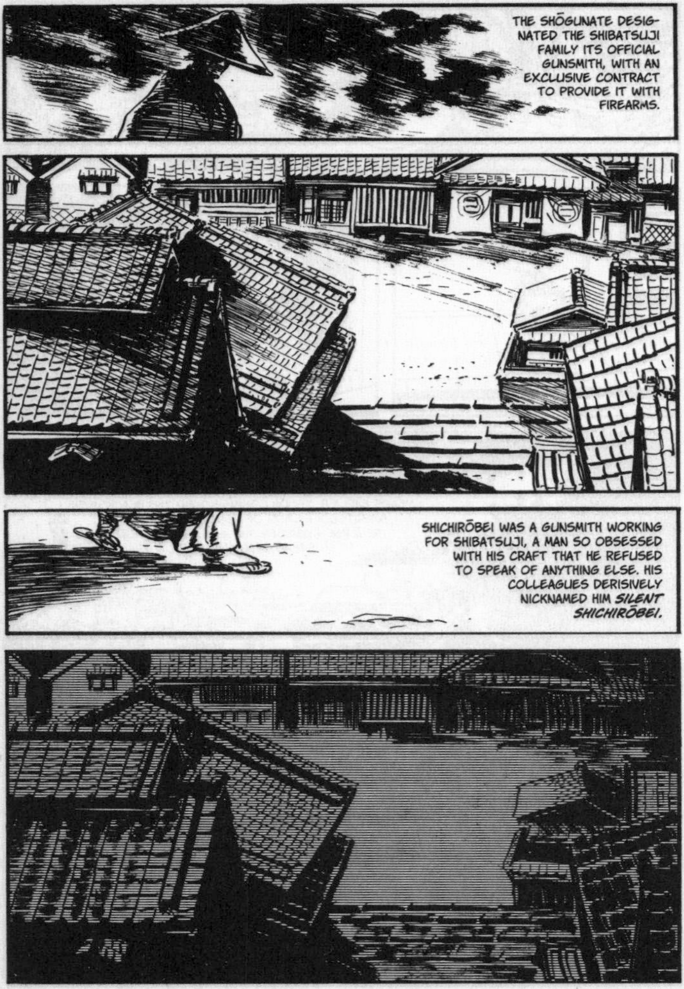
THE SHŌGUNATE DESIGNATED THE SHIBATSUJI FAMILY ITS OFFICIAL GUNSMITH, WITH AN EXCLUSIVE CONTRACT TO PROVIDE IT WITH FIREARMS.
SHICHIRŌBEI WAS A GUNSMITH WORKING FOR SHIBATSUJI, A MAN SO OBSESSED WITH HIS CRAFT THAT HE REFUSED TO SPEAK OF ANYTHING ELSE. HIS COLLEAGUES DERISIVELY NICKNAMED HIM *SILENT SHICHIRŌBEI.*

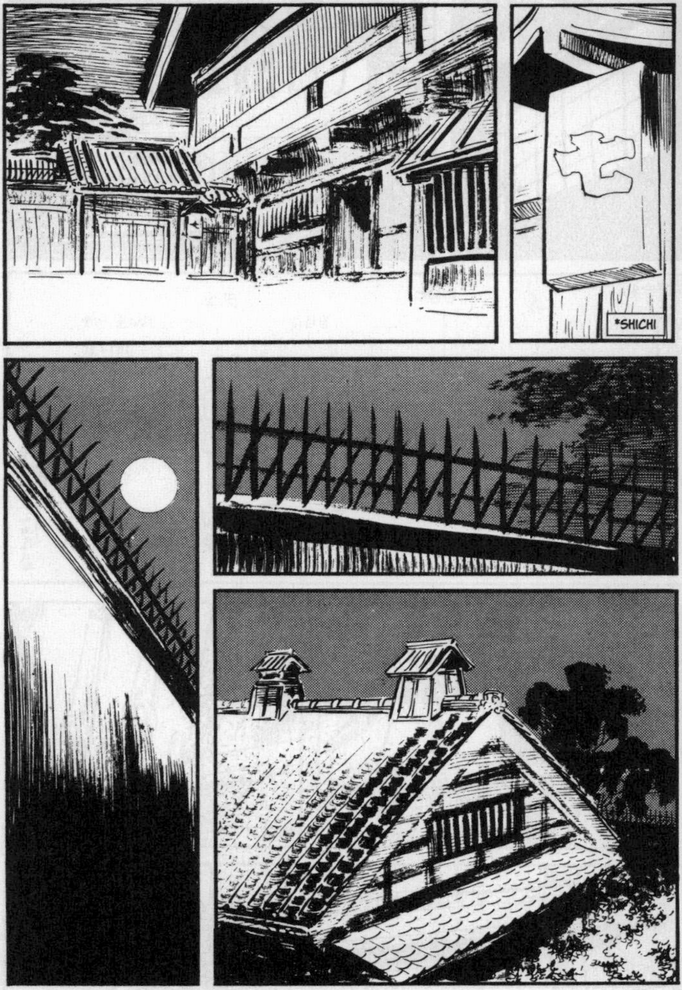
*SHICHI

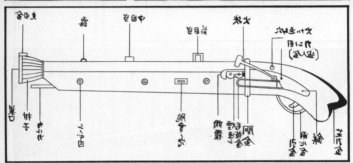

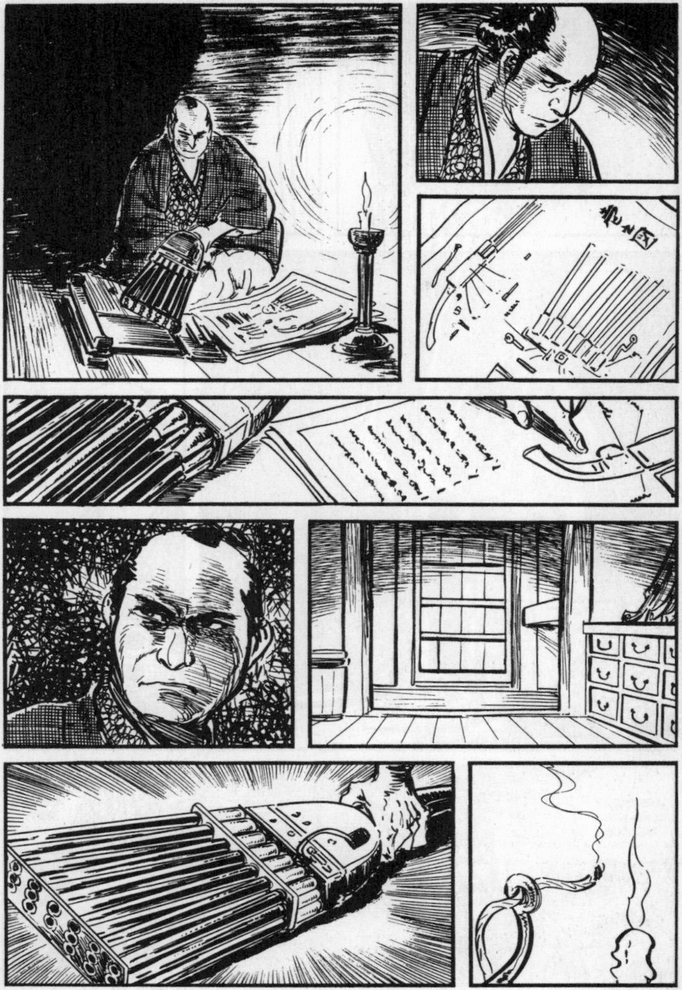

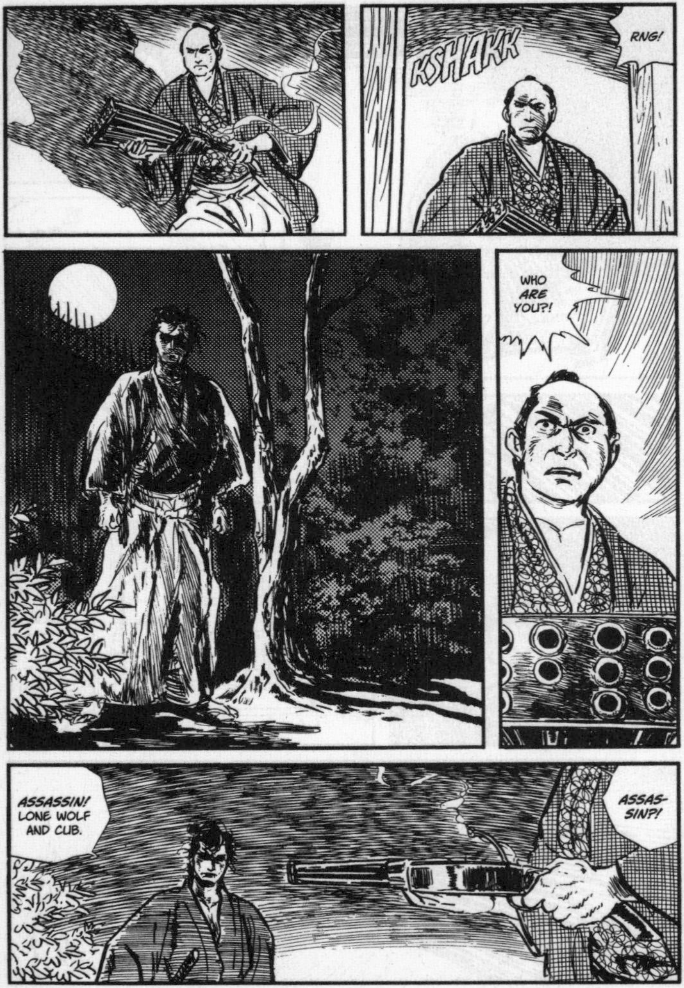
KSHAKK
RNG!
WHO ARE YOU?!
ASSASSIN! LONE WOLF AND CUB.
ASSAS-SIN?!

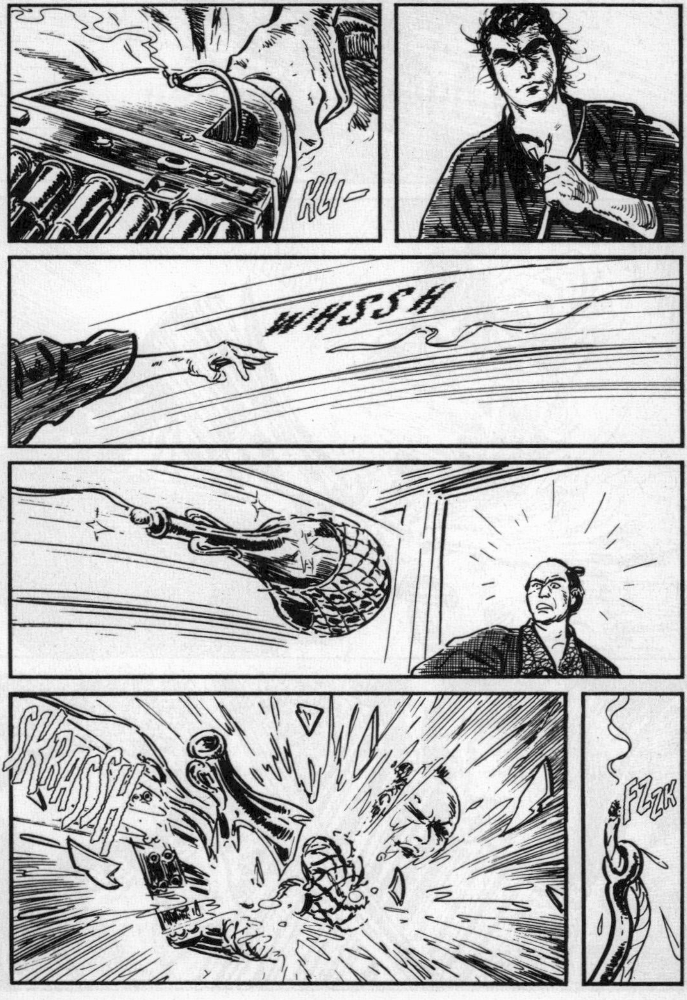
KLI-
WHSSH
SKRASSH
FZZK

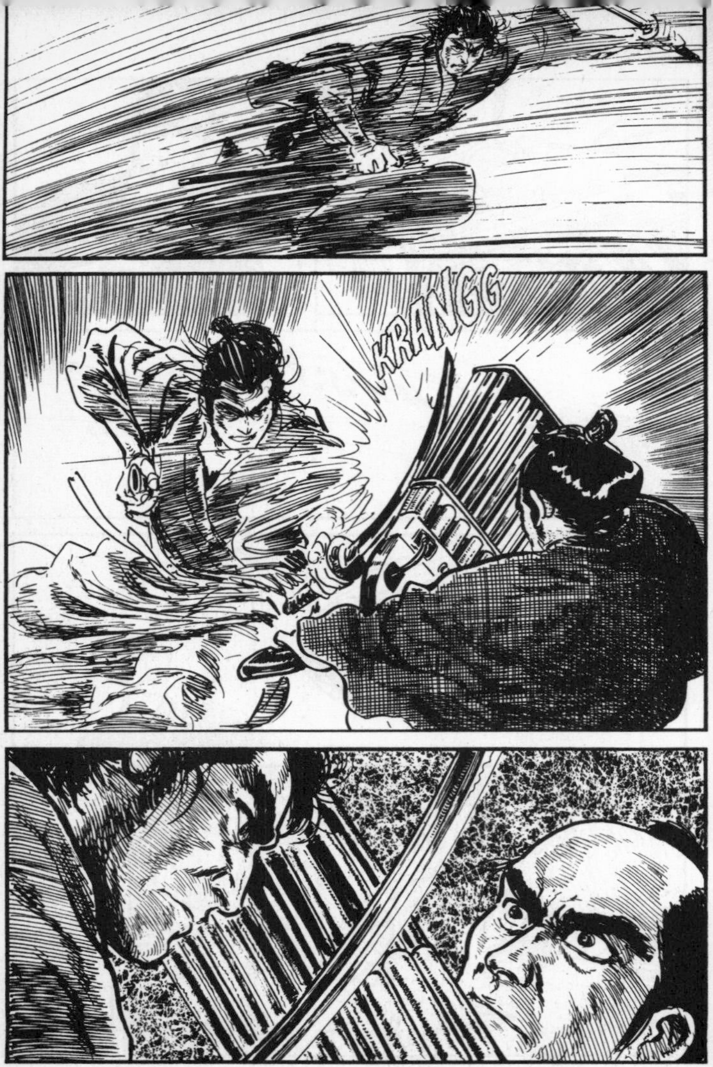
KRANGG

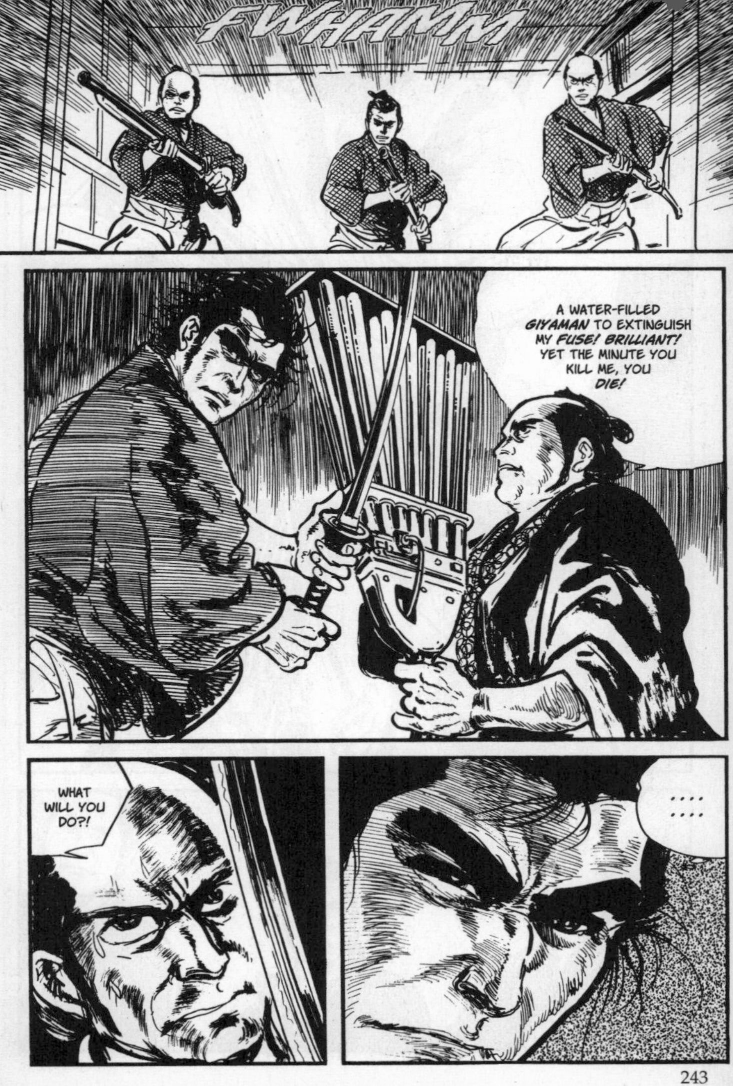
FWHAMM
A WATER-FILLED GIYAMAN TO EXTINGUISH MY FUSE! BRILLIANT! YET THE MINUTE YOU KILL ME, YOU DIE!
WHAT WILL YOU DO?!
....
....

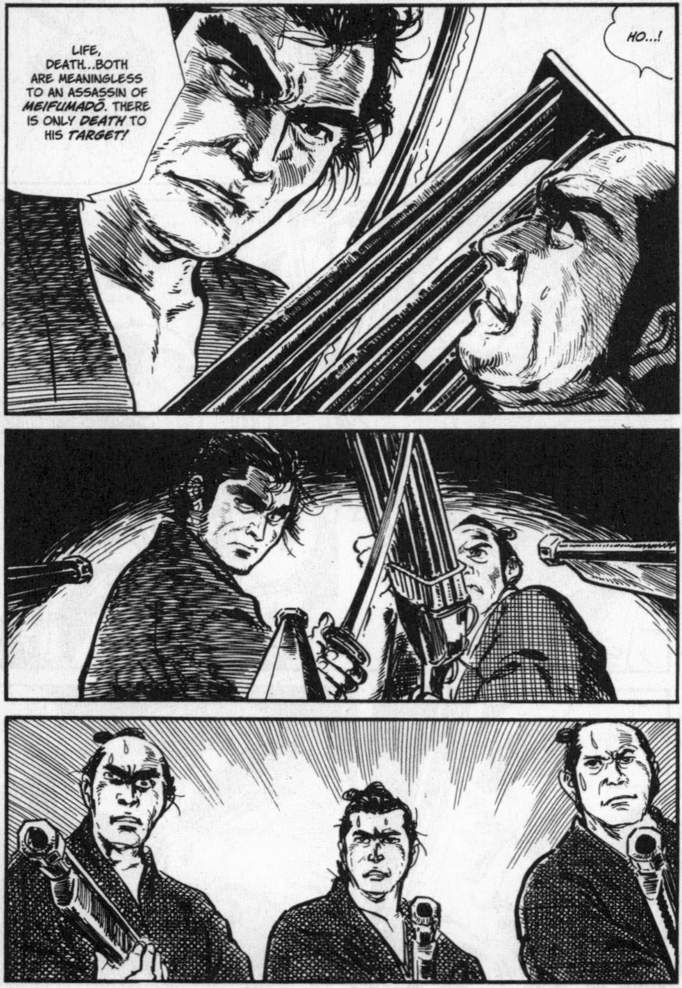
LIFE, DEATH...BOTH ARE MEANINGLESS TO AN ASSASSIN OF MEIFUMADŌ. THERE IS ONLY DEATH TO HIS TARGET!
HO...!

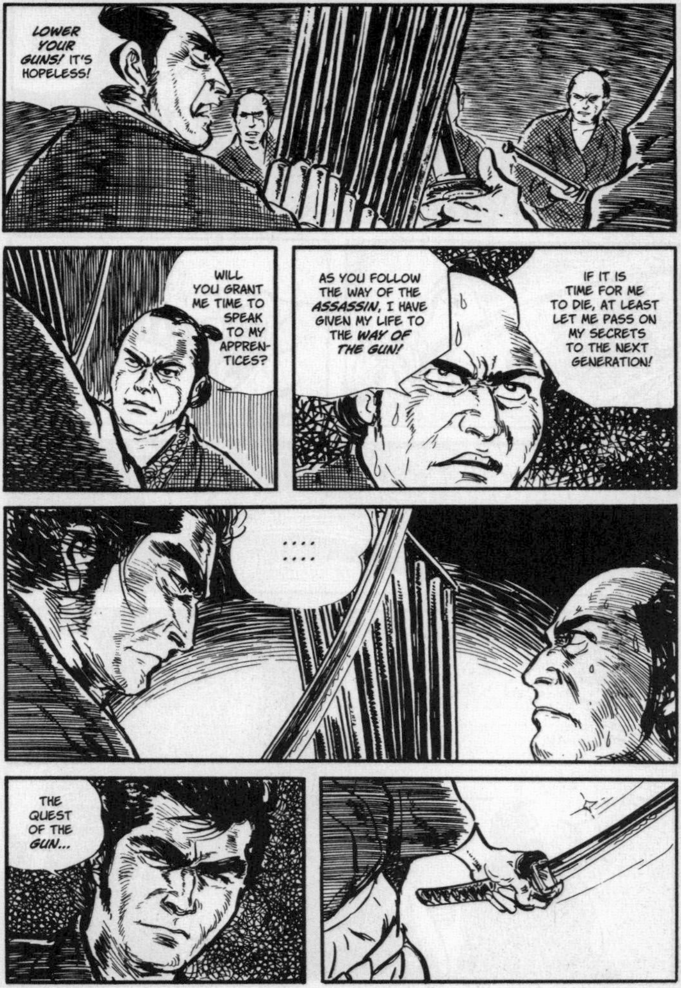
LOWER YOUR GUNS! IT'S HOPELESS!
WILL YOU GRANT ME TIME TO SPEAK TO MY APPRENTICES?
AS YOU FOLLOW THE WAY OF THE ASSASSIN, I HAVE GIVEN MY LIFE TO THE WAY OF THE GUN!
IF IT IS TIME FOR ME TO DIE, AT LEAST LET ME PASS ON MY SECRETS TO THE NEXT GENERATION!
....
....
THE QUEST OF THE GUN...

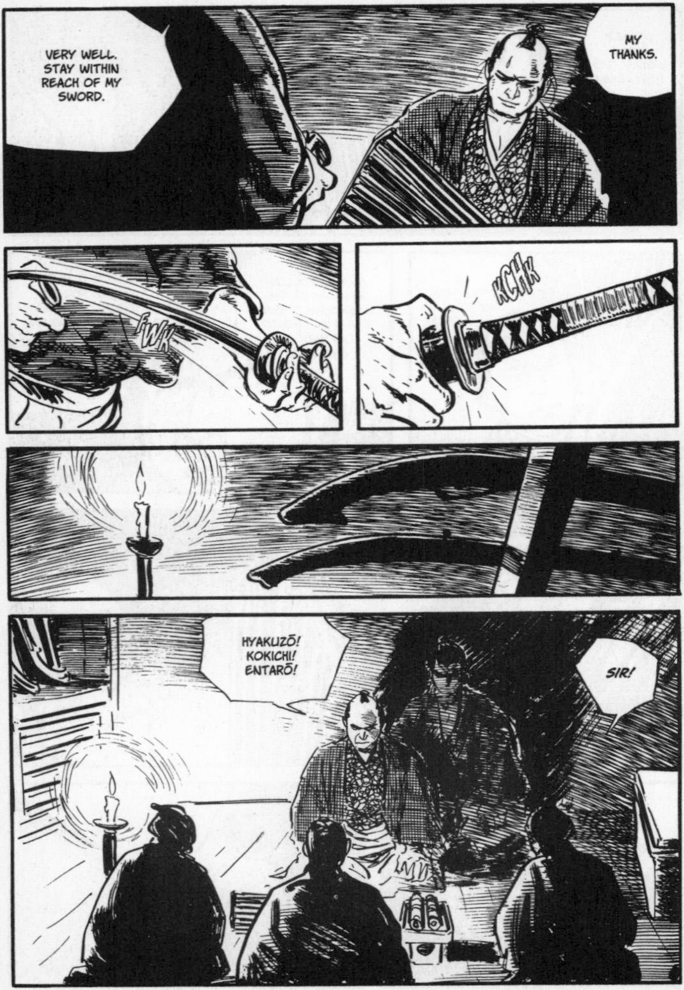
MY THANKS.
VERY WELL. STAY WITHIN REACH OF MY SWORD.
FWK
KCHK
SIR!
HYAKUZŌ! KOKICHI! ENTARŌ!

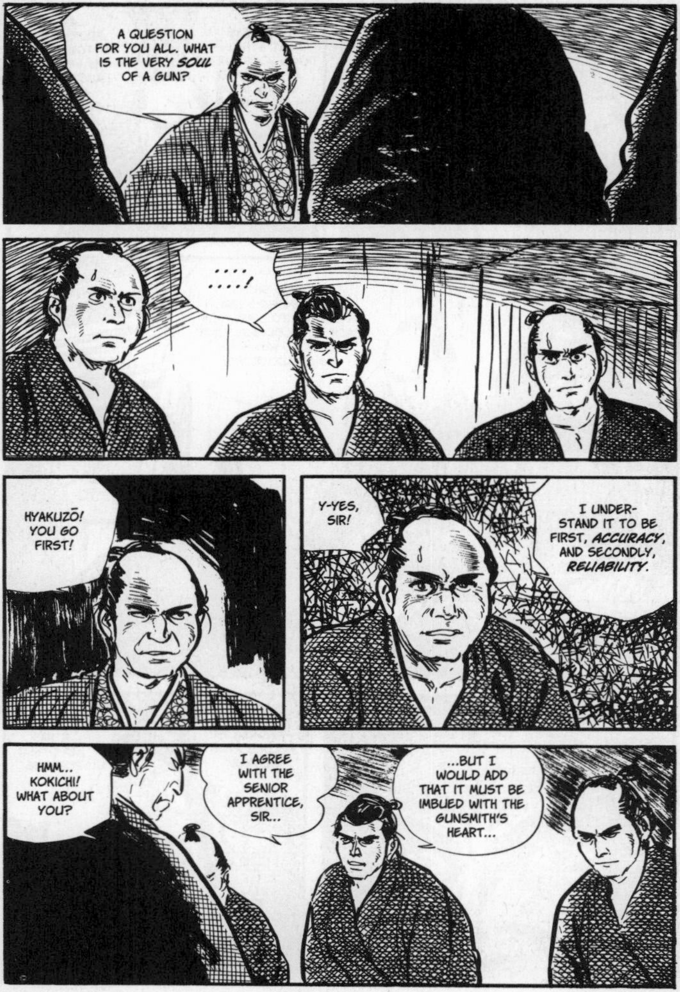

A QUESTION FOR YOU ALL. WHAT IS THE VERY SOUL OF A GUN?
....
....!
HYAKUZŌ! YOU GO FIRST!
Y-YES, SIR!
I UNDER-STAND IT TO BE FIRST, ACCURACY, AND SECONDLY, RELIABILITY.
HMM.. KOKICHI! WHAT ABOUT YOU?
I AGREE WITH THE SENIOR APPRENTICE, SIR...
...BUT I WOULD ADD THAT IT MUST BE IMBUED WITH THE GUNSMITH'S HEART...

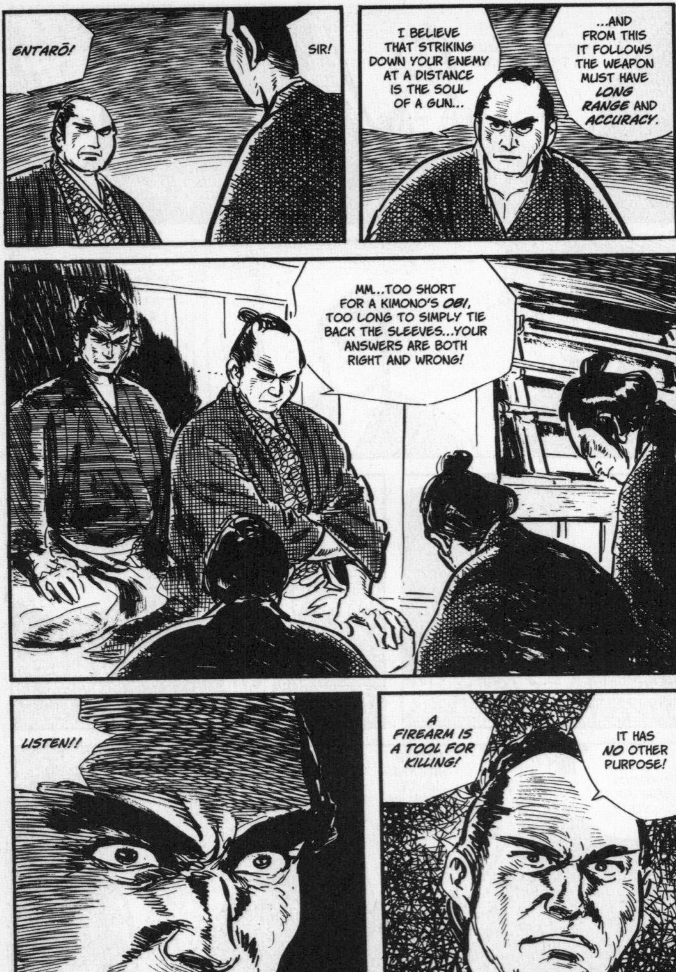
ENTARŌ!
SIR!
I BELIEVE THAT STRIKING DOWN YOUR ENEMY AT A DISTANCE IS THE SOUL OF A GUN...
...AND FROM THIS IT FOLLOWS THE WEAPON MUST HAVE LONG RANGE AND ACCURACY.
MM...TOO SHORT FOR A KIMONO'S OBI, TOO LONG TO SIMPLY TIE BACK THE SLEEVES...YOUR ANSWERS ARE BOTH RIGHT AND WRONG!
LISTEN!!
A FIREARM IS A TOOL FOR KILLING!
IT HAS NO OTHER PURPOSE!

THIS BEING SO, THERE IS ONLY *ONE* CONCERN—HOW TO KILL THE *MOST* PEOPLE *MOST* EFFICIENTLY!

FROM THIS, ALL ELSE FOLLOWS— IT MUST BE EASY TO *CARRY!*

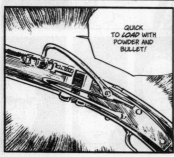

QUICK TO *LOAD* WITH POWDER AND BULLET!

POWERFUL ENOUGH TO FELL A FOE WITH A SINGLE SHOT!

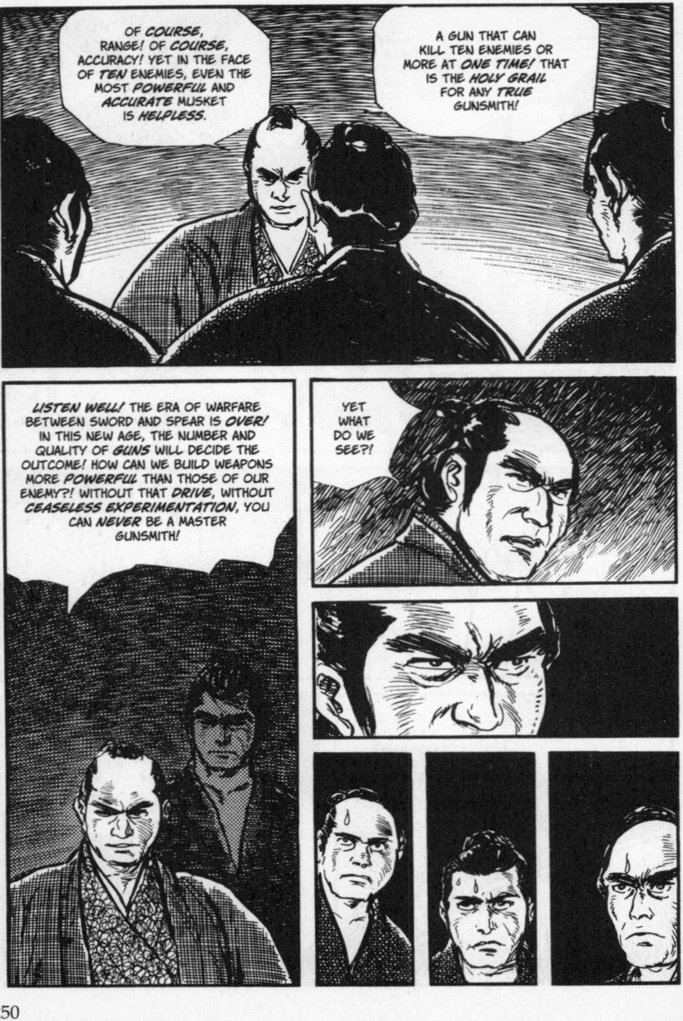
OF COURSE, RANGE! OF COURSE, ACCURACY! YET IN THE FACE OF TEN ENEMIES, EVEN THE MOST POWERFUL AND ACCURATE MUSKET IS HELPLESS.
A GUN THAT CAN KILL TEN ENEMIES OR MORE AT ONE TIME! THAT IS THE HOLY GRAIL FOR ANY TRUE GUNSMITH!
LISTEN WELL! THE ERA OF WARFARE BETWEEN SWORD AND SPEAR IS OVER! IN THIS NEW AGE, THE NUMBER AND QUALITY OF GUNS WILL DECIDE THE OUTCOME! HOW CAN WE BUILD WEAPONS MORE POWERFUL THAN THOSE OF OUR ENEMY?! WITHOUT THAT DRIVE, WITHOUT CEASELESS EXPERIMENTATION, YOU CAN NEVER BE A MASTER GUNSMITH!
YET WHAT DO WE SEE?!

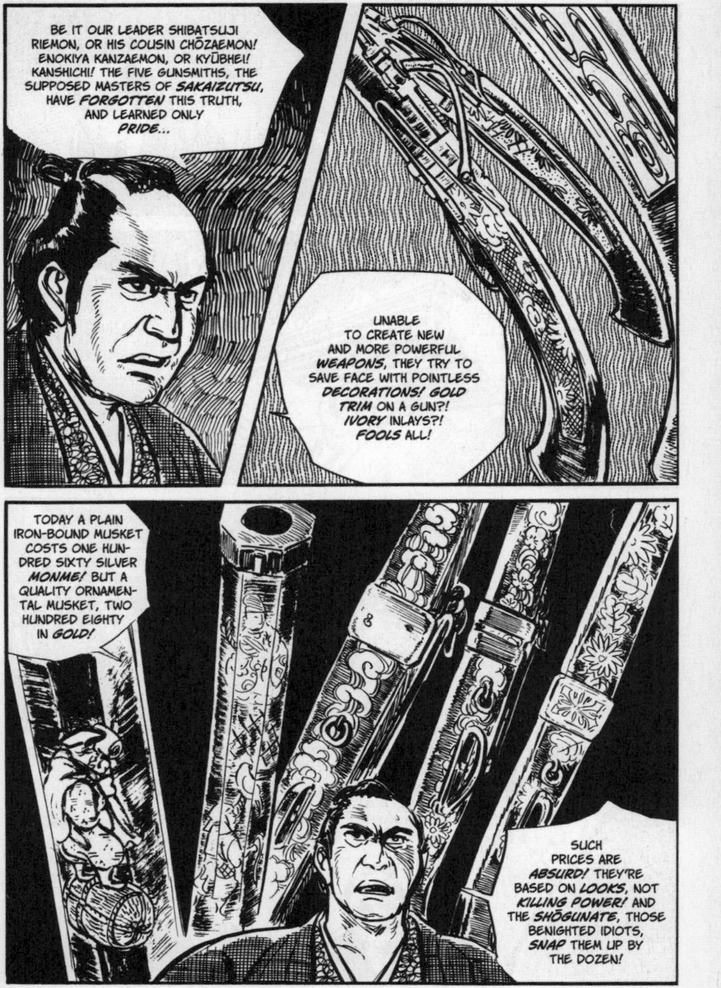
BE IT OUR LEADER SHIBATSUJI RIEMON, OR HIS COUSIN CHŌZAEMON! ENOKIYA KANZAEMON, OR KYŪBHEI! KANSHICHI! THE FIVE GUNSMITHS, THE SUPPOSED MASTERS OF SAKAIZUTSU, HAVE FORGOTTEN THIS TRUTH, AND LEARNED ONLY PRIDE...
UNABLE TO CREATE NEW AND MORE POWERFUL WEAPONS, THEY TRY TO SAVE FACE WITH POINTLESS DECORATIONS! GOLD TRIM ON A GUN?! IVORY INLAYS?! FOOLS ALL!
TODAY A PLAIN IRON-BOUND MUSKET COSTS ONE HUN-DRED SIXTY SILVER MONME! BUT A QUALITY ORNAMEN-TAL MUSKET, TWO HUNDRED EIGHTY IN GOLD!
SUCH PRICES ARE ABSURD! THEY'RE BASED ON LOOKS, NOT KILLING POWER! AND THE SHŌGUNATE, THOSE BENIGHTED IDIOTS, SNAP THEM UP BY THE DOZEN!

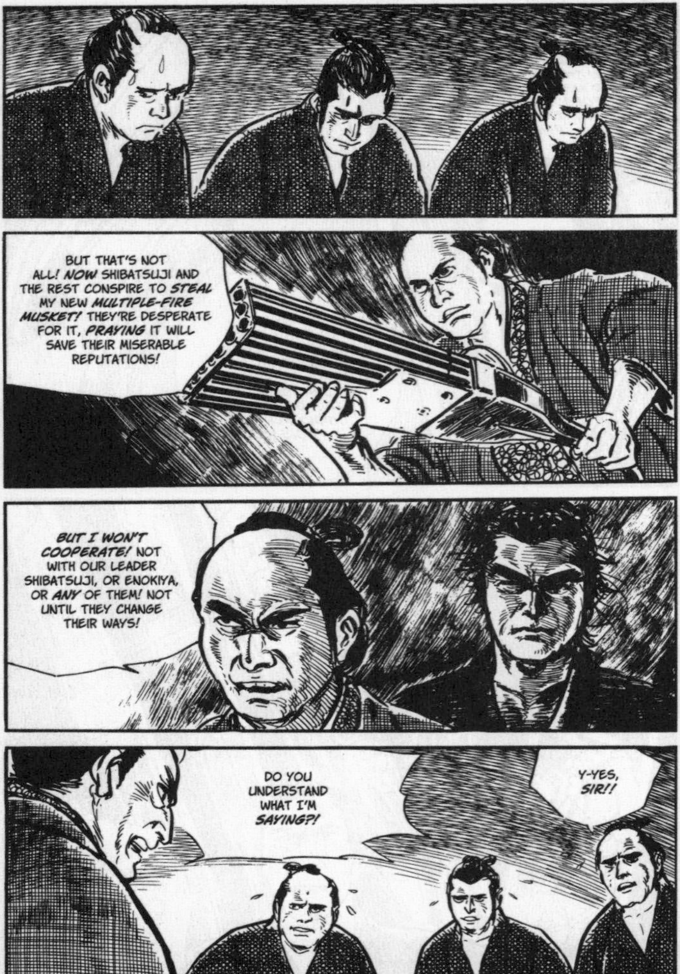
BUT THAT'S NOT ALL! NOW SHIBATSUJI AND THE REST CONSPIRE TO STEAL MY NEW MULTIPLE-FIRE MUSKET! THEY'RE DESPERATE FOR IT, PRAYING IT WILL SAVE THEIR MISERABLE REPUTATIONS!
BUT I WON'T COOPERATE! NOT WITH OUR LEADER SHIBATSUJI, OR ENOKIYA, OR ANY OF THEM! NOT UNTIL THEY CHANGE THEIR WAYS!
DO YOU UNDERSTAND WHAT I'M SAYING?!
Y-YES, SIR!!

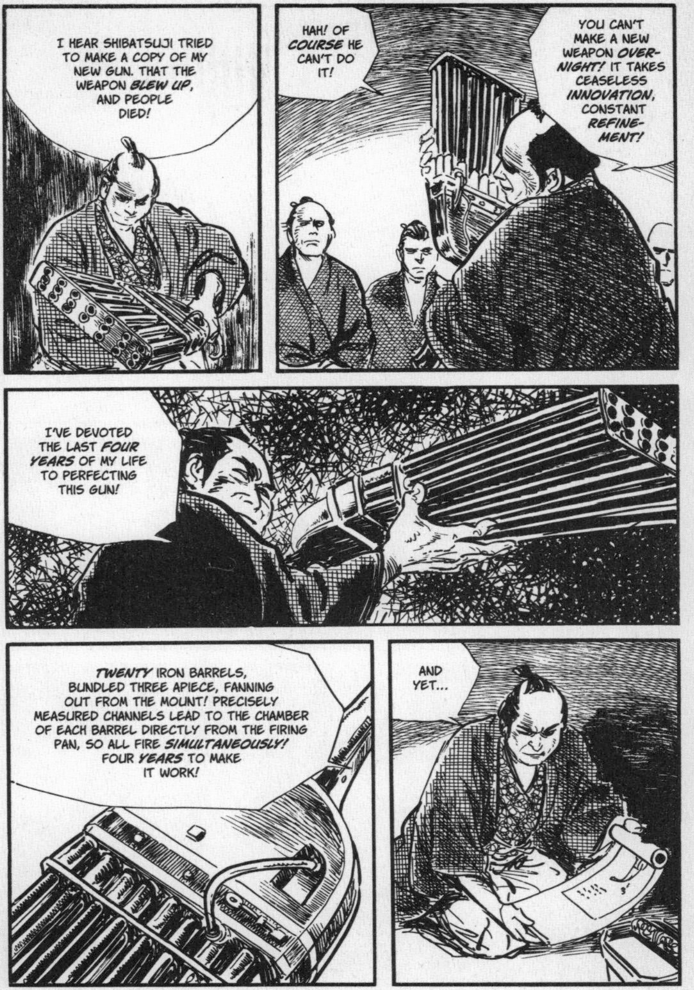
I HEAR SHIBATSUJI TRIED TO MAKE A COPY OF MY NEW GUN. THAT THE WEAPON *BLEW UP*, AND PEOPLE DIED!
HAH! OF *COURSE* HE CAN'T DO IT!
YOU CAN'T MAKE A NEW WEAPON *OVER-NIGHT!* IT TAKES CEASELESS *INNOVATION*, CONSTANT *REFINE-MENT!*
I'VE DEVOTED THE LAST *FOUR YEARS* OF MY LIFE TO PERFECTING THIS GUN!
TWENTY IRON BARRELS, BUNDLED THREE APIECE, FANNING OUT FROM THE MOUNT! PRECISELY MEASURED CHANNELS LEAD TO THE CHAMBER OF EACH BARREL DIRECTLY FROM THE FIRING PAN, SO ALL FIRE *SIMULTANEOUSLY!* FOUR *YEARS* TO MAKE IT WORK!
AND YET...

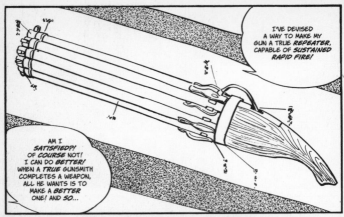

I'VE DEVISED A WAY TO MAKE MY GUN A TRUE *REPEATER*, CAPABLE OF *SUSTAINED RAPID FIRE!*

AM I *SATISFIED?!* OF *COURSE* NOT! I CAN DO *BETTER!* WHEN A *TRUE* GUNSMITH COMPLETES A WEAPON, ALL HE WANTS IS TO MAKE A *BETTER* ONE! AND *SO...*

I SAW THAT IF I COULD MAKE THE GUN BARRELS *ROTATE* WITH EACH SHOT, FIRING OFF IN *SEQUENCE*, I COULD DOUBLE IT'S POWER!

AND... AND *DID* YOU, SIR?!

254

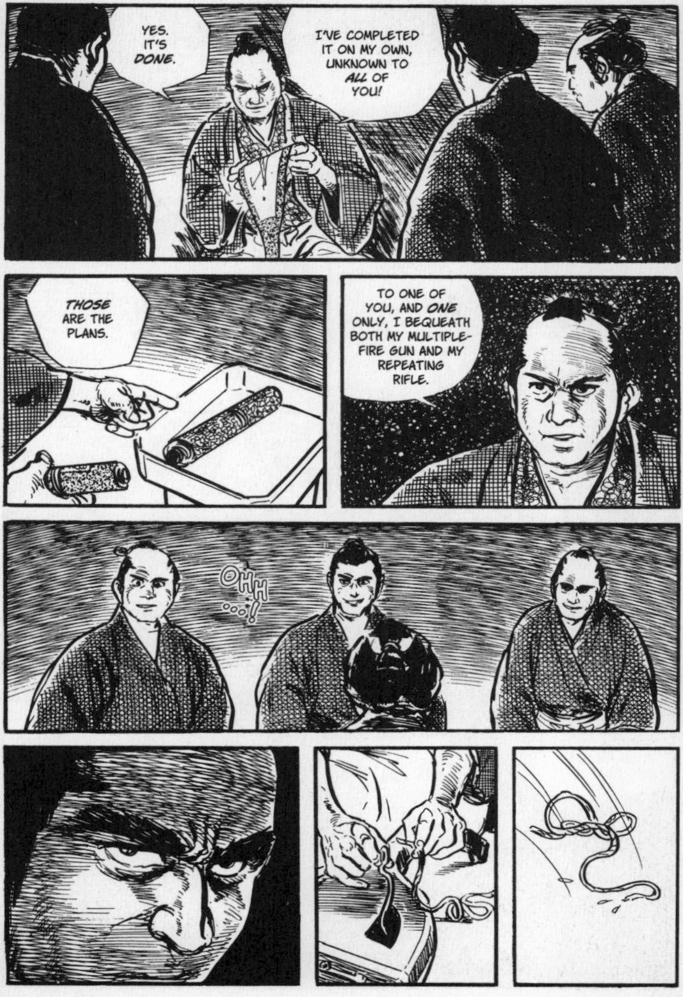
YES. IT'S DONE.
I'VE COMPLETED IT ON MY OWN, UNKNOWN TO ALL OF YOU!
THOSE ARE THE PLANS.
TO ONE OF YOU, AND ONE ONLY, I BEQUEATH BOTH MY MULTIPLE-FIRE GUN AND MY REPEATING RIFLE.
OHH...!

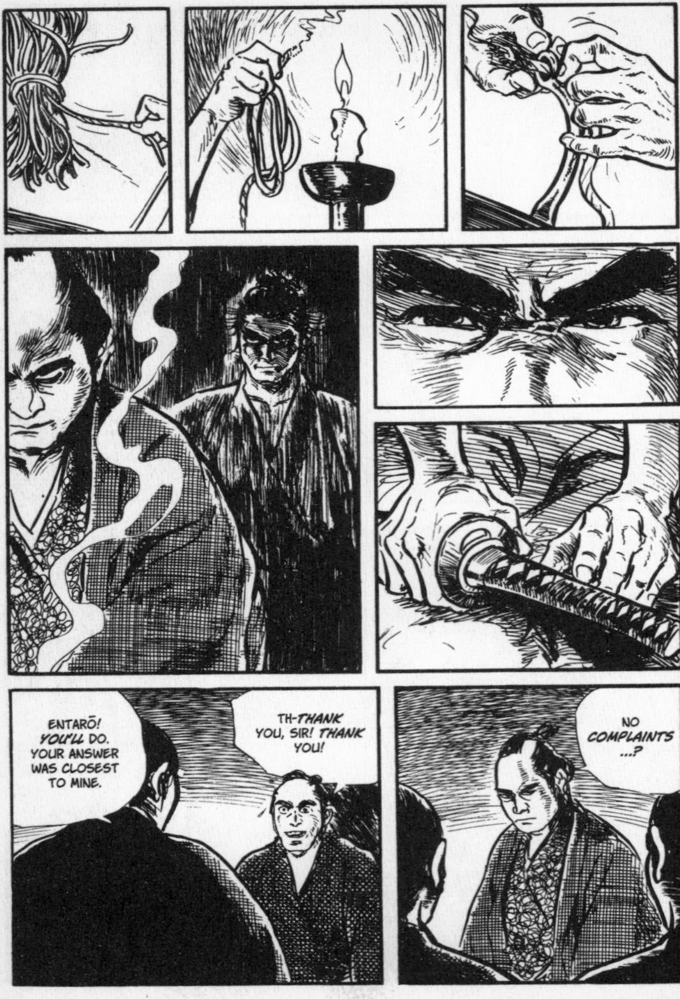
ENTARŌ! YOU'LL DO. YOUR ANSWER WAS CLOSEST TO MINE.
TH-THANK YOU, SIR! THANK YOU!
NO COMPLAINTS ...?

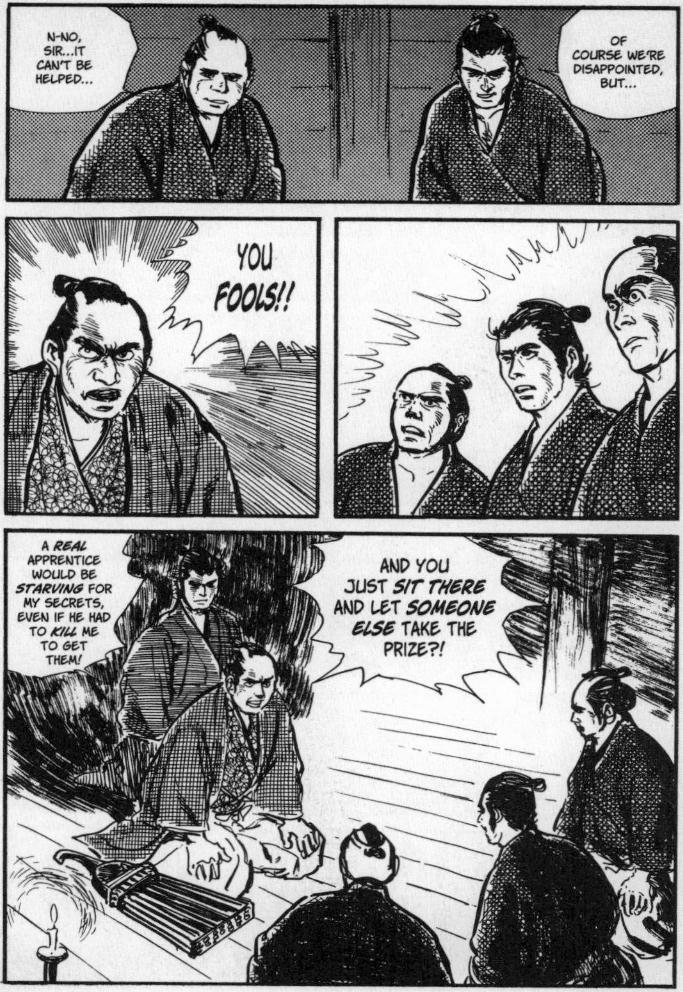
N-NO, SIR...IT CAN'T BE HELPED...
OF COURSE WE'RE DISAPPOINTED, BUT...
YOU FOOLS!!
A REAL APPRENTICE WOULD BE STARVING FOR MY SECRETS, EVEN IF HE HAD TO KILL ME TO GET THEM!
AND YOU JUST SIT THERE AND LET SOMEONE ELSE TAKE THE PRIZE?!

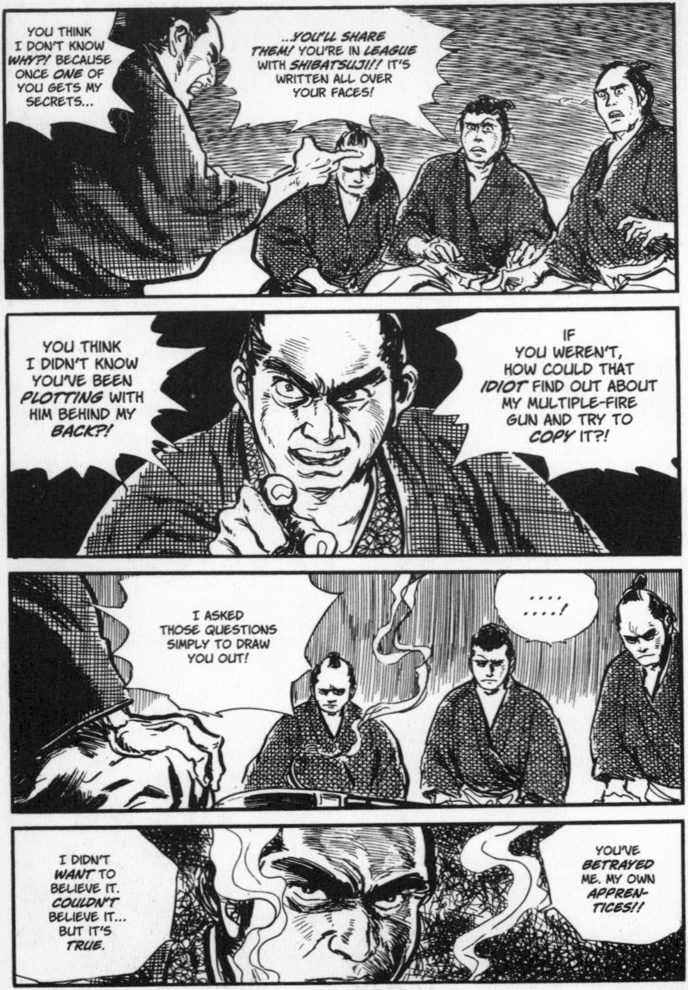
YOU THINK I DON'T KNOW WHY?! BECAUSE ONCE ONE OF YOU GETS MY SECRETS...
...YOU'LL SHARE THEM! YOU'RE IN LEAGUE WITH SHIBATSUJI!! IT'S WRITTEN ALL OVER YOUR FACES!
YOU THINK I DIDN'T KNOW YOU'VE BEEN PLOTTING WITH HIM BEHIND MY BACK?!
IF YOU WEREN'T, HOW COULD THAT IDIOT FIND OUT ABOUT MY MULTIPLE-FIRE GUN AND TRY TO COPY IT?!
I ASKED THOSE QUESTIONS SIMPLY TO DRAW YOU OUT!
....
....!
I DIDN'T WANT TO BELIEVE IT. COULDN'T BELIEVE IT... BUT IT'S TRUE.
YOU'VE BETRAYED ME. MY OWN APPREN-TICES!!

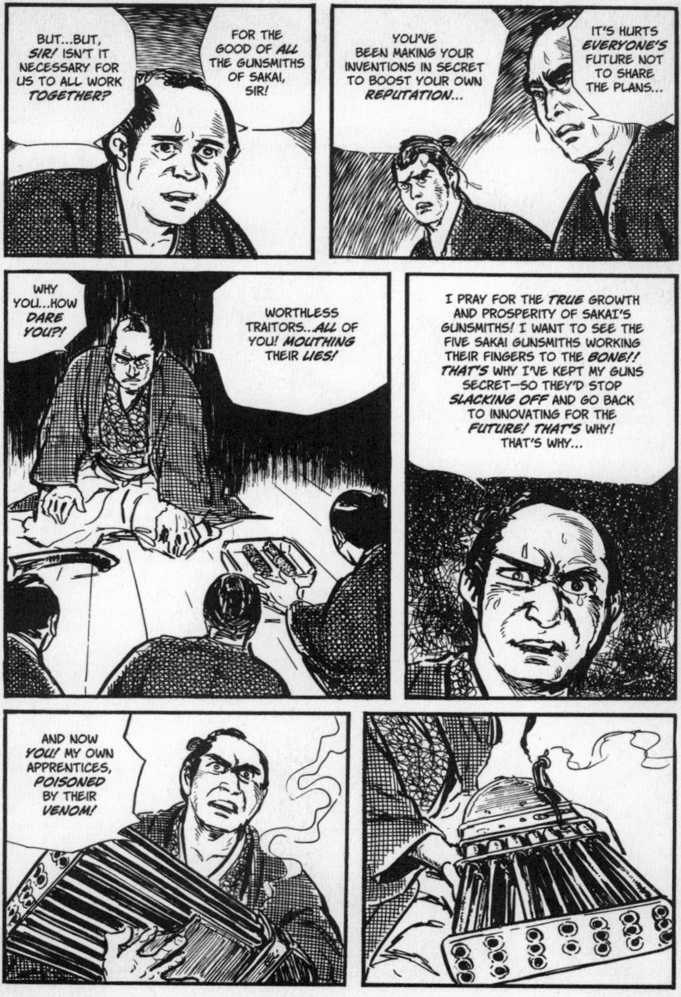
BUT...BUT, SIR! ISN'T IT NECESSARY FOR US TO ALL WORK TOGETHER?
FOR THE GOOD OF ALL THE GUNSMITHS OF SAKAI, SIR!
YOU'VE BEEN MAKING YOUR INVENTIONS IN SECRET TO BOOST YOUR OWN REPUTATION...
IT'S HURTS EVERYONE'S FUTURE NOT TO SHARE THE PLANS...
WHY YOU...HOW DARE YOU?!
WORTHLESS TRAITORS...ALL OF YOU! MOUTHING THEIR LIES!
I PRAY FOR THE TRUE GROWTH AND PROSPERITY OF SAKAI'S GUNSMITHS! I WANT TO SEE THE FIVE SAKAI GUNSMITHS WORKING THEIR FINGERS TO THE BONE!! THAT'S WHY I'VE KEPT MY GUNS SECRET—SO THEY'D STOP SLACKING OFF AND GO BACK TO INNOVATING FOR THE FUTURE! THAT'S WHY! THAT'S WHY...
AND NOW YOU! MY OWN APPRENTICES, POISONED BY THEIR VENOM!

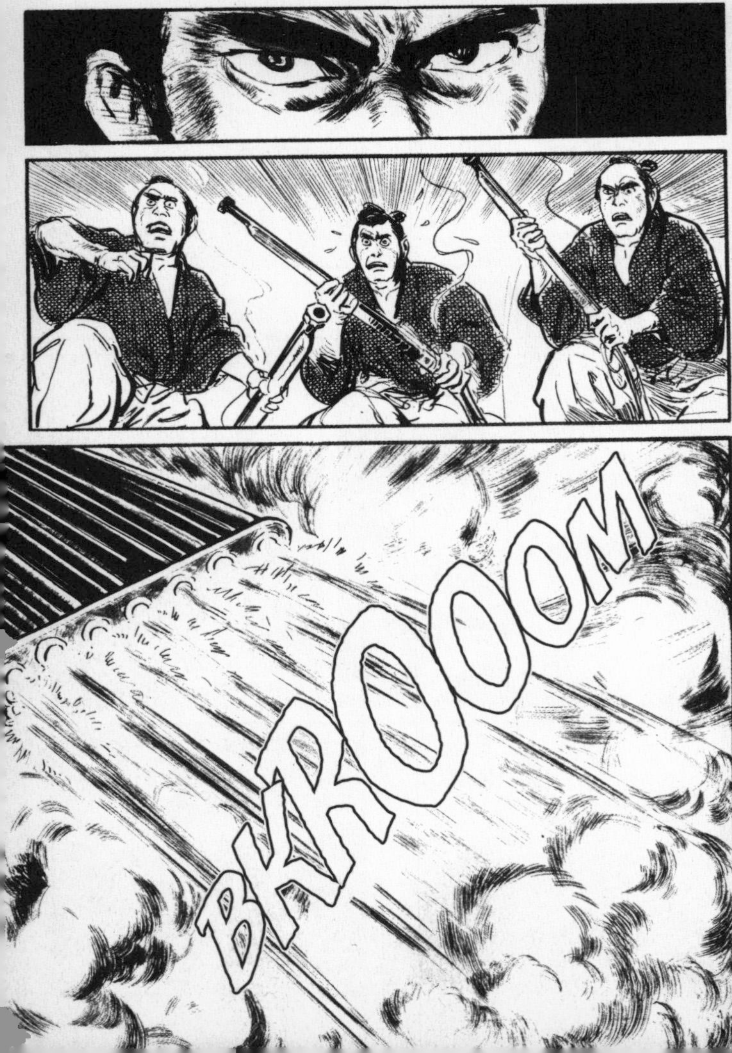
BKROOOOM

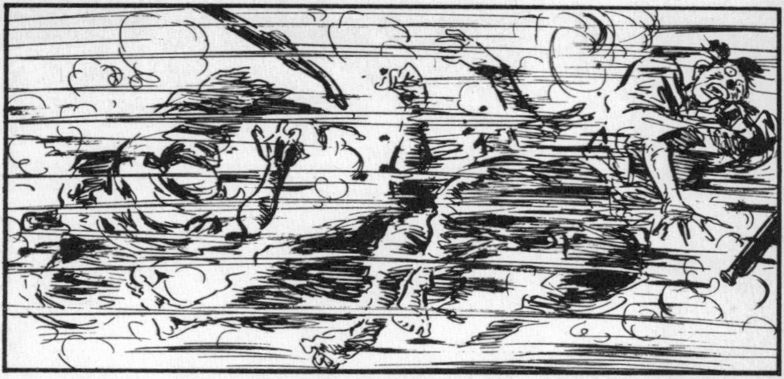

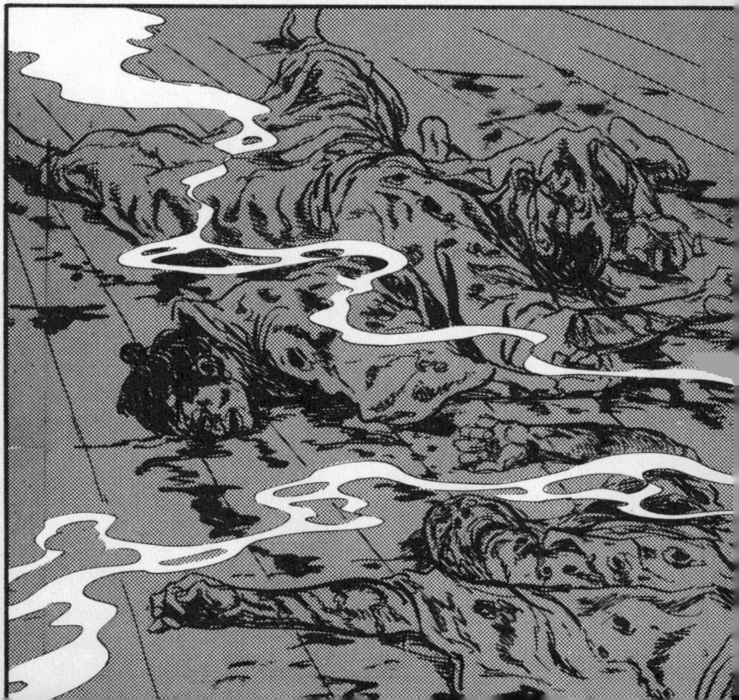

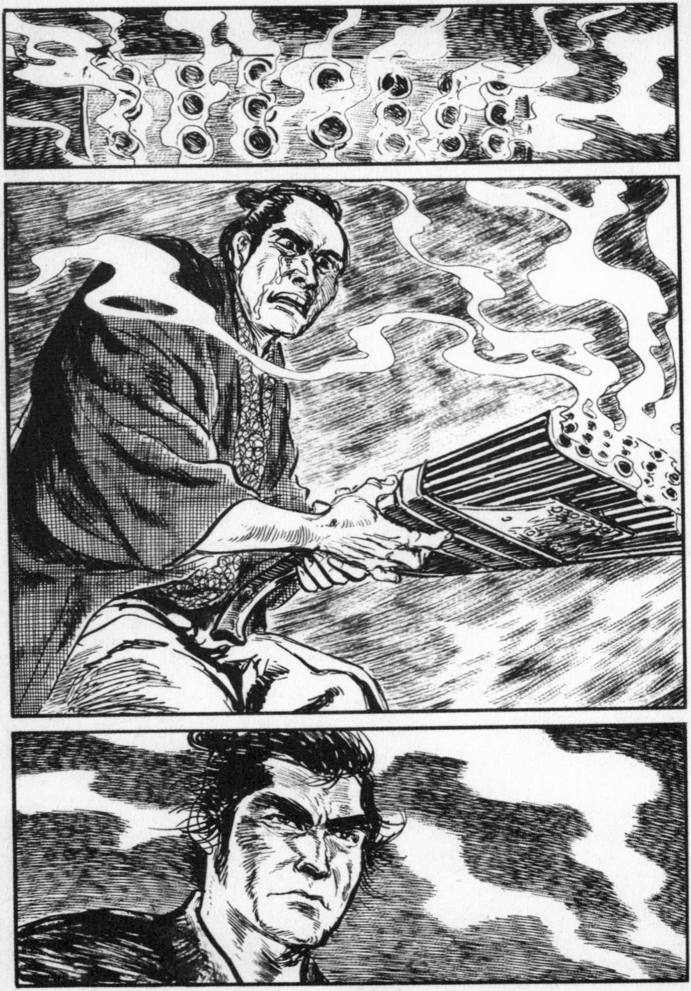

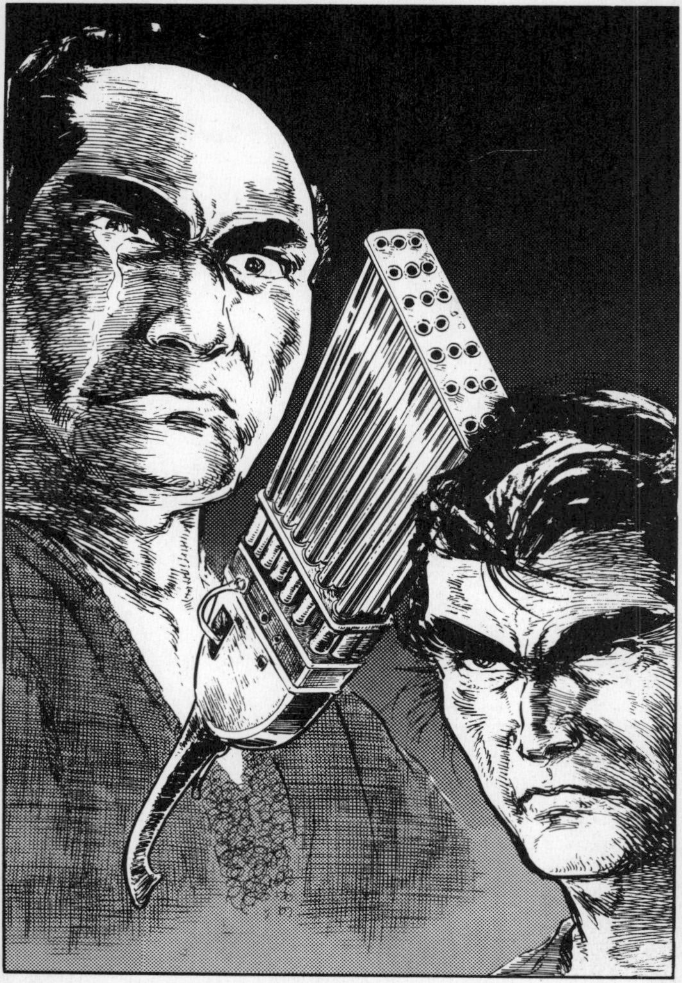

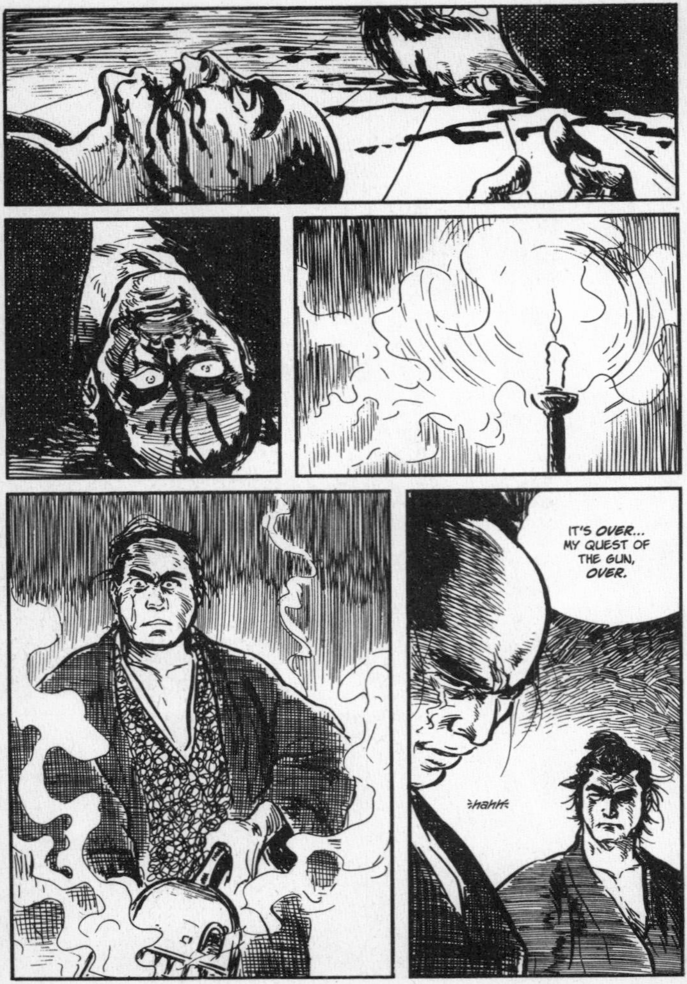
IT'S *OVER*...
MY QUEST OF
THE GUN,
OVER.
≷hahh≶

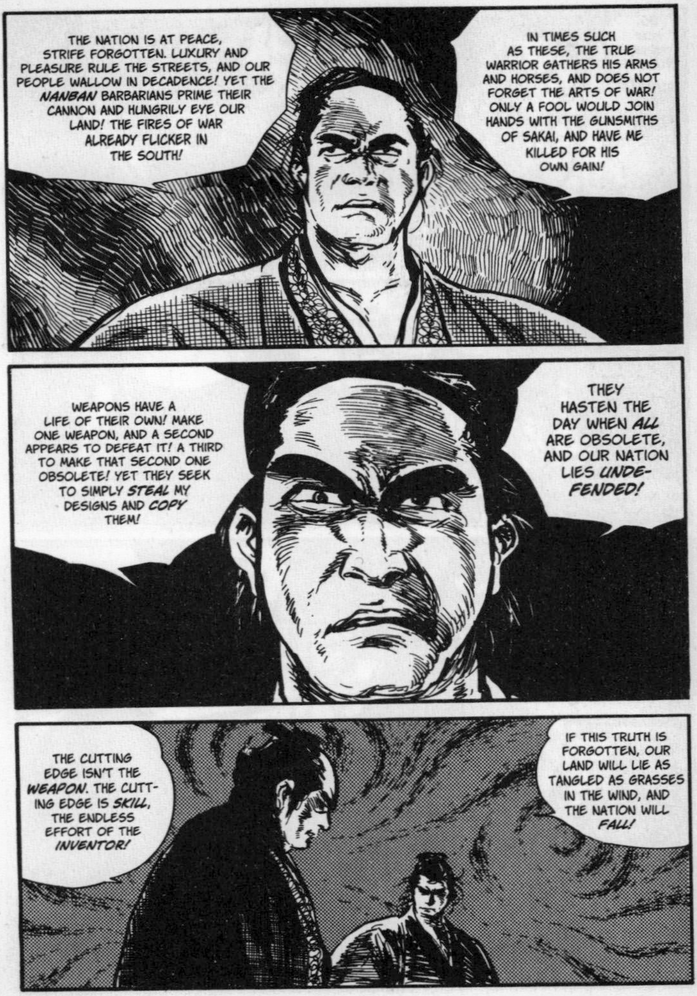
THE NATION IS AT PEACE, STRIFE FORGOTTEN. LUXURY AND PLEASURE RULE THE STREETS, AND OUR PEOPLE WALLOW IN DECADENCE! YET THE *NANBAN* BARBARIANS PRIME THEIR CANNON AND HUNGRILY EYE OUR LAND! THE FIRES OF WAR ALREADY FLICKER IN THE SOUTH!
IN TIMES SUCH AS THESE, THE TRUE WARRIOR GATHERS HIS ARMS AND HORSES, AND DOES NOT FORGET THE ARTS OF WAR! ONLY A FOOL WOULD JOIN HANDS WITH THE GUNSMITHS OF SAKAI, AND HAVE ME KILLED FOR HIS OWN GAIN!
WEAPONS HAVE A LIFE OF THEIR OWN! MAKE ONE WEAPON, AND A SECOND APPEARS TO DEFEAT IT! A THIRD TO MAKE THAT SECOND ONE OBSOLETE! YET THEY SEEK TO SIMPLY *STEAL* MY DESIGNS AND *COPY* THEM!
THEY HASTEN THE DAY WHEN *ALL* ARE OBSOLETE, AND OUR NATION LIES *UNDEFENDED!*
THE CUTTING EDGE ISN'T THE *WEAPON*. THE CUTTING EDGE IS *SKILL*, THE ENDLESS EFFORT OF THE *INVENTOR!*
IF THIS TRUTH IS FORGOTTEN, OUR LAND WILL LIE AS TANGLED AS GRASSES IN THE WIND, AND THE NATION WILL *FALL!*

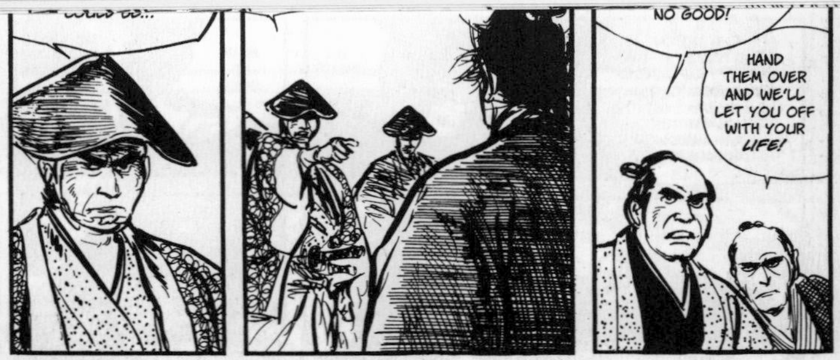
NO GOOD!
HAND THEM OVER AND WE'LL LET YOU OFF WITH YOUR *LIFE!*

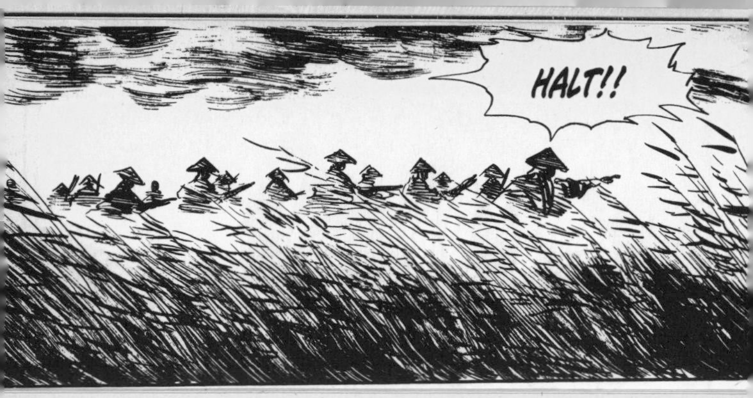
HALT!!

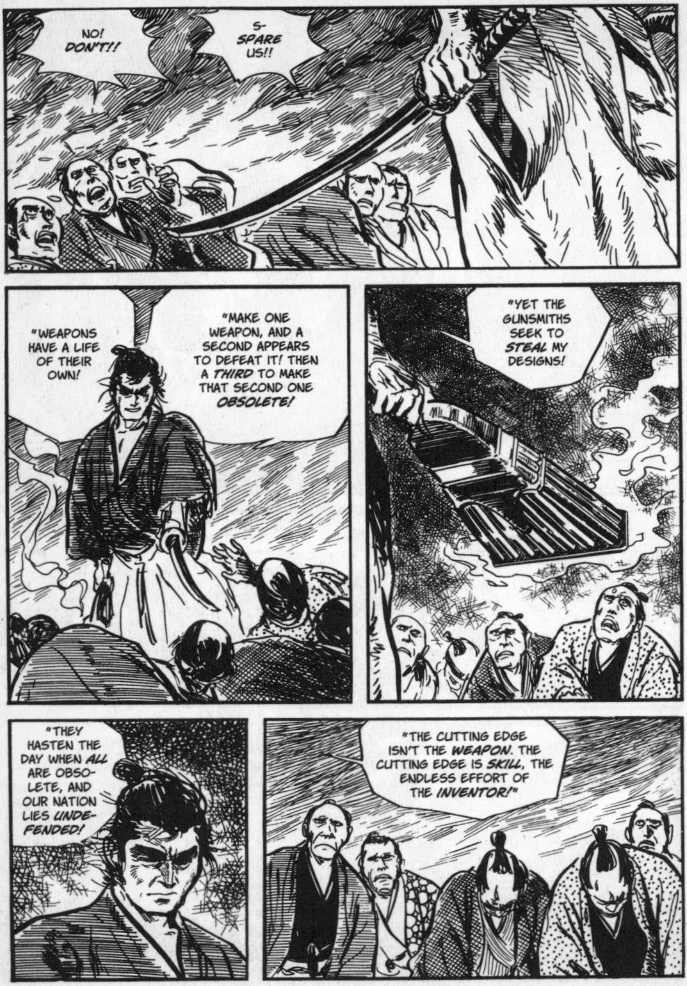
S-
SPARE
US!!
NO!
DON'T!!
"MAKE ONE WEAPON, AND A SECOND APPEARS TO DEFEAT IT! THEN A THIRD TO MAKE THAT SECOND ONE OBSOLETE!
"WEAPONS HAVE A LIFE OF THEIR OWN!
"YET THE GUNSMITHS SEEK TO STEAL MY DESIGNS!
"THE CUTTING EDGE ISN'T THE WEAPON. THE CUTTING EDGE IS SKILL, THE ENDLESS EFFORT OF THE INVENTOR!"
"THEY HASTEN THE DAY WHEN ALL ARE OBSO-LETE, AND OUR NATION LIES UNDE-FENDED!

GLOSSARY

ban
A local policeman, much like a sheriff.

Daikan
The primary local representative of the shogunate in territories outside of the capital of Edo.

daimyō
A feudal lord.

dōtanuki
A battle sword. Literally, "sword that cuts through torsos."

The Forty-Seven Ronin
In one of the most famous stories in Japanese history, forty-seven loyal retainers of a lord forced to kill himself because of the schemes of an enemy dedicated their lives to avenging him, before committing ritual suicide at his grave.

giyaman
From the Portuguese "diamante," or diamond, the tool used to make cut-glass containers.

han
A feudal domain.

jōdai
Castle warden. The ranking *han* official in charge of a *daimyō*'s castle when the *daimyō* was spending his obligatory years in Edo.

kōgi go-yō
The shogun's business.

kōgi kaishakunin
The shogun's own second, who performed executions ordered by the shogun.

machi-bugyō
The Edo city commissioner, combining the post of mayor and chief of police. A post held in monthly rotation by two senior Tokugawa vassals, in charge of administration, maintaining the peace, and enforcing the law in Edo. Their rule extended only to commoners.

meifumadō
The Buddhist Hell. The way of demons and damnation.

metsuke
Inspector. A post combining the functions of chief of police and chief intelligence officer.

nagamaki
A two-handed spear-like weapon taller than a man, with a short shaft and long, curved blade. Similar to the more common naginata, which had a longer shaft.

nanban
Westerners were known as "southern barbarians," after the first traders reaching Japan from the south. By the Edo period, Portuguese, Spanish, and Dutch adventurers, traders, and missionaries were active across Asia.

o-niwaban
"One in the garden". A ninja. the secret agents of the Shōgunate, heard but never seen.

O-Sadamegaki
Short for Kujigata O-Sadamega. The concordance of shogunate laws, compiled in 1742.

obi
The often-ornate bolt of fabric used to tie a kimono closed.

onibōchō
"Demon knife."

Ōsaka Castle
The largest castle outside of Edo, originally built by Hideyoshi Toyotomi, the first unifier of Japan.

Ōta Dōgan
(1432-1486) Japanese military strategist and castle designer, a retainer of the Uesugi clan. He designed the original Edo Castle.

Rikudō Gofu
A talisman of the Six Paths. Used to curse one's enemies.

Rōjū
Senior councilors. The inner circle of councilors directly advising the shogun. The Rōjū were the ultimate advisory body to the Tokugawa shogunate's national government.

rōnin
A masterless samurai. Literally, "one adrift on the waves." Members of the samurai caste who have lost their masters through the dissolution of *han*, expulsion for misbehavior, or other reasons.

ryū
Often translated as "school." The many variations of swordsmanship and other martial arts were passed down from generation to generation to the offspring of the originator of the technique or set of techniques, and to any deishi students that sought to learn from the master. The largest schools had their own *dōjō* training centers and scores of students.

sai
The name of the riverbanks of the river Sanzu, that divides the land of the living from meido, the land of the dead. Legend has it that the souls of dead children would pile rocks on the riverbanks of *sai (sai-no-kawara)* to pray for their parents.

Sakai
A famous trading port, now largely absorbed by the city of Ōsaka, but at the time the industrial powerhouse of Japan.

sō-metsuke
Another name for *"o-metsuke."* The senior law-enforcement officer of the shogunate, reporting directly to the rōjū senior councilors who advised the shogun.

Takama-ga-hara
A heavenly land of bounty in Japan's indigenous Shintō religion.

Wakadoshiyori
Junior councilors. The Tokugawa shogunate was a hybrid government, both a national government empowered by the emperor to govern the nation as a whole, and a daimyō government like that of any han. The council of wakadoshiyori junior councilors was the highest advisory body to the shogun on matters affecting the clan, rather than the nation as a whole.

yakuza
Japan's criminal syndicates. In the Edo period, *yakuza* were a common part of the landscape, running houses of gambling and prostitution. As long as they did not overstep their bounds, they were tolerated by the authorities, a tradition little changed in modern Japan.

yoko-metsuke
A local inspector, reporting up the chain of command to the *o-metsuke* in Edo.